Russian Constitutionalism

For its advocates, constitutionalism provides the resources necessary to allow transitional societies to move away from authoritarianism towards democracy, whilst upholding the vestiges of social and political stability. This book examines constitutionalism in Russia from Tsarist times to the present. It traces the different attitudes to constitutionalism in political thought, and in practice, at different periods, showing how the balance between authoritarianism and liberalism has shifted. In addition, it discusses the importance of constitutional developments for societies in transition, and concludes that post-communist constitutional development in Russia is still far from complete. As an empirical resource, *Russian Constitutionalism* takes a longer historical view than other books on this topic, and it also goes further than this in its interpretive approach, providing a greater understanding of Russian constitutionalism, its significance for other transitional societies and whether the classical model of Western democracy and constitutionalism can be effectively adapted to other regions of the world. Overall, this book provides an incisive and authoritative account of the phenomenon of constitutionalism in Russia.

Andrey N. Medushevsky is Professor at the Higher School of Economics in Moscow, Russia, where he teaches Comparative Constitutional Law and Political Science. He is Expert of the Institute of Law and Public Policy (Moscow) and Member of the Editorial Board of the quarterly *Comparative Constitutional Review.* He is the author of nine books and three hundred articles in various Russian and international learned journals.

Routledge series on Russian and East European studies

Series editor:

Richard Sakwa, Department of Politics and International Relations, University of Kent

This series is published on behalf of BASEES (the British Association for Slavonic and East European Studies). The series comprises original, high-quality, research-level work by both new and established scholars on all aspects of Russian, Soviet, post-Soviet and East European Studies in humanities and social science subjects.

1 **Ukraine's Foreign and Security Policy, 1991–2000**
Roman Wolczuk

2 **Political Parties in the Russian Regions**
Derek S. Hutcheson

3 **Local Communities and Post-Communist Transformation**
Edited by Simon Smith

4 **Repression and Resistance in Communist Europe**
J. C. Sharman

5 **Political Elites and the New Russia**
Anton Steen

6 **Dostoevsky and the Idea of Russianness**
Sarah Hudspith

18 Russian and Soviet Film Adaptations of Literature, 1900–2001
Screening the word
Edited by Stephen Hutchings and Anat Vernitski

19 Russia as a Great Power
Dimensions of security under Putin
Edited by Jakob Hedenskog, Vilhelm Konnander, Bertil Nygren, Ingmar Oldberg and Christer Pursiainen

20 Katyn and the Soviet Massacre of 1940
Truth, justice and memory
George Sanford

21 Conscience, Dissent and Reform in Soviet Russia
Philip Boobbyer

22 The Limits of Russian Democratisation
Emergency powers and states of emergency
Alexander N. Domrin

23 The Dilemmas of De-Stalinisation
A social and cultural history of reform in the Khrushchev era
Edited by Polly Jones

24 News Media and Power in Russia
Olessia Koltsova

25 Post-Soviet Civil Society
Democratization in Russia and the Baltic States
Anders Uhlin

26 The Collapse of Communist Power in Poland
Jacqueline Hayden

27 Television, Democracy and Elections in Russia
Sarah Oates

28 Russian Constitutionalism
Historical and contemporary development
Andrey N. Medushevsky

Russian Constitutionalism

Historical and contemporary development

Andrey N. Medushevsky

Routledge
Taylor & Francis Group
LONDON AND NEW YORK

First published 2006
by Routledge
2 Park Square, Milton Park, Abingdon, Oxon OX14 4RN

Simultaneously published in the USA and Canada
by Routledge
270 Madison Ave, New York, NY 10016

Routledge is an imprint of the Taylor & Francis Group, an informa business

Transferred to Digital Printing 2009

Typeset in Times by Wearset Ltd, Boldon, Tyne and Wear

British Library Cataloguing in Publication Data
A catalogue record for this book is available from the British Library

Library of Congress Cataloging in Publication Data
A catalog record for this book has been requested

ISBN10: 0-415-36368-3 (hbk)
ISBN10: 0-415-54572-2 (pbk)
ISBN10: 0-203-01483-9 (ebk)

ISBN13: 978-0-415-36368-3 (hbk)
ISBN13: 978-0-415-54572-3 (pbk)
ISBN13: 978-0-203-01483-7 (ebk)

Translated by Ekaterina Luneva and Tatiana Baeva

Contents

Introduction

The contemporary scientific research of a worldwide historical process requires identification of the historical situations that show global trends in development and, at the same time, make it possible to examine their consequences within various chronological, geographical and socio-political frameworks. Contemporary historians, political scientists and ordinary citizens in different countries and regions are currently arguing about the extent to which classical (western) models of the transition from absolutist regimes to civil society and the values of a law-based state explain the essence of contradictory social processes emerging throughout the world: in Eastern Europe, Asia and elsewhere. Their attention is concentrated on the formation of modern democracy and, in the first place, on the relationship between a former (authoritarian and absolutist) regime and transition to a new order. In other words, the classical problem for political thought is the relationship between the former regime and revolution.

The development of a worldwide historical process in modern and recent times has shown a stable trend towards the transition from an authoritarian class system to a classless civil society. But the question is how this transition can be implemented, to what extent its implications can be predicted and what actions should be taken by the state and society. Is it possible to carry out evolutionary reforms, which gradually increase social equality, and to ensure and safeguard political freedoms and individual rights? Russia with its serfdom relations resulting in the prolonged conflict of society and state ran the constant risk of social upheaval. Even the authorities realized this. Russia's positive and negative experience of evolutionary development and gradual transition towards the formation of civil society in the nineteenth and twentieth centuries is extremely informative and relevant for solving current problems. As a matter of fact, the study has just begun. And it needs a systemic approach, i.e. a country should be explored as a holistic system: how this complex object is linked to other elements of the system; through which mechanisms the system is maintained; and how its components correlate to the external social phenomena.

To examine the history of a country in the context of worldwide historical process, first, one needs to follow its development in a long-term chronological perspective. This permits identifying factors impervious to any changes. To describe cultural, historical and political events that are typical of diverse societies at different stages of their development, historians and sociologists use such terms as closed and open societies. These societies differ in the ways of interacting with the external environment: while open societies are relatively flexible, self-critical and change-oriented, closed ones tend to escape from external influence by controlling the existing reality.

Second, the phenomenon (a country, a state or society) should be analysed in terms of social statics (how a system functions at a particular moment in time) and social dynamics (what changes take place in the course of historical development; and how some characteristics vary, while others remain unchanged). It thus becomes possible to develop explainable hypotheses, as well as to analyse, compare and obtain new information concerning the issues that are of interest to society today.

The radical constitutional changes, occurring over the past decade of the twentieth century and the early years of the twenty-first century, have prompted modern scientists to rethink a number of classical issues, which may seem to have been already resolved, in the realm of theoretical jurisprudence and the sociology of law. Primarily, they include the models of transitional processes, correlation between social and legal changes, comparison between the adopted political patterns and the traditional national forms of government and society, as well as the impact of political modernization and established constitutional systems. These issues are at the heart of debates in various countries across the world. They are especially relevant for the regions where the dynamics of constitutional changes is most apparent in recent times.

The aim of this book is to discover the nature of Russian contemporary constitutionalism through a comparative approach used within the framework of the historical and contemporary development of constitutionalism. It provides a comparative analysis of Russian and global constitutionalism; including directions of the conflict dynamics of constitutional processes and their links with phenomena such as political regimes, relationships between power and property, society's view of legitimate government, tools for interaction between the state and society in the light of modernization.

The idea of the gradual and cyclical development of worldwide constitutional process forms the basis of the author's theoretical concept. This makes it possible to compare constitutional events from the global and Russian perspective, and to identify typological characteristics and, correspondingly, specific features and vectors of evolving constitutional changes.

The monograph is structured along the following lines. In the first place, the author outlines the theoretical model of constitutionalism that enables us to analyse Russian constitutionalism in the comparative perspective of worldwide constitutional development. On the one hand, the author explores it as a part of the common phenomenon of constitutional development and the actual manifestation thereof. On the other hand, he identifies those particular features that distinguish Russian constitutionalism (as an ideological movement and alternative way of establishing a political system) from classical constitutionalism and characterize it as a specific model of constitutionalism typical of societies shifting from a traditional absolutist state to democracy (Chapter 1). The next chapters analyse the historical and contemporary development of Russian constitutionalism. Constitutionalism emerged as an ideological movement that was reflected in a number of political projects intended to curb absolutism in the course of real historical process. Then it evolved into the first-ever established civil society, thanks to the Emancipation Reform of 1861 that liquidated serf dependence of Russian peasants, and other succeeding reforms (Chapter 2). The research also highlights the importance of theoretical and political experience gained by Russian liberalism in the struggle for transition from absolutism to constitutional monarchy and then to the Republican Constituanta – the Constituent Assembly (Chapter 3).

The fourth chapter explores the phenomenon of nominal constitutionalism widespread in the Soviet era. Finally, the last chapter analyses the type of constitutional development which emerged in post-Soviet times and was embodied in the Russian Constitution of 1993. It also describes the parameters of particular constitutional development reflecting the specific implementation of common features under transition from the traditional authoritarian society to contemporary democratic values.

1 Constitutionalism as a theoretical issue in transitional societies

The history of Russian constitutionalism is of special interest as a case of a transition from authoritarian regime to democratic reforms in recent times. Over a long period, most scholars considered this process to be unique and thus impossible to describe in typological terms. In a contemporary world, as the transition from authoritarian regimes to democracy takes new forms, the need for a typological comparative analysis of its propensity for conflicts is greater than it has ever been. The main issue is how democratic norms and mechanisms can be applied to the societies where both people in power and society at large have inherited traditional features of authoritarian conscience. From this perspective, the existing historiography offers two alternative views. The first assumes that if only the authoritarian government were toppled, society would automatically accept democratic norms regulating market relations and the right to economic enterprise. However, experience has shown that democratic innovations clash with old stereotypes. Here, the second view gains ground: democratic norms in the spirit of western values are totally unacceptable for traditional societies. In that case, the old regime is restored and idealized, i.e. a traditional society regained. These two views are represented in the ideological struggle unfolding today.

The adoption of a new system of democratic values by traditional societies should be viewed as a research problem that can be tackled only through a typological and comparative approach. The world history has demonstrated that traditional authoritarian regimes can shift to modern political systems withstanding challenges of modern and recent times in different ways: either through revolution and complete destruction of the old regime; or through constructive legal self-reforming that is time-consuming and yet fruitful. Russian history has seen both ways in action. However, the experience of constructive and efficient reforms of the state, society and political system – that's what we call constitutionalism – has not yet been synthesized and interpreted as a holistic phenomenon. Neither has the development of Russian constitutionalism been studied in a comparative perspective, unlike the history of revolutionary consciousness. The point is that in the pre-revolutionary science no specific historical study was conducted into this subject, as it would have questioned the very principle of autocracy. The first brief attempts to study the history of constitutional movements that were made at the beginning of twentieth century, when the transition from autocracy to constitutional monarchy was under way. These attempts included such obscure publications as the 1730 political projects, political projects of Mikhail M. Speransky, the scientific publication of Catherine II's *Nakaz* (Instruction) and others. However, each subject was explored separately, and no comparative analysis was conducted.

Constitutionalism emerging in modern times is a reflection of factual social changes and widespread transition from absolutist monarchy to law-based state, on the one hand; and a tool used for influencing modernization with a varying degree of effectiveness due to various reasons, on the other. The legal norms of constitutionalism should be examined in terms of legal control over relations between the state and society and the mechanisms ensuring a stable social consensus.

The chosen research method is based on the essence of this approach. We focus on constitutions (basic national legislation at any particular moment in time), as well as on changes in constitutions and their replacement. Exploring these changes allows us to re-create the socio-political realities that they actually brought to life. Following this approach, the very fact of major constitutional changes or events (such as constitutional revolutions or radical constitutional reforms analysed further in more detail) demonstrates imbalance in the pre-stability period and the lack of a political consensus in society. These changes and events also demonstrate along which lines the consensus is sought for, and what becomes legally binding within a new public legal structure. Then it becomes clear what norms and rules of interaction have been agreed by those involved in political process.

In the study of constitutional process, the actual stages of transformations and their sequences are of equal importance as their historical and chronological course. Therefore, for a better understanding of contemporary Russian constitutional institutions, we should compare them not only with the Western European institutions of recent times but also with the similar constitutional parameters of modern times. That helps to explain the wisdom of legal norms whose social content varies from one historical epoch to another. In modern and recent times, any crisis goes through the following phases: initial stability, instability and regained stability. And the changes occurring throughout these phases are likely to be transposed into political and legal regulations taking a more or less fixed form. The tendency is also typical of certain authoritarian political systems (illegal *per se*) where it is manifested in the phenomenon of either nominal or sham (pretended) constitutionalism.

Like all general notions, the key conceptual notions of constitutionalism and constitutional cycles are applicable only in a rather abstract model of research. In this sense, we refer to the big cycles that cover small ones. Big cycles include three main stages: stability, destroyed stability and regained stability. Why does the normative regulation of social relations never lose its relevance? We believe this is due to the quest for consensus and its embodiment in regulatory norms. The constitution, as a code stipulating legislative forms of utmost importance to society, is an essential element of the mechanisms used for solving political crises. Obviously, constitutions (except for provisional ones) represent society's interests and often present an ideal project for its future development. This instrument, however, can be effective only if the legislative forms are accepted by society and their fulfillment is guaranteed by political power. Thus, constitutions can be broadly divided into effective and ineffective. All social and political crises have common features. They initially destroy constitutional stability, pass through identical stages of development, and eventually restore constitutional stability. Therefore social processes are cyclical in nature. And this is reflected in a constitutional cycle.

According to the theory of constitutional cycles, society is perceived as an existing system and objective reality. Society is an integral system tending towards stability. We view the cycle as a shift from one phase to another. In this process the key role belongs to a socio-psychological component: certain ideas take root in people's minds and then gradually change, following the logic of historical development. This process develops in a certain type of homogenous society and political regime. Unlike natural cycles, social ones can be either spontaneous or controllable and manageable from within society. This fact is very important because it allows changing the system not only through destruction, but also through reform and social regulation. Hence, there are several possible ways to do so: first, social process can be independent of people's intentions (spontaneous); second, it can be destabilizing and aim at dismantling the existing system (the so-called "professional revolutionary spirit"); and lastly, it can be driven by a deliberate process of legal regulation. History knows three main types of changes: spontaneous, destructive and constructive. The possibility of deliberate regulation gives rise to ideologies. And the theory of liberalism is the best and subtlest instrument created by science. This theory is aimed not only at overcoming crises, but also at devising strategies for their prevention. The course of history has demonstrated that destruction takes much energy and costs a lot, while constructive analysis of social implications of the measures taken is most appropriate for society in terms of social costs and outputs. We identify this instrument with the liberal theory of constitutionalism. We believe that social processes are regulated by constitutionalism. Alexis de Tocqueville noted that during transition from the old regime to the new one, France could have fulfilled its objectives peacefully, through reforms, if only it had managed to substitute the evolutionary logic for the revolutionary one.[1] The law emerging from the chaos of destruction is of special interest. Of course, this variant of development, which is in fact the triumph of rational thinking, has certain limitations. The law, as a system of social regulation, may fail to meet expectations under certain historical conditions. It is not applicable in the era of destruction. Yet, the holistic approach to this issue shows a connection between social and legal changes, their mechanisms, evolution, as well as the impact of many other factors. The real historical process seems to be a conflict between various social players defending their views on social processes and, correspondingly, on the state legal structure. This phenomenon can be elucidated within the framework of the theory of constitutional cycles. When social phenomena are analysed in a very broad sense, they appear not as isolated and conflicting, but rather as interrelated and interdependent. This approach can be employed for examining the historical and contemporary development of Russian constitutionalism which has seen both illegal and destructive along with legal and constructive stages of social development.

Therefore, the history of Russian constitutionalism should be explored in a long-term dimension. In Russia, real constitutionalism emerged in the form of constitutional monarchy only back in the early twentieth century. Later it entered the era in which the monarchy gave way to a constitutional republic established in the wake of February 1917 events. After that, the legal development of Russian constitutionalism was halted for many years. And only recently has Russian constitutionalism started to recover (at the turn of the twentieth century) to manifest itself in adoption of the Russian Constitution in 1993.

Having presented the thesis on Russian constitutionalism in comparative perspective, we need to answer the question: what is the historical essence of the constitutional phenomenon that we see today? It is acknowledged that English parliamentarianism began with the adoption of the Magna Carta in 1215, and French parliamentarianism originated from the vassal contractual relations inherent in western feudalism. Logically, the pre-history of Russian constitutionalism should be traced from the first attempts to restrict monarchical power. The official historiography of absolutism, of course, could not fully describe the long tradition of limiting monarchical power. The Soviet historiography, which overemphasized the destructive forms of social upheavals and hampered the discovery of successive legal traditions, is not of big help either. This research is based on a number of sources allowing us to describe the historical and contemporary development of Russian constitutionalism as a holistic phenomenon interrelating its past, present and future. Social players begin to come up with ideas on the political system modernization long before politicians put them into practice. But this period is also chronicled in certain documents. Great importance is attached to the review of political projects that never became legally binding but clearly reflected alternative views on and approaches to the modernization of various social groups pursuing their own interests. These historical documents were familiar to contemporaries as an element of the real political and ideological struggle. They originated from the following sources: papers for constitutional assemblies; proposals on constitutional amendments, both adopted and rejected; political parties' platforms with regard to the constitution and the structure of the state; writings of eminent legal theorists (representing the chronicles and reviews of crisis epochs); legal journalism and notes made by constitutional players, especially the statesmen who streamlined constitutional processes. In Russia's authoritarian past, the programmes of constitutional reforms were for many years based on western constitutional ideas. The ideas explicitly show trends in dynamics; the opportunities and limitations of crisis management; interaction between the government and society; conflict of interests under modernization of a traditional authoritarian system; propensity for conflicts between authoritarianism and democracy in the period of transition.

Historically, Russian constitutionalism has been developing (initially, as a set of ideas and legal guidelines and, only in the twentieth century, as a real political system) in several main areas. It is necessary to define the key notions of our concept in order to interpret comparative, typological and specific parameters of Russian constitutionalism. The cyclical model allows us to compare alternating phases within national constitutional tradition and to explore the typology of constitutional law on a global scale.[2]

Theory of constitutional cycles

In moments of confrontation, a stable democratic transition can be ensured not only by adopting a liberal constitution but also by rendering impossible a reversion to the former authoritarian system. Moreover, it is necessary to establish and maintain the social constitution-based consensus which was previously non-existent. However, the newly created law does not guarantee a stable system: it may take a whole epoch to bring new constitutional norms into compliance with the existing social reality, including the subsequent stages of their rapprochement, confrontation and further merging of new legal norms with the old ones. It forms the basis of emerging constitutional cycles which can be either small (short), because of the so-called "pendulum effect", or big (long). Big constitutional cycles are of great interest to legal philosophers, since they reflect substantial contradictions between constitutional modernization and retraditionalization in transitional societies.

It is appropriate to extend the notion of cycle, used by economists and sociologists for analysing the dynamics of social processes, to the area of constitutional cycles. As a rule, it means a movement through the logically related stages: crisis, depression, revival and growth. One cycle is followed by the other passing through similar stages. The concept of economic cycles, worked out by Nikolay D. Kondratiev and Joseph Schumpeter in the twentieth century, profoundly influenced the development of the sociological theory of cycles. The idea of cyclical political development was pioneered by famous ancient Greeks such as Plato, Aristotle and especially Polybius. They formulated a thesis about the rotating nature of the forms of government. In western political thought, the thesis was supported by Machiavelli and Vico, who believed the idea could be applied to the society as a whole. In modern times, the theory is represented by Hegel's dialectical spiral, Marx's doctrine of the movement of socioeconomic formations and Comte's work on the social statics and dynamics. In recent times, it is conveyed in the philosophy and sociology of Oswald Spengler, Arnold Toynbee and Pitirim Sorokin; in the economic theory of the Kondratiev concept; and in the political sociology of Pareto's idea of the "circulation of elites" and by the "iron law of oligarchy" of Robert Michels. The idea of cycles has spread further across many other branches of knowledge affecting the development of the sociology of knowledge (Thomas Kuhn's theory of scientific revolutions), economic crises (Joseph Schumpeter), the stages of economic growth (Walt Rostow), the sociology of conflict and modernization theory. Thus, the concept of cycles is part and parcel of all the major philosophical, sociological and economic theories that try to describe the typologically similar stages of social processes in comparative perspective.

A study into big constitutional cycles (e.g. classical democracies or Russia) allows us to mark the periods and grasp the logic of various stages of constitutional development; to explain substantial contradictions that arise during transition between democracy and liberal constitutionalism, federalism and unitarism, the separation and consolidation of powers; finally, to examine the specifics and prospects of contemporary constitutional development.

The concept of constitutional cycles is intended to describe the relationship between static state and changes occurring within a single constitutional process, to identify its similar phases in various historical periods and cultures, and to explain the mechanisms used for setting up a new constitutional order.

The constitutional cycle embraces the entire spectrum of constitutional conditions that range from repealing the constitution, which lost its legitimacy, to adopting a new one. Therefore, its stages (emergence, development and termination) should be determined taking account of the new form of constitutional structure. In this sense, the main stages of constitutional cycle are similar to those of economic cycle: crisis (declaring the old constitution null and void and acknowledging the need for drafting a new one); depression (termination of application of the old constitution and the split of opinions over constitutional prospects); revival (reaching a certain agreement on the principles to be enshrined in the new Basic Law); and growth (enforcement of the new legitimate constitution along with hopes for political stability). In terms of institutions involved, different stages are marked by the toppling of former government; coming into play of several opposing forces of the new constitutional power, reaching a compromise between them (e.g. within the framework of a common constituent assembly); and official enforcement of the new constitution and its newly created institutions.

Given this theoretical approach, worldwide constitutional development can be conceived as a correlation between two ideal processes: linear and cyclical.

The first type of process (based on Anglo-American experience) is characteristic of stable democracies with long traditions of civil society and law-based state. Even if there is a need for drastic constitutional changes, the latter are introduced through reforms, without impairing the continuity and legitimacy of constitutional process (it is generally recognized that this process is facilitated by the possibility for judicial interpretation of constitutional norms). However, despite the widespread opinion that the linear development of US constitutionalism is progressive and peaceful, insightful researchers speak about crises and well-pronounced cycles emerging in the process.

There are three kinds of crises involving the fundamental revision of constitutional provisions and their new interpretation. The first crisis erupted in 1787, when the US Constitution was adopted. And it is not without reason considered a constitutional coup. The second crisis blew out during the Civil War in the mid-nineteenth century, when the two opposite and incompatible concepts of American federalism clashed. The third crisis arose when US President Franklin D. Roosevelt was implementing a new policy that stirred up a sharp conflict between the presidential government and the Supreme Court, resulting in new interpretation of the constitution from the perspective of the theory of realism.

Some researchers believe that the USA is again faced with the dilemma of choosing a strategy for radical constitutional transformations. They claim American constitutionalism has unobvious but well marked cycles: stability periodically turns into crisis, then into reform and again into stability. This peculiarity of American constitutionalism was especially convincing in the light of the Soviet fetish for the system stability and rigidity. In this sense, the model in question differs from other cyclical models (e.g. the French model) not so much by the absence of constitutional continuity gaps (they were observed several times) as by the fact that constitutional crises did not lead to the adoption of a new constitution coupled with radical changes to the attributes of political regime. It was the Supreme Court that drastically altered the very paradigm of constitutional interpretation, simultaneously acting as a legal and political institution (specifically, when the new policy was announced and pursued). As such, ensuring legal continuity is a fundamental public value and its achievement is the most important argument in any debate on constitutional issues.

The second crisis is cyclical and typical of unstable democracies and states under modernization, where proclaimed constitutional principles can be hardly observed due to acute social contradictions and society's failure to reach a political consensus, usually achieved by mutual concessions.

French constitutional development is a classic example. The 16 constitutions (including the provisional legislative acts of constitutional nature) reflected successive triumphs of different political forces seeking to impose their political philosophy on society at large. French constitutional cycles arise from a conflict between two theoretical principles established in the Age of Enlightenment: the principle of popular sovereignty (Jean-Jacques Rousseau) and the principle of popular representation (Charles-Louis Montesquieu). These are underlying principles of contemporary constitutions, both of them proclaiming popular sovereignty and establishing the institutions of representative democracy and the separation of powers. However, in their authentic interpretation the principles appear incompatible and contradictory. The first principle underlies the concept of direct democracy, whereas the second one underpins the concept of representative democracy. Their conflict broke out during the Great French Revolution and has remained relevant ever since. Due to this conflict, the parliamentary regime alternated with the presidential one (as a rule, it was the Bonaparte regime advocating the idea of representation in a logically extreme form with all powers concentrated in one person's hands). The cyclical development was observed in a gradual transition from republic to empire and from parliamentary regime to presidential one. The Fifth French Republic proposed its own innovative model to resolve the dilemma of the mixed or parliamentary-presidential republic. The Gaullist model of rationalized parliamentarianism not only played an important role in overcoming the French political crisis but also served as a basis for the alternative concept of government opposed to the pure concepts of parliamentary and presidential republics. However, it is the Gaullist interpretation of the regime as a republican monarchy that was in demand in other political systems during constitutional crises. That is why this interpretation became so widespread in the contemporary world. It has been used by the countries that tried to reconcile the democratic political system retaining strong, effective executive power with an independent head of state. In terms of historical duration, this type of constitutional development is interpreted as cyclical. Its peculiarity rests upon the fact that the main phases of each cycle are fixed in constitutions. Thus, French Constitutions serve as a model for various political regimes ranging from democracy to dictatorship.[3]

The notion of the great periods of historical constitutionalism ("Los Grandes Periodos del Constitucionalismo Historico") is used by Spanish legal and political writers to define the phenomenon of recurrent situations and political regimes in various historical periods. Some researchers claim that this fact allows them to conclude that Spanish constitutional cycles are similar to French ones. Others question their conclusion stating that Spanish constitutional development was ephemeral for a long period of time: the recurrence of constitutional forms was not well-pronounced and the constitutional development was mainly linear and progressive. Though the so-called "pendulum effect" does not work here, according to a contemporary Spanish constitutionalist Alvares Conde, the constitutional regime established by the 1837 Constitution has always preserved a sort of common legitimacy ("una especie de 'legalidad comun'") whose conservative and progressive aspects alternately formed the basis for the next constitutional changes. Of course, it is arguable whether or not to use the notion of general legitimacy with its ideological rather than academic nature. Nevertheless, the opinion of the prominent Spanish scholar actually reflects the process of sinuous transition from the democratic regime to the authoritarian one where each of them promoted its own legitimacy and tried to defend it constitutionally in the course of revolutions and military upheavals throughout the twentieth century.[4]

In Latin America, where they have written a lot about cyclical development, the formula is simple: a conflict between democracy and dictatorship. At a time when there is a deep conflict between the state and society, stability is fictional, and "latent revolutionary situation" is a constant factor, the constitutional deadlock is broken by force. The winning revolution introduces a democratic constitution. Yet, the interference of citizens in politics drastically undermines the stability of law-based state. Democracy gives way to dictatorship acting as an institute adjusting the inefficiency and corruption of democratic regimes. As a result, the republic finds itself in a dead-end situation which may be defined as an imbalanced equilibrium maintained solely by the rotating phases of the cycle. The most important features of such a situation are as follows: dictatorship is needed to impede the disorganization of a government but it doesn't do society's welfare any good, unless publicly supported and approved; democracy is the only regime that can be accepted by the nation but due to its constitutional structure democracy cannot support the government it has destroyed; and lastly, numerous attempts are made to reach a compromise between the two extremes. Having established this pattern ("constitutional deadlock"), one of the classic Latin-American authors, Emilio Rabasa, wrote (referring to Mexico) about the constitutional cycle whose three phases reflect permanent conflicts between the state and society, legislative power and constitutional power, freedom and order. The three phases are dictatorship, democracy and transition from one form of government to another (all of them can be reproduced in positive constitutional law).[5]

Finally, in Asian and particularly African countries, which have just entered the initial stage of constitutional development, cycles are very primitive. They include the following stages: imitation of a western constitution (usually that of a former mother country); its rejection in the light of growing nationalism; and lastly, adoption of a new constitution intended to level liberal constitutionalism and national specificity.[6]

Thus, the comparative analysis of big constitutional cycles allows us to identify general and specific features of various legal systems and to establish a relationship between legal norms and institutions in the democratic transformation of society.

The essence of transitional dynamics is determined by the dialectics of three phases. In order to interpret them we introduce new terminology – the notions of deconstitutionalization (undermined legitimacy and repeal of the old constitution), constitutionalization (adopting a new constitution and specifying its norms in the sectoral legislation), and reconstitutionalization (introduction of constitutional amendments bringing current rules in line with former constitutional rules and practices). Hence, the full constitutional cycle means a return to the starting point of all subsequent changes. That is a question of similarity between phases and not of their repetition (which is practically impossible). The constitutional cycle resembles a dialectical spiral: phases of the new cycle repeat analogous stages of the previous cycle, but at a different qualitative level.

The question is: what gears this system towards the proper order of alternating stages? The dynamics stem from a conflict between the law and the social efficiency of constitutional norms. The logic of alternating phases is determined by their various combinations. Moreover, the next combinations, to some extent, are predetermined by the previous ones. The first phase of constitutional cycle (deconstitutionalization) usually implies the rejection of current constitutional rules and shows a conflict between legal regulation (the old one) and social efficiency (based on a new sense of justice and regulatory legitimacy). The second stage (constitutionalization) reflects attempts to reconcile these two factors by adopting a new constitution (fundamental legal norms are viewed as optimal) by society (the constituent power). Finally, the third phase (reconstitutionalization) usually implies adjusting exaggerated constitutional expectations and levelling constitutional norms with traditional institutions in order to improve their efficiency. This phase may bring an end to the cycle, i.e. restore the pre-crisis situation.

The two extreme conditions of constitutional revolution (illegal modification of the current constitution) and constitutional counter-revolution (illegal re-enforcement of the old constitution) set the time frames for constitutional cycles of all major revolutions in modern and recent times. Joseph de Maistre developed a formula describing the alternation of two extremes: political and constitutional stability can be guaranteed only if a revolutionary "action" is counter-balanced with an equally strong "reaction".[7]

Theoretically, a conflict between the new legal regulation and the existing social reality can be settled in favour of either the former via constitutionalization or the latter via reconstitutionalization. The quest for the rationality of law replaces the search for its efficiency. Therefore, constitutional revolutions are followed by constitutional counter-revolutions or reconstitutionalization which re-enforce the legal norms preceding the newly adopted constitution. Thus, due to the difficulties of constitutionalism, an unprepared society (where the constitution lacks grass-root support, only elite groups are involved in politics, constitutional norms are not protected by courts, and adequate administrative reform is needed) might encounter constitutional retraditionalization occurring directly or indirectly, in one of the ways described below.

As a rule, reconstitutionalization is characterized by three trends. The first trend consists of limiting political space by curbing the activities of political parties. This is achieved through constitutional and other legal methods maintaining the supremacy of one pro-government party over other parties in the area of public policy; and by adopting the legislation compelling parties to strictly observe the constitution (which also undergoes substantial modification). The second trend consists of revising the separation of powers (both horizontal and vertical) with a view to increasing their centralization: restricting federalism; introducing checks and balances systems at the federal level; building the vertical hierarchy of power; instituting the "constitutional" power based on the overwhelming discretionary authorities of the administration. This can be achieved through separating administrative law from the domain of public law and social control (through the adopted legislation on public order, state licensing, greater discretionary powers of administrative institutions and power structures along with limited independence of the judiciary). The coercive administrative supremacy of public law becomes a rationale for reconstitutionalization and concurrently determines its output. Lastly, the third trend shows the prevalence of a special imperial style presidency with the presidential administration ruling over all governmental bodies. Within such a structure, the separation of powers has purely administrative meaning, i.e. a pro-presidential party becomes dominant, especially if led by a president.

The characteristic trends of reconstitutionalization, to some extent, stem from society's unpreparedness to introduce liberal democracy and its response to the inefficiency of democratic institutions. These trends may have different political meaning but, on the whole, they imply new interpretation of constitutional principles aimed at reinforcing centralism and reducing social control over the government through delegating extra powers to administrative bodies within the vertical hierarchy of power and, eventually, to the head of state.

Comparative analyses show that the constitutional cycle completed during reconstitutionalization does not halt the process of development. Rather, it forms the basis for the next constitutional cycle.

Let's take a look at Russian constitutional cycles. The Russian model of constitutionalism, which is mainly based on the French one, can be considered a cyclical model too. Furthermore, the specificity of cycles is very important for understanding the prospects of constitutional development. On the one hand, Russian constitutional cycles appear to be a logical result of the transition to democracy, and in this sense they are far from being just ephemeral formations. Like in other countries, a conflict between the law (as a system of norms) and its social efficiency formed a basis for constitutional cycles and determined their contents. On the other hand, the general peculiarities of Russian constitutionalism could not but affect the configuration of Russian cycles, duration of their phases and the impact of changes. Their peculiarities can be outlined in the following way: i) the absence of social prerequisites for building constitutionalism in the form of a developed civil society and law-based state, on the one hand; and the existence of serious obstacles to its development, such as a traditional class system and a service class system, on the other; ii) a conflict between the state and society, and a conflict between social and legal modernization where the preference was always given to social modernization; iii) constitutional backwardness; iv) constitutional modernization as the principal method of settling differences; v) radical revolution as the main (and the only possible) way for adopting new constitutions during all constitutional cycles.

The cyclical model of Russian constitutional development is a result of the system instability. This instability manifests itself in the regular alternation of periods of deconstitutionalization, constitutionalization and reconstitutionalization, which are every time based on new ideological principles and relevant foreign models. The constitutional revolutions radically rejecting the preceding models (and often the historical tradition), have no constructive elements to ensure political and legal continuity, as well as sustainability of their constitutional achievements. Therefore they don't develop a strong constitutional tradition that would secure the continuity and legitimacy of proclaimed rights and fundamental relations between property and power, thereby impeding constitutional modernization. The danger of new constitutional crises followed by reconstitutionalization is deep-rooted in the Russian society, periodically bringing a cycle to the final authoritarian phase.

Like France, Russia has a cyclical model of constitutional development. Each cycle goes through the phase of deconstitutionalization, i.e. the rise of a new constitutionalism (the phase of exaggerated political expectations); the phase of constitutionalization or practical implementation of constitutional principles revealing their conflict with the reality of everyday life (the beginning of political frustration); and lastly, the phase of transition to reconstitutionalization, limited democracy, and then to tyranny (when society is absolutely indifferent to politics). Cycles recommence after a given interval of time. The uniqueness of Russian cycles lies in their rigid contents: being similar in formal features (developmental phases), each of them tries to radically renounce its predecessor.

This happens for the following reasons: the absence of civil society; inferior legal culture (which until recently has been represented only by a small group of western-minded intellectuals); and the multinational nature of the state with strong monarchial and dictatorial traditions. It was already possible to trace these trends back to the time when the first attempts were made to impose constitutional boundaries on absolutism: drafting projects for restricting monarchical power in the early seventeenth century; making efforts to implement an oligarchic constitution in the eighteenth century; and trying to introduce an octroyed (granted) constitution in the nineteenth century.

Three big constitutional cycles can be highlighted in recent Russian experience. Big cycles are indeed more important than small ones (basically, they correspond to the so-called "pendulum effect" which in the Russian context means the alternation of reforms with counter-reforms in the process of modernization). Small cycles reflect the self-regulating forms of a political system that can be similar in appearance but different in quality. Quite the reverse, big cycles are much more informative in terms of principal qualitative parameters of constitutionalism. Although big constitutional cycles may be of varying duration, they routinely pass through three key phases (some of them may be just perfunctory, whereas others are clearly hypertrophic).

The first Russian big cycle is linked to the 1905–1907 constitutional revolution. It embraces the following phases: the transition from absolutism to monarchical constitutionalism (represented by the progress made from first constitutional drafts to the octroyed Manifesto of 17 October 1905) and then to sham constitutionalism (whose legal form, codified by the Russian Fundamental Law of 23 April 1906 and subsequent legislation, was quite contradictory).

The second cycle was represented by the constitutional revolution that toppled the monarchy to establish a republican regime characterized by one-party dictatorship and nominal constitutionalism. This cycle coincided with a social revolution and collapse of the state. It also included three stages: deconstitutionalization – transition from the monarchy to republic and repeal of the old basic legislation (1917); constitutionalization – the democratic constitution drafted to be adopted by the constituent power (by the Constituent Assembly in 1918); and reconstitutionalization – rejection of both the drafted constitution and the very idea of liberal constitutionalism (1918–1989). At the third phase (which actually covers the whole period of Soviet nominal constitutionalism), the conflict between liberal constitutional law and social efficiency became non-existent. For the law was sacrificed in the name of the abstract and utopian principles of actual equality and social justice (regarded by the population as a guarantor of social significance and legal efficiency). This was achieved through a fine replacement of the real rational constitutional law by the nominal law whose only true social function was to camouflage political reality (the

Soviet Constitutions of 1918, 1924, 1936 and 1977). Besides, the third phase of the second constitutional cycle can be defined as "reconstitutionalization" only conditionally, for it was a return to the pre-constitutional regime with re-established social institutions and practices of the Russian society of the late feudal period (the system of coercive labour and absolute state tyranny).

The third constitutional cycle, which began in the 1990s, has now entered its final stage. This cycle is remarkable because, like its predecessor, it was affected by the collapse of the state. The cycle embraces three main phases: deconstitutionalization – the crisis of legitimacy of nominal constitutionalism in the Soviet Union (1989–1991) and then in Russia (1991–1993); constitutionalization – adoption of the new constitution on 12 December 1993; and reconstitutionalization – the third phase that has been developing since 2000. The question remains: what is the nature of the third phase and can the current constitutional cycle, like other ones, end up reproducing the authoritarian phase in one of its numerous forms?

The comparative analysis of Russian cycles shows their structural similarity: they begin with radical constitutional revolutions, pass through three phases (resembling the Hegelian triad) and come to an end (except for the last one) with radical reconstitutionalization restoring the pre-constitutional order. Each cycle has its own teleology that rests on the previous development and the logic of a constitutional crisis that brought it into life. The first cycle challenged absolutism and promoted the constitutional state, i.e. popular representation in the form of constitutional monarchy or republic. The second cycle tried to overcome the dualism of law and sense of justice by creating democratic institutions. However, it ended up with the introduction of nominal constitutionalism (which fixed the elements of the sense of justice residing in archaic peasants' minds, but turned constitutionalism into fiction). The third cycle was focused on the transition from Soviet nominal constitutionalism to a real one. Thus, its substantial tasks gravitate to the first cycle rather than to the second one originally rejected by the third cycle. The preceding cycles increasingly resemble each other owing to their spontaneous development, broken legal continuity, and reconstitutionalization resulting in authoritarianism and constitutional stagnation during which a constitutional revolution was conceived leading to the next cycle.

The transition from one cycle to another is a complex research problem that cannot be solved without the combination of juridical and political studies. On the one hand, some difficulties were encountered by the researchers who simply analysed Russian constitutional norms and overlooked the extra-constitutional factors of social and political nature that formed public opinion on constitutional norms (e.g. fundamental rights, land ownership or the separation of powers). These researchers noticed that some of the Russian constitutional elements had certain affinities with western constitutions. They genuinely wondered why the elements did not work in Russia and explained it as a collision and cross-impact of various foreign benchmarks. However, what was really needed was a method for selecting norms and institutions which could prove effective in the Russian context. On the other hand, those who used sociological models based on different empiric data describing social transformations outside their Russian legal context faced a different sort of problem. The review of big constitutional cycles highlights continuing trends in the conflict between norms and institutions under changing social conditions of Russian society.

Despite being different in content, duration and consequence, constitutional cycles are always triggered by the same mechanism: a conflict between the constituent power and constitutional power. And it is unclear whether the current Russian Constitution is capable of preventing the mechanism from being set in motion.

Democracy and constitutional changes

Contemporary discussions on democratic issues allow one to formulate two opinions on the role of law in social transformations and constitutional changes. The first opinion promotes democracy and its social parameters as a socio-political structure based on the principles of equality, though providing for the protection of minority and human rights. Following this interpretation, perfect democracy means a social state equally opposed to both a modern consumer society and authoritarian political tradition. Thus, democracy might be defined as a political system adjusting to the objective needs of social development. According to the second opinion, which shares the principles of classical liberalism, democracy in the first place protects and guarantees human rights and civil liberties as well as its own independence from subsistence society. This discussion is a continuation of the controversy between those advocating "collectivist" and "individualist" theories in the first quarter of the twentieth century. As in the past, contemporary discussions revolve around issues such as the contradictory nature of democracy, conflict between the individual and society, conflict between individual social rights and political rights, and the necessity of coordinating these rights within a rational system of public law.

The representative government ("le gouvernement représentatif") in the liberalist interpretation means the "combination of democratic and aristocratic features". There are three perfect types of representative government which emerged one after another in the course of historic development: parliamentarianism, party government and public democracy. Parliamentarianism is the classical system of representation that reached its height in Great Britain in the nineteenth century. Party government ("parteiendemokratie", "démocratie de partis") is a new phenomenon which took shape during the transition from traditional society to mass society in the early twentieth century. This phenomenon was brought about by a shift from rigid class structures and qualification elections to the universal suffrage implemented through the system of political parties. The phenomenon of "party government" was interpreted as a crisis of democracy by Moisey Ya. Ostrogorsky, Hans Kelsen and Robert Michels. The phenomena such as the society divided into political parties, the electorate manipulated by politicians and party bureaucracy are indicative of the "crisis of representation" and of liberal parliamentarianism in general. However, gradually it became clear that though parliamentarianism in its original forms was crowded out by mass parties, the concept of representative government took new forms and remained relevant. Further, there was widespread opinion that the new form promoted democracy by increasing the electorate, engaging the general public into politics, improving competitiveness and consequently ensuring the better expression of *vox populi* (B. Manin).

The recent phase of representative democracy resembles the watershed in its development at the turn of the nineteenth century, since the representative system crisis is again at the core of debates. However, the analysis of new trends suggests that changes are structural rather than substantial. The new term "public democracy" has been proposed to define the contemporary structure of representation dominated by individual representation. The technical features of the new media enable voters to identify themselves with a party leader rather than with the party itself (television, in particular, allows candidates to strongly influence the electorate). Decisions are determined by the media elite rather than party bosses. Public democracy is defined as the domination of media professionals. The political platform is represented by a candidate's image, whereas electoral behaviour (irrespective of political affiliation) is largely predicted by a psychological reaction to this image. As the traditional division of voters (into parties' adherents) disappears, the electorate becomes closer to the public in a traditional sense of the word (i.e. the host of individuals spontaneously reacting to the proposed political initiatives). From an historical perspective, this scheme of representative democratic development is conditional. However, it enables one to identify specifics and particularities of each phase of representative democracy according to the parameters such as the choice of ruler, degree of ruler's independence, freedom of public opinion, and form of political discussion. The ability of representative democracy to adapt to various social conditions arises from its complex nature displaying both democratic and non-democratic features.

The peculiarity of contemporary discussions on democracy lies in the necessity of correlating its classical conception (based on the experience of stable western democracies) with its new interpretations brought about by the era of rationalization, globalization and modernization, i.e. to take account of the regions that have only hypothetically stepped on the road to democracy. Theoretically, the new reality is reflected in the ideas of social processes globalization; in the exhaustion of environmental and demographic resources and the need for discovering effective ways to bridge economic, social and cultural gaps between rich and poor countries and to explore new informational and technical parameters of democracy; as well as in the ideas of communicative democracy.

From this perspective, it is possible to explain the *contradictions of modern democracy*: when rapid social and political changes, aimed at establishing democracy in the countries historically unprepared for it, produce the antipode of democracy a new type of tyranny where real democracy is replaced by an imitation, and legal regulation by nominal or sham constitutionalism.

The main contradiction of democracy lies in a conflict between the idea of popular sovereignty and the principle of law-based state. The absolute power of the people, as shown by history, is often illegal and disrespectful to the law. However, the law itself, as a conservative phenomenon by definition, does not necessarily correspond to the collective vision or the "will of the people" at any given stage of historical development. This fundamental contradiction is typical of all the constitutions written in recent times, since they combine the principle of popular sovereignty with the principle of law-based state. Hence, conflicts are embedded in the constitutional process which has to maintain an equilibrium between society and state, equality and freedom, social guarantees and individual rights. Such conflicts frequently take the form of acute constitutional crises expressed through constitutional revolutions and radical reforms that are most clearly observed during the period of social transformations when the law lags behind the reality or, on the contrary, surpasses it.

Constitutional crisis means radical changes to the existing legal system resulting in replacement of one Basic Law with another. These changes are most visibly reflected in the *constitutional crisis* which can be settled through either the partial or complete restructuring of constitutional system. We are not going to study the origins of the notion "crisis" that has many interpretations in contemporary science. However, it should be mentioned that the crisis implies either the continuity being completely broken or radically modified and yet preserving some of its elements. In this regard, it is important to introduce the notions "constitutional revolution" and "constitutional reform" and to determine their correlation. Revolution, in legal terms, means the broken continuity of political power within a state, accompanied by the radically revised values of public and legal norms. Constitutional revolution means fundamental changes to the Basic Law which are not based on its provisions, hence create an entirely new constitution. The changes may be implemented in a formal way (in the form of the newly adopted constitution) or carried out along with the old constitution being preserved (the phenomenon of a so-called "parallel constitution"). Reform consists of changes to a legal system which do not break legal continuity. Constitutional reform consists of changes to the

Basic Law, which are in line with its provisions and therefore foster its legal development in a new socio-political reality. Being a means of constitutional modernization, such reforms may be accomplished through constitutional amendments or judicial interpretation of constitutional norms. And they can be rather radical sometimes. Procedures for constitutional reforms should be clearly enshrined in the constitution itself or embedded in the liberal culture of citizens as to avoid an unregulated process of constitutional changes leading to the authoritarian re-creation of democratic norms without their formal legal review. Let's now explore a relationship between the notions "social revolution" and "constitutional revolution". American and French revolutions differed so remarkably that their peculiarities were reflected in the difference between the notions of constitutional revolution and that of social revolution. Anglo-American revolutions belong to the first category, whereas French and Russian ones fall into the second. The constitutional revolution is, indeed, a specific type of revolution because it does not fundamentally change the social system, property relations and ruling elite composition. The social revolution is, by contrast, characterized by completely changing the system of public goods redistribution, changing the ways of their allocation, and destroying the legitimacy of the old ruling class. This concept is static and problematic for the analysis of the dynamics of socio-political upheavals: in reality, social and constitutional changes are interwoven; besides, they go through different stages of development (while social revolutions are usually followed by political ones, constitutional revolutions may give rise to radical social changes). This paradigm is very important because it clearly demonstrates the uniqueness of constitutional revolution *per se*. It is relevant in the context of discussions on whether the European Revolutions of 1989 are social or constitutional owing to their evidently specific nature. These revolutions did not have the social pathos of modern-time revolutions with their ideas about progress and social emancipation. Individualistic principles prevailed over collectivist ones. The revolutions were all about an evolutional (peaceful) transition to the new political system. Here, it is probably easier to draw a parallel with restoration than with revolution: the latter should be applied only to the situations where the old discredited system of power is strongly rejected and replaced by a new structural form – political pluralism. All these revolutions were sparked off by political rather than social demands, and the chief demand was to secure citizens' basic constitutional rights. The phenomenon of modernization defined as a "catch-up revolution" is very important too. The synthesis of the two kinds of revolutionary changes has brought forth the concept of new constitutionalism implying that in recent times it is possible (with the help of technical progress, social experience and imagination) to achieve a combination of the previously incompatible principles of social democracy and political democracy. The new type of constitutionalism is expected to bridge a gap between the state and civil society and to create an integral type of sovereignty (a sort of city state), i.e. a dynamic self-regulating system capable of finding adequate legal solutions to crisis situations (to solve the problems of scarce resources allocation, address demographic issues, to ensure the promotion of social information and mobility).

According to Hans Kelsen, revolution (which in a broader sense also covers coup d'etat) means any amendments to the constitution or revision and replacement thereof introduced in breach of effective constitutional provisions.[8] Kelsen stresses that it is the phenomenon of revolution that clarifies the meaning of basic norm. For example, a group of individuals tries to seize power by force in order to replace a legitimate monarchical government by a republican regime. If they succeed in toppling the old regime, the entire legal system with its evaluation criteria for lawful and unlawful revolutionary behaviour will change. Therefore, the same actions may be interpreted in a totally opposite way, i.e. they may be viewed as lawful or unlawful depending on the revolution success or failure. The success of a coup as a criterion of legitimacy or illegitimacy of the new fundamental law lies at the heart of Kelsen's approach. The normativist theory of constitutional revolution, despite its Machiavellianism, is very valuable for legal scholars because it helps to explain the twentieth-century paradoxes when anti-constitutional forces gain access to power in a constitutional way, and the principles of classical constitutionalism are used to legitimate political regimes established by force. Kelsen's interpretation of the constitution as a totality of public and legal norms with state-specific meaning was also very useful for explicating the phenomenon of sham constitutionalism. Liberal criticism of the Kelsen concept of constitutional revolution rested upon the revived ideas of natural law, particularly the new interpretation of relations between the realms of "being" and "obligation" (Sein und Sollen). As one of the critics noted, if we agreed with Kelsen that any operational legal system represents the law in a broader sense, it would be impossible to assess their relations from the perspective of "obligation". This creates a cynical view on the status of the law during revolution. According to Kelsen, the defeated revolutionists are criminals. However, it is exactly the winners who force the next generations of jurists to call the newly established system "law". He considers the obligation to be purely created by constitutional drafters. Yet, it has nothing to do with moral or political principles. The key role here belongs to the concept of legitimacy which is interpreted as a socially determined obligation, i.e. a sort of collective vision of obligation. The purpose of constitutional revolution is to replace one type of obligation with another, paving the way for a new system of norms and for a new legitimacy. The analysis of revolutionary phenomenon focuses on the crisis of legitimacy involving a loss of the old legitimacy and a search for the new one. Accepting the new principles of interpretation with their respective institutions and semantic systems is a factor of transformation and application of the law. It suggests a thesis about the need to supplement the legal study of political upheavals with their moral assessment. Constitutional revolution is a means of transforming the national legal and political structure via conflict. In modern times, the constitutional crisis is coupled with the crisis of a state or political system. Modification or replacement of legal norms is usually linked to or caused by political crises. Legal revolution is in principle interwoven with a political one, the former often being a continuation or consequence of the latter. However, crises can be provoked by the constitutional structure itself: rigid constitutional norms hampering the progress of socio-political changes give rise to revolutionary anti-constitutional movements. Constitutional revolution means the position of state power in the process of transition from one constitutional stage to another, i.e. the very process of constitutionalization of the new power as such.

An ambiguous nature of the relationship between revolution and constitution is reflected in debates on the nature of constituent power and constitutional power and their correlation. If a constitution is created by the power, then a political regime can be established from scratch (*ex nihilo*). According to historical studies, the contemporary concept of constituent power is mainly based on the ideas of medieval European philosophers and it can clearly illustrate what some researchers call "political theology". Thus, the concept of constituent power is a secularized version of the theory of divine power that is able to create the secular order from scratch and arrange it without being put in a position of dependence on the newly created system. The will of constituent power is directed towards transforming itself into a stable formation, i.e. a constitution broadly perceived as any of the Basic Laws. However, this cannot remain the highest secular power without having to depend on its own creation.

During revolution the purpose of constituent power, in parallel to the approach described above, is transformation of the disorganized creative revolutionary force into the constitutionalized power of a certain political regime. As soon as the constituent power establishes its constitution, any other power aspiring to be legitimate must comply with it. In doing so, revolutionaries doom themselves to extinction, for a constitution is the final act of a revolution. At the end of the day, this idea evolves into the transformation of a single constituent power into the pluralism of constitutionalized powers. Therefore, the subsequent political process is regulated by the constitution, not revolutionists. More specifically, this process is regulated by the social forces which benefited from the revolution, though not necessarily initiated it or took part in it. Certain revolutionary groups (seeking to maintain institutional and legal instability), therefore, prefer a permanent revolution to the constitution (U. Preuss).

Though the constitution releases social forces suppressed by the old regime, it frequently creates political and institutional prerequisites for emergence of fresh social and political actors. This observation is proven by the situation in several countries of Eastern and Central Europe where it creates new political actors and presents them, like revolutionists of the past, with the problem of an uncertain political process organized by the constitution.

Given this approach, the constitution represents a self-destructive revolution. The typical feature of all recent revolutions is the split of revolutionary forces into two groups: those trying to escape their political death by proclaiming a permanent revolution or, at least, favouring the institutional structure that perpetuates the ruling of a revolutionary elite; and those trying to use their constituent power in order to establish a new structure of the state. So, we can formulate two alternative interpretations (and self-interpretations) of the political forces divided into "radically democratic" and "institutional", depending on their attitude towards constitutional structure. These trends are discernible in the theoretical discussions of all major revolutions and reflected in contemporary scholars' views on constitutional law.

According to the radical democratic model, constitutions sanction democratic revolutions by formally confirming the fact that via revolutionary actions people gain their constituent power which is immune from any norms, institutions or considerations of higher order and is guided only by its unlimited will to power. Constitutions are the authentic expression and embodiment of this will. According to this statement (typical of Rousseau's interpretation of popular sovereignty), constitutions aim to entrench the main achievements of a revolution and gravitate to incorporate many of its social promises. As the constitution cannot cover all political issues, constitutional framers seek to create an institutional regime that would empower people to act as the highest judge in all political conflicts which will inevitably arise in future. The people are regarded as reliable guards of their revolutionary achievements. Besides, the majority of the people can impose their will on the minority. Radical democratic constitutions, as a rule, put the popular assembly above other branches of power. The power of the people is considered to be the power of their representatives. Additional guarantees are provided by plebiscite, proportional government and imperative mandate of the members of parliament. In the case of major social and political conflicts, power should be delegated to citizens with the permission of the elected delegates, for the power of the people is the highest in democracy. Those advocating this type of constitutionalism count on the people's high morale and adherence to revolutionary principles. Ideally, they would like to maintain the permanent revolution and erase a divide between revolutionary and normal politics. The constitutions of such a revolutionary democratic type are unstable.

By contrast, the institutionalist definition of revolution uses the people's revolutionary spirit to set up institutions that would allow them to return to normal life and normal politics after the attainment of revolutionary goals. Institutionalists rely on the wisdom of the functioning of these institutions and social mechanisms, rather than on the direct principle of the people's will to power and to preserving civic virtues characteristic of revolutionary times. As a rule, the constitutional drafters adhering to the principles of institutionalism reluctantly introduce substantive regulatory provisions (political principles) into constitutions, because these may hinder the implementation of such a policy under new circumstances and therefore undermine the creativity of political institutions. From the institutionalist perspective (primarily represented by the liberal theory), constitutions are "institutional tools for solving problems" rather than ready-made solutions. The people obey norms (separation of powers or independence of judges) not because they want to guarantee stable political results, but because they want to ensure that political results correspond to the original revolutionary goals and to the old principles they want to respect under constantly changing circumstances. The constitutions drafted by institutionalists are not intended to "freeze" the will of a given or any future revolutionary generation. They do not institutionalize decisions. Rather, such constitutons institutionalize the very ability of the people to shape their will in the post-revolutionary period of normal politics, without being urged to reanimate their revolutionary spirit or apply extreme measures under constantly changing socio-political circumstances. Hence, institutionalist constitutions are inimical to any attempts to revive the revolutionary spirit, since they favour social mechanisms that secure political achievements and ensure more effective results compared to revolutionary crises, without incurring the heavy costs typical of the latter.

Constitutionalism is interpreted from two standpoints characteristic of contemporary legal philosophy at large. These are normativist and voluntarist theories. The first relies on the positivist statement that the constitution accurately reflects the state of current positive law. The second (Marxism, in the first place) sees the constitution as an element of the ideological superstructure which eventually mirrors the economic infrastructure. Contemporary science suggests an institutional approach as an alternative to these two standpoints. This approach recognizes a certain independence of legal norms on the one hand; and links them up with the nature of constitutional regime and with the functioning of political institutions on the other. Thus, constitution is sociologically interpreted as the reflection of "force ratio" ("rapport de forces") in society.

Under this approach, constitution is a reflection of the balance of forces existing in society, of a consensus on the general rules of the game. The existence of power relations between the opposing social groups allows the constitution to effectively perform its regulatory functions in society. Resting upon the ideas of functionalism and interactionism, this approach gives a new interpretation for the social nature of the underlying principles of constitutionalism. The concept of social contract is interpreted as a clearly expressed conviction that the constitution safeguards an equilibrium between social partners. The equilibrium is institutionally manifested in the concept of representative government and the separation of powers. Lastly, the interpretation of democracy as a balance of elites stresses the dynamic character of that equilibrium. Sociologists took the notion of dysfunction from biology. It means a situation where normal rational behaviour entails irrational and even destructive consequences under new social conditions. We believe that this approach clearly defines the essential role of constitutionalism in a rapidly changing society. Constitutional behaviour, which is in compliance with the Basic Law, is always more conservative compared with the behaviour not governed by the law. The main contradiction of democracy, as repeatedly mentioned, is a contradiction between popular sovereignty and the principle of law-based state. In the constitutional process, this contradiction manifests itself in a conflict between legitimacy and legality.

When Carl Schmitt raised this issue at the time of Weimar Germany, it generated much interest among those who wanted to alter the constitution, including both right- and left-wing forces. The question "who protects the constitution?" was at the heart of many heated debates.[9] Legal theory gives two different answers: the head of state (Schmitt's viewpoint) and the constitutional court (Kelsen's opinion). Finding a solution to this problem in different political regimes – presidential or parliamentary – is now the focal point of debates on power legitimacy. Clearly, the dilemma can be resolved only through a dynamic constitutional process impeding any blind devotion to the constitution. Democratic legitimization aims to ensure citizens' effective impact on the exercise of power which can take on various forms. There are institutional, functional, structural and individual forms that can be supplementary to and contradictory with each other.

Consociational democracy gives an opportunity to ensure the stability and manageability of divided societies through negotiating a compromise between the elite groups. While the masses of people divided into different social blocks continue to oppose each other, the elite groups representing these blocks can cooperate in order to achieve the highest goal: to guarantee the stability of a democratic process. This becomes possible only if the elites manage to agree on the general rules of the game and on effective resource allocation for the public policy implementation. Such rules are entrenched in a special type of constitutionalism which might be called "consociational". Consociational constitutionalism is indispensable for modernizing heterogeneous societies. The logic of sociological interpretation of constitutionalism allows us to formulate three hypotheses about possible relationships between the constitution and society: the constitution as an adequate expression of social compromise (the constitution acts as an effective instrument of power restriction because it is based on the ability of opposing groups' potential action); the constitution as camouflage for real power relations in society (it can be used as hollow democratic rhetoric based on the belief that the constitution by the very fact of its existence can stabilize social relations); and the constitution as a declaration of desirable changes having mobilizing nature for a transitional epoch.

The essence of transitional dynamics is determined by the dialectics of deconstitutionalization (repeal of the old constitution) and reconstitutionalization (introduction of the new one). Between these two operations a transitional regime is observed which is based on the fundamental act adopted by the assembly and meant for shaping public power during a transitional period. The main legal problem of that period is how to prove the validity of constitutional norms solely relying on their acceptance by public opinion or on the social contract. In the epochs of constitutional revolutions, there are two polar opinions: according to the first one, the very fact of revolutionary changes validates constitutional norms; according to the second one, their validity is determined by the degree of constitutional process' compliance with society's view on the law and democracy. In between the two marginal phases of constitutional cycle, social changes leading to restructuring towards either democracy or tyranny take place in society.

The notion "democratization" and the notion "democratic transition" are different in their scope. Democratization applies to countries with long, stable democratic traditions. And democratic transition refers particularly to countries shifting from an authoritarian regime to democracy. The process of democratic transformation encompasses three periods: from the nineteenth century to the beginning of the First World War; from the end of the Second World War to the 1960s; from the early 1970s up to the present. This process has reached its zenith when extended into Eastern Europe. Currently, even the remaining authoritarian regimes have to resort to "imitated" democracy or "facade democracy" for the sake of self-legitimization. The process of democratic transformations can be spontaneous and mark the first break with the authoritarian past in a country's history; or it can take on a specific form of "redemocratization", i.e. restoration of democratic institutions in the countries where they previously existed. The process of transition goes through the following stages: annihilation of dictatorship; transformation of the old structures and institutions; and lastly, stabilization of the new regime. The analysis of transitional conditions is needed for political forecasting, for it enables one to easily test submitted hypotheses. Using the comparative approach we can classify transitional societies into the following types: those switching from absolutism to democracy in Western Europe in modern times; and those undergoing transition in Southern Europe, Eastern Europe, Latin America and Asia. Retrospectively, depending on the historical duration of an authoritarian phase, crises can be divided into two groups: crises occurring in the countries whose population was either unfamiliar with democratic institutions or already forgot about them; and crises emerging in comparatively developed democratic political cultures partially affected by authoritarian regime. Of importance also is the starting point of this process: individual military dictatorship, populist dictatorship or totalitarian ideology.

Constitutional crises in transitional societies

Constitutional crisis means the conditions under which either the Basic Law loses its legitimacy (a gap between legitimacy and legality appears); or conflicting social forces fail to agree on certain constitutional norms; or constitutional provisions clash with political reality. The most acute constitutional crisis is generally (but not necessarily) linked to the crisis of political regime and it can take on various forms. During transition from authoritarianism to democracy, the ways of solving constitutional crises are represented by two ideal models for adopting a constitution: the first model is based on the contract (consensus-based model), and the second on the disruption of consensus (essentially, the octroyed model). The first model is defined as a deliberate strategy urging political parties to agree on the basic values of civil society and long-term goals of development. The second model, by contrast, is defined as an insuperable conflict between political forces that leads to a situation where one force establishes dominance over the others and bends them to its will. The consensus-based model is preferred to the conflict-based model in terms of stability, legitimacy and continuity of legal development. The first model is illustrated by the Spanish Constitution of 1978, and the second one by the Russian Constitution of 1993.

Globally speaking, the constitutional development is uneven. A chronological comparison permits revealing common factors which determine the specifics of constitutionalism in any given era. From this perspective, recent times are characterized by the factors unknown to classical constitutionalism. These include a new approach to the social problem (integration of social law into constitutional law), new political communications, influence of the international law on the domestic constitutional law, and the constitutionalization of other branches of the law. For a researcher, the stages of constitutional process are as important as its chronology. The constitutional institutions of the present-day Russia should be compared not only to the modern West European constitutions but also to the similar institutions of the nineteenth century. This permits revealing the true meaning of legal norms which acquire different social contents in different historical periods. Let's assume that the linear comparison of constitutional crises in France (1958), Spain (1975–1978) and Russia (1989–1993) shows their differences rather than similarities. Many trends in the contemporary development of Russian constitutionalism can be compared to the West European trends of the nineteenth century, rather than to current ones. For example, let's look at the problems related to Bonapartism or constitutional establishment of authoritarian power. The similar debates, which are currently under way in Russia, highlight a whole range of ideas voiced in France a century ago. Constitutional crises appear even more specific in application to such countries as the Ukraine, Georgia, Kazakhstan and Uzbekistan, where constitutionalism-related issues as such have become a subject of political debates only recently.

A classification of crises leading to revolutionary changes in existing legal systems can be made according to the reasons for their emergence. Firstly, they emerge because of an increasing inconsistency between the traditional legal system and the new social reality (e.g. the rationalistic codification of laws adopted in the eighteenth and the early nineteenth centuries as opposed to the traditionalist legal norms); secondly, they emerge when the problem of inconsistency is solved by adopting a well-drafted foreign legislation (e.g. the French Civil Code adopted by Latin America); thirdly, crises emerge in the course of a real political revolution changing social environment (e.g. the French and Russian revolutions that created new legal systems); fourthly, they emerge when the political elite uses the law to promote a revolutionary spirit among citizens (e.g. the Meiji Revolution in Japan, or the Tanzimat in Turkey); and lastly, crises emerge when the winners impose a foreign legal system on defeated nations (e.g. the Soviet legal system introduced in Eastern Europe after the Second World War).

Crises can be also divided into global (or systemic) crises and internal ones which do not threaten democratic principles. The first type of crises embraces the constitutional crises of all great social revolutions resulting in the establishment of new social and legal systems (e.g. the constitutional crises that erupted during the French, Russian, Chinese, Iranian and Mexican revolutions). The second type of crises includes the crisis that moved France from the Fourth to the Fifth Republic and established De Gaulle's authoritarian regime, or the crisis that is now under way in Italy. In both cases, legitimacy crisis and constitutional system dysfunction took place. However, in the second case, the democratic nature of regimes has never been questioned or at least the hidden danger was not a determinant. This dualism is also characterized, as already mentioned, by a confrontation between "social" and "constitutional" revolutions (although both of them imply the radical transformation of constitutional system).

Crises, as mentioned above, can be linear and cyclical. From the long-term perspective, French constitutional crises can be viewed as cycles or a spiral whose every turn starts with proclaiming parliamentary ideas and ends up with a new authoritarian regime (e.g. Bonapartism, Boulangism, Vichyism and Gaullism). Researchers believe that the reason for this regularity, which makes them think of the famous Vico theory, is the continuous reproduction of a fundamental conflict inherent in the French political tradition: the conflict between the principle of popular sovereignty and republican government.

Some contemporary researchers argue that adoption of the Constitution of the Fifth Republic put an end to the cycles in French political tradition. The purpose of the constitution was to reconcile the following contradictory movements: elitism and egalitarianism, Jacobinism and Girondinism, liberalism and socialism, monarchical tradition and republican dynamic, direct democracy and representative government. In this sense, the constitution in question corresponds to the original Constitution of 1791 with its "royal democracy" ("democratie royale") model.

The constitutional reform of 1958 achieved three objectives: the parliamentary regime was established; the prestige of executive power, undermined by the thorny Algerian problem and weakened in the period of the Fourth Republic, was restored; and the feelings of citizens, who lost faith in representative government in the form of pure absolutism, were taken into consideration. Eventually, a new synthesis – dualistic parliamentarian regime – came into play.

The mechanisms of constitutional structural crises become most visible during revolutions, when a successive transfer of power from one group to another highlights a whole range of possible positions. According to Crane Brinton, power is transferred from the old conservative regime to a moderate political regime and on to radicals or extremists. During this transfer, it becomes more consolidated and loses its link to grass roots because at every important crisis stage the defeated public groups are thrown off politics. In other words, after each crisis the winning party tends to split again into conservatives holding onto power and radicals forming the opposition. At a certain stage, any crisis culminates in the victory of a radical opposition concentrating all authority in its hands. In the course of revolutions, this process may pass through different stages varying in their duration and impact. The structural crisis of a political system expresses itself in transformation of constitutional fundamentals; regardless of the fact whether or not these changes are formally and legally fixed.

Structurally, constitutional crises can be classified using such systemic parameters as centralism and federalism, the separation of powers, the role of parties in a political system, and the procedure for constitutional revision. Revolution as a fact is recognized only if the constitution has been fully rewritten by the sovereign national assembly. The comparative analysis of such institutions (national assemblies and constitutional assemblies) displays both similarities and differences in their functions at a time of constitutional crisis. The features they have in common are the very idea of convening a sovereign national representative body for drafting a basic legislation or part thereof; as well as the key role this political institution plays in the process of revolutionary transition, no matter how it was established (in an upward or downward fashion or by a presidential decree). However, during a crisis the institution's functions vary and can become diametrically opposite ranging from crisis provocation (as it happened when the King called the States General in 1789) to its resolution. During the English, French and Russian revolutions, crises were instigated by the representative bodies that were set up by the head of state to find a way out of crises (primarily, financial crises); and initially they had a limited scope of legislative authorities. As for Russian constitutionalism, it has seen examples of both types of constitutional assemblies: from the Constituent Assembly of 1918 and the Congress of People's Deputies of 1989 to the Constitutional Assembly of 1993.

The internal dynamics of constitutional assemblies is different from that of other political institutions. When researchers tried to understand how deputies of the States General turned into revolutionists, they focused on the internal logic of their collective actions. Furthermore, they challenged the theory of the French Revolution developed by revisionist historians, from Alexis de Tocqueville to Francois Furet. According to this theory, there are no social motives for a revolution in society. However, a researcher finds them in the very composition of the parliamentary corps split into aristocrats and representatives of the third estate. This conflict increased tensions and triggered revolutionary processes in society. The Constitutional Assembly, being a closed political body greatly influenced by the social milieu, not only expressed but also created a new public opinion by crystallizing and intensifying social antagonisms. Under the circumstances, political blocks within the assembly were formed via their division and uncompromising mutual confrontation. Deputy groups, political clubs and parties were shaped following the rule of power consolidation and consistent removal of the forces that could potentially enter the political arena. Over a short period of time, the amorphous political formations gave way to well-organized groups that were later replaced by the Jacobin Club, which was capable of dominating the Assembly and solving the crisis of political leadership.

Constitutional assemblies played a key role in the legitimization of new constitutional authorities during transitional periods in East European countries. The assemblies were formed either through elections (e.g. Albania, Bulgaria and Romania) or self-constitutionalization (e.g. Poland, Hungary and Czechoslovakia). The genesis of constitutional assemblies is very important for the legitimization of newly adopted legislative acts. Democratic procedures for assembly convocation ensure the legitimacy of these acts and their approval by society. However, there may be certain nuances. Constructional assemblies are not always a prerequisite for constitutional consensus (for example, most of the Hungarian constitutional provisions were adopted prior to the first free elections). Assemblies are also composed of different political parties: in Czechoslovakia and Poland, communists not only participated in the establishment of democratic institutions but also strongly influenced their activities (in Poland they even dominated in the Constitutional Commission when it was drafting the Basic Law).

Unlike the national assemblies established by European revolutions in modern times (with the French Revolutionary Convent being a classic example), the constitutional assemblies convened by developing nations in moments of crisis and, paradoxically, do not resist the government but are organized according to the government's activities. Such trends can be observed, for example, in the acts adopted by the national conferences of African francophone developing nations (e.g. Congo, Mali, Nigeria, Chad, Togo, Zaire). Obviously, in some cases the national assembly promotes views of the opposition, while in others it serves as an instrument of constitutional integration. Finally, the assembly may become split and thus trapped in a lasting instability and inaction.

Coup d'etat is usually interpreted as a successful or unsuccessful attempt to seize political power, by means of the threat or use of force. Yet, this general definition does not explain the specifics and particularities of various coups in terms of their position on the Basic Law. Although coups are usually illegal and anti-constitutional, they may lay foundations for a new constitution. This fact drew the attention of such prominent theorists as Aristotle and Machiavelli. They argued that the rational form of legal government could be established through the usurpation of power. The Latin America classical tradition of coups ("el golpismo") suggested that as different as the political nature of coups may be, they are united by opposition to law and law-based state. On the one hand, there lies a similarity between the anti-democratic oligarchic regimes created under the pretext of protecting "Western and Christian democracy" and the Marxist regimes promoting "popular democracy". On the other hand, coups may occur within the framework of the existing constitution, bringing new social and political meaning to its provisions. Finally, there is a specific kind of coup intended to protect the existing constitutional system against external or internal dangers. At a certain stage, even totalitarian ideologists (e.g. Puritans, Jacobins, Bolsheviks and Nazis) used this approach for purely tactical purposes in their pursuit of power. Classical coups d'etat are often carried out in the name of constitution and its "correct interpretation". They are incited by the forces belonging to the governmental elite: high-ranking officials (for example, the coup of Luis Napoleon on 2 December 1851 or the putsch of the Peruvian President in 1992) or military authorities (coups carried out by Franco in Spain in 1936, Nasser in Egypt, and officers in Portugal in 1974). In this regard, we should also mention the special coups which are formally and actually planned to preserve the original constitutional system (e.g. the Turkish military upheavals in the twentieth century). Despite their varying forms, all coups (prepared either internally or externally; carried out either peacefully or coupled with a civil war) have distinct constitutional contents and therefore are an instrument of constitutional changes. Since the respective terminology is vague (coups are called "pronunciamento" in Spanish-speaking countries and "putsch" in German tradition), it is difficult to identify the coups that are formally conducted in conformity with the constitution. The category of "constitutional coups" is very close to radical constitutional reforms with nil or minimal involvement from citizens. The well-known examples of such constitutional reforms are the Bismarck "revolution from above" and constitutional reforms introduced by Kemal Attaturk in Turkey, Charles de Gaulle in France, and Mikhail Gorbachev in Russia. Regardless of their results, the abovementioned reforms were implemented through introducing legitimate and often constitutional changes to existing regimes which, however, gave rise to a substantially new constitutional system.

Introducing a state of emergency is, undoubtedly, one of the ways to suspend or abolish the constitution without undermining its official status. The institution of the state of emergency can be pro-constitutional and anti-constitutional. The real constitutional process illustrates how this instrument can be used in both ways. To analyse this, it is necessary to distinguish between such notions as "state of emergency" and "martial law" (or the stage of siege). A state of emergency can be introduced either peacefully or forcibly. It can be actual and prescribed by law. In Russian political tradition, which is oriented toward authoritarianism, a state of emergency was often imposed to suspend constitutional norms, most notably in the period from 1905 till the demise of the Russian Empire in 1917. In this sense, the institution of the state of emergency is a quintessential element of sham constitutionalism. The history of the Soviet nominal constitutionalism was marked by creation of the so-called institutions of emergency situations under which decision-making on important issues related to the foreign and domestic policies was withdrawn from the scope of constitutional competence, and key decisions were implemented in breach of constitutional and quasi-constitutional norms. It should be mentioned that a state of emergency may be actually imposed without resorting to the whole range of emergency laws but merely by introducing its basic structural elements: censorship, restricted freedom of movement and suppression of the opposition by force. In this respect, it is important to draw a line between the institution of the state of emergency and emergency laws. In federal states, the situations of a state of emergency can be divided into nationwide and local (introduced in individual regions). And one of their forms is direct presidential government in regions. In terms of their legal implications, such measures can be separated into those aimed at preserving and protecting the existing constitutional system and those intended to suspend or abolish the constitution. The first category is typical of stable democracies (e.g. France), and the second one of dictatorial (e.g. the Spanish Constitution "suspended" by Primo de Rivero) or totalitarian regimes. A classic example is Article 48 of the Weimar Constitution which was applied in 1933 for establishing the national-socialist dictatorship in Germany. Thus, the institution of the state of emergency plays a decisive role in levelling legal and political instruments of conflict resolution during acute constitutional crises. Schmitt rightly concluded that only those who had the right and capacity to introduce a state of emergency could protect the constitution in moments of constitutional crisis.

The so-called imitated democracy has a limited potential. The fact was confirmed by the experience of developing nations which encountered many difficulties when they tried to merely imitate the western models of constitutionalism, such as the Westminster model and presidential republic. It became clear that applying the same definitions to political situations in different countries makes them more difficult to understand. We are referring to such basic notions as "democracy", "supremacy of law", and "human rights" whose subject is non-existent in many countries under modernization. This fact explains the quest for a new strategy of constitutional modernization that would pursue the basic aims of western constitutionalism using different means and methods. Constitutional order is supposed to create new rules of the game on the basis of relationships existing within society. That requires a new constitutional reform policy. Instead of having constitutional acts that are drafted by the government and have a zero practical effect for society, constitutional order should be established on the basis of a balance (or consensus) between real social forces. Thus, the constitution is used by society as a tool in its struggle with the traditional regime for establishing a civil society and autonomous political structures.

The situation of choice between models of constitutional transformations characterizes the instability of constitutionalism. A constitutional reform can be modelled on constitutions of either developed democracies or transitional states. For instance, the concept of socio-political reforms in Latin America was considerably influenced by the debates held in the era of Russian perestroika (reconstruction). Similar debates also took place in China, where the existing regime was legitimized not by implementing the constitutional reform but rather by suppressing the liberal opposition. A conflict between the new type of economic development and the remaining one-party dictatorship may provoke a political crisis which can be settled through radical constitutional reform only. Contemporary researchers assert that the crisis of regime legitimacy cannot be solved without the new liberal institutionalization of relations between the state and society. A split in the ruling elite, which showed up in 1989, is yet another characteristic feature of the Chinese transitional period.

Ideally, there should be a combination of national specifics and western patterns revised in such a way that the newly introduced constitutional norms are not perceived as alien and form a true regulatory basis of public life. This kind of successful constitutional modernization is often illustrated by the Japanese Constitution of 1947. On the one hand, it was, no doubt, adopted under the strong foreign influence after Japan's defeat in the Second World War. On the other hand, it ensured the stable democratization of society and broke the traditional stereotypes of patriarchal authoritarianism and totalitarianism. The Japanese pre-war political system represented the modernized version of absolute monarchy. The Meiji Constitution enshrined the principles of sham constitutionalism. Thus, it was impossible to implement the concept of democracy and separation of powers in the western sense. The USA played a crucial role in the transformation of Japanese constitutionalism. It was reflected in the adoption of three fundamental principles: liberal democracy, individual rights and independent judiciary. The Constitution of 1947 proclaims popular sovereignty and introduces the British-style parliamentary cabinet. Finally, Japan preferred the British model to the American presidential system with its separation of powers. Following the British pattern, Japan established a two-chamber system. Yet, the members of the upper chamber are elected by citizens and not appointed by the Crown. There was no sense for Japan as a unitary state to adopt the American bi-cameral system designed for a federative state. However, the two-chamber system was preferred to the one-chamber parliament. At that time, the only way to delimit the competences of two chambers was to introduce one chamber composed of representatives and another chamber formed on a professional basis (like the works councils set up by the Weimar Constitution of 1919). Japan has implemented the radical constitutional reform embracing all three models: American, British and German. So, the Japanese constitution represents both the outcome and the instrument of social changes.

This standpoint permits studying a specific type of constitutional crises breaking out in the traditionalist society that needs modernization. Such crises are distinguished by the fact that they lead to retraditionalization. In other words, society uses, deliberately or impulsively, a set of viable traditional elements (mainly, religious and legal norms) in order to create a special type of constitutionalism. From this perspective we can analyse the Islamic constitutional tradition that produces similar constitutional crises in different countries, no matter how different the forms it takes are. The western patterns of constitutionalism began to penetrate Islamic political tradition in the nineteenth century (most notably, during the Tanzimat in the Ottoman Empire) and became widespread with the adoption of written monarchical and later republican constitutions in the period from the late nineteenth century to the end of the twentieth century. The constitutional revolution, lead by the Young Turks in 1908, became the symbol of modernization and Europeanization for the whole Muslim world. Based on the philosophical synthesis of Islam and Western liberalism, this concept proved that parliamentarian institutions could be incorporated into the traditional authoritarian empire. In 1906, the Iranian constitutional revolution led to convocation of the National Consultative Assembly that adopted the Basic Law introducing a system of monarchical constitutionalism. The classical British, French and later American models played a crucial role in the creation of various types of constitutionalism in the Muslim world. Thus, there emerged a concept of autonomous political law relying on western philosophical positivism, representative government, the legally established division of state power and monarchical power. The concept novelty consisted in the identification of state and law, manifested in the principle of law-based state. However, after achieving independence, along with growing nationalism, this model was substantially altered by attempts to oppose the Islamic religious tradition against western constitutionalism. The conflict between the religious power and the principle of law-based state escalated during the Iranian revolution, when the principle of the rule of law was abandoned in favour of Islamic constitutionalism. The principle of popular sovereignty was interpreted as the principle of national sovereignty. In turn, the principle of national sovereignty was interpreted as the principle of religious sovereignty or theocracy. During the Iranian revolution, an acute conflict arose between the two movements. The first liberal-democratic movement combined the Shari'ah ideology with the principles of western constitutionalism (De Gaulle's Constitution). The second movement, represented by the clergy, rested on Shari'ah and gave all the power to "religious experts". Eventually, the fundamentalist concept of constitutional law prevailed. Similar trends can be observed in other Muslim countries such as Egypt, Syria, Algeria and Tunisia, where Islam has been constitutionally recognized as the single source of law or, at best, as one of its sources. In Islamic tradition, the constitutional conflict clearly demonstrates a contradiction between the principles of traditional Muslim law and the objectives of social modernization and rationalization.

The entire Iberian-American political system marked by the tradition of authoritarian leadership is trapped in a vicious circle: autocracy – unstable democratic efforts – crisis of continuity – autocracy. Throughout the twentieth century, several waves of democratization broke onto difficulties with the stabilization of democratic constitutional systems in Latin America. Nevertheless, Caudillism embracing the old-type dictatorial regimes is a thing of the past. Even the authoritarian regimes needed a new system to secure their constitutional legitimacy. This process unfolded during a revolution in Mexico. The civil war was led by Caudillo-type dictators, not by political parties. However, Venustiano Carranza and his followers, who won the war, had to rely on the political association called "Constitutionalist Party". The ideology of the Mexican Revolution with its underlying pro-agrarian and socialist principles was reflected in the political platform of a liberal constitutional movement known as Moderism (named after its founder); and in the Constitution of 1917 adopted largely as a result of the Caudillo movements emerging during the civil war.

The phenomenon of constitutional instability merits special comments. Constitutional instability is linked to political instability in general, but this connection is not unconditional. Constitutional instability can also be related to the transition from authoritarianism to democracy; or to the sovereign's desire for power consolidation. The notion of republican monarchy ("monarchie republicaine") was introduced in order to identify a situation when the sovereign's power is strengthened in real democracies. For instance, these are states where the rule of presidents or prime ministers was established through elections (e.g. USA, France, Canada) or historical precedents, like the rule of Washington, Napoleon (before the empire was created) and Disraeli. This kind of sovereign power is quite compatible with democratic institutions and universal suffrage ("elective monarchy"). Constitutional consolidation of the sovereign's power is carried out in a different way by traditional patriarchal regimes. Under such regimes, the sovereign personifies the destiny of a nation and the constitution and, like a cardiogram, traces the stages of power reinforcement. In those cases radical constitutional changes, resembling on the surface constitutional crises in developed democracies, are induced not by society but by the sovereign whose interests run counter to constitutional provisions. The constitution is nothing more than a device for sacramentalization or legitimization of power. This type of constitutionalism aims at creating the cult of a nation, a party or a leader through impeding effective control over legitimacy and promotion of democracy among the masses of people. This regime is called "monarchical republic", by analogy with the notion of republican monarchy. The monarchical republic is a political system where the proclaimed republican government and democracy correspond to the consolidation and sacramentalization of monarchical power. This way a presidential dictatorship, which differs from monarchy only by the lack of the title, is established. The characteristic features of the regime are as follows: mono-polar power and presidential monocentrism; nonsensical elections; untouchable sovereign; institutionalization of the sovereign's heir in one form or another (including, the right of inheritance). Political regimes defined as monarchical republics may have more or less visible totalitarian and authoritarian trends in different developing countries. They are united by the exclusive position of the head of state that symbolizes the rebirth of a nation. In view of this, we think it is important to raise the issue of sham constitutionalism as a specific model of constitutional authoritarian regimes established at transitional stages of social development.

Constitutionalism and modernization

Constitutional modernization means the process of introducing changes to a constitution which is going to bring its norms into alignment with a new social reality. Society in general can be modernized in a legal or illegal manner. Legal modernization, in turn, can either maintain or break legal continuity. These two kinds of legal modernization can be defined as a constitutional revolution or coup (they are basically identical, from a legal point of view) and constitutional reform. The latter can be carried out either through constitutional revision by introducing changes and amendments to the existing constitution or via the adoption of a new constitutional legislation aimed at complementing or specifying the Basic Law provisions and their diverse interpretations.

Constitutional modernization reveals the parameters of social development which society fails to unanimously agree upon. The characteristics of crisis are as follows: general scepticism; uncertain social interests; growing nationalism; weak government; lack of viable political parties, charismatic leaders and anti-crisis strategies. Over the past decade, the experience of Central and East European countries has demonstrated that for restoring national sovereignty, implementing the concept of civil society and law-based state, protecting human rights, a government should be strong and capable of reducing social transitional costs and suggesting rational anti-crisis strategies. The classification of new conflicts and political systems, proposed for East European countries, includes three types of conflicts: innovators *versus* conservatives, supporters *versus* opponents of market economy, and ethno-territorial conflicts. These types reflect a general contradiction between the views of collectivists and those of individualists, and hence determine the framework of party-political systems and the course of constitutional dialogue in Eastern Europe.

Let's focus on two problems of structural constitutional modernization: federalism and presidential power in the system of the separation of powers. The end of the bipolar world brought about by the demolition of the Berlin Wall in 1990 was marked by growing political and constitutional instability around the world. These global transformations were mainly reflected in the crisis of state, which spread across East European countries and many developing nations. The crisis had two implications crucial to constitutional development. On the one hand, the national boundaries, previously protected and guaranteed by superpowers, were called into question for the first time after the Second World War. As a result, there was a surge in the political activity of separatist nationalist movements seeking to review the principles of national-state structure (the problems of national self-identity, federalism and autonomism experienced in Eastern Europe, Latin America, Asia and Africa). On the other hand, with abolishment of one-party regimes, the role of central administration was drastically reduced in the period of transition when the state regulation of social processes is needed the most. The struggle for power, which unfolded under the circumstances, was formally reflected in the constitution as a conflict between the branches of power with the problem of presidential power becoming of primary importance. Therefore, federalism and presidential power turn out to be closely interrelated, most notably during the transitional period when national statehood is at stake.

From a legal standpoint, it is difficult to pin down various forms of federalism, since political science offers many varying definitions of the notion based on its diverse modifications: representative federalism, cooperative federalism, centralized federalism, dualistic federalism, fiscal federalism and new federalism. Sometimes these definitions are not mutually exclusive. A great propensity for conflicts emergence in the field of constitutional regulation can be explained by a greater interaction between federalism and nationalism. As for constitutional crises, two models of federalism can be distinguished. The first model helped solve the problem of nationalism (e.g. German federalism in the nineteenth century, and Swiss federalism that created a national political community by uniting different religious and linguistic groups). The second model of federalism, by contrast, is unable to achieve this goal and the nations, which established a federation (e.g. Canada), continually search for a constitutional solution to prevent their confederation from splitting into two sovereign states. The recent studies of Canadian constitutional crisis demonstrate that Canada cannot implement "fundamental constitutional reform" in the situation of a divided society and the general public being actively involved in politics. Another problem is that of harmonizing the concept of federalism with the principle of sovereignty. In the USA, it is acknowledged that the prevailing trend is giving priority to nationalization and centralization instead of strengthening federalism. Even the developed US tradition of federalism, however, faces a problem of the lack of the "working definition and theory of federalism" when it comes to relations between the federal government and states, and juridical intervention by the Congress into the resolution of conflicts between them. From this comparative perspective, the main challenge for East European federalism with its underlying ethno-territorial principle is to find mechanisms for settling conflicts between the principle of national self-determination, which is gaining popularity, and the necessity to maintain national sovereignty.

Constitutional modernization also raises problems related to the forms of government and systems of the vertical separation of powers in the countries developing strategies for a transition from authoritarianism to democracy. The standard division of democratic regimes into parliamentarian and presidential should be adjusted to take into account the specificity of transitional periods and the experience of modern constitutional crises. In moments of crisis, political institutions develop following their own logic, which is not necessarily constitutional. A conflict between the traditional parliament and the president gave impetus to constitutional reforms in many East European countries. However, the conflict reflected social contradictions, rather than formal opposition to the different branches of power.

In the course of political transformations, East European countries have shown a considerable potential for conflict. Dividing new political regimes into presidential, semi-presidential and parliamentarian is a provisional scheme. It is proved by debates on development trends and the role of presidential power under such regimes. Those advocating the parliamentarian form of government during a transition, claim that strong presidential power creates a danger of dictatorship in a political vacuum. This system may generate acute conflicts between a parliament and president, hindering the process of democratization. Such conflicts, though apparently constitutional, may be very destructive when coupled with social or national conflicts. In the course of radical social reforms or struggle for national self-determination, the parliament can seize political initiative. The opponents of strong presidential power argue that there is an alternative way to overcome political instability. They refer to the Russian Constitution adopted in 1993. A collapse of one-party system resulted in the crisis of legitimacy that allegedly could only be resolved via adoption of the supreme law expressing the will of the people. The new constitution, however, exists in the political climate where the personalization of power explicitly manifests itself, thereby allowing for its authoritarian interpretation. The tendency towards the "personalization" of constitutionalism has been stressed by many western observers.

Another standpoint is based on the objective nature of the strong presidential power established in Russia. It is reflected in the concept of super-presidential power which theoretically can evolve into a semi-presidential one. The concept of a semi-presidential regime was worked out by Maurice Duverger drawing on the Fifth Republic's experience. It has three distinctive features: the president is elected on the basis of universal, equal and direct suffrage; the president possesses vast constitutional powers; the prime minister and the government remain at power only if the parliament consents to it.

The three forms of government may have the following interim configurations: the parliamentarian regime dominated by the Assembly (the French Constitution of 1793); the parliamentarian regime in cooperation with the executive power (the Fourth French Republic); and the parliamentarian regime dominated by the Chancellor (the FRG Constitution). In Eastern Europe, we can identify a parliamentary regime in the Czech Republic and Hungary, semi-parliamentary regime in Poland and a specific regime in Russia. The Russian regime can be formally defined as semi-presidential, but actually it is the regime of strong presidential power. Russian experience has already shown that in a situation where the parliament is weak and political parties are non-existent, the semi-presidential regime can be easily transformed into the authoritarian presidential regime.

An analysis of the president's right to dissolve parliament plays a crucial role in the situation. Clearly, this institution cannot function in the same way in parliamentarian and presidential republics. Traditionally, the dissolution of parliament is viewed as an institution that resolves conflicts between the branches of power and secures the integrity and independence of the executive power. The right for parliament dissolution is an essential element in the system of separation of powers because it counterbalances the competences of executive and legislative powers in a parliamentary republic. Today, this theory is relevant to the conflict of two powers. There is another point of view that treats the right of parliament dissolution as a tool for stabilizing government and substituting referendum.

The balance of legal and political factors in the process of consensus building is of utmost importance. If the president wins a parliamentary majority, the situation may shift in favour of the head of state. Therefore, forming a "party in power" is a must for maintaining strong presidential power.

The notion of transition is not precisely defined, hence allows for a number of political interpretations. Firstly, transition can be defined as the shift from a non-consolidated (or deconsolidated) to a consolidated regime in conjuncture with high social mobility. Secondly, it can be defined as replacement of the old political regime by a new, significantly different regime. Lastly, transition can be defined as the hybrid phenomenon that is characterized by continuous confrontation between the principles of the new and old regimes. On the whole, one talks here about an interim period between two stable stages, which is marked by the loss of a social balance and respective review of constitutional law fixing the balance. At the same time, it is necessary to differentiate methodologically between the crisis *per se* and the process of transition. While the former upsets stability and breaks continuity, the latter represents a longer stage marked by the synthesis of old traditions and new processes triggered by the crisis. Having summarized diverse constitutional situations that can emerge under the conditions of the crisis of a transition from authoritarianism to democracy, Juan Linz and Alfred Stepan suggested six basic models. The first model implies preservation of the constitution created by a non-democratic regime by keeping intact reserve domains and introducing complex amendment procedures. While ensuring certain continuity in the development of a political system, the model complicates the process of democratic transition because it is difficult to alter the constitution (e.g. Chile). The second model suggests keeping the former "paper" constitution of the authoritarian regime during transition to democracy. Though this model permits implementing certain democratic constitutional norms that used to be purely fictitious, it is fraught with the danger of "paralyzing" the constitutional norms that do not comply with the conditions of democratic transition (the most important examples are the Soviet-type federative constitutions adopted in the USSR, Yugoslavia and Czechoslovakia). The third model implies a situation when a new constitution is drafted by the provisional government, and legally non-democratic authorities remain at power. By breaking all links with the old authoritarian system, the model sows the seeds of a conflict in the Basic Law. The conflict will have to be solved at a later date. Furthermore, the very fact that the constitution is drafted by the provisional government may hinder the process of democratic consolidation due to the lack of social support (e.g. Portugal). The fourth model suggests using the constitution created under very conflicting conditions and reflecting the actual alignment of non-democratic forces. The constitution is formally democratic and in line with the objectives of democratic transition. Yet, the democratic consolidation faces problems with a real political opposition (this holds for Brazil, to some extent). The fifth model consists of restoring the previous democratic constitution. Though this formula helps avoid any conflicts and arguments about the constitutional alternative and permits quickly solving the problem of legitimization of the new power, it has two shortcomings: it does not take into account: i) the changes that occurred in society under authoritarian regime; and ii) the role of political procedures and institutions of the former constitution in implementing a democratic coup (e.g. Uruguay and Argentina). The sixth model implies creating a constitution based on the people's choice. This is the most optimal variant under which the democratically elected constitutional assembly drafts and adopts a constitution that is further approved by popular referendum (e.g. Spain).[10]

Transitional situations unfolding in Southern and Eastern Europe, Latin America and Asia in recent times have been compared and classified according to the nature of process. The model of treaty ("pacto"), illustrated by the Spanish Constitution of 1978, is set off against the model of broken continuity ("ruptura"), illustrated by constitutional changes in the post-war Germany (the Constitution of 1949) and in Portugal where the Constitution of 1976 was introduced through a military coup carried out in the name of social reforms. However, this dualistic model of pact-rupture does not explain so well the cases where features of both models are observed, e.g. the Brazilian Constitution of 1988.

The Spanish model of constitutional reforms provides a classic example of peaceful transition from the authoritarian political regime to the democratic system. Spanish constitutional tradition is of a fickle nature: all constitutions, apart from the one adopted in 1876, were rather ephemeral and the Basic Law was non-existent over a long period of Franco's dictatorship. Thus, the constitution served as an instrument for struggle between political forces, rather than a legal base of public life. It holds for all constitutional initiatives undertaken in the period from 1812 to 1931, and resulted in a failure to tackle such fundamental national problems as the regional structure, role of the church, education and enlightenment, social issues and the choice of form of government. The deep constitutional crisis of recent times manifested itself in the conflict between the Franco political structures and social needs in the period of rapid transformations. Despite its affinity with the fascist dictatorship of Hitler and Mussolini, the Franco regime had some specifics that predetermined the essence of constitutional reform in transitional period. This regime came to power via a military coup, not through elections. It enjoyed another type of legitimacy and was not as much totalitarian. The dominant military nature of the regime and its loose ties with the ideology opened new opportunities for a transition from the totalitarian fascist regime to the authoritarian technocratic system. Franco's dictatorship has three distinctive features. First, the party played a less important role in the political system (the Falangist movement, unlike the parties of Hitler and Mussolini, did not play a key role in the seizure of power and establishment of a new regime; and it was more controllable and less ideological). Being a one-party system, the Franco regime had some sort of internal pluralism combining elements of various ideologies ranging from the fascist-totalitarian and monarchical to conservative-catholic and republican ones. Second, the regime was characterized by the absence of massive political mobilization of citizens who were rather pessimistic about the system. And finally, the Franco regime did not have its own ideology, for it combined the elements of different ideologies which rendered it more flexible and disposed to change. These specifics and particularities allowed Juan Linz to conclude that the Franco regime was authoritarian rather than totalitarian. Although Spanish scholars criticized Linz, they did not argue against his thesis that the regime was very flexible and had a very long lifetime thanks to the endogenous evolution of its nature. Some scholars, claiming the Franco regime was different from other fascist regimes, described it as an original and innovative system for regulating political and constitutional crises. Interior social changes, international climate and the individual role of the monarch created a unique opportunity for establishing democracy by constitutional means under the crisis of the Franco regime.

The Spanish transition to democracy can be schematically described in the following way: General Franco's death as a catalyst for crisis; restoration of the monarchy and change in the legitimacy of power; erosion of political dictatorial institutions, appearance of new politicians and political symbols; amnesty; adoption of the law on political reform; achievement of social consensus through reciprocal concessions. This type of political transformation became referred to as "reforma pactada" (negotiated reform). An alternative scheme is represented by the thesis concerning a greater role of evolution in the process of democratic development. The crisis demonstrated that the Franco regime had no potential for evolution. However, continuity was maintained to some extent. And this fact allowed the country to change the legitimacy of power and replace the previous ruling elite. Institutionalization of the new principles was based on a compromise between various political forces, which became possible because of their weakness. The Spanish model of transition has greatly influenced the entire logic of similar processes worldwide. At the same time, it is an exception rather than a rule as the transition from authoritarianism to democracy is often carried out by force, in a illegal way. The recent experience of Eastern Europe and Russia along with transitional processes in Southern Europe, Latin America and Asia have shown a very important cognitive role of the Spanish model regarded as a perfect transformation. The Constitution of 1978 is indeed recognized as the final outcome of the whole Spanish transitional process, irrespective of how the process is interpreted.

Spanish constitutional process might be defined as the period during which the constituent power was accomplishing the task of establishing a new state via creating a new constitution for it. This process began with the first democratic elections held after many years of dictatorship, and ended with the adoption of the new constitution in 1978. It is noteworthy, unlike its predecessors, that the new constitution adequately reflects social reality and has a truly national character: it is based on a compromise between all the political forces that express the will of the people. Particular attention should be paid to the democratic procedures of constitution making and consensus building: the procedure of constitution adoption was stipulated in the special law on political reform that was approved by a referendum in 1976, and adopted by the Congress of Deputies and then by the Senate. Further, the Constitutional Commission comprising representatives of all political parties was set up for discussing the Basic Law. This ensured a greater legitimacy of the constitution appearing as a nationwide pact of consent. The key issues on the political agenda included the concept of sovereignty in the light of Spain's accession to the EC; the official status for Catalan and other minority languages; the status of autonomous communities; the legalization of political parties, free trade unions and political pluralism; the official status of the army and of the church; and constitutional recognition of the general principles of the international law. The constitutional reform was based on the idea of social contract: agreement on fundamental issues such as the structure of the state, political freedom, party pluralism, the political form of the state (the parliamentarian monarchy) and the territorial organization of the state (the problem of autonomous communities).

A solution to the intricate problem of autonomous communities was found in the political and legal redistribution of legislative and executive powers on a territorial basis among emerging autonomous communities. The decision was democratic and rational because it combined the basic liberal principle of the separation of legislative, executive and judicial powers with the idea of autonomy and communal pluralism ("pluralismo communitario"). Thus, Spain represents a united or total society comprising limited communities such as Catalonia or the Basque Country. The integration of various communities into a united state community serves greater integration of the Spanish nation as a whole.

There were several logical reasons for establishing a parliamentarian monarchy as a form of government. First, the institution of monarchy promoted political stabilization, consensus building and legitimation of constitutional reforms. Second, it was viewed as an important tool for resolving future constitutional crises. The thesis proved the possible and rational combination of elected authorities with an irremovable head of state within a democratic system. Democratic systems contain a certain contradiction expressed in competition and struggle for competencies between the different branches of power – parliament and president. Besides, being elected via general elections, they enjoy equal legitimacy. Democratic dualism is typical of presidential regimes (e.g. the USA) and semi-presidential regimes (e.g. France and Portugal) where it may sow the seeds of constitutional crises. Throughout the nineteenth century, similar situations developed in the constitutional monarchies where a parliament and a monarch had different sources of legitimacy. According to the architects of modern Spanish models of constitutional monarchy, such conflicts are prevented by the newly established structure of power where the parliament takes sovereignty in its hand and the monarch, being excluded from political decision making, becomes the symbol of a nation and acts as the highest judge in such a capacity. The third argument in favour of the system is that the monarch guarantees the consolidation of democratic forces in a transitional period.

The Spanish transition (1975–1978) ended with the adoption of the constitution. That was followed by a new important process: the constitutionalization of significant legal areas via adoption of new laws. To be implemented, the constitution should lay down such principles that serve as a basis for the activity of legislative authorities, administrative bodies and courts. Foreign analysts underline that the process was very rapid in Spain compared to France, for example. They explain this phenomenon with the following reasons: i) sacramentalization of the Spanish Constitution; ii) its "interventionism", i.e. the degree of involvement in law and regulation; iii) its normativity, i.e. the constitution includes a large number of regulatory provisions that specify all legal proceedings and therefore can be used by courts of general jurisdiction; iv) the independent Constitutional Court enjoying great prestige and vested with vast powers; v) a system for resolving the issues of constitutionality including the remedy of amparo (a simplified emergency procedure for appeals to the constitutional justice for protection of fundamental human rights). The first three reasons are determined by the constitution's general characteristics, whereas the other two are immediately linked to constitutional justice.

Despite constitutional stability, many disputes arise in relation to the future of Spanish constitutionalism. Some argue that the current constitution should be prevented from becoming sacred and stolid. They even state that there are "lacunas and flaws in the wording of the constitution" and therefore it should be partially revised. The revision would presumably involve introducing changes in the light of Spain's accession to the United Europe (similar to those discussed after the ratification of the Maastricht Treaty in France, Germany and Portugal); transforming the Senate from the upper parliament chamber to the federal chamber; as well as regulating gender relationships and resolving issues related to political parties. As the generations of the political elite are changing, discussion between those supporting the unchangeable constitution and those opposing "paper barriers" continues.

Thus, constitutional crises in transitional societies provide very valuable material for a political theorist who wants to analyse the mechanisms of constitutional changes. The concept of constitutional cycles seems to be promising because it demonstrates a correlation between the main phases of constitutional process during transition: crisis (loss of constitutional legitimacy), upset balance (political discourse on constitutional issues), and stability regained at a new level (consensus on the next constitution). The problem of constitutional dysfunction is manifest in a conflict between the notions of legitimacy and legality and in the way they are revealed in the process of constitutional modernization. The mechanisms of constitutional transformations can be understood through analysing different types of constitutional crises, their developmental stages and the role of the constitution as a factor of social changes. Hence, the theory of constitutional cycles enables one to see the correlation between the broken political and legal tradition (in the form of constitutional crisis), consolidation of a new constitutional regime (solution to the crisis) and restored continuity.

The problem of democracy and authoritarianism has become one of the key issues these days. Put simply, democracy is a truly new social regime. In the past, there was the traditional society where each individual was incorporated into a rigid social structure. In modern times, traditional structures collapse and give way to a phenomenon which Tocqueville called "universal equality". The phenomenon has a number of serious implications, namely: the ill-prepared masses of people begin to influence politics through elections; traditional monarchical regimes collapse; the divine law gives way to the necessity of legitimizing the will of the people, new technical tools for manipulating mass consciousness appear.

So far, we have described the process of transition from the absolutism as a political superstructure of a traditional society, to the modern state systems evolving under democracy. In this regard, the relationship between legitimacy and legality is of utmost importance.

Legal material is not enough to solve this problem. It is necessary to take into account the collective consciousness and psychology of the people. At present, most Russians have no knowledge of constitutional process and are very sceptical about the changes occurring in society.

Many scholars still believe that the Soviets represented a specific form of parliamentarianism. Many argue that parliamentarianism and constitutionalism stem from the idea of communal existence. This necessitates an articulate approach to the issues of democracy and authoritarianism; correlation between direct and representative democracy; and definition of circumstances under which democracy transforms into authoritarianism politically reproduced in the systems of either sham constitutionalism or nominal constitutionalism, which is in essence a totalitarian regime.

From this point of view, the author was interested in issues relating to the correlation between legitimacy and legality and to the modification of constitutional system. The author was thinking about the appropriateness of studies that link legal formulae with their social realization and that study them in a certain legal context.

The social function of liberal constitutionalism in Russia

To explain the phenomenon of Russian liberalism, one needs to describe its typology in a comparative perspective. It is important to specify the basic notions historically formulated to reflect the public consciousness of past generations. However, a lack of precision presents difficulties for contemporary researchers when they use the notions of democracy, liberalism and constitutionalism in different fields of their studies. These notions, as simple as they may appear, do not have a single meaning. We need to explore the scope of notions in order to achieve our main objective: to identify the essential, general and specific features of the Russian model of political development in a comparative perspective. First of all, we ought to explain the hierarchal and logical relationships between the three notions. They are different. Each notion narrows and specifies the preceding one and thus has a distinct logical scope. Being a broad notion, democracy means the movement that is dedicated to promoting the interests of citizens and aimed at expressing most adequately the will of the majority of people. Understood in this way, the content of this broad notion is associated with the achievement of a certain goal. The traditionally imprecise and vague notion of democracy (allowing for its numerous interpretations) has been narrowed and enriched by the notion of liberalism introduced in modern and recent times. The notion of human rights is the backbone of liberalism. It is necessary, however, to explain the main problem with a study of liberalism that includes its insecure social base, variable political platforms and comparatively unstable views of liberals. These characteristic features of liberalism, discussed so many times, can be clarified by its underpinning element: the minimum and essential human rights which ensure the fundamental integrity of liberalism, and its continual revival in new forms and conditions. The shortage of specific human rights (economic, social, political, religious, demographic, etc.) brings changes to the platform of liberals and to the social base of society, in part. Liberalism is a sensitive indicator of social conditions, especially those of a larger segment of society – the middle class – who, on the one hand, seek to make things better and, on the other, resist any extreme measures endangering their human rights. This is the reason why the problem of liberalism becomes very important in modern societies. Thus, we associate this notion with the essence of liberal ideology. Lastly, the notion of constitutionalism, yet more specific, is exactly the political (or legal) ideology of liberalism. Drawing on the experience of the great revolutions of modern and recent times, liberal philosophers have concluded that the revolutionary achievement of democratic goals does not prove its worthiness. To find out what political mechanism is most suitable for achieving democratic goals, it is necessary to devise a theoretical model of transition. From this perspective, constitutionalism is the notion that clarifies the very fashion in which transition is achieved.

Contemporary international legal literature knows three different meanings of the term "constitutionalism": i) the Basic Law of the state and the system of secondary legislative acts; ii) the system of political, public and legal institutions ensuring the implementation of constitutional norms; and iii) the social movement aimed at establishing civil society and law-based state, and at enshrining them in Basic Laws and practices of civil society institutions. The third definition is particularly relevant to the interpretation of the Russian model of constitutionalism. Russian constitutionalism is at a fundamental stage and it is constantly compared to other developed systems. Therefore, it is important to dispel the prejudice that Russia has known only the authoritarian forms of political culture. And this can be done by displaying its constitutional traditions. Does Russian constitutionalism represent a specific model of global political development? If yes, what are its particularities, mechanisms and parameters of scientific study? To answer these key questions, we need to conduct a typological and comparative analysis of Russian liberalism and constitutionalism in the context of its internal dynamics and main forms in Europe and Asia.

The social function of constitutionalism in a broad sense is to create a certain legal system: rules and norms governing the activities of principal political institutions. The normal constitutional process assumes that the system already exists and just needs to be regulated, rationalized and made more efficient. However, constitutionalism fulfils an essentially different function in a modernizing society: the old traditional system is no longer relevant and the new one has not been yet established. Therefore, a conflict between the constitutional ideal and the actual government is inevitable because the constitution (or drafts thereof) does not reflect reality. Rather, it outlines expected changes and the scope of their social implications.

To understand the relationship between democracy and authoritarianism in modern and recent times, one needs to systemically analyse the nature and specificity of interactions between the state and society, reforms and counter-reforms, power and government, ruling elite and bureaucracy in a period of modernization.[11] The specifics of Russian historical process and the resulting position of Russian liberalism have provided, as mentioned above, the main incentive for development of a legal school and political sociology in Russia. The role of Russian constitutionalism in establishing a modern democracy as well as its types, development trends and prospects is examined under separate cover.[12]

Speaking about the experience of modern and recent times worldwide, Russian constitutionalism appears to be one of the manifestations of a global social conflict provoked by the transition from a traditionalist society (class system) to a mass society evolving into a democracy. On the one hand, this conflict develops on a worldwide basis, however on the other, its manifestations are not similar and simultaneous in different political contexts. Thus, it is advisable to focus on three aspects of the conflict. The first aspect includes issues relating to modern democracy: the theory of transition from a traditionalist society to a mass society; and reconstruction of the main stages in comprehension of the fundamental conflict between the government and society as described by prominent political philosophers in their theoretical concepts. The second aspect embraces absolutism and revolution: the exercise of power and the types of constitutionalism, i.e. the study of actual constitutional systems whose historical destinies were shaped differently by the mechanisms used in exercising the power. This approach allows us to carry out a typological analysis of Russian constitutionalism represented by the third aspect: the Russian model of constitutionalism in the global political process. The three aspects mentioned above were analysed using information from relevant sources. Among them are the fundamental classical works that created the political philosophy of constitutionalism; sociological and legal paradigms of constitutional systems; constitutional legislations adopted as a result of the great European Revolutions in modern and recent times; and all informational sources related to the main stages of Russian liberalism and constitutionalism. Russian constitutional development was compared to western practices and studied in a long-term historical perspective. This approach helped to explain the logic of the Soviet and post-Soviet political and legal development from the historical perspective of both Russian and global constitutionalism.

At the end of the twentieth century, worldwide development was marked by a prevailing tendency toward transition from authoritarianism to democracy. The past decades have given us a unique opportunity to see the rapid collapse of the world's most ambitious authoritarian regimes and emergence of new ways of socio-political development based on the ideas of democracy, parliamentarianism and multi-party system. Concurrently, the situation has shown that rapid democratic transformation of an unprepared society is not a cure-all for its social problems, because it often poses even greater challenges to such society. On the one hand, as a result of this situation the majority will is imposed on the minority (that threatens their civil liberties and human rights). On the other hand, rapid democratic transformation of an unprepared society may lead to a qualitatively new democratic Caesarism that uses democratic principles and forms of social organization to establish its anti-legal power. Most philosophers, starting with Aristotle, saw a major danger where a new tyranny was potentially based on the manipulation and monopolization of the electorate's will and consciousness by political parties. Contemporary political experience has demonstrated that the paradigms of legal thought in modern and recent times were formulated in anticipation of the great European Revolutions: English, French and Russian. It became necessary to expound the notion of social order from the perspective of understanding a revolutionary crisis and searching for its solution. According to classical English philosophers, Thomas Hobbes and John Locke, there are three essential elements: natural law, social contract and the concept of power. By the seventeenth century, following the theories of natural law and social contract, English philosophers argued about which was the best way of dealing with social crises: either to establish a monarchical absolutism or to develop a representative government. By the time of the French Revolution, the issue of law and democracy was at the heart of theoretical debates.

Rousseau and Montesquieu formulated two alternative political-legal doctrines of revolution. Rousseau idealized the "general will". He held that it was different from the "individual will" and from the majority will comprised of "individual wills". However, Rousseau himself assumed that the "general will" might be in conflict with certain individual interests. In this case, he believed, the problem could be solved only through coercive and constraining measures used by the government against individuals. This doctrine has been traditionally contrasted with the Montesquieu theory idealizing representative government. Montesquieu formulated the principles of state structure that were radically different from Rousseau's totalitarian democracy and antithetical to the principles of liberal democracy, by following Locke's tradition in the field of political thought. Rousseau enriched the science with his theory of the sovereignty of people which justified their struggle against monarchical tyranny. As for Montesquieu, his main achievement was the concept of law-based state and the separation of powers that is enshrined almost in all constitutions of contemporary democracies. Contemporary science and the twentieth-century experience have proven that the teachings of Rousseau and Montesquieu represent the two fundamentally different world views: the prototypes of an authoritarian state and a modern liberal democracy, respectively. And it is not incidental that the chosen way of constitutional building lent a fresh perspective to this discussion on the eve of the first Russian Revolution. Political experience of the French Revolution and monarchical restoration gave a new impetus to the discourse on the correlation between democracy and authoritarianism.

Like Montesquieu had previously done, Tocqueville, through comparing the different types of societies, wanted to solve one problem: the emergence of democracy as a new socio-political regime. He tried to find a solution in the interpretation of transition from a traditional, feudal and aristocratic society to a society based on equality of opportunities. The key issue here is the correlation between the principle of equality and that of freedom: the concept of democracy as an internally contradictory formation is based on the reciprocal opposition of its underlying principles. This explains the search for a new political ideal – the combination of democracy (as a universal equality) and liberal institutions – which is politically implemented in the form of constitutional monarchy. The Tocqueville theory of democracy is still relevant today, because many similar problems arise during a swift transition from authoritarianism to democracy.

In the countries whose social order was compatible with the French Revolution experience, political philosophers concentrated on two main types of problems: the problems of modern democracy in countries where revolutions were successful; and the problems of transition from old absolutist regimes to new regimes in countries under modernization. The French Revolution clearly demonstrated the destructive consequences of a spontaneous social outburst. It also showed that the new legitimization of power structures by no means prevent them from returning to authoritarianism. This experience gave a strong stimulus for the interpretation of constitutional ideas in the countries that, unlike countries with classical liberal and constitutional traditions, had to build up their institutions in the period of modernization, namely: Germany and Russia. Thus, the classical western model is corrected by the German liberal theories of civil society and law-based state in modernization periods.

At the turn of the twentieth century, the problem of legal rationalization and modernization of society, which is carried out by the government in a rapidly changing social context, came into the spotlight. From this perspective, one can clearly see the importance of political philosophy of German and Russian liberalism which show that social conflicts can be settled not only through revolutions, but also through radical social, political and economic reforms purposefully implemented by the government. In this respect, we should mention the very important concept of rationality developed by the famous German sociologist Max Weber. His substantive and friendly correspondence with the representatives of Russian constitutional movement (for example, with Bogdan A. Kistyakovsky) allows us to compare the outcomes of constitutional reforms of the countries where the process of modernization is strongly influenced by the government. These countries employ a specific approach when it comes to the relationship of modernization, liberalism and bureaucracy. German liberalism, like Russian liberalism, had to comply with national particularities and therefore was far from the classical model. Due to the lack of grass-roots support, it had to appeal to the government and enlightened bureaucracy, and therefore to observe the rules of the game and respect the monarchical principle in the first place. Attitude toward the government was ambivalent. On the one hand, it was viewed as an enemy (when the government violated the rights and freedoms of citizens) and, on the other, as a friend (when the government protected order and legality, and implemented democratic reforms). When analysing the situation, there emerges a sociological concept of the so-called "sham constitutionalism", i.e. constitutional changes that might put a country back on the path of authoritarianism. When Weber and Russian constitutionalists examined the Russian and German revolutions of the early twentieth century, they highlighted a problem that turned out to be highly relevant to subsequent worldwide political development.[13]

Following the pattern of social development as mentioned above, German philosophers, unlike Russian constitutionalists, were much more cautious about mechanically implementing western democratic institutions into a society with traditional norms of authoritarian social regulation. Interestingly enough, Russian and German philosophers observed a typological resemblance between the political models implemented by Russia and Germany in the course of their historical development. Recent experience allows us to assert that this type of development constitutes the model of transition that offers modernizing countries an alternative to revolutionary outbreak viewed as the only and thus optimal way of democratic development. Hence we pay particular attention to both positive and negative trends in its development. One of the key problems arising on the way to democracy is the universal right of suffrage. In the early twentieth century, German and Russian constitutionalists began to work out strategies for liberal transformations. And at the heart of many heated debates was the problem of universal suffrage without qualifications related to the objective level of civil consciousness. They believed that this problem was the main danger to real constitutional norms as it could transform them into nominal ones.

A turning point in interpretation of the phenomenon of modern democracy came with the concept that, for the first time, linked such issues as the transition from traditional society to democracy, the role of universal elections in political mobilization of citizens, interaction between the masses of people and political parties, as well as the process of bureaucratization of political parties which produced a special political apparatus called "caucus" (Moisey Ya. Ostrogorsky). The term "caucus", which derives from the Anglo-American political tradition, became widely used in the contemporary sociology of political parties. It means the nucleus of a party that puts the whole party mechanism in motion. The caucus was originally (during the emergence of political parties) established as a specialized body enabling parliamentarian parties to communicate with the electorate. But later it was transformed into the machinery which mobilized the masses in support of political platforms, coordinated party propaganda, selected and appointed functionaries to leading posts in local and central governments, and advocated party ideology. According to researchers, this institution promoted the bureaucratization of political parties and provoked the crisis of classical parliament at the dawn of plebiscitarian democracy.[14] The collapse of a traditional society removes old barriers between classes in society and changes the positions of groups and individuals in relation to power. The process of modernization breaks old stereotypes and liberates the people, but at the same it isolates them and leads to the detachment, dehumanization and depersonalization of society. Democratization gradually extends to spiritual, social, and economic life. And it is politically reflected in the creation of democratic power structures and political freedoms. The general public that used to be a recipient becomes an actor in politics, and gets an opportunity to directly (via the electoral system) influence political and even decision-making processes. Drawing on the experience of classical democratic institutions, Ostrogorsky revealed the mechanisms used for political manipulation of public opinion. However, this problem became particularly urgent not in the countries where democratic traditions and institutions were well developed, but in the regions where such traditions and institutions were non-existent or set up on an ad hoc basis in the light of social changes. It is not surprising that a greater contribution to the analysis of issues related to constitutionalism was made by scholars from the countries – like Russia, Germany, Italy and Spain – that have passed through the stage of accelerated and catch-up development and modernization in recent times (Gaetano Mosca, Vilfredo Pareto, Robert Michels, Carl Schmitt, Moisey Ya. Ostrogorsky, Jose Ortega y Gasset and Hannah Arendt). However, the theoretical discourse is only one aspect of the study into democracy and authoritarianism in modern and recent times.

It is impossible to interpret the political philosophy and practice of liberalism without comparing different forms of constitutionalism and different mechanisms used for exercising the power in the first place. The comparison should be made in the context of transition from absolutism to constitutional monarchy and then to contemporary political systems: parliamentarian and presidential republics. So far, we have examined the development of principal theoretical paradigms of constitutionalism in the context of great revolutions. Further, we employ this comparative approach for exploring the functioning of political regimes during the transition from absolutism to constitutional monarchy. In between absolutism (characterized by an absolute and indivisible monarchical power) and modern republican democracy (characterized by the supremacy of representative government) there is a specific transitional form that has long traditions in world history. This form is generally defined as a constitutional monarchy. In the real political process, it comes in different shapes, and each of them imposes different limitations on monarchical power. The limitations become minimal under certain circumstances. As a result, absolutism is restored or new authoritarian forms are created. That is why it is so important to scrutinize all the components of the political system. Under the mixed form of government, the mechanisms used for exercising the power are determined by the existence of three opposing forces: popular representation (parliament), governmental bureaucracy and monarchy. The first force produces and promotes an organized representation of leading parties in parliament and their fractions or caucuses actually decide on matters regarding the destiny of any given cabinet. At the end of the day, the process of party bureaucratization will create a political machine to be used by leading administrators and ideologists for seizing and retaining power. The second force, governmental bureaucracy, goes through the different stages of rationalization to become more differentiated, functionally specialized and corporatively consolidated. The third force, which has been historically the strongest one, is represented by the head of executive power: a monarch who is formally placed at the top of the pyramid. However, between the monarch and society with its representative institutions expressing the will of the people there emerges a new force – the highest bureaucracy – that actually acts as a judge and exercises real power.

Given this alignment of forces, there may be two fundamentally different kinds of alliances in society: i) an alliance between parliament and monarchy against bureaucracy; and ii) an alliance between bureaucracy and monarchy against parliament. Also, there can be an intermediate option of unstable compromise between parliament and monarchy. Such compromise, though conflicting in nature, represents a transitional form between the two forms of government. Having analysed the mechanisms used for exercising the power within the system of constitutional monarchy, we can now identify three main types of political regimes that have taken place in history. The first type is represented by the British model of constitutional monarchy which is basically the disguised form of a parliamentarian republic. The alliance between an all-mighty parliament and a powerless monarch enables the former to effectively control a government (the cabinet of ministers) and the entire administrative-bureaucratic system. The second intermediate type of constitutional monarchy is defined as a dualistic form of government. Under such a regime, a parliament and monarch enjoy equal legislative and partially executive powers, and they also control and constrain each other. In several countries of Western and Central Europe, the dualistic form of government was established following major revolutionary upheavals as a result of unstable historical compromise between the two forces; and it gravitated toward the strengthening of monarchical power. Lastly, the third type of constitutional monarchy constituted the so-called monarchical constitutionalism. Under this regime, the alliance between monarchy and bureaucracy against parliament became fully-fledged. The historical function of monarchical constitutionalism was to preserve the essence of a monarchical system under new circumstances through the restructuring of state power and introducing a new form of government. This type of constitutional monarchy – initially implemented by countries of Central and Eastern Europe and then by Russia and Asia – gives the best fit for our vision of sham constitutionalism. Sham constitutionalism emerges only in the countries where democratic forces do not enjoy social support, lack unity and therefore have no other choice than to appeal to the government. The power is distanced from society, and the monarch is trapped by bureaucracy because the parliament is weak.

The phenomenon of sham constitutionalism clearly manifests itself in a comparative study of monarchical constitutionalism in Europe and elsewhere in the eighteenth to twentieth centuries. When analysing a Russian constitutional process in a legal comparative perspective, one needs to examine its historical and legal precedents. The first type of constitutional monarchy is characterized by a transfer of real power from the monarch to the cabinet of ministers that fully depends on the representative power. The parliament controls all budgetary allocations and, correspondingly, the activities of administrative branches and the executive power at large. If the cabinet loses parliamentary debates on a key subject or the government receives a direct vote of no confidence, this leads either to the resignation of the cabinet or to the dissolution of the parliament. Two other types of constitutional monarchy were, for the first time on the continent, fully represented in the French political system in the epoch of the Great Revolution. They were alternately enshrined in two main types of constitutions – in the contractual Constitution of 1791 and in the octroyed Constitution of 1814 – which set the pattern for such states as Belgium, Italy, Germany, Austria-Hungary, Japan and Russia. A transition to the limited monarchy and then to the republic formed the political content of constitutional process by the time of the French Revolution. The initial stage of the process was completed when the Constitution of 1791 was adopted and the constitutional monarchy modelled on the British political system in its American interpretation was established. However, the system of monarchical constitutionalism was most consistently described in the Charter of 1814, the first historical draft of the so-called "octroyed constitution". The Charter set an example for all subsequent legislative acts of a similar nature, for it was the first document that combined a new post-revolutionary social reality with the old political traditions. The Charter of 1814 (revised by Louis-Philippe in 1830), for the first time, stipulated the underlying principles of monarchical constitutionalism: the monarch is the real head of state, embodiment of all powers and constitutional guarantor; the true separation of powers is replaced by a false and purely functional system; the legislature is powerless; the government is completely dependent on the monarch and not controlled by the parliament; and the judiciary is not autonomous. The Charter of 1830, in turn, had an impact on the constitutions of Italian states (namely, Sicily's Constitution of 1848; and Piedmont's Constitution of 1848 which ceased to be the all-Italian Basic Law only in 1922, when a dictatorial regime came to power).

It is particularly interesting to draw a comparison between Russian experience and the German constitutional monarchy that followed the path of monarchical constitutionalism. Germany implemented a specific political form unparalleled in the parliamentarian democracies (the USA, Great Britain, and France) and the countries of Eastern Europe that at that time did not have any constitution at all. Despite being modelled on the Charter of 1814, German constitutional monarchical tradition had its own political style, best defined as a monarchical principle. As the first step in this process, one should recognize the 1815 Confederation Act that introduced monarchical constitutions in all the German states. The Prussian Constitutional Charter of 1850 specified monarchical elements and provided theoretical rationale for their implementation in the political system. This document played a crucial role in the history of monarchical constitutionalism. Following the principles of sham constitutionalism, it laid the foundations for their further implementation in the united Germany through influencing Bismarck's politics during the constitutional crisis of 1861–1862, the 1871 Constitution of the German Empire, and partially the concept of the strong Reich President enjoying the right (under the well-known Article 48) to introduce a state of emergency under extreme conditions. In this respect, we should note that Germany saw the succession of three main types of sham constitutionalism: monarchical principle, presidential dictatorship and the Führer principle. Thus, the principal French and German models of monarchical constitutionalism became the prototypes of similar legislative acts adopted in Eastern Europe and Asia, namely, the Monarchical Constitution of 1876 in the Ottoman Empire and the Meiji Constitution of 1889 in Japan. These prototypes were also directly used by the Russian Empire for drafting the Fundamental Laws in 1905–1907, and indirectly used by several contemporary states for drawing up their legislative acts. These models became so widely used because they (especially, German public and legal tradition) formulated most concisely the main idea of sham constitutionalism: the precedence of monarchical principle over popular representation.

The monarchical principle concurrently represented the framework of legal science (theoretically formulated by Friedrich Stahl and sociologically analysed by Otto Hintze); the norm of public law enshrined in the fundamental legislation of East European monarchical states; and lastly, the ways of practical political organization of relations between the monarch and the institutions of popular representation. German analytical jurisprudence has another theory that is essential to the interpretation of sham constitutionalism. The theory whereby state sovereignty is viewed as a legal entity was described in the famous writings of Paul Laband and Georg Jellinek, and in the writings of the Russian scholars Sergey A. Muromtsev and Fedor F. Kokoshkin. This concept rests on the compromise-based model of constitutional monarchy as a form of government opposing two extreme doctrines: the revolutionary sovereignty of people and the feudal monarchical principle. Furthermore, the state-as-legal-entity concept does not carry the idea of the separation of legislative, executive and judicial powers to the extremes of their opposition and independent existence. Rather, it interprets the separation of powers as the division of competences within a single managerial system headed by one judge: an emperor. The concept of the state as legal entity was very important for establishing a relationship between the principles of federalism and unitarianism, for it provided the best combination of autonomy and unity of the state as a political formation. Being a legal entity, the state itself creates laws, applies them and acts as a judge in the case of a conflict. The contradiction can be solved only by viewing the separation of powers from a perspective where the state itself acts in different capacities. On the whole, the teachings of German philosophers were quite metaphysical and authoritarian. Their main conclusion was that the political will and the head of state represented the embodiment of a nation. The posterior synthesis of the Rousseauist concept of popular will and the German concept of political will is reflected in formulation of the ideological doctrine of a total state (from the teachings of Carl Schmitt and Andrey Y. Vyshinsky to contemporary interpretations).

So far, we have explored how the phenomenon of sham constitutionalism emerged and developed in the course of the three major revolutions occuring in modern and recent times. Now we have to analyse the general historical functions of sham constitutionalism, taking into account the conflicting nature of social development in modernization period. In fact, every traditional society experiences the crisis of an existing legal system at the stage of modernization. The necessary restructuring of the old legal system can be carried out in two ways, either via revolution or radical reform. Despite using different methods of transformations, these approaches pursue the same goal. They are aimed at bringing the political power in line with the nature of social changes. This can be achieved either through introducing a new formula of legitimization and or by changing the nature of political regime. Ideally, the two approaches should go hand in hand. Practically, under revolutionary transformations they often become separated, giving rise to transitional forms that are inevitably conflicting in nature. The stage of sham constitutionalism is unavoidable during the transition from absolutism to law-based state. In other words, sham constitutionalism (in one of its myriad forms) is a natural stage in the political transformation of any traditionalist authoritarian regime. It emerges because of inconsistence between the declared goals of democratic restructuring and the reality of political confrontation. However, sham constitutionalism, like many other transitional forms, exists only in the climate of political changes. Its social content can vary greatly and even become diametrically opposite, depending on a direction in which the whole political system moves. Sham constitutionalism can be (and has been historically) representative of the transition from the absolutism to a parliamentarian democracy. Yet, under certain circumstances it can mean the reverse direction of transition: from the parliamentarianism to a constitutional monarchy or to Bonapartist dictatorship. And lastly, sham constitutionalism can be a formal, temporary concession implying the transition from one form of authoritarian government (a traditional absolutism) to another (a rationally organized bureaucratic monarchy). So, revealing the nature of pseudo-constitutional phenomenon in a certain socio-political context will enable one to tell where the political regime moves. The final answer, of course, can be given only after the establishment of a new regime, i.e. when sham constitutionalism gives way either to true constitutionalism in the form of constitutional monarchy or presidential republic, or to their combination introducing a new form of sham constitutionalism. Forecasting trends in the development of sham constitutionalism is of great interest to political analysts and constitutionalists. Such work, however, requires the researcher to study political regimes, systems of government and mechanisms of power.

For interpreting the political philosophy of liberalism in the twentieth century, it is important to determine its attitude toward a transitional political system, as well as toward such interrelated phenomena as sham constitutionalism and nominal constitutionalism. In our systemic analysis of the transitional political system, these notions have the following meaning.

Sham constitutionalism might be defined as a system where political decision making is withdrawn from the sphere of constitutional control. This is accomplished through: i) conferring vast legal powers on the head of state; ii) maintaining flaws or lacunas in the constitution; and, consequently, iii) adjusting these flaws or omissions depending on the actual balance of social and political forces. As an alternative option, there may be established a new form of authoritarianism.

Nominal constitutionalism can be defined as a system where the constitutional norm is not effective at all. The classical principles of liberal constitutionalism which are governing human rights and power relations (the separation of powers) are not entrenched in the political system. The constitution legalizes an unlimited power, a dictatorship, which is *per se* unconstitutional. Therefore, this system is constitutional in name alone. And it does not have constitutional norms for power restriction in reality. Nominal constitutionalism embodies new principles of legitimacy (the sovereignty of people or classes) and establishes an authoritarian government (the dictatorship of a party in power).

The dialectics of sham constitutionalism and nominal constitutionalism makes it possible to better understand the logic of Russian political system development in a comparative perspective.

The theoretical approach has allowed us to interpret Russian constitutionalism as an integral historical phenomenon of modern and recent times. Russian constitutionalism is specifically characterized by contradictions inherent in the modernization process. These are contradictions between the law and the necessity of rapid social changes; between the newly established democratic institutions and the consolidation of power needed for reform regulation; and lastly, between the classical West European models of constitutional development and the indigenous forms of political development.

In the public consciousness of society or a part thereof, constitutional institutions are usually associated with the positive participation of citizens in public administration. The regimes, which cannot and thus do not want to implement adequate legal norms or institutions of government, tend to use constitutionalist terminology in a demagogic way. Constitutional modernization in transitional societies may begin or continue with this terminology, which acquires a new meaning therein.

To be clearer in interpretation of emerging gaps between the notion and reality, it was important to find a terminology for transitional process (though in reality, they sometimes imperceptibly evolve into one another). Hence, we describe nominal constitutionalism and real constitutionalism as two polar opposites divided by a changing space of conflicting interests and development. Like Max Weber, we call the space "sham constitutionalism". Weber, together with Russian liberals, studied the instability of sham constitutionalism using German constitutional law and drawing on the Russian specific experience of the early twentieth century. In particular, German and Russian liberals meticulously studied prospects for implementing the right of universal suffrage in the societies that are not ready for liberal thinking. In the late nineteenth and early twentieth centuries, Russian liberal philosophers focused on the issues linked to transition from the authoritarian regime to a constitutional system. They believed that under the circumstances the best way of transition was to introduce an octroyed model of constitutional monarchy. Thus, the enlightened monarchy could restrict its powers by establishing representative institutions, the right of universal suffrage and parliament (the Russian Duma). This was done by the Tsar's Manifesto of 17 October 1905. However, the key problem for Russia has always been the non-readiness of its citizens to coexist with the universal right of suffrage and democratic institutions whose functions oblige the masses of people to have an adequate level of legal background and political culture. Despite being politically irrelevant, this scientific problem captured the attention of leading liberal scholars with political, historical and legal knowledge of Russian realities and Western models of constitutional development. Among Russian legal scientists, historians and politicians involved in the study we should mention Pavel N. Milyukov and the whole Russian legal school represented by its founders: Konstantin D. Kavelin, Boris N. Chicherin and Sergey M. Soloviev.[15] Moisey Ya. Ostrogorsky, Russian political figure and legal scientist, approached the same issue from another angle. He explored the realities of political life drawing on the experience of western democracy. Ostrogorsky analysed how political culture was raised among the masses of people, and how the British and American electoral institutions were functioning over the period from their formation to modern political realities. Ostrogorsky's classical work along with the writings of other legal and political scientists laid the foundations for Russian scientific and political sociology.[15]

Classical constitutionalism, which took shape in Western Europe, set an example for social thought in many other countries. Throughout the eighteenth century, Russia followed the European patterns of economic, cultural and political development. Contemporaries associated the period of Europeanization with modernization. In modern and, especially recent times, representative institutions and the Code Napoleon has become a model for liberal thought. Constitutionalist political terminology was used for incorporating new elements into existing structures. For instance, many political terms coined during the French Revolution came into use under new circumstances in the wake of the 1917 Russian Revolution. Of course, the meaning of French terms applied to the functioning of Russian institutions was inadequate from the start and became inconsistent with their original meaning in the course of time. In modern and, especially recent times, classical West European constitutionalism has been regarded by the liberal movement as an example for countries under modernization. Constitutional modernization means modifying constitutional norms and institutions in the context of social changes. In general, society can be modernized in a legal or anti-legal way. Legal modernization, in turn, can either maintain or break legal continuity.

2 Proto-constitutionalism in Russia's traditional society

It would be reasonable to start a study into constitutionalism in transitional societies with a review of the original situation that it actually evolves in. This is a crisis of traditional society, which transforms from the intrinsic self-sufficiency and stability of its grounds to a state of new self-identification, recognizing the necessity of upholding its place by interacting with other political systems in the world. As decision making is outside public control here, the driving forces of modernization are connected by power structures and administrative mechanisms. History of autocratic Russia is represented by different types of reforms and ideological justification thereof, pursuing modernization (initially conceived as Europeanization) of social relations. The first type implies a rapid "catch-up" development exercised exclusively through government administration, seeking the accomplishment of the authorities' strategic goals as fast as possible. Since the public rated the power's place within the hierarchy of a global political system by its military potential, this modernization option is more or less indirectly linked to the effectiveness precisely along this line. This is best illustrated by the reforms of Peter the Great in the early eighteenth century, who managed, in a short space of time, to establish an effective army, navy, industry, taxation and secular education systems. A special significance of this historic type of reform was imparted by the charismatic reformer, who viewed the objective process of modernization as a personal responsibility and choice. This type of reform required an absolute power and resulted in establishment of absolutism in Russia.

Absolutism and constitutional projects

Transition from the traditional system of a service class – where each class was obliged to perform any service to the state of an absolutist hierarchical system, be it military or administrative as the representatives of nobility did, or to perform compulsory obligations (so called tax) on behalf of rural peasantry and ordinary citizens – started at the beginning of wartime in Russia.

Contemporary science views absolutism as an era of building national centralized western-type states, and in this sense it is contrasted with the preceding phase of feudalism. Given this approach, absolutism comes to be an integral social system which, despite national specifics, has a number of stable attributes: presence of a certain level of national self-consciousness, economic and social integration (taxation system), a fixed (though far from uniform) network of legal and political institutes; it is characterized by a centralized administrative procedure, a significant role of regular army and rationalized bureaucracy in consolidating political power and; finally, an ideologically consolidated principle of monarchic sovereignty.

In modern times, an important historical modification of absolutism evolves in the form of enlightened absolutism, which is interpreted by contemporary science as an essential step towards a law-based state. Enlightened absolutism means attempts of traditional entities to adapt to new terms of development, to exercise modernization through top-down reforms and an active interference of the state in public life by regulating social relations, a stronger legal regulation thereof. This model is also interpreted as a police state known for a rigid legal and administrative regulation of all facets of life, whereas supreme power as such is not restricted by law. Therefore, the gist of the enlightened absolutism policy manifests itself most explicitly in its plan of legal reforms (the eighteenth-century codification). Virtually everywhere, absolutism ceases to exist in the course of revolutions of the new and the latest times, giving way to a variety of constitutional forms of government, primarily to constitutional monarchy. Absolutism, in the wide sense, is any regime renouncing the idea that the sovereign power can be limited by any power other than its own. In this sense, the concept of absolutism is applicable to both monarchic and democratic regimes ("absolutism of popular will"). The absolutist forms of government are, therefore, opposite to pluralistic regimes. Absolutism (and theories legitimizing it) took on its classical form in French monarchy. There are two concepts underlying the absolutist doctrine, namely, sovereignty and monarchy making up a notion of monarchic sovereignty (in contrast to popular sovereignty in democratic nations).

This transition and entrenchment of absolutism in Russia required a special desk study.[1] The focus of attention was the choice of key parameters used for exercising comparative research: these parameters are the network of political institutions subject to modification in the course of deep reforms at the time of Peter the Great; the structures of the ruling circle and changes in its composition, and ways of regulating its status, prestige and well-being; and its relations with the specific group which is both a tool for reform and its independent force, whose efforts can be directed both at continuation of reforms and the conservation of the traditional system. The study into the mechanisms of absolutism consolidation also focused on the issues such as capacities of and limits to the authoritarian power of the monarch and the impact of the charismatic personality of Peter on the course and outcomes of the deep reforms. This made it possible to produce comparable data on quantitative and qualitative changes in power structures and administration, the ratio of new and old political institutions, and especially composition of and changes in the administrative structure in the course of transition from the traditional system of institutions to participative one. This model of deep reform gave a boost to the process in the course of which the traditional power system ended up in consolidation of absolutism. We interpret the consolidation of absolutism in Russia as a first step in building an authoritarian system, which determined, for centuries, the development vector and the type of relationships between the government and society in this country in modern and recent times.

The modern era radically modified the process of government rationalization. While the world is increasingly turning into a uniform civilization, owing to economic, geographic, technical and cultural discoveries, a slower pace of development and rationalization puts national sovereignty at risk. The organization of government in advanced countries acts as a model of desirable reforms under the circumstances. Hence, it becomes necessary to step on the road to "catch-up" development and modernization. All these modifications of a rationalization process – "catch-up" development, radical government reforms and Europeanization – first found their explicit expression in the reformatory activities of Peter and later of his followers in Russia in its biggest reforms. A comparative analysis showed that the administrative transformations, while meeting the objective tasks of the "catch-up" development and modernization, were the first in a series of similar reforms of modern times, manifesting a number of stable signs, which can then be found in the reforms of absolutist and authoritarian regimes in general: Prussia, Austria, Denmark, Turkey, Japan and other developing nations of modern and recent times. The traditional organization of power and government in the world history is opposed by the rationalistic structure thereof. The process of government rationalization, manifesting itself in the reforms, encompasses quite diverse facets of life: the economy, social relations, politics, culture. Most explicitly, however, it manifests itself in the organization of public administration, notably, in reforming the administrative machinery, the ruling class and the bureaucracy. Keeping this in mind, the entire logics of reforms and counter-reforms in Russia's history becomes more comprehensible. In order to interpret Peter's reforms in a wider historical perspective, we turned to the legal programme of enlightened absolutism, which is a brave attempt at transforming traditional structures by way of top-down reforms. In the light of modernization theory, enlightened absolutism in East European countries constitutes a desire of entrenched entities to adapt to the new conditions of development, exercise modernization through top-down reforms and an active interference of the state in public life by resorting to regulation of social relations, more intensive legal regulation thereof.

A comparative analysis of law in countries such as Russia, Prussia, Austria and other nations in the reviewed region helped identify a number of significant legal initiatives having much in common. In treating big codification initiatives as milestones on the road to social reforms with policy of the law, we segregated three major stages of legislative activities in the era of Enlightened absolutism. These are the beginning of codification activities (Peter's Codification Commissions in 1700, 1714 and 1721; in Austria – 1709 Commission, and in Prussia – 1713 Commission), a new boost to their activities was given in the middle of the eighteenth century (Codification Commissions of Elizabeth and Catherine II in the 1750s to the 1760s in Russia, 1747 Commission in Prussia, and 1753–1755 Commission in Austria); and finally the third, closing phase of codification after the French Revolution (Prussia's Local Code of 1794; Austria's Civil Code of 1811, and codification projects in the beginning of the reign of Alexander I in Russia). In this perspective, Peter's codification efforts can be viewed as the first attempt, in modern times, at purposeful utilization of law, legal policy for reforming and modernizing social relations. There is a distinct similarity between the motives behind codification (undertaken in countries with absolutist regimes) and methods of their execution (by setting up bureaucratic committees). As similar, in principle, were the results of their activities, which were characterized by incompleteness, which in turn was due to a desire to adapt West European law to feudal structures in Eastern Europe. This holds also for the Codification Commissions of Peter's time, especially with respect to regulating the possession rights of the ruling class.

The Code of 1649 fixed the original construct of combining land and power within the frameworks of serfdom, which served as the core of the service state up to the beginning of its transformation. The directions of this transformation are represented by the projects developed by the Codification Commissions in the eighteenth century. The political stability of the Russian state was historically linked to the economic and social power of land resource ownership. As collectively perceived by the public, the state, the authority (personified by the monarch) was the embodiment of both the unity of territory, supreme government, supreme disposal of land resources. In the second half of the seventeenth century, some processes important for the further development of the nation evolved: the geopolitical situation, which acted as a factor of public consensus, came to be more stable; new opportunities for a wide-ranging colonization of new farm lands opened up. The authorities, in turn, became capable of limiting people's migration to the regions free of farming: peasants were assigned to the land, hence, to the landed gentry, who formally registered them (Code of 1649).

Privatization by the gentry of land resources, which the authorities had been historically using for handing out for qualified tenure for military service, increasingly intensified in the second half of the seventeenth century. Land provisions of the Code drew a distinct line between patrimonial and estate law. Subsequently, it had to be revised with decrees issued by the authorities on concrete cases, and acted as a sort of case law, under the circumstances. Peter I attempted to take this process under the authority's control as early as the beginning of his reign. The attempt involved a more intensive codification of the effective laws and potential development of a new Code, for which a special Code Chamber was established. However, the attempt failed, and the process of modification of authority and property relations went on.[2]

As is seen from legislation analysis, social policy in Peter's time largely pursued the creation of a new ruling class, namely, gentry. Of course, this class emerged on the basis of previous privileged sections. However, it differed from them in a bigger homogeneity and unification; the degree of connection with the government; status and prestige; separation from the rest of society; and, above all, in the nature of recruitment and social mobility, intra-estate organization and relation to landed property. Lying in the core of this process of consolidation of the new ruling class was the evolution of property relations, which proceeded throughout the second half of the seventeenth century and ended up precisely in Peter's era. The main social gist of this evolution was equalization of the legal status of the *pomeste* (estate dependent on state service) form of land ownership and the *votchina* (unrestricted hereditary estate) form thereof. The legal recognition of this fact became possible, however, only in Peter's era. Unification of land and peasant property relations has once and for all separated the ruling class from the rest of the population, promoted its consolidation on the basis of uniform economic conditions, service functions, role in administration, social psychology and culture, as well as regrouping of forces within its own self. The fragmented and archaic class division of Sovereign court, which existed in the seventeenth century, gave way to a new type of closely-knit and uniform class. An active role in building this ruling class was played by the state, which sought to mold it into an effective management tool and make it greatly dependent upon political power. One of the explicit manifestations of this social policy became an attempt to limit landowners' succession by instituting entailed estate (1714) with a view to preventing economic degradation of the ruling class resulting from endless fragmentation of estates, and simultaneously provide personnel for military and civil service. The decree of Peter I, as of 23 March 1714, sought to stop the process of endless fragmentation of the country's available land under the impact of demographic factor, for it pursued the goal of introducing a form of a single heir, which was new for Russia. However this attempt at stabilizing the strength of the class of civil servants by enacting a new law was hard to implement in practice too. The orthodox bureaucracy managed to emasculate the new rule, which was later recognized by the lawmaker himself. This situation exposed the independent role of the administrative machinery in the process of reforms. It is precisely this transition from traditional administration forms to creating a rational bureaucracy that the critical significance was attached to in the course of absolutism consolidation.[3]

The main regulator of the state's efforts towards creating a new ruling class was its transformation on the basis of the Table of Ranks issued in 1722. Its idea was as follows: the ruling class received a uniform structure; new principles of social mobility were introduced (the local principles of nomination on the basis of gentility have once and for all given way to the length of service, business competence); the ruling class dependence on the government increased (for careers and performance of functional responsibilities for a salary ruled out or heavily limited other sources of income); also improved the ruling class rationalization and its organization, which was now exercised, first, along civil servant rank rather than intra-class subdivision and, second, by functional characteristics (affiliation with military, civil or court hierarchy). All these features of the new social order promoted bureaucratization and concentration of power in the hand of the ruling elite (the generals) and the monarch.

The comparative analysis made it possible to match the Table of Ranks with a series of other laws of the late seventeenth century to the first quarter of the eighteenth century, which modified, to some extent, the traditional hierarchy of the ruling class for a more rational one. The Table of Ranks, viewed in a broad historical context, is not a purely Russian phenomenon, but represents a trend, common for all (and especially for East European nations) in switching from traditional to a more rational government and development of a new ruling class and bureaucracy. The other side of this process in Russia is regrouping of forces within the ruling elite, a gradually decreasing role of boyar aristocracy as a specifically exclusive class corporation, whose members were connected by the commonality of social status, bonds of relation, social psychology.

In Russia, class formation generally proceeded under a direct influence of the state. The society and state form as if an integral whole, each class and social group perform their functions occupying a respective place in the social hierarchy, which is in turn fixed in law and administrative practice. And it is government that is the main method of regulating social relations. This promotes consolidation of bureaucracy, concentration of huge real power in its hands and puts government and administrative machinery in special conditions. All this makes the administrative system the necessary, increasingly visible component of social structure, a tool of interaction between the authorities and society, whose attitude to transformations strongly bears upon their feasibility. The administration is vested with a great deal of power, even more so now that the opportunities for public control are rather limited (the influence of Boyar Duma comes to naught, the class representative institutions are scrapped, church influence is limited). In conducting top-down radical reforms the state, which initiated them, was unable to rely on the old, entrenched system of institutions and administrative procedures, which came to be not only inadequate as a tool of transformation but actually impeded them. Hence, the agenda of Peter's reforms was topped by the transformation of the network of political institutions and public agencies. Modernization of the state machinery manifested itself in rational principles of its structure, establishment of new institutions (senate and boards) and higher administration efficiency. Qualitatively new features of Peter's administrative system, compared to the departmental administration of Moscow state, came to be unification, centralization and differentiation of administrative functions and, to an extent, its militarization inherent in absolutist regimes. It is the uniform system of legal norms, various regulations, procedures of board and other institution activities that were the key features of rational organization of the government; a new formal hierarchy of the levels of administration, institutions and officialdom was developed; also developed were definite principles and rules determining the status and well-being of different categories of officials and their career progression. All this promoted development of corporate psychology of bureaucracy as of a specific social group.

Reorganization of the state machinery is an outward manifestation of the deeper changes in the social foundation of absolutism and in the correlation between various social structures: the ruling elite, the evolving bureaucracy and the army.

The other important prerequisite for subsequent development came to be the country's affiliation with the global (the then European) system, which marked the beginning of a modernization era. It became necessary to correlate the maintenance of existence stability and the nation's prosperity in the future with the system of European powers. At the same time, the joining of the European system caused a significant informational shift in the public's consciousness: the new informational space enabled people to identify themselves amid other European nations, to change quality of life and culture of the ruling circles, change national self-consciousness. It was precisely the time when a certain contradictory perception of the nation's self-identification emerged: the natural but formerly unimportant question arose as to why the state so rich with resources (in European terms) is so poor for its own population.[4]

Quite understandable against this background are the changes in the forms of ownership – from power over land as a territory, as a reserve of national wealth and a source of subsistence (through the use of its resources by the population) – to a narrow interpretation of land ownership as class privilege. The initial power of the state over land is, in theory, a kind of a social contract closely resembling its interpretation by Thomas Hobbes, where the government receives an exclusive prerogative for maintaining internal and external stability. Hence, the interpretation of relationships between society and the government, which is responsible for defence, organization of the army, providing for administration, state machinery (landed system). Max Weber defined this type of relationship as "liturgical state". In Russian historical and legal science, it was traditionally referred to as "service state". Functioning of the given system was based on the systematic registration of lands and their taxation (three types of land: service, church, public or state-owned). And the major function of the state was to provide for accounting and controlling the distribution of land resources, which placed demand on the respective personnel.

Joining the system of European states and modernization challenge, the necessity of preventing its trailing behind the more advanced European states, and providing for implementation of nationwide objectives turned out to be a factor determining the modification of social structure of society. The government is no longer in a position to keep the entire land resource under its control. The traditionalistic interpretation of the notion of "land" (as a tri-unity of territory, of the people and of the government) has long expressed the formula of social consensus, which found its sound expression at the time of doing away with discord and formation of a new dynasty, as well as repulsing the intervention at the beginning of the seventeenth century. It was legally consolidated and inscribed in the Code of 1649. The assignment of peasant homesteads to the land, depriving peasants of any choice, made the possession of inhabited lands the goal of the service class. Along with redistribution of ancestral-patrimonial resources, the struggle was also waged around the land resource of conditional landed estate under government control, which happened to be outside state control for a historically short period of time. The service conditional landownership gives way to private (unconditional) landed estate. The social group, which grabbed the land, has changed configuration of the class system and government/society relations. The entire stock of land came to be at the disposal of gentry exerting a powerful pressure on the government with a view to concentrating all potential rights and privileges in the hands of gentry corporation. Liberation of the latter increases the enslavement of the possessory segment of the peasantry.

Nationwide interests are identified with the interests of the privileged corporative class. The gentry turn into a link between the government and the population attached to the land. It secures tax obligations of peasants, it has to supervise their discharge (tax collection). The periodic censuses of taxed population produced general data on the strength of taxed population and enabled supervision of tax obligations to the state. The remainder becomes the internal affair of the landlords, depends on their goodwill and is regulated by the state only indirectly. Naturally, it has an adverse effect on agricultural development, on the condition of possessory peasants. Peasants were denied the right to purchase real estate in the district and town (1730) and were only allowed to engage in leasing and contracting (1731); they were to have the right to personal property only. As a result, peasants are freely separated from land and sold separately from the family. Selling people separately was prohibited only later (1843).

Turning peasants into house serfs, moving them to other lands and in fact solving the issue of marriage choice also belonged to the landlord. At the latter's disposal were not only all of the peasants' property but also the effective tools of repressive influence such as the right of deportation to exile (to Siberia), giving into recruits, various statutory forms of punishment. The restriction of forced labour by introducing a three-day statute labour was formally announced only in 1797, but it didn't have any real significance. This model of social development resulted in economic stagnation, the lack and conscious suppression of any initiative on the part of peasants, collective prejudices hindering development of entrepreneurial ethics and spirit of capitalism in the Weber sense. In interpreting this phenomenon by comparing America and Russia, Alexis de Tocqueville spoke of the existence of democracy in both countries, yet he stressed that in the former case democracy was based on synthesis of equality and individual liberty, and in the latter of equality and slavery.

The fundamental conflict of society and state, being the focus of attention of prominent political philosophers in Western Europe of modern times, was especially acute in Russia. The establishment of absolutism in Russia in the first quarter of the eighteenth century, manifesting itself in the reforms of Peter the Great, marked the dominating trend towards concentration, bureaucratization and militarization of state power, which was realized later on. The Russian political thought deemed it necessary to look into the possibilities of creating public control over the autocracy, legal guarantees of political system, development of mechanisms regulating interaction of the government and society. The evolution of political ideas here was proceeding in specific conditions of absolutist power exerting a huge and, in effect, determining influence on ideological concepts and the respective interpretations of political movements and transformation projects. The first constitutional project of restricting the autocracy in Russia dates back to 1730. In historiography, the problems and developments in the beginning of the reign of empress Anna Ivanovna were first treated as an unimportant event involving an attempt by a group of aristocrats, close to the authorities, to compel Anna, who was invited for reign, to commit herself to their leading role in administration. As the candidate did not have any reign experience, the failure was immediately interpreted as an abortive plot, a court intrigue. Kept as a secret was the other event, notably, a public design by metropolitan and representatives of provincial gentry of a series of projects restricting monarchical power by establishing a representative institution in the interests of the upper circles.

The projects of autocracy limitation proposed during the political crisis of January–February 1730, which raised empress Anna to the throne, have a special place in the public movement of the eighteenth century. They reveal that the idea of an unlimited autocracy as an optimal system and the only possible for this country was far from exclusive in the Russian society in post-Peter times. The authoritative government of Peter the Great, on the one hand, and the lack of a charismatic personality of the ruler during the years of reign of Catherine I and of under-age Peter II, on the other hand, produced a great deal of occasions for the thinking segment of society for comparisons and reflections on the forms of civilized government and ways of their accomplishment.

In the history of political process in Russia, the events of January–February 1730 have not yet become a subject of comparative analysis, yet it is precisely under this approach that their non-ordinariness becomes more apparent: advancing alternative projects of monarchical power limitation; open and public discussion thereof in society involving compilation of numerous texts, design of political reform projects; radicalism of a suggestion linked to convocation of a representative assembly on the basis of universal suffrage (for privileged layers of society) called to solve the issue of the form of monarchical rule by the majority vote; uncommonness of a direct appeal to the supreme power with a petition on modification of the form of government. Naturally, none of these projects was realized. Moreover, the scale and meaning of the events have undergone drastic changes in the subsequent historiography. A negative labelling of the bigwigs as state criminals prevailed. But the event revealed society's preparedness for change, and the compilation of no less than 10–12 texts of political projects recording about 1,000 signatures of the representatives of gentry, aristocracy and officialdom supporting the projects, took only a few days.

The political crisis of 1730 rendered the issue of constitutional limitation of autocracy on the part of society highly acute. The alignment of forces was not confined by the existence of oligarchic alternative. Indeed, the bigwigs sought to establish an aristocratic control over monarchical power in Russia like the one existing in Sweden in the seventeenth and eighteenth centuries.

The project of oligarchic way of government produced the most negative response from the wider gentry circles. The gentry have unambiguously opposed the attempt at establishing oligarchy – "a crowd of sovereigns instead of one". According to De Liria, Spanish Ambassador, "They were afraid to get as many tyrants as many members there were in the Council". The same was written by Artemy P. Volynski, a junior employee of Peter, one of the most intelligent political figures of that time. It would be a considerable simplification to believe, however, that in opposing oligarchy the gentry, and especially its enlightened representatives such as Volynski, were upholding just the ideal of autocracy. On the contrary, the point was about the introduction (within the frameworks of the ruling class, though) of a wider public control over the monarch to be exercised through class representation.

In the decisive days of the 1730 political crisis, not only metropolitan but also a great many of provincial gentry were in Moscow. The point is that Peter II's wedding party was scheduled for that time, therefore the events received a wide public response. The forms of government and the advantages of limiting autocracy were debated everywhere. The foreign diplomats, closely watching the public sentiments, left numerous evidences of different approaches to this problem. The common impression thereof boiled down to ascertaining wide-ranging suggestions, from more radical to quite moderate. "The doors of the room, where the Supreme Council of Russia sits" – Danish envoy Vestfalen wrote on 9 February – "were for the whole week open for all those willing to speak on the issue and suggest anything pro or cons the suggested transformation of the then way of government in Russia". He also noted a high intensity of debates.

The gentry, not confined by political discussions alone, designed more than a score of draft reform projects signed by a large number of people (over 1,000). The fact that it became possible to draft complex political documents over a few days is a clear indication that they had been thoroughly prepared, and the stated demands thought over in advance. Hence, as early as that period of time, the political life was rather saturated by reflections on the problems of a perfect government, and the information about a variety of political systems in European states was quite accessible and was part of the political culture of the educated segment. As for the projects as such, they primarily reflected the common idea of the necessity of control over the government, in particular allocation of government funds, by the elected representatives of gentry. The specific transformations have not, however, been developed in detail. Most integral of those documents is the project of changing the form of government, developed in cooperation with Vasily N. Tatishchev.[5] In considering the existing forms of government, to which he referred, monarchy, aristocracy or a government of elite, and democracy with a mixed representation, Tatishchev arrived at the conclusion that only monarchic form of government was suitable for Russia. Given the dynastic crisis, he suggested the election of a sovereign, but by consent of the subjects, "by the whole people" defining the latter as gentry only. Being fully aware that that legislation may not be entrusted to one person, he suggested the establishment of a Higher Government – Senate, made up of 21 people to assist the monarch. Apart from this, a two-chamber body of a complex composition was suggested. It would be subdivided into a higher assembly (for consideration of especially important issues) and a standing assembly (for their extra discussion and execution). Rather important was a project thesis on election, by secret ballot, to a number of top posts in the state, and one of the elected candidates would be approved by the monarch. It is interesting to note that a restriction on representation of one family in the higher government and other representative bodies was to be introduced (no more than two representatives thereof), which clearly points to gentry's desire to resist the oligarchic ambitions of the orthodox aristocracy. Other projects, too, contained similar suggestions on the election of a representative assembly from out of the gentry ranks for drawing up a plan of state reforms. Quite apparent in all of them was the class nature of gentry's projects paying special attention to granting considerable benefits and rights to this class and its transformation into a privileged one. It is precisely this side of the issue that was immediately grasped by the monarchic power, which was fully and persistently realized later on, in the legislation of Anna, Elizabeth and Peter III, by turning gentry from service to noble class.

The fact that political systems and teachings of western powers were so attentively studied in Russia should, no doubt, be attributed to a sort of influence of Europeanization. This interest goes back to the reforms of Peter I, who systematically demanded and received from Russian diplomats rather detailed information about the state structure of England, France, Sweden, Prussia, Denmark, Austria and even Turkey and Venice. In so doing, he was largely interested in the administrative system in these nations, the organization of officialdom in them, which was directly related to the board reform and development of the Table of Ranks. Also, a great deal of attention was given, however, to political systems of western nations, and their comparison with Russian ones. One of the features of turning to western political and legal experience was the interest shown in parliamentary institutions and ways of restricting arbitrariness of the power. Many representatives of the Russian aristocracy, who had a chance to be abroad, say in England or Sweden, have unwittingly drawn certain parallels between their systems and that in Russia. This was precisely the source of the critical attitude towards the monarchic power that was inherent in the evolving Russian intelligentsia.

The political campaign of 1730 culminated in an appeal of a representative group of reform proponents to Anna Ivanovna herself, which took place in the Kremlin upon her arrival to Moscow on 25 February. A group of noblemen (up to 800, on some estimates) who arrived to the Kremlin, carried an earlier compiled and signed petition, which was read aloud by Vasily N. Tatishchev. It requested the monarch's consent for calling (from all the generals, officers and gentry) a representative assembly, with representation of one or two members from one family, which in its turn could "by consensus and majority vote design a form of Public Government" and submit it "for endorsement" to the empress. The monarch fixed her agreement on this document too (as she had done earlier on the text of standards). The situation in the palace, however, changed within hours. The guards and officers, filling up the palace, "raised a clamour" demanding immediate acceptance of autocratic rule. This provided opportunities for simultaneous renunciation of both restraining options: the bigwig standards (who didn't dare to object) and the just read out petition. A rapid rearrangement of positions of the event's participants occurred, and yet another delegation (headed by Nikolay Trubetskoy) arrived before the monarch, with a new petition read out by Kantemir. It contained a request from all the subjects to assume autocracy, do away with the signed "items" and restore the Governing Senate. In return and for demonstration of her agreement, Anna Ivanovna ordered to bring in the text of standards and tore it slightly in an emphatic manner. Tatishchev's petition seemed to be forgotten, and he himself was appointed manager of state plants in the Urals. But the gentry's demands for both cutting the period of service, revocation of the primogeniture were realized during the so unusually commenced reign and in the course of subsequent ones, including those of Peter III and Catherine II.

Upon confirming her reputation of real politician, Anna Ivanovna used the gentry's opposition to the Supreme Privy Council for its destruction and establishment of absolute rule, disregarding all the ideas of restraining monarchy. The gentry project came to be, in effect, of no real significance. But the very fact of its development is rather interesting. While only the authorities' initiatives concerned with social transformation are observed in the era of Peter's reforms, the 1730 project acts as an evidence of bottom-up initiative. Of course, not of society at large but only of a segment thereof, namely of the gentry, realizing one's identity as a class and eager to formulate a programme of its corporative interests.

The establishment of new relations between public opinion and power was launched by Catherine in connection with her *Nakaz* ("Instruction").

Catherine II drew up her Instruction for the activities of a Commission, set up for drafting a new Code, which was published on 30 July 1767. The Code Commission of Catherine II was formally a collegiate body set up for codification of statutes enacted after 1649 Code (Russia's main body of laws). The evolution of general social conflict linked with the establishment of absolutism in Russia, spreading and consolidation of serfdom set the government a task of choosing a reform strategy. The only way out under absolutism suggested a statutory regulation of class relations and a tougher administrative and military control. Catherine did not, however, give up her intentions to act, in public opinion, as an enlightened reformist ruler. A quite peculiar political step of the new reign was a convocation by Catherine, in 1767, of the Code Commission, which was charged with drafting a new Code. This was announced in a Manifesto on 14 December 1766. Formally, the Commission was an ad hoc collective body – an assembly of class representatives from all over Russia. This was society's will on the major economic, social and political issues, quite unusual in the history of Russia and absolutist Europe. The right of drafting mandates (suggestions delivered to deputies) was given to classes: gentry, town-dwellers and countrymen, small-holders and some peasants. The mandates were also compiled by central government agencies. The Code Commission was not offered any original version of the Code. It is the Instruction on drafting a new Code, written by the empress herself and issued to the Commission, that served as the main guiding document.

It is the Catherine II Instruction prepared for members of the 1767 Code Commission that came to be an officially endorsed programme of socio-political transformations of enlightened absolutism.[6] The gist of the programme boils down to the implementation of enlighteners' ideas (in the first place, of Montesquieu) on the introduction of the principles of lawful monarchy in contrast to despotic regimes, where the varying will of the ruler is the law. Hence the interest of Catherine II in the writings of Sir William Blackstone, who interpreted the unwritten English Constitution and the principle of separation of powers in favour of autocracy, whose existence serves as a guarantee of stability and continuity of legislation. Accordingly, social reforms had to be carried out along with mandatory observation of the key laws and natural rights of the individual confronted with society and state. The idea of calling the Code Commission becomes more understandable against this background. It is an attempt by supreme power to appeal to society for developing a more optimal strategy of socio-political development with due regard to the interests of various social strata and groups. It is quite possible that the hidden purpose of the Code Commission was to probe into public sentiments on the crucial issues such as abolition or limitation of serfdom, civil and criminal law reforms along these lines, expansion of the social base of a monarchic system by making it more law governed. Serving as a social basis for raising a serfdom-related question were the well-known differences in attitudes to it on the part of the bulk of gentry (who were satisfied with the status quo and did not want any changes) and a narrow group of court aristocracy who (being more rich, sharing liberal sentiments and familiar with the experiences of West European countries, and especially of Baltic provinces) deemed it possible to raise agricultural labour productivity by relaxing serfdom, introducing the respective changes in the existing laws. Also, Catherine II was well aware of the difference between despotism and genuine monarchy, she was eager to transform the traditional Russian political system into enlightened absolutism.

The Instruction was not a ready-made body of laws but a declaration of general principles for the society and state to be guided by. In so doing, Catherine II did not proceed from the existing system but from the vision of an ideal one. Remember the general belief at the Age of Enlightenment in the opportunity for the development of laws meeting the principles of reason with no correlation with reality.

The concept of fundamental legal principles underlying the political system assumed that the new laws might disagree with them, hence, provided for an opportunity for their revision in a legal manner. Thereby an important step was made towards delimitation of the three types of statutes: basic laws (which, ideally, remained intact), ad hoc short-term instructions (temporary institutions or regulations) and provisions (orders and decrees). Chapter XIX interpreting this issue proceeded from the fact that "laws" should carry fundamental provisions not subject to revision, and may not abound. Accordingly, the absolute power shall be exercised within certain fixed limits. Fundamental laws, few as they may be, are permanent, exist independently from the sovereign regnant and create frameworks within which the sovereign must act. The recognition by monarchs of laws compulsory for them is limitation of power. The area, where the ruler's arbitrariness dominates, is narrowed by delimitation of the ruler and the state. This concept was not quite new in Russia, yet it was, for the first time ever, presented in the form of philosophical formula and declared from the throne.

In historiography, the Catherine II Instruction is simplistically interpreted as a sort of intellectual game of the young empress, or even as a naive, if not hypocritical, philosophic treatise – a compilation of ideas of enlighteners of her time. However, this is because the document is not related to the history of the constitutional movement evolving in Russia. The history of reform projects in eighteenth-century Russia, for all their unreality, is a bright illustration of the typical, characteristic socio-political situation in a transitional society. The body text of the Instruction carries a clearly worded key problem of the situation: unless solving the issue of personal liberty of citizens and their property rights the nation will be unable to secure progress and prosperity. The empress states bluntly that the country where people are afraid of looking rich, and even simply well off, has no future. The Instruction is a question to society, primarily to its more educated segment: are reforms feasible? The answer was apparent – the serfdom foundations are stable. Reforms can undermine stability of the traditional system. The subsequent policy of the empress showed that she grasped the gentry's sentiments perfectly: quite in the spirit of traditional value orientations she did her best for extending traditional serfdom to the new lands. She also inscribed in laws a special status of gentry consistent with their economic might and political ambitions. But first the empress made yet another attempt at securing support to her reform dreams: she turned to scholars of the Free Economic Society and offered a topic for the contest – should peasants be given property, and if yes, then what? Alexey Ya. Polenov, a jurist, developed his own project, where he answered this question.

This project involved the introduction of perpetual land lease for peasants (Alexey Ya. Polenov),[7] which outlined the subsequent reform initiatives (from Mikhail M. Speransky and Nikolay S. Mordvinov up to Pavel D. Kiseliov reform of state peasants). Its evolvement marked the search for a way out of the tough formula of a villainous state. The model of solving the agrarian issue, suggested in Polenov's project, is one of the most integral and significant in the history of this country. A note by Alexey Ya. Polenov was written for the contest announced by the Free Economic Society in 1767 on the topic of peasant land property. This was initiated by empress Catherine II at the time of calling deputies for designing a new Code and commencing active debates on this problem in society. The prize was won by a hardly-known foreign author – Bearde de l'Abaye (died in 1771). This writing was against continued slavery and for the advantages of freedom, handling the issue positively in principle. Yet it drew conclusion on the necessity of postponing the solution to the problem: "First it is necessary to prepare slaves for liberty before any property would be given to them".

At this background, Polenov's contribution is quite significant, for virtually 100 years prior to liberation of peasants the author formulated the problem solution. The suggested concept of handling the agrarian issue seems quite rational even from today's perspective. It is very close to the one evolving in the later liberal projects of Konstantin D. Kavelin *et al.* advanced in the course of 1861 reform. As for Polenov, he can be viewed as a prominent Russian jurist, law theoretician and enlightener. In reviewing Polenov's notes, attention is drawn to a number of aspects: firstly, its very clear philosophical, historical and legal language (reflecting, as is shown below, the basic directions of the evolution of thinker's views); secondly, the well-known internal contradiction between the general (theoretical) section (proving the necessity of private property for any society) and applied one (stating the concept of land handover to peasants on perpetual lease terms). This contradiction, in fact inherent in entire philosophical thought in the Age of Enlightenment, reflected the conflict between the social ideal and the reality of traditional society. Only in reform projects of the nineteenth century, the contradiction disappears in the concept of transitional period, for which a special type of contractual relationship between landlords and peasants and a special type of land tenure is designed. It is hard to find analogues of this type of land use right in rational legal norms of civil codes of modern and recent times. Of prime importance, therefore, is the issue of genesis of Polenov's ideas, which he formulated primarily in the categories of Roman law.

The Polenov solution model can be defined as a conditional hereditary possession of land by peasants with no title, and the continued limited dependence thereof on the landlord. It is difficult to interpret this solution in terms of contemporary civil law, which in principle operates only around the concept of property (private or public). Polenov fails to push his conclusions to accepting this thesis (on the contrary, he rejects it as unacceptable for Russian reality). He writes about "allotting property in lands to peasants along with an appropriate limitation and about ceding full power over private property and other benefits to them". Nevertheless, it was a serious attempt at protecting peasant land tenure from landlord arbitrary interference. This construction can be interpreted as a kind of perpetual land lease with no right to dispose of it other than for agricultural purposes. Land remains in landlord hands, but the peasant acquires a right to its perpetual lease for agricultural production (it most closely resembles the notion of emphyteusis). The peasants' situation can best be described as colonatus. This solution forestalls the following Kavelin model, realized in the course of the Peasant Reform, suggesting preservation for the transition period of a certain status of the provisionally obligated. In suggesting his model, Polenov keeps in mind precisely Russia's specifics. He wants to secure, on the one hand, the interests of the farm and, on the other, prevent arbitrariness with respect to land on the part of peasants themselves.

To accomplish the first goal "each peasant must have enough land for sowing bread and tending livestock, and possess it in hereditary manner so as landlord shall not have even a slightest power to oppress in any way, or take it away for good". The peasant's right to independent disposal of land shall be limited not by landlord's arbitrariness (which rules out efficient farming) but by rationality of behaviour of the peasant himself, by the extent to which "the peasant will duly labour". In case of a conflict between peasant and landlord, the latter may deprive the peasant of land only by decision of an independent external court: the issue shall be examined in a "decent court" (note, which suggests its interclass and out-of-class function of dispute resolution).

In order to accomplish the second goal – guarantee of rights of landowner (landlord) from its misuse by peasants (which may result in ruin thereof) – the succession right of peasant land tenure is subject to considerable limitations. Polenov specifically stresses that the point is not of land transfer to private property of peasants but of its provision to peasants on terms of conditional lifelong and succession use, whose scale is defined as an opportunity for the peasant to "to use (landlord's land) in a free and unrestricted manner and thereby earn one's living". Peasants were supposed to be given full "power and liberty" only with respect to the private property (defined as livestock and crop).

The formula of peasant/landlord relationships is as follows. The peasants were still due to pay an annual "statutory" fraction of their crop to their master (unfortunately, nothing was said about the amount and form of this tribute). It was said about a possibility of limiting the statute labour (work for the master) to one day. An important side of the problem is not even the amount of statute labour and tribute but a desire to legalize them. This is a model of colon, emphyteuta, usufructuary and tenant but not a farmer. In terms of this model, it is therefore clear as to why Polenov introduces (as Kavelin later does) substantial limitations to the application of civil (private) law: the peasants are not allowed on any account "to sell their land, or present, or pledge, or share it out to many children, but following death of the father, one of the sons shall own it" (the principle of entail, which Peter failed to realize with respect to gentry estates earlier).

On the whole, Polenov's model was a trade off, seeking to balance the interests of peasants and landlords: "Thus," he concluded, "the landlords will always retain their right, and the peasants will freely use the authorized benefits".

In reviewing political projects of Russian reforms in the eighteenth to nineteenth centuries, one may see that agrarian reforming is present in them as one of the key components. The bulk of Polenov's note is devoted to comparing terms of peasant liberation: either without land, or with land, and the author is a staunch supporter of the latter option, and defending its advantages and specific terms is the author's goal. In considering the issue in an historical perspective, we see that this alternative does not appear in this note for the first time, and it could be observed, firstly, in the historical retrospective review of Russian history and, secondly, as a key issue of the type of civilizations wherein there exists peasantry and labour on land as business of the bulk of the population. The most appealing project – Polenov's – was subjected to concealment, and its author was deprived of an opportunity to develop his concept and continuation of jurist career.

Why, on the one hand, is there a continuous revival of this discussion and, on the other, power's passivity in its solution? The problem is not so much in gentry's class egoism, but it has deeper reasons. This problem was rather explicitly outlined by yet another figure of that time, namely, Mikhail M. Shcherbatov in his famous writing "On inconvenience of liberating peasants in Russia", where it was explained that the abolition of the established dependence would result in irreversible destructive processes. Naturally, Shcherbatov was not a proponent of peasant liberation with land, but he drew attention to the fact that the freedom of movement of one's own free will would as such destroy Russian agriculture and result in destruction of the administrative system. Naturally, Shcherbatov was a loud mouthpiece of the gentry's stance proper, but his associate – Nikolay M. Karamzin – too, in his "Note on ancient and new Russia" once again drew the authorities' attention to the fact that attempts at changing the peasants' situation would put the system at risk of getting out of control and thus rendering it unmanageable. At this point, Radishchev (unlike the above two thinkers) does not even raise the question of reform implications and the nature of a future social system. It is precisely this peculiarity and even weakness of his stance that become the focus of Alexandr S. Pushkin's judgements of Radishchev.

In his draft political reforms, Nikita I. Panin, an experienced politician, perfectly explained the gist of the problem: a step towards reforms can in no time destroy the state system.[8]

Liberation of peasants would immediately create in this country a category of people deprived of work, of a possibility to support themselves, hence, turning into a destructive force. The point is, apparently, of which share of society this destructive component broken free would account for. It can be crushed, destroyed or dispersed. An association with English enclosure arises, when peasants left without land become tramps, like Robin Hood, become people with no pursuits. In Russia, where peasants accounted for the bulk of the population, this alternative (according to project authors) was ruled out. It is a risk of agrarian revolution that was the most dangerous sequence of reform failure. An alternative to it is, as was perfectly demonstrated by August Haxthausen, changing the status of peasants, their education, rationalization of agricultural production.[9] But this is an issue of protracted development.

The documents of the era – second half of the eighteenth century – permit us to perceive, on the one hand, the scale of the socio-economic crisis and, on the other, the lack of real opportunities for getting out of it. The educated contemporaries of that time, more so those familiar with liberal ideas of West European enlighteners, including the recently enthroned empress, Alexey Ya. Polenov, a connoisseur of Roman law, were quite aware of the lack of prospects for national development without extending at least minimal economic freedoms to the wide strata of the rural and suburban population. But it was quite clear to the real politicians that any attempt at radical reforms may bring about implications becoming fully out of the authorities' control. During over one and a half centuries of binding peasants to land (finally consolidated in 1649 Code, governing a permanent search for runaway serfs) there was established and entrenched a traditional system ruling out any initiative and maintaining the type of economy that had not undergone any modifications for centuries. The ideal of people's consciousness is fully directed backwards, where one sees a free use of unlimited land, water, forest resources, plus free pastures for the nomadic population.

The stability of this utopian ideal and the scale of destructive force conflict potential was demonstrated by the Peasant War of 1773–1778 under the leadership of Yemelyan Pugachov. In his proclamations, this ideal of the ruler, providing his subjects with free lands, grasses and waters, is quite pronounced and embodied in a number of decrees and manifestos allegedly emanating from the tsarist power of pretended emperor Peter III.[10] Suppression of the Peasant War required huge efforts of administrative and military forces. The war demonstrated the necessity of strengthening regional authorities, administrative resources, development of communications and the need for reforming the administration system (provincial government reform of 1775). The constitutional projects developed by representatives of the ruling circle ignore socio-economic basis of reforms. They focus on the areas linked to the restriction of power – of autocracy – by general legislative settings, i.e. by laws, which may not be revoked by the ruling sovereign. These fundamental, not-subject-to-revision laws were drafted by prominent figures of Catherine II's era as a programme for future reigns. Of these, most of the complete projects (yet unrealized) were developed by count Petr I. Panin. His first project appeared in the beginning of Catherine II's reign. In his project, Panin suggested improvements to the procedures of decision preparation and making by establishing an Administrative Council attached to the monarch, and expanding the advisory functions of Senate. Catherine did not realize the advanced project as a limitation of her powers. Later, Panin and people around him (including Fonvizin, a noted literary man) developed a detailed project – a kind of a programme of legislative reforms for Catherine's successor, the future emperor Paul I. Paul tried to realize some of the provisions of this legislative project during the years of his reign. One of these was the introduction of legislative control of the position of the tsar family and the procedure of throne succession.

In comparing legislative projects of Nikita I. Panin, developed in the beginning of Catherine's reign,[11] and his projects of the 1780s,[12] one may note that the reformer's thoughts evolved towards a bigger expansion of legal framework of the state. The issue of a network of institutions, which could regulate the power functions of the monarch, figuring prominently in the 1762 project, is no longer of interest to the author. As for Catherine II, she turned to reforming government institutions quite persistently throughout her reign.

A review of 1762 papers makes it possible to trace continuity of the concept of oligarchic limitation of monarchy, manifest most explicitly in the idea of Imperial Council. On the one hand, this supreme institution can be viewed as yet another attempt at strengthening oligarchic principles within monarch administration, formerly represented by a number of more or less similar high institutions. On the other hand, one may treat it as an important link between the purely oligarchic attempts at monarchy limitation and subsequent consolidation of administrative and legal principles of power (expressed in legal-advisory and expert-supervisory role of the Council of State). In any case, the very status of the designed institution – Emperor Council – and its structure make it possible to state that its introduction would be an important step towards bureaucratization of autocracy and diminishing the personal role of monarch in making crucial decisions. This is, apparently, the main reason that the project was never realized, though it was first approved by the empress (1762). Some time later, the above idea was embodied in the Council under royal court, established on 17 January 1769.

In this epoch, the constitutional issue appeared to be the protection of human rights, separation of powers and limitation of autocracy as opposed to a synonym of a structure of government in general (as it previously was in eighteenth-century Russia). In the wake of French revolution, especially in restoration environments, constitutionalism becomes a generally accepted form of legitimation of any power, including a monarchical one. However, this creates a basis for discussion on the issue as to what should be considered constitutionalism, and what meaning should be attached to the notion of "constitution". Firmly established now is a thesis that it is precisely that time that constitutionalism is subdivided into two strands: governmental and revolutionary. Serving as a criterion of constitutionalism division into the two types is the nature and scale of constitutional guarantees, as well as ways of meeting them. In the former case (governmental constitutionalism) the outcome is a constitution, essentially limited, octroyed and bestowed by a monarch, which in practice hardly differs from the rationalized and systematized administrative system of monarchical state operating on the basis of fixed laws. In this sense, governmental constitutionalism of both the current and the future times is a form of sham constitutionalism, making use of the respective principles for legitimation of traditional monarchical (autocratic) regime. The second type of constitutionalism – revolutionary – was to a greater extent consistent with its current interpretation, and could be realized only along the lines of bourgeois development of society. And it is the bottom-up pressure on the government that served as the means of its accomplishment, either by way of revolution or a wide public movement. In theory of constitutional law, these two types of constitution were quite distinctive, depending on the principle behind its emergence, i.e. traditional monarchical (octroyed constitution) or that of popular sovereignty (contractual constitution). Accordingly, the West European sources thereof were also different. The first type combines all monarchical constitutions generally based on the restoration French Constitutional Charter of 1814. The second, constitutions of the main bourgeois revolutions in Europe and America in the eighteenth to nineteenth centuries. In Russia, both types are represented quite clearly in a series of projects of governmental constitutionalism, from Speransky to Witte and Stolypin, on the one hand, and in a series of radical revolutionary projects, from Decembrists to Constituent Assembly, on the other.

Acting as connecting links between the projects of enlightened absolutism and Speransky transformations are projects developed in-between the seventeenth and early nineteenth centuries. Under new socio-political circumstances, the authors were also guided by the experience of the French Revolution, referring to its attempt at solving social problems as a search for "pseudo-equality".[13]

Chancellor Alexander A. Bezborodko turns to the idea of Governing Senate, advanced in the preceding projects, as "Russia's supreme government". Considerable attention in his project, addressed to emperor Paul I, is given to the issue of legal control in the state. It was suggested one must establish a special post of Chancellor of Justice, who would perform this function. First mention is made of the term "person and citizen" in the sense of individual, whose life and rights are protected by law (which, undoubtedly, is a component of the concept of civil society). Underlying it is Montesquieu's idea on the difference between despotism and monarchy, restricted by fundamental laws. He recognizes reasonability of autocracy (necessary due to spatial length and multi-ethnic nature of the state), yet he suggests a rational organization considerably limiting personal arbitrariness. To this end, it was suggested to undertake legislative regulation of the position of all classes, ordering of administrative and judicial systems, introduction of a consultative bureaucratic institute under the monarch for drafting better laws.

The beginning of Alexander I's reign was marked by intensive discussions on constitutional issues. Prior to coming to the throne, the future tsar had discussed with a group of "young friends", under the influence of enlightenment ideas and their interpretation by La Harpe, the principles of reasonable state structure – a concept of enlightened monarchy limited by fundamental laws. Upon assuming power, he set his mind on practical implementation of this concept. In institutional terms, this was embodied in the Secret Committee set up in 1801 (made up of Stroganov, Novosiltsev and Chartoryisky) – an actual headquarters of future reforms. The materials resulting from the discussion of this problem – coronation projects authored by Alexander R. Vorontsov, Victor P. Kochubei and Nikolay N. Novosiltsev – were most fully embodied in a key ideological document entitled "Charter to the Russian People" (12 August 1801).[14] Apart from this, two more documents – a manifesto on peasant issues and a Senate transformation project – were drafted for the time of coronation.

A solemn coronation of the new emperor was scheduled for September of the same year. Huge work had been done during these few months, which ended up with the development of the project "Charter to the Russian People". The respective document was drafted by members of the Secret Committee, with considerable contributions made by Victor P. Kochubei, Nikolay N. Novosiltsev and Platon A. Zubov, young pushing politicians keen on enlightenment ideas. An important role in drafting this paper was played by Alexander R. Vorontsov.

The great expectations linked with the document, which members of the Secret Committee treated as a kind of constitution, failed to be realized. Contrary to expectations and constitutional intentions, the charter was not proclaimed in the course of Alexander I's coronation, which took place on 15 September 1801. The fate of these projects was traditional too: having raised certain hopes of their liberal proponents they, following protracted wavering and doubts, were rejected by royal power again. A new address of governmental circles to state structure reforms is linked with the name of Mikhail M. Speransky, an outstanding statesman of Russia. Unlike representatives of higher aristocracy and bureaucratic elite of the preceding time, Speransky was raznochinets by origin, virtually an intellectual in the modern sense of the term.

In Speransky's project,[15] the idea of fundamental laws, making up the base and structure of a political system, is developed in detail and in a perfect legal manner. One may observe this project continuity with the preceding monuments of Russian constitutionalism. There are, however, new liberal ideas in it too. The point is not only of public laws, determining personal attitude to the state, but also of civil laws, determining relationships of private persons between themselves. Further developed was an idea of legal regulation of not only privileged but also of dependent strata of society ("rights of working people" interpreted along with rights of the middle class and gentry). While denying the "working people" political rights, the project author confers "general civil rights" to this class. As he refers to the "working people" not only artisans, workmen and house servants but also landed peasants, then just imagine the potential scale of social reforms. Considerable attention in the project was given to the political system policies. Quite interesting is the idea of separation of legislative, executive and judicial powers, though the author fails to carry it through to its logical conclusion: the separation of powers within the frameworks of constitutional monarchy. The suggestion first involved a gradual introduction of individual transformation phases, such as the setting up of the Council of State, of State Duma, transformation of Senate and of legal procedure.

This project was not realized. Only the Council of State was set up, and then the reform deadlocked. In 1812, Speransky was exiled. Upon coming back to Petersburg, Speransky became member of the Council of State and focused on codification of Russia's legislation.

Yet another attempt at reform was made during the reign of Alexander I. Long discussions on constitutional issues produced two monuments: Constitution of Polish Kingdom of 1815 and "Constitutional Charter of Russian empire" of 1820. Both monuments have clearly expressed the gist of Russian governmental constitutionalism of the age of Vienna Congress and subsequent regulation in Europe, and were largely connected with the monarchy's vision of European countries. Hence, the Seym and constitutional system were preserved in Finland after its annexation in 1809. The enactment of constitution in the Polish Kingdom was at the same time a test on the way to constitution in Russia. This is precisely what Alexander I said in his speech at the opening of Polish Seym in 1818.

The ideas of governmental constitutionalism found their more logical expression in a document such as the Constitutional Charter of Russian empire. Its compilation is linked to Alexander I's enthusiasm for liberal plans going back to 1818.

The Constitutional Charter of 1820, drafted by Novosiltsev under continuous control of the emperor, is an apex of all attempts at governmental constitutionalism of the first quarter of the nineteenth century and, in a sense, of all attempts at such political reforms prior to the twentieth century in general.[16]

Speransky's project of 1809 and, to an extent, the Charter of 1820 are the most complete products of official political thought. These monuments are quite a definite type of legalization of society/state relationships, known as "octroyed" constitutionalism. Russian liberals, in drafting their own constitution of constitutional monarchy at later times, prior to and during the revolution of 1905, used them as a starting point for their reflections. The influence of these projects (primarily that of Speransky) also tells on the development of fundamental laws of the Russian empire at the time of the Duma monarchy. It is no accident that the key projects of Speransky were published as a separate book in the years of the first Russian revolution.

The concept of a gradual development of power/society interaction mechanism was not realized in the first quarter of the nineteenth century. The autocracy political practices came into a sharp conflict with the proclaimed legal principles, which were quite appealing to liberal noble intellectuals. The aggravation of social conflict (largely due to the outstanding main issue of serfdom) found its expression in the Decembrist movement: an open military revolt of noble revolutionaries in December 1925. The most radical group of noble political figures came to the conclusion that gradual transformation of the existing system was impossible. They were inclined to see a way out in power replacement, in political coup d'etat, which would bring to power new politicians capable of top-down reforms. One of the plan options is more radical as it suggested the establishment of republican order; the other associated reforms with constitutional monarchy. It is common knowledge that the new emperor Nicholas I put down the Decembrist revolt in December 1825. The Decembrist policy documents reflect the revolutionary concept of changing the political system in this country. Underlying them is renunciation of attempts at peaceful reformatory interaction with the regime, the idea of overthrowing the autocracy and introducing a new form of government. These documents have been developed for a number of years, and they are quite detailed. The key policy document of the Southern Society – "Russian Truth" – was written by Pavel I. Pestel, the ideological leader of the Society. The key provisions of the Russian Truth were discussed at the Kiev meeting of the Southern Society leadership in 1822, where a decision was made to give one year to the organization members for reflection of the constitution concept. In 1823, at the next gathering of the Society leadership in Kiev, Pestel made a presentation of the document, which was approved as a policy document by voting. Other leaders of the Southern Society, in particular Sergey I. Muraviov-Apostol, also contributed to the preparation of the final text. The Southern Society proposals were debated by the Decembrist movement as a whole, and it was suggested to hold further discussion of Southern and Northern Societies' projects for drafting a uniform text of the constitution. This suggestion never materialized for Decembrists had to act at the time of interregnum following the sudden death of Alexander I (on 14 December 1825 in Petersburg and Chernigov regiment in Ukraine in late December/early January 1826). Russian Truth (named so in 1824) was designed as a mandate to an interim revolutionary government of Russia. Its core ideas were as follows: the establishment of the republican form of government in the country, abolition of serfdom, class system, and equal protection of the law.[17]

The main ideological paper of the Decembrists' Northern Society was written by Nikita M. Muraviov, one of the founding fathers of the Union of Salvation and Union of Welfare, member of the Supreme Duma and governor of the Northern Society. He worked on the text of the Constitution during 1821–1825. In contrast to Russian Truth, Muraviov's Constitution designed constitutional monarchy as a political system in Russia. The lawmaker paid special attention to the problem of federative government. The Constitution proclaimed citizens' equal protection of the law, freedom of speech, of press and religious freedom, serfdom was to be abolished, but landowners' land rights were declared inviolable. Public participation in representative institutions was limited by a high property qualification.

The Decembrist constitutional projects constitute a combination of teachings of the Age of Enlightenment, the then advanced ideas of western political thought and their reflections on the constitutional practices and the developments of constitutional movements in Western Europe and America. The comparison of the two major programmes of Decembrist movement, those of Pestel and Muraviov, acts as a core problem of the study into Decembrist ideology and, from a wider perspective, of the nature of social conflict of society and state in Russia. The researchers note a contradiction between the authoritative doctrines of Pestel political concept and the liberal reforms he had planned. Interpretation of the programmes of Decembrist movement from a wider comparative perspective indicates that the point is not of the contradiction solely in the concept of Decembrist movement, but of a deeper objective social conflict, which is quite distinct in recent times: this is a question of the way of transition from authoritarianism to democracy, given the modernization of traditional agrarian society.

In Russia's history, constitutional projects of the first quarter of the eighteenth century evidence an undoubted continuity relative to the projects of bigwigs and enlightened absolutism with their ideas of limiting royal power by fundamental laws, which it may not violate. In this sense, Alexander I just continued the business started by Catherine II involving convocation of the Code Commission in 1767. Accordingly, the difference between constitutional projects of the early nineteenth century and the preceding ones comes down not so much to principles and goals as to methods of implementation. A trend towards a wider social base of public control, rationalization and bureaucratization of monarchical administration, in lieu of class representation under a monarch, evolves and gets increasingly stronger in the late eighteenth century. This necessitates establishment of an advisory body under a monarch. In effect, all reviewed projects do not go beyond this idea. Implementation of Speransky's projects and ideas of Constitutional Charter would result, at best, in the development of a more rationalized bureaucracy, reduction of personal power of a monarch and, probably, restriction of arbitrariness, but not in creation of constitutional monarchy like the one in Great Britain, France and even Germany, which Russian autocracy most resembled.

The Muraviov constitution[18] and views of members of the Northern Society in general developed under the influence of constitutional ideas of the USA, England, German states and, in part, of revolutionary France. As Nikolay M. Druzhinin showed in a special exploration of this problem,

Nikita Muraviov was familiar with the contents of major European constitutions, which were expressly collected and studied in the course of drafting his own constitutional project. These include a three-volume Leipzig compiled constitutional laws, the Paris edition of 1791 Constitution, Madrid and Leipzig editions of Spanish Constitution of 1812, the Russian–French text of Constitutional Charter of Polish Kingdom with Muraviov autographic notes, a two-volume overview of French Constitutions, authored by Lanjuinais Jean-Denis, a manual of constitutional law of the USA authored by Jefferson and Adams and manuals on state law of Switzerland and France of the Age of Restoration, on Roman law. Muraviov was familiar with the constitutions of all 23 North American states. A predominant influence of the US Constitution on the Muraviov project was manifest in its generally democratic nature, federative structure of the state, structure of legislative and executive entities. The concept of constitutional monarchy, as the most acceptable form of government, also resembles the American institute of strong presidential power. In the constitution, social issue is solved from qualification democracy perspective: while abolishing serfdom and class differences, it left virtually landless peasants fully dependent upon landlords, and the qualification system of election to supreme power bodies also left them politically dominated. The moderate character of the constitution is identified upon its comparison with other monuments of West European constitutionalism. In drafting this project use was made, apart from American constitution, of the experience of constitutionalism in other European nations, in particular France (1791 constitution), from which the idea of limited monarchy in England, whose "unwritten constitution" was traditionally appealing to the liberal intellectuals in Russia, was borrowed. Also illustrative is how Muraviov interprets American experience proper: he formulated the key provisions of his programme (federalism, theory of separation of powers, representation) largely guided by the constitution of the state of Massachusetts – most similar to the European, primarily English constitutional tradition. Accordingly, a considerable influence on the Northern Society programme was exerted by the political ideas of European Enlightenment represented by authors such as Montesquieu and Constant de Rebecque, who had thoroughly substantiated the political doctrine of liberalism (human rights, representative government, separation of powers). Key to the entire tradition was conservation of the principles of political liberties, prevention of power usurpation, and the major guarantee of this was seen in the system of checks and balances best realized in constitutional monarchy. Thus, perception of western experiences by Muraviov and his associates was quite purposeful. Sometimes they made a quite original interpretation of the terms of western constitutionalism. Thus Muraviov had somewhat modified the concept of federation, treating it as a certain balance to centralized monarchy or centralized-Jacobinic republic (which figured in the Pestel dictatorial project). For this purpose he, in reviewing the American system of states, tried to find an intermediate form between a federation of autonomous states (in fact, confederation) and a system of autonomous provinces. Finally, the suggested transfer of capital to Nizhny Novgorod and the deliberate use of terminology of traditional Russian representative institutions served to deck the project out in national form. The social technology of introducing this constitution is clearly described in the "Manifesto", written by Sergey P. Trubetskoy on its basis, carrying the plan of power seizure and its consolidation. The major steps involve elimination of the current system, establishment of an interim government, which would then conduct radical social and political reforms: abolition of serfdom, introduction of democratic liberties (civil court procedure, freedom of press, elimination of military settlements).

Pestel's "Russian Truth" set off a quite distinctive concept of unitary state against the principle of federative state. Like Napoleon France, it would exercise uniform – purely geometric – principles of administrative division. It is worth noting that Pestel, unlike Muraviov, had given much more attention to national issue. The latter, when dealing with federative structure of the state, in no way linked this structure with the multinational nature of the nation. Pestel, on the contrary, took this factor into consideration, yet he tried to overcome it by integrating all non-Russian peoples in the uniform Russian culture, proceeded from the necessity of cultural assimilation and Russification policy and planned expulsion of Jews from this country. The political structure of the state had nothing in common with the principles of liberalism either. It is republic that was set off against limited monarchy as a form of government. Worth noting is the exercise of power in this political regime, notable for pronounced authoritative features. Finally, Pestel saw quite different ways of building the new society. He was for revolutionary dictatorship rather than constituent assembly, mentioned in Muraviov constitution, for regicide and not for peaceful agitation.

All of the above allows one to agree with those researchers who, in comparing the two projects – those of Muraviov and Pestel – see in them the origination of two drastically different trends in the Russian liberation movement, liberal and revolutionary, which increasingly diverged as sociopolitical crisis aggravated. Accordingly, the significance of these projects for the fate of Russian constitutionalism is different. The first one provides a basis for a genuine solution of constitutional issue, while the second leads to an impasse of quasi-constitutional authoritarian regime.

The beginning of transition from traditional society to civil society

At the time of transition from traditional society to civil society, the very existence of constitutional ideas and even projects acts as an indicator of the new state of mass consciousness. A real step was made, however, with a legislative reform from above. This step was indeed necessary, for it opened up the way to subject conversion into citizens. The concepts of civil society and law-based state have become since then a real political requirement of liberalism. Civil society is the model of social organization realizing the basic rights and the respective obligations of citizens to the state acting as a guarantor of these rights. Civil society involves three dimensions: legal (equality under law), political (universal suffrage) and socio-economic (e.g. right to healthcare). This approach was further developed and adjusted in the recent studies into the problem. First, by proceeding from the European model of movement towards civil society, classical theory ignores the specifics of movement towards it in other regions, where the development of civil rights may have (and has) specific features linked to traditions of these societies; second, the dominant model of western democracy (with the established correlation between rights and obligations) does not encompass the extremely unique and contradictory dynamics of a contemporary world, where meeting some (e.g. economic) parameters of civil society is frequently accompanied by weakening or suppression of other parameters (legal and political); third, account should be taken of the ambiguous status of various social categories (e.g. women, foreigners, ethnic minorities). A contemporary approach to civil society involves parameters such as ethnic and national make up of society, its class, sex and age division, problems of self-identification of various social minorities and implementation of rights thereof and, finally, politicization of these rights within the boundaries of national states and in a global perspective.

Law-based state is a state which, pursuant to its constitution, is obliged to exercise the law approved by way of popular will or popular representation, not to violate this law in its own activities, and be subject to control by an independent court (along the lines of theory of separation of powers). The concept of law-based state proceeds from an ancient idea stipulating that it is laws rather than people that must dominate; from medieval ideas of meeting laws as the main mission of the state and, finally, a holistic theory of state and law developed by European (specifically German) liberalism of modern times. The concept of law-based state was advanced by theoreticians of liberalism as distinct from the dominant concept of absolutism or police state – of administrative and police control and regulation of business and the social life of subjects, limitation of rights and liberties in the interests of centralized and class hierarchical absolutist power.

It is precisely because of this that the concepts of civil society and law-based state were most pronounced and became a strategy of social transformations not so much in countries with developed traditions of social equality and political democracy as in the nations where liberalism had to fight the preserved class orders and strong absolutist power, such as in

Germany and Russia. The principles of civil society and law-based state, which were most holistically formulated in the philosophy of law and in the writings of German lawyers of the nineteenth century, were further developed by Russian proponents of liberal political and legal thought, which turned into a theoretical foundation and the policy provisions of constitutionalism. The historical typology of forms of law-based state distinguishes a liberal law-based state (proclaiming supremacy of law, principle of separation of powers, and individual liberties); democratic law-based state (adding to this concept a wide-ranging right to political involvement) and social law-based state (including principles of social guarantees and implementation thereof).

It became possible to turn to these modernization models in the 1860s, when they found support amid the wider strata of the educated segments of society, who had recognized the urgent necessity of reforms. By proclaiming a radical social transformation the goal of great reforms, the power promoted the involvement of a fragment of society in the reform process whose distant yet desirable goal was creation of civil society and constitutional government. It is the alliance of educated bureaucracy and liberal intellectuals that was the motive force of the reform.

It is the perception of the concept of civil society and law-based state that was of special significance for the development of political culture in Russia. This concept, borrowed from German law philosophy, served as a basis for liberal political reforms of the second half of the nineteenth century. According to this doctrine, society and state enjoy an equal status, and the relationships between them are regulated by law. This logic finds the highest expression in the constitutional limitation of power, wherein bureaucracy serves society rather than the monarch. This was behind the evolvement and development, in the course of big reforms, of the so-called liberal bureaucracy recognizing its duty of serving society. It is precisely this type of liberal bureaucracy that turns into a key driving force of reforms in Russia.

The objective relationship of peasant issues and political modernization tasks came to be specifically pronounced prior to and in the course of the peasant reform of 1861. Both the conservatives and liberals observed this relationship, deeming it necessary to take it into account during the reforms. Evidences of this can be found in theoretical writings of Konstantin D. Kavelin and Boris N. Chicherin, in Alexander I. Hertzen's essays, notes of prominent figures of liberal bureaucracy (e.g. Alexey I. Levshin, Nikolay A. Milyutin), writings and political speeches of leaders of public movements (e.g. Alexey M. Unkovsky, Alexander I. Koshelev, Nikolay P. Semionov-Tyan-Shansky). Tsar Alexander II was aware of it, too, especially in the closing years of his life. With regard to the aforesaid, the key objective was to develop priorities of government policy, determine the sequence of steps towards solution of social issue, and later of political reform too.

The unfolding public discussion of the peasant issue would inevitably pass over to the problems of the political system. The reform required a stronger feedback between society and state. This task was handled by non-traditional institutions – Main Committee on peasant matters and Regional Committees (1858) which served as central units of reform preparation and implementation. As early as this phase, the conservative elite fretted that the regional committees may become a kind of regional states, turning later into government states. The grounds for such fears did exist for the regional committees, in particular the most liberal of them (like Tver-based) turned into the forums for debating issues of political structure. The struggle for ways of handling the peasant issue, giving rise to a great deal of appeals on the part of regional committees and individual members thereof to central authorities, could not be resolved locally. But the main thing was that the reform preparation proceeded on a scientific basis. There was a specially developed model of a gradual liberation of serfs along with preservation of traditional forms of ownership: allotment of land to peasants along with retaining a long transitional period and traditional communal institutions. Valuable information within this context is provided primarily by the major projects of peasant liberation, which had a real impact on the progress and outcomes of the reform. These are the projects of liberal proponents of the reform (in the first place, Kavelin's project and its implementation in the course of peasant reform), gentry committee projects, the case of their consideration by editorial boards. The review of this model helps follow the progress of the entire peasant reform: from its design to implementation. Kavelin's project[19] is not only of considerable interest for a researcher, but can be treated as a scientific forecast which came true. Social sciences in general face a scarcity of successful scientific forecasts, as they are extremely rare in history. When conceiving transformations, reformers usually have only a general and rather vague picture of the future social structure, which undergoes multiple transformations and adjustments in the course of reforms proper. Hence, there are continuous discussions in historiography about the correlation between spontaneous and planned character of some or other reforms (e.g. Peter's). There is usually a negative rather than positive motivation of reforms, which leads to a mechanical negation of the existing institutions and relations (recognized as ineffective, by definition). With this in mind, the general direction of reforms is set not by a positive scientific forecast but sooner by a retrospective criticism of the preceding system. It is precisely this reform model (as was demonstrated by their implementation at contemporary stage) that leads to spontaneity and absence of rational control of their progress.

Kavelin's project, on the contrary, falls into a rare category of forecasts realized with a high degree of accuracy. A simple comparison of its provisions with laws governing the peasant reform and its implementation procedures renders it quite apparent. The point is of similarity in both the fundamental principles and technological parameters: the reform contents as a trade-off of two classes; determination of scale of this trade-off; a clear legal registration of mutual concessions; procedure of reform implementation over time (introduction of "provisionally obligated peasants" institution); computation of economic and financial feasibility of implementation (determination of quantity and quality of allotted land; procedure of buy-out operation); lastly, assignment of institutions in charge of reform and even the procedure of their selection. Kavelin made a precise forecast of the situation of different social strata relative to reform, and even their potential response to it, from different groups of peasants, the gentry and urban population to officialdom and court circles. This made it possible (back on the eve of peasant reform) to outline a whole number of other specific transformations, which came true at the next phase. Of course, it would be right to assume that the effectiveness of Kavelin's forecast was due to knowledge of the analogous reforms in Central and Eastern Europe, as well as in the Russian empire in the past. But this assumption is only a partial explanation, for the accepted concept of peasant reform in Russia differed markedly from them. The fact is that Kavelin stated the provisions of the reform, proclaimed by Alexander II on 19 February 1861, back in 1855.

The only acceptable explanation of this phenomenon is Kavelin's deep scientific insight into the reform problem based on extraordinary erudition, practical experience and, probably, political intuition. Indeed, Kavelin's concept was a real alternative to agrarian revolution. This becomes clear from the comparison of his recommendations with those exercised in the countries, which managed to prevent agrarian revolution or, in any case, minimize its destructive implications (the Meiji Revolution, agrarian reforms in India, reforms in Eastern Europe). For him, social revolution was a consequence of the appropriately unresolved agrarian issue. The destruction of stable social relations in agrarian society (as a result of peasant alienation from land and the emergence of masses of destitute population) led to erosion of social foundation of the power, emergence of destructive elements turning into a tool of revolution, overthrow of autocracy and the establishment of Bonapartist regimes. The Kavelin conclusion on impossibility of social revolution in Russia, which now seems erroneous, should be correlated with the conditions, which he operated with in justifying his conclusion, i.e. preservation of peasantry as a social foundation of power, continuation of agrarian reforms by the state, development of new political consciousness of the ruling class.

That was also the time of the development of a holistic philosophical and sociological concept of Russian historical process, the so-called state or legal school founded by Boris N. Chicherin, Konstantin D. Kavelin and Alexander D. Gradovsky. Its contribution involved settling the problem of the relationship between the state and society, development of theoretical principles of Russian constitutionalism.[20] Kavelin's views are of interest as he was directly involved with the ideological struggle at the time of reform and its implementation. This was reflected in his scientific papers, and can be recreated in more detail from his correspondence with like-minded people.[21]

Kavelin's project was an integral programme of preventing agrarian revolution in Russia. Therefore, he actualized the components of social reality, whose projection into the future permitted the achievement of such a result. This is, primarily, a thesis of objective unacceptability of the western model of handling the agrarian issue, which resulted in revolutionary crisis, and its negative manifestations boiled down to capitalism (a new class conflict), constitutionalism (as pseudo-legal guarantees given the establishment of Bonapartist type of dictatorships), and socialism as an extreme form of social demagogy with its "uncontrollable theories of equality". Acting as an antithesis is an assertion of unique national foundations of Russian historical process, whose evolution "does not resemble any other history". Finally, the synthesis is represented by a concept of a special third way of permitting implementation of the social ideal of law-based state by persistently applying the technology of traditional society modernization. In so doing, a special guiding role is assigned to constructive forces: monarchical state, rationalized bureaucracy and gentry, acting as a "conservative aristocratic basis" necessary under reform circumstances.

The successive replacement of reform and counter-reform ideas, public and government initiatives, characteristic of the Russian historical process in modern times, is of considerable interest as a real experience of development of state undergoing transformation of traditional foundations into civil society with legally regulated rights. Of special interest, from the cognitive standpoint, is Russian experience of radical reform opening up the way to civil society: this is an experience of the great reform of 1861 involving the abolition of serfdom. The history of modern times is unaware of any other such radical reform of the very foundations of social system, which was implemented in a legal manner, avoiding revolutionary outburst. It would be logical to compare this experience with the other great event, chronologically roughly coinciding with the great reform in Russia in the 1860s. This is the abolition of slavery in the USA. There, they did not manage to prevent the civil war (1861–1865). Researchers raise a question as to why the USA failed to avoid a protracted war, drawing in wide layers of the population, while Russia, where serfdom was a long entrenched core of social system, managed to do this. The Code of 1649, finally inscribing serfdom in law, effectively continued into the nineteenth century (its edition opens up the "Full Body of Laws of Russian Empire" compiled in the 1830s).

The great reforms were, no doubt, promoted also by the components, key to the reform success in general, such as a deep theoretical, legal, hence, technologically rational concept of reform, developed by liberals.

That time witnessed coordinated actions, ideological consensus of the educated segment of society as well as of educated, rationally oriented bureaucracy, having the central administrative resource at its disposal and implementing the political will of the legitimate bearer of supreme power – the monarch.

The peasant reform has drastically altered the situation of the two major classes: peasants and gentry. Subject to reform came land ownership relations, which had developed historically and served as a foundation of the mode of production in that society. The point was to transform, within an historically short span of time, the position and lifestyle of scores of millions of people. And the regions, known for widespread predominantly serfage relations, were part of the general system of the huge territory of empire with a huge diversity of geographical, ethnic and cultural specifics. This radical transformation gave a powerful boost to future democratization. Building of civil society started with provision to former serfs of personal liberty and land (settling on land and allotment per registered head) for which a big purchasing price had to be paid. To purchase the field plots, peasants were granted government instalment loans for 49.5 years. The purchase prices were repeatedly reduced, and were finally abandoned by 1907. Subsequent years also witnessed a judicial reform, establishment of local self-government institutions (Zemstvo reform), military and education reforms, and liberal law on press. The formation of new democratic institutions opened up the way to the development of market relations, entrepreneurship, which in its turn placed demand on initiative and free choice, the search for new business forms, which came into deep conflict with the social psychology of the traditional communal system. The reforms in the 1860s gave rise to a situation, which can be defined as the interaction of bureaucracy and various privileged groups with a view to jointly developing mechanisms of restructuring social relations for conducting transformations and preventing a revolution. This alliance was possible only at the most dynamic phase of transformations, and was undermined by the more powerful conservative forces.

The most important monument of governmental constitutionalism in the 1860s to 1880s was Petr A. Valuev's project of reorganization of the Council of State, which no doubt took account of the preceding experience of involving the public with the activities of editorial commissions, and of the requests of representatives of gentry. In early 1863, known for the preparation of zemstvo reform, Polish revolt, more intensive political activities of the gentry and radical opposition, Alexander II requested Valuev draft a note on the possibility of representative element involvement with lawmaking. The effort resulted in "A note of Secretary of State Valuev" describing the concept of arranging popular representation in an autocratic state.[22] The key thesis of the note – a possibility of instituting a representative principle given conservation of autocracy – determined the volume of reform deemed admissible by liberal bureaucracy. From the very beginning, it was suggested they replicate the German (Prussian) model of monarchical constitutionalism, proceeding from stability of monarchical principle as a guarantee of stable political course of the autocratic state towards a persistent institution of rational norms of legal regulation with no changes in the essence of the political system. The principal idea of this policy is a combination of western constitutional forms and of Russian monarchical contents. The major component of innovations boils down, therefore, to the possibility of local representation with a view to performing advisory functions, and the purpose thereof is to ease social tension at the expense of partial concessions to liberal opposition. The starting point of Valuev's reflections is an idea, entrenched in the educated segment of Russian society, that the availability of class representation is an integral feature of a civilized European state. The political modernization of Russia must, therefore, inevitably proceed the same way.

The gist of the suggestion is a reform of the Council of State, involving its conversion from a purely administrative institution to an administrative and advisory one.[23] The point was to invite a certain number of representatives of gentry and townspeople, and several members of high Orthodox clergy to this body for "deliberative participation in the discussion of issues under its jurisdiction". This political formula leaves no doubt about the note author's desire to avoid the very possibility of drawing any analogies between the designed administrative and advisory institution and western parliamentary type of institutions.

Accordingly, the structure of the designed class representative institution gives rise to associations largely with traditionalist feudal institutions like Zemstvo council, General States, Landtags, Cortes, Seym of the period of class-representative monarchy, rather than with representative institutions of the people of modern times. In a sense, this is also a continuation of the case of Code Commissions of the eighteenth century, legislative commissions of the first half of the nineteenth century and editorial commissions of the period of peasant reform in the 1860s. Of key importance in this respect is the issue of balance between zemstvo-class and central administration principles, bearing upon the outcome of the planned transformation of the autocratic political system. The Valuev project handles this problem by instituting a kind of two-chamber representative body, where the role of the upper chamber is conditionally played by the Council of State, and the lower one by the Congress of state councillors. The above construction was justified in detail and legalized in a special document authored by Valuev. This was "A draft new institution of the Council of State".

The great reforms set off a gradual movement towards civil society and law-based state. The next step would have involved the establishment of representative institutions. Valuev's project simply outlined but did not solve the problem. Yet, the necessity of changing the political system along the line was apparent for the most radical representatives of ruling circles. The attempts at moving towards constitutional monarchy merit a careful study. The educated segments of Russian society shared the ideas of and desire for convening a national representative institution, but they were rather hazy and did not materialize in specific political projects. These sentiments can in part be traced in personal files of prominent figures of this era.[24] The link between social reforms and reforms of political system is observed throughout the history of Russian constitutionalism. By the 1880s, the government circles were preparing to give a new boost to the reform process. This political course was embodied in the programme of Mikhail T. Loris-Melikov, whom Alexander II delegated wide powers with respect to both fighting the oppositional movement in the country and preparing a political reform.[25] The monarch supported the idea of setting up a legislative advisory institution, whose membership would be in part appointed, and in part elected. Even this careful step towards political reform was treated as rather resolute. The tsar himself, upon signing off and giving the go-ahead to the project, did not hide the association with the assembly of notables from his court circles (which served as, as is well known, a prologue to French revolution).

As for western sources of these documents, it would be reasonable to point to the entire tradition of monarchic constitutionalism, especially its German version. Literature frequently underestimates factors such as the high degree of recognition of constitutional guarantee problems in monarchic states by the heads themselves, the emergence of monarchic solidarity. An important document in this respect is a special message of German emperor to Russian tsar Alexander II, summing up similar transformations in Bismarck Germany, and practical recommendations on how not to forgo the main thing in the course of reforms, namely, monarchic principle.

"Constitution of Mikhail T. Loris-Melikov", as it was figuratively referred to by Maxim M. Kovalevsky, is among the major monuments of governmental constitutionalism in the closing years of Alexander II's reign. The point of the documents is, initiated by the tsar and institutes a limited public representation with a view to expanding monarchy/society feedback. In literature, this attempt is evaluated quite ambiguously. Some researchers treat it as a careful but quite deliberate step towards constitutional monarchy, while others believe that it was yet another autocracy manoeuvre in conditions of sharp political crisis, objectively directed against genuine constitutionalism. The former opinion, represented by Kovalevsky, was stated in liberal pre-revolutionary papers, striving thereby to legalize the idea of constitutional reform and demonstrate that it had long been discussed in government circles. According to this standpoint, the failure of reform objectively marked victory of conservative bureaucracy over the liberal one, continued pursuance of the authoritarian course, which resulted in a final separation of autocracy from society, and brought about revolution. According to the other, articulated largely by soviet authors, that attempt was a forced trade-off on the part of autocracy under revolutionary circumstances, which, due to its limited nature, was doomed to failure from the very beginning. There is, however, a potential third approach to the problem considering it from a different perspective, notably, performance by the state of administrative functions in a society undergoing modernization. From this perspective, that attempt at political reforms should be reviewed in connection with the general course of social and administrative reforms of traditional agrarian society, treated as a closing phase thereof and, at the same time, a desire to raise to a new level of their implementation. The purpose of the reform was to make the regime more efficient, create a system of more rational discussion of decisions made, control of their execution, and seek a wider social basis. This political course was embodied in the so-called Loris-Melikov's "dictatorship of heart" whose proclaimed goal was, on the one hand, stabilization of situation in this country and, on the other, a persistent continuation of reforms on that basis. The institution of components of public representation played, therefore, an auxiliary, technical role in Loris-Melikov's programme. That was the formula of modernization, which was then developed in Stolypin's policy. This approach helps provide a deeper insight into the entire logic of this policy, which was apparently the only one possible for keeping the course of reforms intact under the aggravating political crisis.

The considered project of political reforms can be perceived in the context of other attempts at governmental constitutionalism systematically evolving in the pre-reform period. All of them were part of the course of liberal reforms carried out by educated bureaucracy. Among its representatives in the considered time period there was, first, Mikhail T. Loris-Melikov himself, who was given wide powers as head of supreme administrative commission in charge of fighting political terrorism (set up in the wake of the explosion in Winter Palace in 1880) and later minister of internal affairs and emperor proxy; Dmitry A. Milyutin, war minister; Alexander A. Abaza, minister of finance; senator Kohanov, deputy minister of internal affairs; Dmitry M. Solsky, state inspector, who were closely involved in discussions. Decisive, however, was the fact that the reform idea was shared by Alexander II himself, who treated it as a sort of completion of the entire transformation cycle. As early as 1879–1880, the emperor himself initiated a discussion of the representation issue at a special conference. Serving as a basis were the earlier projects of Valuev (1863) and that of grand duke Konstantin Nikolaevich (1866). The outcomes of these discussions found a specific embodiment in the documents presented by Loris-Melikov.

The key issue of the scale and forms of the given representation was handled, however, exclusively with an eye on autocracy conservation. Being guided by the general attitude, the project author rejects both western type of parliamentarianism, and traditional Russian version of zemstvo popular representation. The former is unacceptable due to its inconsistency with national conditions. As far as Russia is concerned, the document stresses:

> No scheme of popular representation in forms borrowed from the West is acceptable: these forms are not only alien to Russian people, but could even shake all of its basic political views and give rise to confusion, whose consequences is hard to foresee.

On the contrary, the revival of ancient Russian forms such as Zemstvo Duma or Zemstvo Council were rejected because they are obsolete and inconsistent with the modified geographic boundaries of the state, ideas of the population and new conditions of development, under which "a simple recreation of ancient representation would be hardly feasible and, in any case, a dangerous case of bringing back reasonability of popular representation as such in any of its forms". These arguments, fully consistent with the ideology of autocracy, point to impossibility of treating the project as a "constitution", even in the most restricted understanding of this term.

Thus, the project implementation would not have led to constitutional restrictions of autocracy. It is important to note, however, that given social tension this attempt could become a prologue to legal discussion of constitutional issue. This, in its turn, created prerequisites for uniting and institutionalizing all the forces in opposition to autocracy. In spite of "absolute confidentiality" of the special conference activities involved with discussion of the reform project, some information about it got into press, both Russian and Western. In particular, promulgation of the constitutional act was expected to take place on 19 February. The absence of this act already by itself would turn into a significant destabilizing factor. It is, apparently, precisely this that was meant by Alexander II himself who, during meetings with ministers on Loris-Melikov's project, said:

> We are suggested nothing else than an assembly of notables of Louis XVI. Do not forget the consequences, yet, if you deem it beneficial for the nation, I shall not resist.

According to the other source, Alexander referred to the suggested convocation of zemstvo representatives as "general states". Being a staunch proponent of autocracy Alexander II recognized, however, the necessity of rationalizing its form. Hence, he played some role in drafting a series of important documents of governmental constitutionalism. It is precisely because of this that he agreed to the meeting of the council of ministers for the final discussion of Loris-Melikov's "constitution". Alexander II signed Loris-Melikov's project on 1 March 1881, and the same day he died as a result of a murderous assault by a terrorist revolutionary. The very first decisions of his son Alexander III, calling off the beginning of the political reform, marked the policy of counter-reforms in Russia. Alexander III, who was the opponent of class-representative institutions in any form, put a characteristic comment on the document, after the assassination of his father: "Thanks God, this criminal and hasty step towards constitution was not made". This train of thought was also characteristic of the main ideologist of unlimited power Konstantin P. Pobedonostsev, who initiated the well-known manifesto of Alexander III entitled "On stability of autocracy" (29 April 1881). It was soon followed by yet another key document called "Provisions on measures for maintaining national security and public peace" (14 August 1881). Issued as a temporary act (valid for three years), the Provisions were persistently renewed at the end of each three-year period, and were valid up to the February revolution of 1917, serving as an actual Russian Constitution. This act virtually introduced a state of emergency, legalizing a wide-scale application of force to political opponents of the regime (declaration of state of emergency in any locality, possibility of arrest, exile and court-martialling any citizen). The concept of autocracy stability was then repeatedly reproduced in a revised form, in the well-known note of Sergei Y. Witte on incompatibility of autocracy and zemstvo, in Petr A. Stolypin's statement on inadmissibility of parliamentarianism and the necessity of strong monarchic power in Russia. Underlying this concept was a sufficiently realistic idea of impossibility, under extreme circumstances, of weakening monarchic power, which was the only integrating factor in a multinational state, a guarantee of stability, given the rising socio-political conflicts, and a tool of reform policy. The split of the ruling elite on constitutional issues reflected the two strategies of handling the crisis: firstly, pursuing the course of modernization with public involvement and, secondly, preservation of the intact system exclusively by repressive methods. Hence, resignation of the liberal cabinet virtually immediately after the assassination on 1 March 1881 implied a turnaround of the political course involving revision of the reform policy. The conservative strategy, which led monarchy to revolution, prevailed.

The strategy of the traditional society modernization by way of gradual reforms, on the one hand, and revolutionary severance with the old regime and establishment of a new order, on the other, markedly differ in terms of tactics too. The key stance can be gauged by the attitude of proponents of some or other strategy to the problem of law. The two attitudes are diametrically opposite relative to the creation of a legal basis for future transformations. It was already noted that a bright example of professional legal preparation of this type of reform is provided by the great reform of 1861 and subsequent reforms in the 1860s. The historians of Russian constitutionalism have so far somehow bypassed yet another phase, namely, legal preparation of new law of the age of transition from absolute monarchy to constitutional system. The focus of attention for prominent lawyers came to be an issue of drafting a new Civil Code, in particular, legal regulation of property rights, primarily land ownership under the new circumstances. This intensive lawmaking activity went on for several decades and ended in the beginning of the twentieth century. The subsequent course of events rendered the new draft code unimportant. As for the transitional period analysis, however, this problem is of prime interest. The gist of the problem is that radical reforms inevitably give rise to a situation of legal dualism, with concurrently coexisting traditional ideas and new laws, inevitably giving rise to legal problems and conflicts. The development of a new legal system acts under the given (typological and inevitable) circumstances both as a kind of decisive point in the reform success, and a guarantee of their acceptance by society.

The two main draft constitutions evolved in the course of the first Russian revolution. In the very beginning of the revolution, the leading liberal organization of Russia – Liberation Union – suggested a draft constitution. This document can be treated as a programme of the entire movement. This document was the focal point of discussions at the first (1904) and especially second (April 1905) zemstvo-wide congresses. The draft Fundamental Law of the Russian empire was actually developed by two main units of the Union – Petersburg and Moscow – in late October 1904 as part of the preparation for the first (November) congress of zemstvo activists. Vladimir M. Gessen and Iosiph V. Gessen were among the authors.

State Duma was deemed a key prerequisite for the transition to law-based state, a major tool of political reforms and institution of its control over monarchic power (a responsible ministry). Some signs of the Muromtsev draft influence on the basis of the legislation at the time of the first Russian revolution can be traced in a number of provisions of the Fundamental Law, in the first place, chapter eight – "On Rights and Obligations of Russian Subjects" and chapter nine – "On Laws".

The legal dualism was manifest in the existence of two legal systems in Russia at the time of reforms: a positive law (increasingly manifesting itself in the reception of laws of western origin) and common law (mostly rules of unwritten peasant law), which was only partially reflected in the effective legislation but constituted a real base of legal awareness of the overwhelming segment of the population. The above (comparison of the two types of law) may serve as a basis for the exposure of the conflict of the old and new laws; identifying the causes and parameters of legitimacy crisis of the land ownership concept, which was inscribed in positive law (body of civil laws). In the focus of attention is an attempt of doing away with legal dualism linked with updating the national legal system, rationalization and modernization of traditional rules of Russian land law. It was embodied in the draft Civil Code of the Russian empire. Special attention was given to the problem of legal regulation of traditional forms of land ownership under the new circumstances, as well as of transitional forms of ownership, use and disposal of land. This approach helps to interpret scientific discussions in the considered period in a new way, in particular, the idea of utilization of a number of categories of Roman and western law for the expression of the complex reality of land relations in Russia under transition.

The draft Russian Civil Law[26] was a serious initiative towards the modernization of the Russian private law in general and of land law, in particular. The Draft Code came to be a natural product of Russian empire transition from an absolutist state to a civil society and law-based state, which commenced since the great reforms of the 1860s. It can, in fact, be treated as a major government initiative aimed at overcoming legal dualism in this country. The exploration of the very Draft, its western sources and discussions in legal and historical literature of that time helps forgo the one-sided perception of the causes of failure to implement that initiative. Naturally, conservatism of the gentry and ruling circles played a major role in this. As important was the time factor (the draft was prepared virtually by the beginning of the revolution).

The most fundamental reason of the impossibility of realizing the provisions of western civil law in Russia, however, was as actual preservation of traditionalist concepts of land law, proceeding from the possibility of converting virtually feudal institutions into civil society ones. Hence, the appeal to the principle of private property, which really implied, in Russian conditions, inviolability of the forms of land ownership emerging back at the time of service state and linked to preservation (if not legal then actual) of class privileges. At the same time, the Draft Code contained an idea of the tools of conflict resolution in a legal manner, i.e. by exercising a state-guided judicial and administrative reform. Being a real project of land relation transformation (by extending rules and principles of private law to all categories of land ownership, use and disposal) the Code suggested an idea of resolving the legal dualism. Its development and discussions helped to provide a deeper insight into the difficulties facing the reformers of agrarian relations, in particular, the necessity of identifying and describing real land relations, which were far from the formulas of western codes. The analogies thereof were discovered in the formula of Roman law expressing transitional forms of ownership – an unstable equilibrium, and capable of evolving in diametrically opposite directions depending on the state of the entire social system and political regime.

It is justification of the Russian strategy of creating a law-based state of modern times that was the key theoretical problem of Russian constitutionalism in the second half of the nineteenth and beginning of the twentieth centuries. Addressing the issue of revolution/reform balance as a means of accomplishing that goal came to be in the focus of scientific and political discussions. A special significance in this connection was attached to the analysis of French Revolution; a certain analogy of the situations was well perceived by the Russian liberal thinkers. Common for Russian constitutionalists, the majority of whom were philosophers, lawyers, historians, was turning to the ideas of historical law school. They attached a great importance to the development of the type of legal conscience of the people, political reality established in the course of protracted evolution.[27]

The reforms of the 1860s, by promoting interest in the study of law and institutions, gave a new boost to the development of sociological concept. The new direction is represented by scholars such as Alexander D. Gradovsky, Vasily I. Sergeevich, Vasily N. Latkin, Mikhail F. Vladimirsky-Budanov, Sergey A. Muromtsev, Nikolay M. Korkunov. The objective position of Russian constitutionalism reveals both its strengths and weaknesses. Falling to the former are a high theoretical level of political analysis, accumulating the advances of global science and practical struggle for a law-based state, development of an objective and realistic concept of a Russian state system; to the latter the lack of social mechanisms for putting theory into practice, an extreme degree of political isolation.[28] This situation, typical for states under transition, is most apparent in Russia.

3 Constitutional platform of Russian liberalism and its implementation under the transition from a monarchy to a republic

The political philosophy of Russian constitutionalism is an integral system of views on society and state at large, as applied to Russia, in particular. The philosophy can be adequately interpreted within the framework of a broader socio-political system in which it emerged and developed as an independent social institute and a sort of stabilizing factor. This allows one to better understand the nature of the Russian constitutionalism and the prospects of its development.[1] The political philosophy of Russian constitutionalism of the nineteenth and beginning of the twentieth century is viewed as a philosophical and political paradigm that interpreted in a comparative perspective the relationship between the state and society existing at that time.

Constitutional transition at the beginning of the twentieth century

The theory of Russian constitutionalism appears to be the most important independent component of the political culture of the society, a basis for its harmonic legal development and therefore a stabilizing factor. So, the philosophical meaning of the paradigm remains relevant to the modern methodology of the philosophical analysis of political process along the following lines: reasoning of the possibility to solve a fundamental social conflict not via a revolution, but rather via radical socio-economic and political reforms consistently carried out by the state; development of the model of transition from the authoritarian regime to the modern pluralistic democracy while keeping the power continuity and the government legitimacy; determining the specifics of the theoretical base, strategy and tactics of constitutionalism under accelerated political modernization.

Liberalism of this type is observed in modernizing countries; its specific features can be revealed primarily in a comparative historical perspective. Such an approach inevitably suggests highlighting the problems of the social base of liberalism and its bearers; the character of its relations with the state; the peculiarities of its platform and the tactics of political struggle. Contemporary science, specifically that focusing on the recent historical periods, has created a significant knowledge base covering these issues. Of special importance here is the German historical and legal studies traditionally paying a lot of attention to the problem of genesis of the modern civil society and the law-based state. The specificity of German liberalism as compared to classical Western European models, such as French and British, is determined by the time of its emergence (it was formed much later); greater vagueness of its social base due to the backwardness and weakness of the bourgeoisie; as a result, the peculiarities of its ideology, chiefly of its legal platform (historical legal school versus traditional natural law rationale typical of the Enlightenment Age); the view of the role of the state in the development of society (attributing primary importance to the state as opposed to proclamation of the struggle with the old absolutist regime); and accordingly, the ways of attaining goals (top-down support of the reform versus a revolutionary coup).

The main reason why liberalism, or to be more exact, liberal ideology has become widely spread in Germany and other countries of Eastern Europe currently undergoing modernization, lies in the fact that the ideology has not been affiliated with a single social layer, but rather expressed the aspiration of all the advanced elements of the society for modernization.[2] From this perspective, one can better comprehend the significance of the concepts of civil society and law-based state elaborated by German legal philosophers, for mankind. A closer look at the social bearers of liberal ideology in different countries reveals that they represent not only and not as much of the bourgeoisie, as aristocracy, intelligentsia and bureaucracy. From this arises a problem of correlation between modernization, liberalism and bureaucracy in the process of modern and recent time transformation of a traditionalist society of Eastern European countries. The debates on this issue revealed the existence of different approaches specific to each individual country of Eastern Europe, such as Germany, Austria-Hungary and Russia, and displayed the necessity of expanding the scope of the comparative method application.[3]

The beginning of the twentieth century was marked by important new trends in the development of the European society. Among prevailing tendencies was a rapid and in many respects forced transition from traditionalist society characterized by pronounced remnants of the class system to democracy based on the universal suffrage – the process closely linked to escalating differentiation of the emerging civil society along ideological and partisan lines (the era of "party democracy") – and finally, a crisis of traditional monarchical legitimacy and its replacement by the democratic power legitimacy. A surge in public political involvement, on the one hand, and inadequacy of the old forms of state structure, on the other, constituted the essence of constitutional crises in many countries in Europe. This conflict was especially acute in the empires of Eastern Europe, first of all in Russia, where the transition to political democracy collided with ill-preparedness of the traditional agrarian society and the state power for the new forms of political organization. Everywhere in the world, these revolutionary changes resulted in modification of the classical ideological theses formulated back in the nineteenth century, in order to adjust them to rapid social and political modernization. This process found expression in the shaping of two key strategies of modernization: a reform-based strategy implying preserving the continuity of legal development, and a revolutionary strategy negating such continuity. In the conditions of political competition of the two approaches, classical Western European liberalism of the epoch of parliamentary democracy of the eighteenth to nineteenth centuries underwent significant modifications on the path of transformation to neo-liberalism. A distinctive feature of neo-liberalism was its taking into account new factors of social development, primarily the necessity to address social and agrarian issues, and recognition of the role of state in the social transformation process. In Russia, until recently, the process of the genesis of neo-liberalism, first and foremost linked to the stance of Pavel N. Milyukov, has been given little special attention. The importance of the problem is determined by the good prospects of the neo-liberal concept in the conditions of modern social and political transformations. Reconstruction of the neo-liberal model of the constitutional crisis in Russia dating back to the beginning of the twentieth century is possible by comparing it to the radical social revolution theories, on the one hand, and to the views of the advocates of classical liberalism, on the other. Being in essence a modification of the classical European liberalism in the new conditions of social agrarian revolution and accelerated modernization, neo-liberalism suggested a new strategy of political changes. The radical doctrine of permanent social revolution negating the law as an instrument of social regulation was countered with the neo-liberal approach of resolving a social conflict in a legal way, while maintaining the classical principles of civil society and law-based state. Classical liberal ideas of evolutionary social development through minimal political reforms rendering conflicts impossible were countered with the thesis of constitutional revolution carried out by the state under wide public pressure.

In the Russian history of constitutionalism of more recent times, constitutional drafts created by liberalists are of special interest. Their underlying theoretical model and the specific influence the drafts had on actual political process, suggest that they are interpreted not merely as constitutional drafts, but first of all as documents adding to the better understanding of liberalism political strategy issues.

It is expedient to consider the key constitutional drafts of Russian liberalism at the beginning of the twentieth century – to explain the history of their conception, dwell on the theoretical model they are based on and assess the character of their influence on Russian political process. Comparison of this model to that underlying the Fundamental Law of

Germany will enable one to point out the trends in the statehood development the two countries have in common.

Useful information on this topic can be found in *Osvobozhdeniye* ("Liberation") magazine, edited and published in Germany by Petr B. Struve. The magazine contains information on a number of initial drafts of the key constitutional documents of Russian liberalism. The drafts reflect gradual crystallization of the constitutional principles along the development of the zemstvo movement and organization of Soyuz Osvobozhdeniya (Union of Liberation).[4] The main goal of the zemstvo movement was formulated in the manuscript of the platform article "Zemsky Sjezd i Zadachi Oppozitsii", 1904 ("Zemstvo Congress and the Objectives of the Opposition") as "creation of common formal political conditions for existence and activity of all the social groups of contemporary Russia". The platform of the movement – the "factor structuring public attitude" – includes such principles of national democratic character as universal suffrage and the peaceful struggle of all the social classes for their rights. The idea of incompatibility of the zemstvo movement with the autocracy is formulated quite clearly: "the movement is fundamentally antagonistic towards autocracy, for the latter is organically unable to incorporate legitimate activity of individuals and social groups". The activity implies "wide social movement expressing the idea of the necessity of a constitution". This concept of political change is delineated ever more clearly in the platform documents of the Union of Liberation of 1904–1905. One of them, namely the declaration adopted at the Union conference, formulates the main goal of the movement as the "political liberation of Russia" and establishment of constitutional regime in the country.[5]

There is a special group of documents in Struve's collection which make possible the reconstruction of the main stages of work on constitutional drafts by members of the Liberation movement in 1904–1905. The so-called Gellert's draft deserves special attention, for it implicitly lays out the main principles of the Russian Constitution to-be.[6] Formally, the document concerns the state structure of Austria-Hungary; however, the context of the whole document demonstrates that the author precisely implied Russia, resorting to the disguise solely for the sake of conspiracy. This initial sketch already contains all the key provisions of the future liberal constitutional drafts. The document reasons introduction of the new form of government, namely constitutional monarchy. The first chapter of the document entitled "Fundamental Laws and Constituent Assembly" defines political rights and puts special emphasis on one of them, namely universal suffrage (Section I is entitled "Political Rights," and Section II is entitled "Universal Suffrage"). Foreseeing possible differences on the issue of expedience of universal suffrage, the author sets forth special arguments in its defence. So, the author believes that given the poverty of the country, introduction of the qualification system will in fact result in voters' oligarchy. The situation is compared to that of "contemporary Russian zemstvo bodies, where the ratio between the number of voters and total population of the provinces is a completely negligible figure".

The constitutional draft touched upon an issue important to both Austria-Hungary and Russia, that of the status of the national regions of the empire (Section VI, "Remote Areas"). When writing about conferring local autonomy status on Galicia and restoration of the status quo of Czechia, the author undoubtedly had Poland and Finland in mind.

The provisions on introduction of the Fundamental Law of the state specify the procedure of elections to the National Assembly, and the rights of the latter to approve the state budget and appoint a cabinet. The analysis of the "Gellert's draft" allows one to recognize it as the first constitutional document of Russian liberalism at the beginning of the twentieth century containing the key elements of a constitutional monarchy concept elaborated in greater detail in subsequent documents.

Among these documents one should definitely mention a manuscript found in the files of "Liberation". The manuscript is entitled "Basic Provisions" and contains a preliminary list of the most important constitutional requirements.[7] A note on the document indicates that these theses for the draft were created by the Union of Liberation, subject to discussion by its members, which means that the document can be considered the first draft of the "Fundamental Laws" to-be.

It is already in the course of elaboration of the constitutional drafts that discussion on them unfurled. In particular, a question arose as to which materials could be published on behalf of *Osvobozhdeniye* editors. An opinion was voiced that instead of publishing several documents, in particular, the "foreigner's draft", only one draft reflecting the stance of the circles supporting the Union of Liberation should see the light. In pursuing this goal, it was decided to translate the draft in question into foreign languages and consult with European scholars. One of the recommendations read: "It would make sense to translate the draft into French, send it out for discussion and possibly ask Ademar Esmein and Georg Jellineck to critically review the document". The recommendation was followed later.

Seeking to respond to the critique voiced by the German scholars, Russian liberalists made an attempt to find guidelines for their future work on constitutional drafts in the French and English models of constitutional development. Struve's notes contain criticism of Jellinek's thesis about "constitution emerging in a nonlegal sphere, sometimes even by means of a crime".[8] The author states that Jellinek and Paul Laband wanted to sacrifice society to the state, and to justify all the deeds of the latter. The opinions of these German scholars highly respected by Russian legal philosophers, were countered with the views of their Western European opponents, such as Albert Venn Dicey, James Bryce, Leon Duguit and Anton Menger.

The constitutional draft can be viewed as a platform of the movement as a whole. This explains why the draft became the main subject of discussion at the first and especially the second zemstvo congresses held in November 1904, and April 1905, respectively. At the end of October 1904, in the course of preparation for the first congress of zemstvo leaders to be held in Moscow in November, a group of activists developed a draft of the Fundamental Law of the Russian Empire founded on constitutional democratic principles.[9]

The project on the whole was politically orientated. It is demonstrated by the fact that the envisaged form of government was not that of a republic or even a parliamentary monarchy, but rather that of the limited monarchy of the German kind, which was considered to be the best model for Russia, as opposed to the English-style of monarchy. The principle of separation of powers serving as a basis for their delimitation was therefore implemented with significant exemptions benefiting the monarchical power. While formally introducing dual monarchy, the constitutional draft, however, did not provide a clear-cut legal formula of the relationship between the monarch and popular representation. The document stated that "the supreme power of the Russian Empire is exercised by the Emperor with participation of the State Duma" (Article 1). However, the character of this participation remained extremely vague, which in a conflict situation would inevitably result in the triumph of the monarchical power. The monarch reserved the right of vetoing the decisions of legislative power, of dissolution of the chambers, as well as all the prerogatives in interior and foreign policies and the right to supervise the armed forces of the state (Articles 28, 30, 32).

According to the authors, the constitutional draft represented a platform of the political movement rather than a document ready to be adopted. The drafters stated:

> The only correct way to implement the program outlined in the draft is convocation of the Constituent Assembly freely elected by nationwide, direct and secret vote for the purpose of development and implementation of the Fundamental law of the state. This is the only way to ensure that the law will stem from the appropriate source – the will of the people.[10]

This second opinion led to the creation of another draft, referred to as "Muromtsev's Constitution", which formed the theoretical basis for subsequent constitutional movement in Russia. The draft in question aroused great interest of the contemporaries and undoubtedly influenced the development of the most important legislative documents of the Russian statehood of a post-revolutionary period. However, the draft has not received adequate attention from the modern scholars. The constitutional model offered by Sergey A. Muromtsev aimed not so much at replacing current legislation as at gradually filling it with the new content. Therefore, the main ideological principles of the Russian liberal constitutionalism were manifested here the clearest. Muromtsev who developed the draft together with Fedor F. Kokoshkin, a prominent lawyer of the young generation of constitutional democrats' party, cut down the number of changes to be introduced to existing laws, and poured maximum effort in stipulating these changes in a more formalized legal parlance than before. While revising the sections on legislation, which underwent significant changes, the authors deliberately mitigated many of the definitions of the previous constitutional document.

In this regard, it makes sense to dwell on the general principles that the authors of the document who unquestionably were the leading Russian specialists in constitutional law, sought to put across. Sergey A. Muromtsev (1850–1910) was a representative of the older generation of Russian liberal intelligentsia, one of the most prominent legal philosophers and theorists, a recognized leader of the constitutional movement in Russia, a senior member of the constitutional democrats' party and the chairman of the First State Duma.

Whilst being a staunch supporter of the constitutional monarchy and the representation of the people, Muromtsev, however, denied blind adoption of the western forms of political structure, and considered necessary their adjustment to Russian conditions and political practice. This explains a general moderate nature of Muromtsev's constitutional draft, which was accepted as a guideline by the majority of the liberal public and enlightened bureaucracy. The second active drafter of the constitutional document in question was Fedor F. Kokoshkin (1871–1918), a representative of the younger and therefore more radical generation of Russian constitutionalists. Kokoshkin, who was of raznochinets (from "various ranks": intellectuals not belonging to the gentry in nineteenth century Russia) origin, was one of the most prominent experts in the field of state law and a public figure. He was one of the initiators and active members of zemstvo-constitutionalism movement, and of the Union of Liberation – the liberal organizations which subsequently served as a basis for the Constitutional Democratic party formation. As a lawyer and a politician, Kokoshkin participated in the drafting of the first constitutional draft developed within the Union of Liberation, and played an important role in zemstvo movement during the first Russian revolution. Later, he became one of the leaders of Kadets party and the deputy of the First State Duma. Just as Muromtsev did, Kokoshkin developed the theory of law from the positivist positions, seeking to analyse legal norms within the framework of the social political system, as a whole. The approach is demonstrated in his paper "On Legal Nature of the State and State Bodies" published in 1896. Following Jellinek, Laband and other German lawyers, Kokoshkin regarded the state as a legal person.

An individual printed copy of the draft has been kept in Muromtsev's archive; it is entitled "Draft published in *Russkiye Vedomosti* of 6 July 1905, issue No 180".[11] This document, subsequently revised by Muromtsev, and additional materials, touch upon a number of important issues. These revisions are partially accommodated in the abovementioned edition published in memory of Muromtsev. However, the publication of the revisions does not appear to be exhaustive. These are the texts of Muromtsev's draft that a contemporary researcher had at his disposal. Most probably, the initial manuscript has not been preserved; at least, it is missing from the scholar's archive. Memoirs of prominent leaders of the Kadets party dedicated to the constitutional movement in general and to Sergey A. Muromtsev and his work on the draft, in particular, significantly enrich the picture. Biographic articles written by Pavel N. Milyukov, Gavriil F. Shershenevich, Alexander A. Kisewetter, Igor A. Kistyakovskiy, Nikolay I. Astrov, Dmitry I. Shakhovskiy, Maxim M. Vinaver, Vladimir D. Nabokov, Sergey A. Kotlyarevsky and Nikolay A. Gredeskul, deserve special mention. Among these memoirs written specifically for the book of collected articles published in 1911, the article of Fedor F. Kokoshkin entitled "S.A. Muromtsev and Zemstvo Congresses" occupies a special place. In the article, the constitutional draft in question is analysed, and the history of its creation is revealed.[12]

Although Muromtsev deemed monarchical power limitation necessary, he believed limitations should be derived from the whole totality of other norms stipulated by the draft of Fundamental Laws, rather then being fixed in its individual section. The author thought it would secure continuity in the course of transition from the old law to the new one (without a drastic substantial disruption). Being placed into such political context, monarchical power inevitably becomes subject to certain limitations, at the same time serving, however, as the highest guarantor of the legality and supremacy of the law. It is emphasized in the first article that "the governance of the Russian Empire is firmly based on the laws issued in the order stipulated by the Fundamental Law". All other provisions of the section are derived from this key principle of the law-based state. They include the order of interrelation between general and local legislation which should not be conflicting; the principle of irreversibility of the law; and lawmaking strictly in accordance with the constitution (Articles 2–4).

The model of the future state order of Russia suggested by the draft represented a constitutional monarchy of the German kind. Its key distinctive feature was an aspiration to combine strong executive power concentrated in the hands of the monarch, with well-developed representation of the people, the most important element of social control. This was the model implemented in the constitution of the North German Union of 1867, and specifically in the German constitution of 1871.[13] The comparison of the German constitution of 1871 with Muromtsev's draft reveals that there are fundamental similarities in the structure of the two documents, as well as in the interpretation of a number of key issues. Both opuses suggest an essentially identical concept of the state as a legal person. The concept was substantiated to the fullest extent by Georg Jellinek and Paul Laband in Germany, and by Muromtsev and Kokoshkin in Russia. Within the framework of the concept, the state is regarded as a subject of the law, which maximally corresponds to the idea of the unity of its organization, will and purpose. From this point of view, constitutional monarchy represented a type of unitary state, as opposed to countering dual monarchy. The principle of separation of powers gave way to the principle of separation of functions. According to this idea, the parliament as a whole and its chambers are considered to be specific state bodies. They are established collectively, and their functions include participation in a lawmaking process by ratifying the basic legislation of the state, and exercising control over administrative authorities, thus essentially implementing the principle of ministerial responsibility. These institutions, however, are not independent legal persons. Along with the monarch, whose power is limited, they represent a part of the single state. This concept of constitutional monarchy as a unitary state, being a legal rationale behind the existing political system, was largely of metaphysical and teleological nature and pursued the goal of legitimizing strong monarchical power.[14]

At the same time, according to the constitutional document, the monarchical power reserved the prerogative to issue decrees elaborating or interpreting the provisions of laws. In order to prevent these decrees from turning into by-laws, Muromtsev specifically defines their status and places the procedure of their promulgation on the same footing as that established for the laws *per se*. The significance of this norm for both Russian and German legislation is demonstrated by the fact that henceforth the monarchical power frequently resorted to issuing decrees to circumvent the constraints on its legislative competence imposed by the Duma. In such a way, the principle of monarchy was in fact implemented.

Another important element of the political system – primarily, of legislative power – was the State Duma. In his constitutional draft, Muromtsev gives special consideration to the regulation of the legal status of the body. Section III of the draft focusing on this issue is entitled "Establishment of the State Duma"; 52 articles (out of total of 113) make up the section which in its volume significantly exceeds all other parts of the document, and is distinguished by greater detailing.

The assessment of the constitutional experiment at the moment of its performance by its participants themselves deserves special attention. We have at our disposal the notes of the French researcher Paul Boyer which contains results of his interviews and correspondence with the prominent public and political figures of Russia. From the end of the nineteenth century up to the 1930s,[15] Boyer systematically and with great attention gathered information on the most important developments in cultural and political life in Russia and other Slavic countries of Eastern Europe. The official status of Boyer as the Director of the School of Living Oriental Languages ("L'Ecole des Langues Orientales Vivantes") enabled him to converse with representatives of different political forces, to compare the declaratory stance with the views of the opposition, and the opinions of scholars with those of the politicians, as well as to get into direct contact with key actors of various political events. Boyer frequented Russia – at least, he visited the country in 1906–1907 and then in 1909–1912, which is proven by numerous notes dating back to these years.

A question of the degree of influence liberal constitutional drafts exerted on the existing legal system deserves special consideration. The analysis of the drafts' content demonstrates that they were essentially integral and highly legible platform documents of the constitutional movement in Russia. Building on the German theoretical concept of constitutional monarchy, Russian lawyers tailored it to the conditions of the Russian Empire and the revolutionary crisis experienced. Whilst clearly realizing the practical difficulties of implementation of the project, they nevertheless state creation of civil society and law-based state as a prospective objective. Seeking to avoid an unbridgeable gap in the legal tradition, Russian constitutionalists considered incorporation of the new principles into the current legislation to be one of their key objectives. While preparing the constitutional draft, Sergey A. Muromtsev had in mind the possibility of its direct inclusion into the *Svod zakonov* (Code of Laws) in place of Articles 47–81 of the first part of the first volume, without directly affecting other sections and leaving more profound synthesis of the new and the old legal norms to the discretion of future legislators. This paved the way to the gradual transition to constitutional monarchy, which was facilitated by the overall moderate nature of the draft, absence of special sections on the emperor's power, allowed modifications of the principle of separation of powers, and specific terminology maximally approximated to the existing legislation. For instance, the author of the draft preferred the term "Fundamental Law" to "constitution", "supremacy of the law" to "constitutional monarchy", and "the State Duma" to "parliament"; and avoided such terms widely used in western constitutions as "civil list" and "responsible ministry".

In the liberal political spectrum of Russia conservatives, moderates and radicals were separated by the concept of the statehood formed in the course of the revolution, and to an even greater degree by the attitude to its reform. The position of Oktyabrists, the conservatives of Russian liberalism, remained unchanged throughout the old regime. The theorists of Oktyabrists party unanimously supported the new political system established by the manifesto of 17 October 1905.[16] The platform documents of this movement claimed that the main goal of the political reform, that of setting up constitutional monarchy, had been achieved. The political system was modelled on the dualistic type of monarchical constitutionalism, with the Duma exercising legislative power and the government appointed by the monarch. In contrast to the English parliamentary monarchy, the sovereign here remained an autocrat and was supposed to govern the country not only *de jure*, but also *de facto*. It was in fact a question of the political reform aimed at democratization and rationalization of the regime without radically changing the principles of its functioning. According to the theorists of the party, e.g. professor Vladimir I. Gueriet, the main danger of implementation of the model emanated from the radical political parties influenced by the ideas of non-critical adoption of the western experience, and advocating parliamentary monarchy and responsible ministry principle, i.e. the concepts totally unacceptable for Russia. In the conditions of acute political crisis and power destabilization, the solution was seen not in setting up the party government, but rather in the elaboration of the traditional principle of "unity of the monarch and the people".

The Kadets (constitutional democrats) in their draft presented a theoretical model of resolving the agrarian issue through reallocation of the land resources while guaranteeing the property rights of the landowners. This neo-liberal model demonstrates elaboration of the formulae of social functions of the law and of social state, with the view of settling the agrarian issue by constitutional means. The model appears especially relevant in the light of reforms nowadays. Three main problem blocks can be identified in the model: the theoretical liberalism approach to the resolution of the fundamental social conflict; the programme of the agrarian issue settlement, its content and elaboration; and the political strategy stemming from the programme.

On the whole, having examined the three stages of the development of the constitutional democrats' agrarian programme, one can conclude that it steadily shifted to the left. At the first stage, the dominant ideas were those of fixity of the private property right on land, and the possibility of its alienation only under the condition of fair reimbursement. At the second stage, the idea of forced alienation of the land with minimal or zero reimbursement emerged, which is illustrated by various interpretations of such notions as "nationalization" and "expropriation". This turn can already be regarded as a certain bias towards the adoption of the social democratic ideology of the right-wing relativism. Finally, the third stage was the one where internal contradictions were observed to the full: while sharing the general ideology of the government of strengthening the private property institute, which was the underlying principle of the constitutional democrats' platform, the party, however, refused to accept the authoritarian methods of the "revolution from above" initiated by Stolypin.

There were not enough social prerequisites for implementation of this Bonapartist-style strategy in Russia, but it could be well carried out, should the state and liberal opposition have made active attempts to start a dialogue. Later on, similar reforms were implemented in developing countries. They were based on overcoming extremities, manoeuvring, centralization of the government, implementing changes in a stringent and consistent way and thus creating a gap between technological and social parameters of the reform. This opportunity was realized in Germany and other countries, but not in Russia. The Russian Empire of recent times, like, previously, the Roman Empire, appeared unable to respond to the agrarian challenge with an integral programme of reforms.

Sham constitutionalism as a problem of the transitional period

The transition from absolutism to a constitutional system reveals a number of contradictions that have not received theoretical elaboration within the framework of the classical theory of western constitutionalism. This problem became central in the theoretical and political heritage of Russian liberalism. This contradiction revealed itself already in the works of the founders of Russian liberal theory via the occurrence of discussions about the advantages of constitutional monarchy before the transition to a republic. This was the reason why Russian liberals considered constitutional monarchy to be the optimal form of such a transition. This transition should be analysed in connection with the problem of power legitimacy in the periods of radical reforms. Legitimacy is a consensus achieved in the relations between society and political power, under which the right of the latter to govern is recognized. Being a fundamental feature of a political regime, legitimacy has two components: the perception of the government order as acceptable by the major part of society, on the one hand; and comprehension on the part of the ruling upper crust of their right to exercise power, on the other. Legitimacy and the law are related in certain ways: traditional legitimacy accords with customary law, whereas rational legitimacy corresponds to codified norms of modern legislation, and charismatic legitimacy implies recognition of extraordinary achievements of a person under the crisis of replacement of the existing legal system by the new one. However, legitimacy is not the same as formal legality. For example, regimes established as a result of revolution or other forms of power encroachment, may become legitimate in the people's opinion without having become legitimate with respect to positive constitutional law in force at the time of their emergence. And vice versa, formally lawful regimes do not always enjoy legitimacy and social support, which is expressed in constitutional crises. Thus, modern democratic regimes interpret the problem of legitimacy in many different ways: monistic legitimacy is typical of the parliamentary regime and is exemplified in general parliamentary elections, whereas mixed and especially presidential regimes are characterized by the phenomenon of dual legitimacy illustrated by general elections of both the parliament and president, which sows seeds of discord between the branches of power.

The legitimacy of the monarchy is a form of society modernization which emanates from the power; it is traditionally perceived as customary. In this context, one can better understand the meaning of paternalism as determining the social position or the right to power in accordance with the status inherited from the common ancestor. Neo-paternalism in transitional societies rests upon a specific mechanism of power typical of traditionalism regimes, where the rulers relying on a branched system of familial, clannish and estate-based relations legitimize their power using the traditional stereotypical perception of leader as the head of the kin, and of the state as his hereditary patrimony. Such perception was typical of the Russian peasantry until the beginning of the twentieth century; and the official monarchical ideology perfectly corresponded to it. Being one of the most stringent types of authoritarianism, patrimonialism gravitates to sham or even nominal constitutionalism.

This approach allows one to interpret the neo-liberal concept of constitutional crises, and the strategy of their resolution. A constitutional crisis is viewed as a natural phase of development in the process of transition from a traditional agrarian society to an industrial civil society, and from absolutism to a parliamentary democracy. This transition is carried out in the course of radical legal reform or in case of the impossibility of the reform implementation via a constitutional revolution under which new political institutes are formed. The absence of developed civil society and of democratic political tradition practically rules out the possibility of a linear character of this process. Therefore, the process has a cyclical character expressed by fairly consecutive alternation of constitutional and authoritarian regimes. This explains the fact that the greatest achievements of constitutionalism at the beginning of the twentieth century ended up returning to stringent authoritarian regime. To break away from the vicious circle of the cyclical recurrence and to ensure a linear progressive motion to constitutionalism, it is necessary to secure active support from society, primarily on the part of intelligentsia.

At the culmination period of the revolution, in October 1905, Sergei Y. Witte, the author of the Manifesto of 17 October 1905, consistently pursued a policy of enhancing cooperation between the power and liberal community. He believed that the transition to a constitutional regime, which was theoretically enabled by the Manifesto of 17 October, and getting liberal opposition involved in constructive activity would allow one to overcome revolutionary crisis. The political goal of Witte was to form an alliance between enlightened bureaucracy and liberal intelligentsia. However, the political plan failed. Zemstvo congress held in November 1905, resulted in the split of democratic forces instead of their consolidation. The report by Sergei Y. Witte delivered on 18 October 1905 can be considered as a platform of gradual achievement of consolidation of power and society on the liberal base. The hopes for "political tact of Russian society" expressed by Witte were not justified, and his loyal report submitted to Nicolas the Second turned out to be a sort of a political project, which was never further developed.

For the Kadets party, the issue of the constitutionality of monarchy boiled down to exercising social control over the latter. However, when deciding upon the kind of control, the party theorists suggested at least three approaches based on different western models, namely parliamentary monarchy, dual monarchy and a republic. When formulating his position, Petr B. Struve distinguished between two types of European constitutional monarchies: parliamentary monarchy where the people's representation does not only exercise legislative power, but also governs along with the monarch (as in England, Belgium and Hungary); and constitutional bureaucratic monarchy where the parliament carries out legislative functions, but the country is governed by the monarch via the government he appoints (as in Prussia). In this perspective, the regime established by the Russian revolution should have been recognized as constitutional, but with significant reservations. The essence of the "constitutional coup of October 17" was perceived as follows:

> The monarch yielded to public pressure and renounced autocracy. Russia became a constitutional country. Nicolas the Second became a constitutional monarch. But Russian constitutional monarchy stumbled over bureaucracy. And the whole country which had made a big step forward, suddenly stopped. The bureaucracy proved unable to advance it.[17]

A conclusion could be drawn about the necessity to exert pressure onto monarchy and bureaucracy, with the view of implementation of the principle of responsible ministry composed of representatives of public movement. The position of Vasiliy A. Maklakov was similar to that of Struve. Maklakov countered the legitimate constitutional reform of 1905 with the non-legitimate revolutions of 1917, and interpreted the Manifesto of 17 October as the absolute victory of liberalism by stating that "it was a great reform carried out by legitimate power; the constitution that the liberalism had long dreamt of, was octroyed. In terms of its depth and the aftermath the reform of 1905 was comparable to the reforms of the 1860s; but neither back then nor now revolution occurred".[18] Retrospectively assessing the development of the Russian political system of that period, Maklakov saw the key objective of liberalism in supporting the reformed power rather than in destabilizing it. The main contradiction of the post-reform political system was seen in the overall ill-preparedness of the traditionalist society for democracy, in declaring political freedoms before implementing actual social and economic transformations, in proclaiming the principles of parliamentarianism before forming political parties reflecting the will of the people in an unbiased way. To declare political freedoms without having suggested an acceptable solution for the agrarian issue meant clearing the way for extremely dangerous revolutionary demagogy, aimed no longer at implementation of the legal reform, but rather at establishment of dictatorship disguised by the utopian slogans of building socialism. In these conditions, power vacuum became a real threat; and in an underdeveloped country with lack of political culture the most likely way out of the situation was to set up anti-liberal and anti-legal dictatorship. This is the reason why Maklakov, unlike radical members of the constitutional party, shared the views of Tocqueville, and deemed it necessary for liberals to form an alliance with the authorities to oppose the revolution, rather than with the revolutionary forces to oppose the authorities. This alliance was seen as obligate in order to preserve liberalism *per se* in Russia. And Maklakov suggested a special strategy and tactics of relationship with the authorities, which tolerated constitutionalists' cooperation with the bureaucracy in order to safeguard the course of the reforms. The philosopher emphasized that "constitutional monarchy was something that liberalism wanted to have in place, and something useful for liberalism itself to prevent it from being carried away by the revolutionary chaos". Maklakov continued:

> If Bismarck is right in stating that a compromise is a basis of constitutional life, then the compromise with the constitutional monarchy was no longer treason, but the only reasonable policy to follow. Moreover, at that moment reaching an agreement with the monarchy was even easier, for the latter had already made the necessary step. It consented to the constitution having legislated it in the manifesto. After all, it appointed Witte the Head of Cabinet. Could there possibly be a more remarkable choice?

Other active members of the party, too, with hindsight acknowledged that the confrontation with the regime was an erroneous policy. Ariadna Tyrkova admitted that:

> even after the Manifesto of 17 October the Kadets remained in opposition. They made not a single effort to cooperate with the government in the activities at the State Duma. Despite the political logic that suggested the cooperation, it proved impossible due to psychological reasons. This was not the platform which was the hindrance. We stood for the republic, and not for constitutional monarchy. The Kadets were to become the mediators between the old and the new Russia, but failed to perform the function. Besides, they did not want to.[19]

The main reasons why the strategy was erroneous are believed to be the emotional atmosphere in which Russian constitutionalism developed, excessive reliance on the German legal tradition, and false perception of Russian autocracy and its objective historical role.

Pavel N. Milyukov, the leader of the constitutional democrats, criticized Russia's political regime from a somewhat different standpoint, focusing on the consistency of introduction and implementation of the principles of parliamentarianism. In assessing the Manifesto of 17 October, not only did he emphasize its inconsistency and limited scope, but also refused to stress an act of constitutional limitation of power therein. He saw the main drawback of suggested political system in the Duma's lack of real legislative power which it shared with the state council and the monarch. Such a system did not allow the people's representation to exercise effective control over the government, and therefore to implement the principle of responsible ministry. From this a conclusion could be drawn about the necessity of relentless pressure from the opposition on the power with the purpose of wringing additional concessions. Tactically, it meant refusal of the opposition to participate in the coalition "bureaucratic" government or to cooperate with it. According to Dmitry N. Shipov, it was this compelling standpoint which partly accounted for the failure of the idea of a coalition government with the involvement of constitutional democrats. The idea was discussed by Stolypin and Milyukov.[20] The prospective goal was to create the government of public trust comprised of the Duma majority party representatives. It was moreover suggested that Kadets play a leading role in the government. This political crisis came to an end with dissolution of the Duma by the decree of 8 July, and appointment of Stolypin as a Chairman of the Council of Ministers. Milyukov in his conceptual work on the second Russian revolution characterized a Russian constitutional monarchical system even more intelligibly from the sociological standpoint, having seen in it pretend constitutionalism. He wrote:

> German publicists already came up with a good name for this period: an epoch of 'sham constitutionalism' (Scheinkonstitutionalismus). If it is possible to briefly formulate the reason why with the first concessions from the government the conflict did not end, but assumed a lingering character and eventually resulted in a real catastrophe, the explanation is in the word Scheinkonstitutionalismus. The concessions on the part of power authorities could not satisfy the people and society not only because they were insufficient and incomplete. There were moreover insincere and mendacious, and those at power who made the concessions not for a single moment considered them to be definitive and irrevocable.[21]

Milyukov based his judgement on the fact that there existed two competing centres of legislative power in the Russian political system, namely the Duma expressing the interests of the people's representation, and the State Council expressing the interests of the old-regime bureaucracy. Their conflict paralyzed legislative work, and eventually blockaded the constitutional reform as a whole. In these conditions the wide gap between the liberal opposition and the power became unbridgeable, and cooperation between them advocated by the Oktyabrists and the right-wing Kadets appeared to be political hypocrisy. So, the spread between the constitutionalists' positions on the attitude to power and the prospects of cooperation with it was so great that it accommodated polar and mutually exclusive standpoints: for some, the fact of establishment of constitutional monarchy was beyond all doubt; whereas for the others, it was a pure fiction.

The position of Fedor F. Kokoshkin deserves special attention in this regard. As a staunch supporter of law-based state and a prominent lawyer, he strived for putting the projected statehood changes maximally in line with the legal tradition. However, being one of the leaders of the political party opposing autocracy, Kokoshkin could not help taking into account key principles of the party platform. His position can be therefore defined as a compromise, as compared to the views of Maklakov and Milyukov. Kokoshkin assumed that constitutional monarchy already existed in Russia, and perceived the Fundamental Laws as a real, although contradictory, constitution of the country. As his position in the course of the Vyborg Appeal demonstrates, he sought to respond to the challenge of autocracy by means of legal arguments. At the same time, Kokoshkin shared the stance of the party leaders on key questions of strategy and tactics. Kokoshkin's somewhat ambiguous position within the party leadership failed to escape criticism on the part of his contemporaries Maklakov wrote:

> In November 1904, Fedor F. Kokoshkin objected to the establishment of the Constituent Assembly while the monarchy still existed; even in July 1915 at the like-minded gathering at Alexander I. Konovalov, which I remember well, he still defended monarchy as a great and useful power. But as a member of the Central Committee of the Kadets party, in contradiction to what he stated elsewhere, on 20 October 1905 he presented a drastic ultimatum to Witte demanding Constituent Assembly introduction.

Maklakov considers Kokoshkin to be a person who sacrificed his views for the sake of party unity. Even if this is an exaggeration, there is a grain of truth in it. From Milyukov's memoirs we know about his argument with Kokoshkin about the structure of the parliament in which the latter advocated a pre-eminently bicameral system. After all, close cooperation between Kokoshkin and Sergey A. Muromtsev in the course of the constitutional draft development indirectly confirms the moderate character of his views.

In addition to studying the constitutional process in the two dimensions considered above, namely public legal and sociological analysis, it should be viewed from the phenomenological perspective, i.e. in the course of its historical development. Such analysis clearly demonstrates that sham constitutionalism is an unstable and internally contradictory system anywhere, and it can evolve in diametrically opposite ways depending on more general trends of social and political development. This phenomenon is in fact typical of a transitional period. Theoretically, such a system, representing a combination of constitutional legitimization of power with preservation of its authoritarian nature, can be a well-justified starting point of both constitutional and anti-constitutional development. The overall situation that emerged in Russia at the beginning of the twentieth century objectively favoured the second variant; this fact, however, does not rule out the possibility of a different outcome at the end of the century.

The concept of law-based state was elaborated by Russian constitutionalists based on the analysis of both western and Russian socio-political practices. Fedor F. Kokoshkin ranks among a number liberal philosophers focusing on problems development, the most eminent being Boris N. Chicherin, Konstantin D. Kavelin, Alexander D. Gradovsky, Maxim M. Kovalevsky, Petr B. Struve, Bogdan A. Kistyakovsky, Pavel I. Novgorodtsev and Pavel N. Milyukov. At the same time, Kokoshkin offered a non-standard synthesis of law and sociological theory at the beginning of the twentieth century, and made a significant contribution to the practical implementation of the ideals of a law-based state.

Kokoshkin developed legal principles in connection with the analysis of the socio-political system as a whole. When considering the state, he tended to perceive it as a social relationship, on the one hand, and as a legal person, on the other, depending on whether the phenomenon was interpreted in terms of sociology or legal theory.

The most important platform document of Russian constitutionalism, the draft of the Fundamental Law, was developed by the Union of Liberation and published in 1905 in Russia and France.[22] The draft was compiled by the most prominent contemporary lawyers, including Fedor F. Kokoshkin and Sergey A. Kotlyarevsky, as well as Sergey A. Muromtsev who subsequently participated in the revision of the document. The draft was an important prerequisite for the Fundamental Law of the Russian Empire of 23 April 1906. On the whole, this document very distinctly manifested political aspirations of the most rationally-minded representatives of Russian constitutional liberalism, who already in 1904 called for convocation of the State Duma. The draft was developed on the basis of a thorough analysis of main European constitutions, primarily French and German ones, and therefore in many regards turned out to be extremely radical for Russia. This probably explains the dual reaction of the French and especially German lawyers to it. While approving of the goals of the movement and its platform as a whole, and even fully identifying themselves with the movement, as Max Weber did, some western scholars, such as Esmein, Jellinek, Weber, and some Russian philosophers, such as Maxim M. Kovalevsky and Sergey A. Muromtsev, criticized the draft for being excessively radical for Russian conditions. While taking satisfaction in the spread of the principles of Western European constitutionalism in Russia, the scholars at the same time fairly pointed out the ill-preparedness of the country to the immediate adoption of such a radical reform. They saw the main danger for the reform emanating from the absence of the stable social base, radicalism and legal nihilism of intelligentsia, as well as from absolute power of bureaucracy. This explains the quest for a moderate strategy of constitutional reforms in Russia.[23]

Therefore, it was the German model of constitutional monarchy with its strongly pronounced monarchical principle that the Russian moderate constitutional liberals of the end of the nineteenth and beginning of the twentieth century attributed the most importance to, rather than the French republican model of the legal state or the English model of parliamentary monarchy. The German model represented a significant modification of the principles of Western European – namely, English and French – constitutionalism, their new synthesis, enabling combination of the principles of law-based state and strong monarchical authority. The model was deemed rational due to the character of historically evolved relationships between society and the state, and the role of the latter in the modernization process. Fedor F. Kokoshkin who took part in all the stages of developing the constitutional draft, faced a dilemma of combining the classical liberal requirement of universal suffrage with the platform statement of the constitutional monarchy as the form of government. Theoretically, the contradiction was resolved through adoption of the German model of a political system and putting it into practice. However, the question remained as to which legal character, contractual or octroyed, the Fundamental Law would assume. In the first case, it had to be adopted through the expression of the will of people, whereas in the second case resolution of the monarch was necessary and sufficient.

In this regard examination of two practically unknown legal documents prepared for the anticipated convocation of the Constituent Assembly of 1905 appears quite interesting. There is every reason to believe that it was Kokoshkin who played a significant role in their drafting, because he was considered the main specialist of the party in these matters, although did not approve of the idea of convening a Constituent Assembly while preserving the monarchy. One of the documents is entitled "Project of Sub-Commission of the Bureau: Regulations for the Elections to the Constituent Assembly of People's Representatives". The document gives a detailed account of the overall structure of electoral bodies, their working procedures and operations of the district, municipal, provincial and metropolitan election committees.[24] Another document is entitled "Regulations for the Constituent Assembly of the People's Representatives of the Russian Empire for Elaboration of the Fundamental State

Law". This draft regulates the composition of the Constituent Assembly and its election procedures, the mechanisms of its functioning, legal status of the deputies, as well as the competence of the body in the process of developing a constitution, i.e. the Fundamental Law.[25] According to these drafts, the Constituent Assembly is elected by the total population of the country on the basis of "universal, equal, direct and secret vote". The body regulates its own structure, the working mechanisms and elects a chairman by majority vote. The body "can not be dissolved before the ratification and promulgation of the Fundamental State Law where the target date of convocation of the legislative assembly of people's representatives stipulated by the given law, is to be specified". The analysis of the documents demonstrates that Kokoshkin advocated contractual constitution. If adopted, it would maximally ensure that autocracy in its original form would not be restored. At the same time, constitutional monarchy appeared to be the most desirable form of law-based state in Russia. According to the constitutional democrats, in the difficult conditions of the transitional period constitutional monarchy creates an optimal balance between the key principles of liberal democracy worked out by the Western European experience, namely popular sovereignty, separation of powers and effective executive power.

Thus, Fedor F. Kokoshkin demonstrated a unique combination of academic activity profoundly elaborating the theory of law-based state with the practical work of setting up the state in the form of constitutional monarchy. This was a central problem for Kokoshkin at all the stages of his scientific work and political struggle: when he became one of the founders and active members of constitutional zemstvo movement and of the Union of Liberation, from which the constitutional democratic party emerged later; when he as an expert participated in developing drafts of the constitution and of the electoral law; when he played an important role in the zemstvo movement during the first Russian revolution, was one of the leaders of the Kadets and the First State Duma deputy; and finally, when Kokoshkin was one of the key figures of the Provisional Government engaged in preparation of the principal documents for the Constituent Assembly.

Russian constitutionalism represented by Kokoshkin suggested an integral concept of law-based state, the significance of which becomes fully evident nowadays. The concept combines key achievements of the European political thought with the tasks of society modernization. The political crisis Kokoshkin witnessed and actively participated in, helped to verify many provisions of the theory as applied to Russian conditions. It became clear that a mere transfer of the political experience of European liberalism does not yield expected results in Russia. The conservatism and political inertia of the wide public did not allow peaceful implementation of constitutional reform. Society and the state faced a dilemma traditional for Russia – the necessity to choose between anarchy and autocracy.

In these conditions, liberal intelligentsia saw their primary task in the fostering of the new political culture, i.e. implementation of legal principles via zemstvo activities, teaching at universities, conducting civic disobedience campaigns in order to prepare the minds of the public for prospective establishment of civil society and law-based state.

In the conditions of revolutionary crisis, the concept of law-based state became the theoretical paradigm enabling Russian liberalism to cherish the ideal of a strong democratic state and at the same time to play a political role of moderate opposition to the monarchy.

Has constitutional monarchy ever existed in Russia at all? If yes, what kind? Is the Russian model typical or unique for the global political development process? It is important to respond to these questions in order to identify possible ways of creating a constitutional regime nowadays, to foresee the difficulties it might face, and possibly formulate its prospective trends.

The necessity of transition from absolutism to law-based state was acknowledged back in the eighteenth and especially nineteenth centuries; it was reflected in drafts of political and constitutional reforms. However, in actual fact this problem was stated only at the turning point of the first Russian revolution. Despite the general continuity of the main legislative acts, one can observe three main phases in the constitutional policy of the monarchy of that time: establishment of monarchical constitutionalism, its transformation towards dual monarchy; and the formation of the regime of the monarch's individual reign.

The first phase represents an initial stage of the new basic legislation development. At this stage, autocracy sought to keep the existing political system intact having imparted a new legal design to it. The overall relationship of the people's representation and the monarchical power fit well into the traditional scheme delineated in the drafts of the so-called governmental constitutionalism back in the nineteenth century. The essence of the documents was in complementing autocracy with deliberative bodies of a representative or quasi-representative nature. The concept was consistently pursued in a legislation package drafted by the Ministry of Interior in the first half of 1905 as a response to requirements of the liberal public. Already at the Congress of zemstvo and municipal leaders that took place on 6–8 November 1904 in Saint-Petersburg a resolution was adopted on the necessity of engagement of elected persons in legislative work. After certain fluctuations in the governmental policies, which in fact served as a public opinion monitoring tool, a manifesto was issued on 18 February. The document was formulated as a re-script addressed to the Minister of Interior, Alexander G. Bulygin; it promised convocation of the representatives of the people.

The draft developed at the Ministry of Interior was further submitted for consideration by the special conference in Peterhof chaired by the tsar and attended by ministers, some of the Great Dukes, members of the State

Council and special invitees, such as Vasiliy O. Klyuchevskiy. As a result of the conference a number of key documents were promulgated. These were to be the supreme manifesto of 6 August 1905; a document on the Establishment of the State Duma, and Regulations for the State Duma Elections.

Main legislative documents of the so-called Bulygin Duma have a number of features characteristic of a quasi-constitutional power structure. Already in the manifesto of August 1905 a certain form of the monarchical principle adjusted to the Russian reality is found. The manifesto does not even formally limit the prerogatives of the tsar, and in this regard presents a contrast to the Western European monarchical constitutions. The leitmotif of the legislative act in question is inviolability of the "Fundamental Law of the Russian Empire on the essence of the autocratic power".

The scope of Duma's competence corresponds to its status as a deliberative body, and is subject to strict regulation by the government (see Chapter 5). The Duma can be by no means regarded as a legislative power body, for it lacks its main attribute – the right of legislative initiative.

Certain conflict potential existed in the relations between the two chambers, the State Duma and the State Council, because the authority in consideration and implementation of legislative policies the latter was endowed with became even greater. This imbalance had to be redressed through establishment of the conciliatory commission specially set up by the two chambers on parity basis. However, it was the chairman of the State Council or one of its departments who chaired the commission and therefore had an upper hand in it.

The general political strike that unfurled in October 1905 signified dissatisfaction of the society by the government's concessions.

The second phase of the reforms in Russia saw the most prominent achievement in the sphere of the limitation of power by constitutional means. It coincided with the greatest upsurge of revolutionary activity, and to a large extent represents an emergency measure taken by the monarchy in the extreme conditions. The matter in point is the manifesto of 17 October 1905, and complementary legislation issued at the end of 1905 to the beginning of 1906, including the law on changed regulations for elections (dated 11 December 1905); the manifesto on changed procedures of the State Council establishment and on revision of the State Duma establishment process, as well as the document regulating establishment of the new State Duma (dated 20 February 1906). These pieces of legislation formed the legal basis of the First State Duma in Russia. The concept of relations between the representative bodies and the monarch they suggested was in many regards similar to that underlying monarchical constitutionalism in a number of western countries, first of all, in Germany. Unlike previously, two chambers of parliament, the State Duma and the State Council, were vested with equal rights in the field of legislation. In the case of unanimity, they could theoretically oppose the monarch in the areas of budget control and new legislation enactment. However, the rights to amend fundamental laws, to manage the work of the government and to use the armed forces were totally withdrawn from the scope of competence of the Duma and State Council, and were reserved exclusively for the monarch. Therefore, it would not be fair to state that constitutional monarchy in its integrity was established in Russia because of a great number of legislative exemptions favouring the monarchical component of the political system. One could at best talk about introduction of the first elements of the dual government regime in Russia.

Being a typical act of octroyed constitutionalism, the manifesto of 17 October 1905 formulated the "steadfast will" of the tsar in solving the following problems: i) to confer fundamental civil freedoms on the population on the basis of real personal immunity, freedom of consciousness, of speech, of assembly and of congress; ii) without interfering with planned State Duma elections, to immediately involve in participation in the Duma the classes of population currently totally deprived of suffrage, insofar as the short period of time left before the convocation of the State Duma permits, leaving further expansion of suffrage at the discretion of the newly established legislative order; iii) to set an irrevocable rule that no law may come into force without prior approval by the State Duma, and that elected representatives of the people are given an opportunity to exercise real control and supervision over legality of the activity of the authorities set up by the will of the tsar. These three guidelines were further elaborated in more specialized legislative acts focusing on separate aspects of the political system reform. Expansion of the suffrage was regulated by the personal decree directed to the Senate dated 11 December 1905 entitled "On Changes in Regulations for State Duma Elections". The document declared the lowering of the property qualification limit which enabled the participation of the new categories of population, such as factory workers, in elections. The Duma itself became the leading institution overseeing the legality of elections. The changed status of the State Duma and the State Council stipulated by the manifesto of 17 October was further fixed by the manifesto of 20 February 1906. The document was entitled "On Changes in the State Council Establishment and on Revision of the State Duma Establishment". It stipulated that from the moment of the convocation of the Duma and the State Council a law can come into force only if the bodies agree on it. Accordingly, the status and structure of both entities, as well as the nature of their relationship with the monarchical power, underwent a change.

As opposed to what was envisaged by Bulygin's draft, the State Duma and the State Council now received equal rights in exercising legislative power, namely in amending an annulment of existing laws, and in issuing new legislation. This right, however, was not applied to fundamental laws; the prerogative to revise them was retained by the monarch. Hence, one can talk here about the advancement of the Russian political system towards a bicameral parliament per sample of the western constitutional monarchies (English, French, Italian and especially German), where legislative power was formally exercised on a dual basis (by the two chambers of parliament and by the monarch). However, this advancement was quite inconsistent, with the monarch reserving the exclusive right to amend fundamental laws.

Conferring equal prerogatives on the State Council and the State Duma was a deliberate step, because it evidently reduces the role of representative government. Even in the case of absolute unanimity, the Duma and the State Council did not have the right to pass a law if the monarch rejected it. This rendered the status of the two bodies even more vague. Therefore, representative institutions of Russia can not be even theoretically viewed as actually limiting autocracy by constitutional means; they rather act as legislative advisory bodies under the monarch exercising at the same time some functions of public control over the power. Such were juridical and institutional prerequisites of the third phase of the transformation of Russian monarchical constitutionalism. The stage concluded the process, and its distinctive feature was the strengthening of the individual role of the tsar in implementation of the political course.

The third phase of the constitutional legislation process in Russia evidently bore a purely formal character, and was mainly perceived as such by contemporaries. Its main goal was to codify laws in order to complement the Code with the new acts issued in the preceding period.

The results of the legislation work of the preceding period were summed up by the publication of the new Fundamental Laws on 23 April 1906, and of the law "On the Establishment of the State Council" on 24 April 1906. A new political system was created whose operating principles were often a subject of heated debates by many scholars, starting from the contemporaries of the events and ending with researchers of our time. A question of correlation between the people's representation principles and monarchical power became the central point of the debates. Indeed, one can draw diametrically opposite conclusions based on the texts of the Code. The document "On the Establishment of the State Council" published on 23 April 1906 clearly reveals the nature of the relationship between the supreme legislative body, on the one hand, and the monarch and his government, on the other.

At the same time, the Emperor enjoys a number of exclusive prerogatives in the legislative domain: the rights of legislative initiative, of revision of the laws in general, as well as an exclusive right of initiative of introducing changes to the Fundamental Laws, and finally, an exclusive right of approval of the legislation.

Judicial power is exercised by courts in the name of the Emperor. The law fixes the existing order of succeeding to the throne in the regnant Tsar House. The monarchical power is a core of the political system, and the monarch factually stands outside the system of social and legal control.

After the overthrow of monarchical power in Russia as a result of the February Revolution of 1917, the Provisional Government was formed which became the central authority of the state. Its main goal, as stated on 2 March 1917, was convocation of the Constituent Assembly as a representative body meant to define the form of government and work out the constitution of the country. By the decree of the Provisional Government, a special conference was convened for preparation of the document regulating elections to the Constituent Assembly on the basis of universal suffrage.[26] The decree paid close attention to the composition of the special conference in order to ensure a high level of legal expertise in development of the documents for constitutional reforms. The decree read as follows:

> The Conference will be composed of specialists on the state law issues, a statistician and other competent persons; political and public figures representing key political and national-political movements in Russia will be invited to participate in it.

For "initial technical development of the issues on the conference agenda", a drafting committee was set up. Its objective was to finalize the drafts elaborated in the course of the Conference. The possibility of inviting experts in a consultative capacity to attend the Conference was also stipulated. In accordance with these decisions, the most prominent experts in the state law took part in the Special Conference chaired by the Senator Fedor F. Kokoshkin, a leader of the Kadets party.

The prospective political system became a subject of discussion in the course of the work on the draft of the Fundamental Law.[27] One can reconstruct the projected model of the political regime based on the legislative drafts developed. It was evidently a model of the republic with strong presidential power. Initially, the political power had to be concentrated in the hands of the Constituent Assembly, the president and the government elected by the Assembly. Later, as far as fundamental laws were developed and adopted, a final decision on the form of government was to be made. In this regard, the key issues of any constitution were discussed, namely the nature of safeguards of individual rights and freedoms, federative or unitary organization of the state; structure of the legislative power (the chambers of parliament and referenda), and, which was the main issue, the place occupied by the head of state in the political system. The first issue – declaration of civil rights – revealed two different approaches to its settlement. Deeming it necessary to include such document into the preamble of the Fundamental Laws, Russian liberals were guided primarily by the experience of constitutional organization in France. However, there are two types of constitutional safeguards distinguished in the French model, negative and positive ones. The discussion revolved around the issue of whether the Russian declaration of rights should include only traditional political rights, or social rights, too, such as a right for work, land, education, insurance, medical help, etc. The confrontation of these two positions corresponding respectively to the French Constitutions of 1789 and 1875 reflected a real choice to be made between the social state and parliamentary monarchy. Another problem, that of correlation between unitarity and federalism, was essentially resolved in favour of the first variant. Building on the assumption that the Russian state is "united and indivisible", the authors of the respective draft deemed it possible to reflect the rights of the regions by according them "regional autonomy" rights. This status did not allow the autonomies to issue local legislation contravening with the laws issued by the central authorities. There was to be only one exception to the rule, namely Finland, which "enjoyed independence on the grounds and within the limits stipulated by the law on mutual relations between Russia and Finland" adopted by the Constituent Assembly. Therefore, in this matter, the trend to preserve the unitary state typical for previous drafts prepared by Constitutional Democrats, was adhered to. The very notion of the federation was interpreted as nothing more than conferring some degree of autonomy on the regions.

The third key issue, that of the organization of legislative power, caused the most heated debate, due to the aspirations of the theorists of constitutionalism to avoid two dangerous situations – power usurpation and power inefficiency. In order to do this, they suggested that as many guarantees as possible be created against power usurpation either by the legislative authorities (i.e. the constituent assembly or the parliament) or by the executive authorities. It was also suggested that at the same time an efficient political system be kept in the crisis situations. The central points of discussion were the structure of parliament, namely the question whether it should consist of one or two chambers, as well as the role of referenda.

The question about the form of government and the place occupied by the head of state remained open, however, the problem was somewhat elaborated in relation to the status of the Provisional Government and its work in the transitional period. This is demonstrated by the constitutional document, which was prepared in advance, entitled "The Draft Law on Organization of Provisional Executive Power under Constituent Assembly, and the Draft Form of Issuance of Laws under Constituent Assembly".[28] In accordance with this document, full executive authority is vested in the "provisional president of the Russian republic" elected by the Constituent Assembly by secret ballot and keeping his authority until re-election in the same way. Certain coherence between the position of the provisional president and that of the constitutional monarch comes under notice. The former enjoys significant authority in the legislative domain: he has the right of legislative initiative; issues decrees on structure, composition and working mechanisms of governmental agencies excluding judicial bodies; and addresses the Constituent Assembly for credit extension. In the executive domain, the president's prerogatives are even more substantial: he "settles all governmental affairs", appoints and displaces the Council of Ministers and its chairman, supervises external policies, and is in charge of the armed forces; the president is exempt from any inquiries. The fact that the power of the provisional president is of an emergency nature, and lasts for no more than a year does not eliminate the impression that this is quite an authoritarian model of presidential republic. The power of the president is in fact limited only by the theoretical possibility of being re-elected, the undertaken obligation to communicate in written form with the Constituent Assembly, as well as by the special procedure of approval and promulgation of the presidential decrees which have to be countersigned by the head of the Council of Ministers or by the corresponding minister and promulgated by the Governing Senate. Therefore, the president, just like the constitutional monarch, is in fact rendered jurisdictionally immune, and assumes no legal liability while wielding absolute authority. The structure of the presidential power very much resembles that developed in the Weimar Constitution of Germany, where the president elected by all-nation vote assumed a right to act practically independently of the parliament in critical situations. With the dissolution of the Constituent Assembly the question about democratic constitution was postponed for an uncertain time period, although the attempts to develop it were taken later, after the establishment of Bolsheviks' dictatorship. According to indirect evidence, one of these attempts formed the basis of the so-called Tagantsev's Case when discussants of a constitutional draft were incriminated in a political crime.[29]

The concluding republican stage of Russian constitutional development basically consisted of preparation and brief operation of the Constituent Assembly. This is where the preceding monarchical period of constitutionalism is divided from the essentially new republican constitutionalism, on the one hand, and from subsequent Soviet sham constitutionalism, on the other. The constitutional documents of the Constituent Assembly therefore represent the most important element linking the preceding liberal tradition of constitutionalism with modern democratic constitutional reforms. The main problem that arises in this regard is legitimization of the new principles of the statehood, its forms and their legal expression. The Constituent Assembly is a unique political institution in Russian history with no direct analogues observed either previously or afterwards. The Constituent Assembly is an elected body created on the basis of popular will; its objective is to adopt constitution and define the structure of the future state order. The idea of its convocation was a practical conclusion of the liberal constitutional thinking of the nineteenth to the beginning of the twentieth century, grounded on the belief that adoption of the Fundamental Laws should be done on the basis of universal suffrage, receive the support of the population, and fix the system of people's representation in the norms of the constitutional law. This is how two central principles of constitutionalism of recent times, namely those of popular sovereignty and of people's representation, are implemented in practice. Therefore, work on preparation and convocation of the Constituent Assembly became the most important direction of the activity of the Provisional Government, the very name of which was pointing out the limited, 'provisional' nature of its power extended only until the moment when a new representative body vested with full authority starts its activity. The most prominent contemporary lawyers, such as Vladimir M. Gessen, Nikolay I. Lazarevsky, Alexander E. Nolde, Sergey A. Kotlyarevsky, and others were members of the Provisional Government and took part in the development of the key political documents. Creation of the "programme of fundamental laws", a constitutional draft, in fact, was one of the most important issues on the agenda.

The overall logic of the constitutional process required active effort to legally substantiate the relations between the Constituent Assembly and the Provisional Government in the transitional period. The task was accomplished in the special report of the Legal Conference chaired by Nikolay I. Lazarevsky on 21 September 1917. The document was entitled "On the Opening Procedure of the Constituent Assembly and the Legal Status of the Provisional Government after the Opening", and despite being of a recommendatory nature, was to be definitely taken into account. The document suggested a radical way of solving the problem and it stated that:

> in no respect would the Constituent Assembly take over any of its authorities from the Provisional Government. The authorities of the Assembly stem directly from the supreme will of the people. From the moment of the will having been manifested in an organized way, the role of the Provisional Government in this regard essentially comes to an end.[30]

When analysing historical precedents of such a situation, the experts took a close look at two key models observed in France in 1848 and 1871. In the first case, Provisional Government made an effort to determine the very institutionalization of the Constituent Assembly; whereas in the second case the government of national defence on principle did not interfere with the work of the Constituent Assembly and did not consider it possible to even formally open its sittings. In the first case, the government continued to work for some time after convocation of the Constituent Assembly; whereas in the second case, it resigned immediately with the start of the activities of the Constituent Assembly. Being more in conformity with the principle of popular sovereignty, the second model was found more acceptable by Russian constitutionalists. However, while being in line with the doctrinal considerations, the model in fact totally deprived the Provisional Government of the right to actively participate in the work of the supreme legislative institution, giving away the initiative into the hands of the political parties represented in the institution. The situation that had been repeatedly observed in the countries of Western Europe under acute political crises was repeated in Russia: while strictly following the logic of the concept of popular sovereignty or separation of powers, active politicians, being members of the government, could not participate in the decision-making process. Seeking to somehow correct the situation, the Legal Conference allowed the possibility of the Constituent Assembly being opened by the minister-chairman, and presenting to the deputies the "Provisional Mandate" developed by the Provisional Government. However, it was stipulated right away that from the formal legal viewpoint the document will be viewed merely as information material. It is not for nothing that the draft documents contain reservations of that kind; they express great respect of the authors to the will of the people. This myth hypnotizes the drafters' consciousness leading to a totally erroneous conclusion that "setting any rules of any sort to guide the work of the Constituent Assembly is absolutely out of question".

The issue of the projected time of the Provisional Government resignation is also dealt with from a purely doctrinal standpoint. The very fact of the opening of the Assembly automatically means resignation of the government that becomes a body exercising day-to-day control and expects the legislative authorities to decide on its destiny. The government may submit legislative proposals to the Constituent Assembly, but by no means enjoys the right of legislative initiative. Therefore, by delegating the full authority to the Constituent Assembly even before it elects the permanent presidium, the Provisional Government loses any control over the development of the situation.

This approach led to a situation where the only problem the Provisional Government was concerned with in the light of the Constitutional Assembly convocation, was detailed development of the regulations governing the elections to the Assembly. For this purpose, the Provisional Government issued a decree adopted already on 25 March 1917, according to which a special body was formed called "Special Council for Preparation of the Draft Regulations for the Constituent Assembly Elections". The guiding principle of the body's operations was publicity: it was suggested that the council be composed of "specialists on the state law issues, a statistician and other competent persons, political and public figures representing key political and national-political movements in Russia".[31] The status of the Council, whose reports were submitted to the government, its atmosphere of free discussion implying existence of individual opinions, the possibility to attract other experts with an advisory vote right – all these factors rendered the institution a real think-tank of the constitutional reform. The result of the work was formulated in the exhaustive legal document entitled "Regulations for the Constituent Assembly Elections".[32] In the document, the most important principle of liberal constitutionalism was codified, namely the creation of civil society and law-based state on the basis of free universal declaration of will. The first article proclaimed:

> The members of the Constituent Assembly are directly elected by the population on the basis of universal and equal suffrage, without making sex-based distinctions, via secret vote, following the principle of proportional representation.

The system of proportional vote, when lists of candidates were voted for, facilitated representation of political parties in the supreme legislative body of the country.

The projects of creating the legal mechanisms and transfer of power to the Constituent Assembly have never been implemented. After the events of the October Revolution of 1917, the Constituent Assembly could not start its activities on the target date, 11 December 1917. It was opened on 5 January when Petrograd was already in the state of siege, and was forced to cease its activity. Russian constitutionalists in their struggle for civil society and law-based state, faced such challenges as extremely low levels of political and legal culture of the population, in general, and of the ruling groups and intelligentsia, in particular; absence of the traditions of parliamentary activity and of respective social practice of interaction between the state and society; class-based egoism; domination of attitudes favouring short-term gains with no long-term transformation perspectives taken into account. This is why social problems were resolved primarily by force, which resulted in the establishment of the authoritarian regime. Various forecasts of the trends of social development with confrontation either growing or declining were annulled by the mere fact of forced dissolution of the Constituent Assembly.

The dissolution of the Constituent Assembly was immediately characterized by French observers Joseph Noulens and Petit as a coup-d'etat, according to their telegram of 20 January 1918.[33] Noulens reported that "all of those present at the first sitting of the Constitutional Assembly had an impression feeling of a night-mare (l'impression d'un cauchemar)". While marking unprecedented violation from the Bolsheviks' deputies and a mob of their sympathizers, threats and insults from the armed soldiers and mariners present inside the conference hall, the observer notes extreme composure and heroic calmness of the socialists-revolutionaries majority until the very last minute of the sitting. The overall atmosphere of the development of the situation was determined by the sanguinary crackdown on the manifestation in support of the Constituent Assembly. At the same time, the French observers noted how easily the Bolsheviks became convinced that the opposition did not have a massive support. Socialists-revolutionaries and other opposition socialist parties put forward a thesis concerning restoration of absolutism in Russia.

Dissolution of the Constituent Assembly and formal transfer of authority to the Soviets made analysts take a closer look at this type of power.

The problem of relationship between the Constituent Assembly and the Soviets was important for the political assessment of the trends of the new regime. According to the author of the analytical report sent from Petrograd on 11 January 1918, the convocation of the Constituent Assembly was not only the last hope for salvation of the country and, in a sense, of the revolution itself. It was indeed a dream cherished by all the liberals and revolutionaries since the era of Alexander the Second, and subsequently a goal strived for equally ardently by all the political parties, including the Bolsheviks who reproached the Provisional Government for procrastination in solving the problem. However, after execution of the coup d'etat on 25 October (7 November) 1917 the Bolsheviks, flushed with success, proclaimed the beginning of the new era for the whole world, and announced the idea of the constitutional assembly to be a bourgeois prejudice. This doctrine is defined as proletarian sovereignty; it is politically expressed through the thesis about transfer of authority to the Soviets. The Soviet electoral system was impaired due to its dependence on the administration, certain individuals, and on exclusion of the mass population from the electoral process. These peculiarities of the system are revealed in the course of detailed analysis of such aspects as "how, with whose help, on which guarantees of independence, regularity, proportionality to the constituency size" the Soviets of all the levels were elected – up to congresses and their executive committees (permanent bodies of government and administration). This electoral regime on the whole and the pyramid of institutions created on its basis represents a deliberate distortion of the will of society for the purpose of supporting the dictatorship by reducing the will of the country where the peasantry represented the majority of the population, to the will of the proletariat, reducing the will of the latter to the will of the workers of the capital city, and in turn reducing their will to that of the communists and internal Bolsheviks' machinery. After discarding the ideological formulas disorienting the mass population, one can state that the power of the Bolsheviks was based on the mere fact of its existence and was therefore grounded at the point of bayonets.

In this respect, the fate of the Constituent Assembly was predetermined. The type of constituent that suited the Bolsheviks was determined by the ability of this assembly to reject its own sovereignty in favour of the Soviets, thus accepting their preceding, present and subsequent legislation. In the context of the thesis about the prevalence of the Soviets over all other forms of people's representation one can better understand the efforts of the Bolsheviks to disrupt the Constituent Assembly sitting by prompting a situation when the local Soviets declared void the mandates of undesirable deputies; by introduction of the necessary quorum of 400 people for the opening of the assembly; by establishment of control over the deputies' mandates exercised by the special Bolsheviks' bureau headed by Moisey S. Uritskiy (rejection of the control voiced by the socialists-revolutionaries allowed the authorities to declare lack of the quorum). In addition, one should take into account all kinds of administrative and political measures taken to prevent opposition deputies from actual arrival to Petrograd, primarily via declaring Kadets outlaws and public enemies, introduction of arrest practice against them and later resorting to this measure against the socialists-revolutionaries who were forced into hiding and thus could not actively participate in the polemics (take the arrest of Nikolay D. Avksentjev as an example); usage of the Red Guards and of the mariners to disperse the Constituent Assembly and pursue its supporters; finally, a disinformation campaign in the press announcing the opponents, including socialists, accomplices of the bourgeoisie and abettors of Kaledin and Kornilov, which could provoke lynching of the opponents, which Fedor F. Kokoshkin and Shingarev became victims of.

The mechanism of the conflict was displayed most clearly in the confrontation of different approaches to the elaboration of the Fundamental Laws. The Bolsheviks suggested that the Constituent endorse without discussion the key document they developed, "Declaration of Rights of the Working and Exploited People", according to which full authority was transferred to the toilers and their representatives in the Soviets, i.e. to the Bolsheviks themselves. The alternative platform developed by socialists-revolutionaries offered a different solution to the power issue, as opposed to that offered by the Bolsheviks; the autonomous nature of the Soviets was underlined. The main reason why the mass population did not support the Constituent Assembly is their political inexperience: the promises of the peace and the bread made them forget about the victims of war, and to recognize the authoritarian demagogic regime of the dictatorship of the proletariat leading to the civil war, as the result of the class struggle and the promise of better life.

In the historical perspective of the twentieth century, after the Russian revolution, the struggle for the right in different countries of Europe appeared typologically similar in many respects. In terms of ideology, it is undoubtedly similar to the struggle being unfurled in the last decades of the twentieth century. Therefore, the liberal model of settling a social crisis developed during the revolution has a more universal, typological significance.

Liberalism, striving to overcome the social crisis which manifested itself so mightily in 1917 in Russia, faced a number of problems, the solutions to which appear significant from a theoretical point of view. The tasks in question were as follows:

1 To create a legal barrier to the split of society leading to the civil war.
2 To prevent unlawful seizure of power and its instruments, i.e. basically a coup d'etat, carried out under demagogic slogans of the will of the

people, but in fact aimed at power usurpation and distortion of this will. The concept of a constituent here is countered with the concept of a coup d'etat.

3 To stop uncontrolled dissolution of the state and the law via creation of a rational model of state order and government.
4 To oppose the fundamental civil principles of a law-based state to a class-based principle of election of revolutionary authorities (the Soviets).
5 To stop using national contradictions to split the society, leading in future to the upset of public consensus and to preference given to national rights versus individual rights as implied by the key liberal principle. The contradictory activity of Russian liberalism on the eve of the Constituent Assembly opening will be examined further, and its strategy under the conditions of social crisis will be analysed.

The development of the concept of constitutional revolution appears quite timely under the conditions of the transitional period of recent times. Liberal legal philosophers define constitutional revolution as carrying out radical reforms coupled with the rupture of legal continuity. As opposed to social revolution, however, these changes are implemented through the transformation of the norms of public law and revision of their values, rather than by breaking up social relations and replacing the political elite. Social and constitutional revolutions may coincide, but there may be situations when drastic social changes are not reflected in legal changes and thus are implemented by unlawful means. On the contrary, there may be constitutional revolutions which do not bring about certain social changes. Despite the radical nature of the constitutional revolution, it largely preserves the legitimacy of the regime and continuity of the state power. The difference between the concepts of constitutional and social revolution underline such an important feature of social change as its correlation with the law, showing whether they are implemented by unlawful means or, vice versa, based on the new concept of constitutional order. In the course of all large-scale revolutions and radical reforms the issue of correlation between social and legal changes was of decisive importance, as well as the question of correlation between the forms and means of its accomplishing, whether these be spontaneous or based on an integral concept of future political order. During the Russian revolution, the problem was expressed via the attitude of various political forces to the Constituent Assembly and the concept of the state order it suggested.

Contrary to the concept of social revolution disregarding the preceding legal tradition which is accompanied by destabilization of the whole system of political and legal relations, the concept of constitutional revolution suggests a legal formula of democratic transitional period. It implies delimitation of the constituent and constitutional power: the former, being grounded on wide public consensus, becomes a legitimate source of the new Fundamental Laws. Implementation of the model in worldwide political process makes it possible to avoid spontaneous social outburst and subsequent establishment of authoritarianism, which is almost inevitable. This is done through usage of the potential of public consensus. A classic model of the social pact concluded for democratic transition, which was implemented in post-Francoist Spain, illustrates this approach. In this regard, the historical experience of representative institutions of Russia during the epoch of the Constituent Assembly, deserve special examination. External events influencing the history of the Russian Constituent that existed for only one day, and subsequent interpretation of the principles of civil society and law-based state led to a paradoxical situation of researchers paying no attention to the positive experience of the drafts of representative institutions developed by Russian lawyers on the eve of the Constituent Assembly. Based on experience of recent times, contemporary political science distinguishes between two models of transitional period, namely a contractual model (a model of a pact) and a conflict one (a model of rupture). While analysing the contractual model, modern political philosophers have identified its backbone features. Applying the model in historical retrospective to the epoch of preparation of the country for the Constituent Assembly, allows one to find these features in the actions of the political forces in Russia in 1917. A comparative approach enables one to answer the question as to why this model was not implemented and gave place to its opposite, as well as to interpret from this standpoint various concepts of representative power in Russia.

The key feature of the model of contractual transition in the divided society is the ability and readiness of various political forces to accept the principles of liberal democracy as the highest value, for the sake of which they are able to give up their individual political interests. This consent is fixed in the contract specifying the procedures of adopting a legislation during the transitional period. The result may be the adoption of the legislative act about the political institutions of the transitional period, i.e. about the constituent power, about the mechanism of discussion and adoption of the new Fundamental Law.

Another feature of the democratic transitional period, typical of the contractual model, is ensuring of wide public consensus, which is achieved, on the one hand, by adoption of the principle of civil rights, and on the other hand, by securing deliberate participation in this political process of set minorities distinguished by their cultural, national and political interests.

The third distinctive feature of the contractual model is an agreement between main political forces, primarily large parties, on the future state order and the form of government.

The process of achieving the agreement is very complicated and unfolds in a conflict atmosphere. If successful, it results in creation of a legitimate constituent institution, such as Constituanta, National Assembly, etc., which develops a draft of the Fundamental Law subsequently submitted for a referendum or plebiscite. When addressing in this perspective the documents drafted in the process of preparation for the Constituent Assembly opening, one can reveal the key trends of the contractual model, and understand when the participants of the political process chose to refuse it.

The legal development of the procedures of adoption of the transitional period legislation becomes a key problem. Over the time of preparation of the Russian constituanta this activity was carried out by a special institution, Legal Conference under the Provisional Government. Experts on legal theory who developed key drafts for the Constituent Assembly formed the Conference. The documents they created, different variants of the texts and comprehensive discussions unfurled in the course of their preparation, provide rich factual material for analysis. The areas of the Legal Conference activities were determined by the political process itself, but examination of the contents of the drafts discussed reveals the greater influence the Conference exerted on the formation of representative institutions. Of specific interest are materials of the Legal Conference of September 1917, when the Draft Regulations for the Interim Soviet of the Russian Republic was in the focal point of debate. At that time a situation emerged that can be characterized as the culmination of the political process of the transitional period: the attempt to reach a consensus between various political forces on the basis of democratic principles was being taken. Practically right after the failed attempt of the armed coup in Petrograd on 14 September initiated by the General Kornilov, upon the decision of the Executive Committee of the Soviet of Peasant Deputies and other public associations and political parties, the All-Russian Democratic Conference was opened. It was attended by 1,582 deputies. A decision was taken to pick from among the Conference participants representatives of all the groups and factions on a pro rata basis and set up a new permanent institution – All-Russian Democratic Soviet or Provisional Soviet of the Russian Republic (VSRR). The general idea was to create a democratic institution vested with the right of legislative initiative. Its status had to correlate with that of the Provisional Government; the prospects for creation of a Constituent Assembly had to be taken into account, too. The reviewed process coincided with the formation of the new coalition Provisional Government. Therefore, a deliberate initiative was undertaken to create a representative institution of the new type composed of representatives of the groups and factions delegated by the Democratic Conference, as well as of representatives of the Kadets party, commercial and industrial unions and other public movements. Despite its evidently vague character, the attempt was directed towards uniting heterogeneous forces with the purpose of supporting the course of the reform. It goes without saying that the institution required a more elaborated legal base. The Legal Conference was dealing namely with this problem; it considered several drafts of Regulations on VSRR at its sittings. These drafts and the discussion accompanying their development deserve close attention within the framework of the democratic transitional period model.

Discussion revolved around the resolution of the Provisional Government about establishment of VSRR fairly referred to as Pre-Parliament. This supreme representative institution existed from 7 October to 24 October old style and was dissolved in the afternoon of 25 October 1917 when the armed forces of the Military Revolutionary Committee (RVK) surrounded the Mariinsky Palace. The Legal Conference paid maximum attention to detailed elaboration of the Regulations for VSRR, because this body was to play a decisive role in the consolidation of democratic forces on the eve of the Constituent Assembly. The relationship between the Pre-Parliament and the Provisional Government was the first issue requiring constitutional substantiation. On 25 September 1917, the Provisional Government issued a declaration establishing general principles of VSRR. The Provisional Soviet of the Russian Republic received the right to address the Provisional Government with questions and to receive timely clarifications from the latter; the right to develop legislative proposals and to discuss the issues which were submitted to VSRR by the Provisional Government or emerged upon the initiative of the former. However, after discussion of the mechanisms of relations between the two institutions, the participants of the Legal Conference amended them somewhat.

Two drafts of the Regulations for VSRR were submitted to the Legal Conference. The first one was drafted by Moisey S. Adzhemov and was discussed on 27 September 1917; the second one was developed by Nikolay I. Lazarevsky and was discussed on 28 September 1917. Adzhemov's draft specifically stipulated the nature of the representation: a total of 443 people representing the Democratic Conference, qualification elements and national groups were to comprise the institution.[34] Thus, in addition to the pro rata representation of the political forces attending the Democratic Conference, social and national representation was suggested. According to this draft, the Provisional Government had an upper hand in relations with VSRR: the scope of competence of the Soviet was limited to the issues submitted for discussion under the special resolution of the Provisional Government; the first sitting of the Soviet was opened by the government plenipotentiary. The government as a whole and individual ministers were not responsible to VSRR, and the decisions of the Soviet were not only non-binding for the government, but could also be repealed by the latter. It is also emphasized that the government has a right to agree with the opinion of the minority of the Soviet, rather than its majority. On the whole, the draft models relations between VSRR and the Provisional Government after respective sections of the Regulations for the State Duma and the State Council of the preceding period. The Provisional

Soviet enjoys the right to address the government and individual ministers with inquiries and requirements of clarifications (the right of interpellation); however, the latter are not unconditionally bound by the resolutions of VSRR. The draft stipulates that the total number of the members of the Soviet will be 443, and considers the moment of the convocation of the Constituent Assembly to be the moment of termination of the Soviet's activity.

Another draft was prepared by Nikolay I. Lazarevsky; it was on the whole characterized by greater attention to the conflict side of relations between the given institution and the government.[35] The issue of the composition of VSRR is addressed in the following way: the Soviet was to be comprised "of 475 members appointed by the Provisional Government from among the representatives of existing public associations", and the lists of its members were to be published in the *Vestnik Vremennogo Pravitel'stva* (Provisional Government Herald). The dependence of VSRR on the Provisional Government was emphasized by the right of the latter to determine the date of the termination of the Soviet's activity. Regarding the prerogatives of VSRR, the draft provides not only for discussion of legislative proposals, submitted by the Provisional Government, but also for discussion of "other issues" upon the Soviet's own initiative, i.e. within the framework of its right of legislative initiative. The ministers, as in the previous draft, are not accountable to the Soviet. The issue about according permission to attend the sittings of the Soviet to representatives of the press and outsiders is of certain interest: the chairman of the Soviet has the right to decide on the list of people to attend the sitting; the first sitting of the Soviet is to be chaired by the plenipotentiary of the Provisional Government, all subsequent sittings are to be chaired by the elected chairman.

The composition of the representative institution reflected certain public consensus, which determined the fundamental novelty of the body. Instability of the consensus in the political life of the country was manifested in the debates on the principles of its composition revealed at the Legal Conference. As mentioned above, a part of its composition derived from the Democratic Conference was defined more or less clearly: it was a pro rata representation of the parties attending the Conference. The idea was to integrate them with representatives of liberal parties and movements, such as Kadets and other "qualification elements", into a single institution. However, the representation norms of these elements were neither elaborated nor concretely stipulated in the draft. This issue was raised in the course of discussion. Irakly G. Tsereteli representing the Democratic Conference at the sitting of the Legal Conference voiced his objections to the draft in question. If the number and composition of the representatives of the Democratic Conference is already known, then, according to Tsereteli, any change of the total number of members of the future Pre-Parliament will be able to distort the pre-defined proportion.

According to Tsereteli, by stipulating a different number of the members of the Soviet, the draft "allows for a possibility to expand the membership in breach of the previous agreement". A member of the Legal Conference Vladimir D. Nabokov explained the fact by growing ambitions of "various groups of population" to take part in VSRR. He assured Tsereteli that the changes in the membership of the institution would be introduced only under the condition of keeping percentage correlation between the parties. In response to this, Tsereteli suggested that the constant ratio of 75 to 35 be established between representatives from the Democratic Conference and envisaged new public associations. A question was raised about the right of the Provisional Government to dissolve VSRR, which Tsereteli considered illegitimate. Adzhemov and Nabokov, on the contrary, claimed that the Provisional Government had the formal right to dissolve the Soviet. The question about the relations between the two power institutions, however, was not defined by formal legal norms. Besides, the situation was changing rapidly, leaving practically no encouraging prospects to the emerging institution. The jurists and the politicians participating in the discussion understood it quite well. Vladimir D. Nabokov fairly concluded that the argument about the amendments did not matter much, "for the relationship between the Soviet and the Provisional Government is determined not as much by the wording of formulations, as by real conditions of the objective life of the people".[36]

As a result, the Legal Conference developed a final draft of the Regulations for the Provisional Soviet of the Russian Republic which underlay its activity. The issue of the composition of the Soviet was dealt with in a somewhat vague way: the draft stipulated that the Soviet was formed under invitation of the Provisional Government "according to the opinions of the public and political organizations", and the list of its members was officially promulgated via *Vestnik Vremennogo Pravitel'stva.* The scope of the Soviet's competence included discussion of the two types of legal drafts – those submitted by the Provisional Government and those created upon the initiative of the Soviet itself. Therefore, it combined legal advisory function with legal initiative function. The Ministers were not accountable to the Soviet and could delegate their deputies to attend the sittings of the Soviet. The carefully elaborated mechanism of exchange of inquiries between the members of the Soviet and the Provisional Government was characterized by certain bureaucratic formalization. Thus, there was undoubtedly some rational idea of achieving a social consensus in society, for the concept even received certain institutional manifestation. Pre-parliament started its work; however, coordinated solutions of the most acute problems of internal and external politics were never taken.

In the course of subsequent preparation for the Constituent Assembly convocation, the contractual model of Russian constitutionalism was developed along the following lines: firstly, transition from the concept of nationality to that of citizenship, and creation of the legal base for the universal suffrage; secondly, solution of the problem of federalism and centralization, and discussion of the rights of ethnic minorities in this regard; and, thirdly, devising the mechanisms of separation of powers, mainly legislative and executive. All three areas of work reflected in the sources of law (legislative drafts) allow one to characterize the nature of the planned constituent as an institution aimed not only at solving the problems accumulated, but also at establishing the new legitimate power supported by the population.

4 Nominal constitutionalism under Soviet dictatorship

Soviet constitutionalism, which is, on the one hand, a historical continuity in relation to the sham constitutionalism of the preceding period of time and, on the other, a quite different, qualitatively new political phenomenon, merits a special consideration within the frameworks of this study. Characteristic of it is a new way of power legitimation (which is now of a "revolutionary", "popular" and "Jacobinic" character) and at the same time much tougher (compared to the preceding monarchic phase) authoritarian forms of government (in the form of dictatorship of proletariat, the party and the leader). In none of the preceding forms of sham constitutionalism did the conflict between liberal norms and absolutist reality achieve such a huge dimension: there, the point was more of a certain prevalence of monarchical institutions over representative ones but not of negation of the latter. Under a communist dictatorship we witness a unique combination of declaration of constitutional guarantees, an outright negation of law and of constitution in particular as a means of regulating relationships between the state and society. Law under the circumstances loses its separate value turning into a form of ideological education and coercion. It is no accident that all idiocratic regimes have so persistently opposed Kelsen's theory, who was a proponent of a "pure doctrine of law", that is its perception as independent of any philosophical interpretation.[1]

The main distinguishing characteristic of this type of constitutionalism and power organization is the gap between the reality of communist dictatorship and the written constitution, taken to its extremes. Therefore, Soviet Constitutions were hard to analyse with traditional legal tools. Explorers of European constitutionalism suggested classifying all Soviet-type constitutions (in countries of people's democracy) into a specific variety of legal acts, negating the entire philosophy, the internal logic and practice of genuine constitutionalism.[2]

A theoretical underpinning and a legitimizing formula of Soviet regime, as well as of its analogues in other countries, came to be the concept of Marx, Engels and Lenin on dictatorship of proletariat as a form of state under transition from capitalism to socialism. A thesis of dictatorship of proletariat was first advanced by Marx. Researchers note, however, a deliberate inscrutability and uncertainty of his interpretation of this concept (largely developed in the course of polemics with Blanquists). Its original interpretation, therefore, more likely corresponds with the perception of dictatorship as a system of class domination rather than a form of government.[3] For Lenin and subsequent Soviet law, the concept of dictatorship of proletariat came to be the key conclusion of Marxism. What is more, it began to be perceived in quite a specific manner. It is already interpreted not so much class domination as a form of government, a political regime meeting all formal attributes of dictatorship. While its original interpretation did not negate, in theory, parliamentarianism and a multiparty system, then in Lenin's interpretation dictatorship of proletariat became identical with the regime of one-party dictatorship ruling out any political pluralism. In this interpretation, dictatorship of proletariat turned to be quite close to its Jacobinic prototype as well as to the traditions of Blanquism and of Russian populism (of Narodniks).[4] In other words, dictatorship of proletariat, formerly an abstract Marxist philosophical principle, turned into a practical theory of seizure and use of power by revolutionary elite in a backward modernizing society. The very concept of law (and justice) acquired a new modification in this system. The theory of socialist law treats it not as an absolute value but rather as a body of rules, laid down by society and dependent upon it. Accordingly, law acts exclusively as a component of superstructure (along with politics, religion, morals) which, on the one hand, is a reflection of socio-economic relations and, on the other, a tool of the ruling class for consolidation of its power (in particular, of the working class and the party, expressing its will). The key task of law in socialist society comes down to the creation and consolidation of new social conditions and relations: law is a tool of class struggle, and serves for implementation of political decisions; legislation and the application of laws are guided by political expediency, politics gains precedence over law; law defends, in the first place, collective communities rather than individuals; individual rights are recognized insofar as they are not in conflict with cooperative social interests determined by the party.[5] These specifics of the Soviet interpretation of law were exposed in emigration literature.[6]

A number of phases are discernible in the legal doctrine of the Soviet regime, which in principle reflect its consolidation – an outright negation of law, permissibility as a sort of substitute and, finally, justification of a specific "class law". The starting phase is represented by the ideas of direct abolition (or "withering away") of law and by suggestions to liquidate the very notion of it (as counter-revolutionary), its comparison with a devolved "perpetual disease" (Petr I. Stuchka), its treatment as "opium for the people" (Alexandr G. Goihbarg),[7] a "fetish" (Eugeny B. Pashukanis) or, at best, warnings against a "boundless legalization of our system even on the basis of proletariat dictatorship" (Mikhail A. Reisner).

All of the above theories, somewhat differently treating social nature of law (as social psychology, manifestation of commodity-money relations, will of victorious class), agreed on one thing: negation of law as a universal means of regulation of social relations, its treatment as a temporary phenomenon. "Withering away of categories of bourgeois law" – stressed one of Bolshevist theoreticians – "will under the circumstances imply withering away of law as such, i.e. a gradual disappearance of legal aspect in human relations".[8] This nihilistic idea of law was first expressed in a theory of Mikhail Reisner, who argued for the determining nature of political struggle for the development of the so-called revolutionary self-consciousness of masses, which in turn served as a source of new class law replacing traditional (bourgeois) forms thereof.[9] According to this concept (whose main principle was borrowed from Lev I. Petrazhitsky, a pre-revolutionary liberal scholar, but transformed into its antithesis) law is treated as an intuitive idea of social justice, and its development in revolutionary conditions proceeds from subjective individual law to class law, and on to common law. In attempting to overcome the class character of "bourgeois" law, this theory pushed to the fore people's sense of justice by restoring components of traditional common law, which in Russia's environments could be nothing more than anarchic ideas of peasants and lumpen urban segments. In fact, this implied not only renunciation of objectivity of law and its regulating role in society, but destruction of the very foundation of legal culture trampled by ignorant revolutionary crowds.

Consolidation of dictatorship necessitated a more explicit and dogmatic interpretation of law. In so doing it was necessary, on the one hand, to do away with the legal vacuum and chaos of laws engendered by the cancellation of the entire previous law in the course of power seizure and, on the other, creation of a new, stronger punitive legal doctrine legitimizing and strengthening the one-party regime. Under the circumstances, the uncertain and polysemantic (especially in NEP – New Economic Policy – conditions) psychological concept of Soviet law gives way to the official doctrine of "proletarian law". Recognized as bourgeois and counter-revolutionary, the concept of legal awareness (implicitly containing notions of natural law and justice) is replaced with the principle of class domination and interest. The problem was solved by borrowing the concept of law as a way of social relations and social protection, accepted in liberal jurisprudence (Sergey A. Muromtsev) and by "class transformation of this formula to the benefit of Bolshevist dictatorship". As a result, it gained a quite opposite meaning, for the point was already of an anti-legal order and its protection from all dissidents. This nihilistic interpretation of law was quite candidly formulated by Petr I. Stuchka, people's commissar of justice.[10]

Worth noting is an objective gap between the real social contents and the legal form (including the entire political and legal system) which is bridged with the metaphysical concept of class nature of law. Under revolutionary modernization, law acted not so much as the function of legal assistance as ideological mobilization and coercion, hence was rendered a repressive character (virtually, the principle of "club rule" – "rule means force" – is revived). This process has objectively ended up with restoration of the principles of absolutism – a political or "regular" state with an all-embracing legal regulation of social relations. Under the new circumstances, this meant, however, a qualitatively new phase of totalitarian state.

Given the establishment of totalitarian dictatorship, law performs two main functions: legitimation of the regime and suppression of its opponents (both real and potential). This relates to a significant modification of the Marxist legal doctrine – renunciation of the previous thesis of "withering away" of law, justification of the new system of authoritarian state, and a much bigger punitive role of law. All of these changes have largely led to evolvement of the so-called "theory of Soviet state and law", which has prevailed throughout Stalin's period, and the most essential aspects of it continued into the future. The main practical purpose of this doctrine was legal justification of the party course towards "top-down revolution": running collectivization and industrialization associated with mass repressions, primarily annihilation of the old Lenin party and state elite (in the course of political processes in the 1930s) and highlighting the personal power of the leader. Subsequently, yet another purpose of this doctrine was the support of the ideological turn from the idea of global revolution to the idea of "Soviet patriotism", which turned into the main argument in the foreign policy of the state. This legal doctrine was most fully justified by Andrey Ya. Vyshinsky, whose writings served as an official programme of law reorganization.

The entire preceding legal doctrine is rejected not in parts but rather as a holistic outlook and the practical codification of individual branches of law. The main flaw of these doctrines for Stalin's regime consisted in the negation of an active role of law as a tool of unification, mobilization, modernization of society, and justification of the inevitably repressive role of the state. Indeed, these tasks are not related with the problems of "withering away", on the contrary, "with the necessity of using law and state, hence, with the necessity of reinforcing law and state".

The constitution of socialist state formerly assigns rights to citizens, defines society/state relations, structure of state power, sets prerogatives of public agencies. All these rules prove to be a fiction, however. The purpose of this constitution is not so much consolidation of legal system as performance of propagandistic and policy functions – disavowal of real power, fixing the stages of progressing towards communism, and advancing perspective political targets. Really operational, therefore, is only one constitutional norm – that of political monopoly and leading role of the party, which is above the law. This implies a number of fundamental conclusions: firstly, party resolutions and directives are not bound up by law, but create law themselves, and, secondly, all state bodies shall pursue party goals irrespective of their conformity with constitutional norms. This construction reproduces, in a new form, the monarchic principle of octroyed constitutions of the past taking the monarch out of social control and making the monarch the only source and guarantor of constitution. The issue of continuity in Soviet constitutionalism, in contrast to other constitutional systems, is also handled in a specific manner. It would be wrong to speak of the continuity of really functioning norms, but sooner of legal declarations. It would be right to state, in this sense, that the entire Soviet constitutionalism is based on the Jacobinic theory of "functioning parliament", treating the supreme representative assembly as the supreme power body. Accordingly, all Soviet Constitutions rejected the principle of separation of powers, and the constitutional boundary between legislative and executive powers was not clearly drawn. It is sooner the reverse that holds, and it would be right to speak of a purposeful convergence of the two types of power into a single administrative system under which legislative power makes its decisions directly through executive power bodies, thereby turning out to be functionally dependent upon them.

The sources of the system of nominal constitutionalism are to be found in the relations of the Soviets and the party. February revolution (on 27 February) gave rise to a specific form of government – a diarchy, which was in existence up to the establishment of the Bolshevist dictatorship (on 25 October 1917). In outward appearance, the dual power first looked like a balance of two branches of government – the legislative power was represented by the Soviet, and the executive one by the interim government. Remarkably, many people, such as for example Sukhanov, believed that this system of supreme power bodies would continue into the future.[11] As a matter of fact, the two institutions were in deep conflict emanating from the differences in their social nature, organization and political orientation. It was generally accepted that this conflict was to be resolved by the supreme legislative body – the Constituent Assembly. Its convocation, for the first time after the overthrow of monarchy, opened up a way to a legitimate resolution of the constitutional issue. Being fully aware of the fact that they would be unable to receive a power mandate from the Constituent Assembly (for the bulk of the electorate – peasants – would vote for socialists-revolutionaries) the Bolsheviks preferred to forestall its convocation with a coup d'etat. In this case they were faced, however, with an acute problem of power legitimation. An ideal method for its resolution came to be a convocation of the Congress of Soviets which, due to its organizational amorphism and dependence on Bolsheviks, permitted them to gain advantages. The fact that they treated the Congress as an auxiliary means too is best illustrated by the discussion (between Lenin and Trotsky) on whether it would be worth waiting for the seizure of power until the convocation of the Congress, or whether it was necessary to present it with the power takeover by Bolsheviks as a fait accompli. If first it was suggested to limit its agenda to drafting legislative proposals for the Constituent Assembly, then later the main function of the Congress turned into authorization of power transfer to Bolsheviks. By making use of the Soviets for legitimation of power seizure, Bolsheviks have tended to use this mechanism, thereafter, as a basis for the entire system of nominal constitutionalism.

After the October coup, the organization of political system suggested several basic alternatives such as dilution of the party in the government; transfer of government functions to the party; preservation of the party and government as autonomous structures and execution of administration functions, without government or through it, by party leaders taking up top posts in the executive branch. In reality, the latter option prevailed: the party and the state retained autonomy by uniting at the level of staff of executive power bodies. This system allowed Bolsheviks to make political decisions within the frameworks of the party and then implement them through the network of public institutions. As is well shown in modern literature, this model of political system happened to be the most original invention of Bolsheviks and was used by all subsequent one-party dictatorships irrespective of their political orientation. This is explained by its huge efficiency in terms of concentration of legislative, executive and judicial power through centralized distribution of posts within the frameworks of a single non-governmental organization – the ruling party. The historical prototype of this organization of power are Jacobinic clubs in the era of French Revolution which, while not merging with government bodies, practically overrode the government (by strict internal discipline, voting by consensus, allocation of key posts in state machinery). The subsequent variations are totalitarian one-party fascist-type dictatorships.

Reconstruction of the key phases of nominal constitutionalism evolution, unlike that of the real mechanism of power (which is thoroughly concealed), is not very difficult for the researcher. It is precisely by virtue of its affectation, declarative nature and even forced imposition from above, Soviet nominal constitutionalism is rather explicitly represented by distinct phases, whose boundaries are marked by five constitutions of 1918, 1924, 1936, 1977 and, finally, 1993. Of course, all of these (save the last version) are not so much legal as primarily ideological monuments. The shared feature thereof is, according to the jurist, "falsification of political and state reality" – "concentration of unlimited political power in the top party and political machinery (nomenclature, partocracy)". The specific nature of nominal constitutionalism (as of the whole law of totalitarian states), however, is precisely the practical impossibility of differentiating law and ideology. In analysing, it is therefore useless to proceed from the formally legal logic of the documents as such, as is frequently done in analysing real legal documents. It is more important to fix the relationship of some or other declarations with actual changes in power structures and political interests. In so doing, the changes in configuration of public institutions – trends in their merger and separation, reshuffle, written regulation of their functioning – can well serve as a point of departure. This analysis will be helpful, in particular, for understanding as to how the ruling elite itself defined its achievements and goals, what it deemed to be the main obstacles to their accomplishment. We find this approach also rather promising for understanding the latent springs of the political regime, whose effects were, voluntarily or not, reflected in laws and trends in their development. Hence, the setting of the problem of law and power balance, as the gap between them reaches a qualitatively new level in the given political system, converting the very constitutional law from power restriction into the tool of its social policy – a means of society modernization or conservation of the existing relations.

The reviewed specifics of socialist constitutionalism manifest themselves, on the whole, rather clearly in all Soviet Constitutions. The first of these, the Constitution of 10 July 1918, does not disclose the real structure of power at all. By declaring the Soviets the key institutions of power, it describes their hierarchy from the local level to the topmost one – the All-Russian Congress of Soviets. The latter is proclaimed the supreme body of legislative power. In-between the congresses, the decisive role is played by their executive body – Central Executive Committee (CEC), formally appointing and controlling the supreme body of executive power – Council of People's Commissars (CPC). In fact, however, the 1918 Constitution was a camouflage of real power. Despite the fact that the party controlled the supreme bodies of legislative and executive power (Sverdlov – CEC chairman, and Lenin – CPC head), the party elite did not treat them as bodies of real power. It was concentrated in the party machinery using "constitutional" state institutions and public organizations for pursuing their policy. This line was fixed in the resolutions of the eighth party congress (convened in March 1919) urging the communist party to preserve an indivisible political domination in the Soviets and supervise all of their activities in practice. It is no accident that Lenin, generally not inclined to absolutize the significance of legal institutions, paid much attention to this side of Soviet constitutionalism.[12]

The main contradiction of the entire Soviet constitutionalism, which was apparent in the very first Constitution of 1918, is a desire to justify, in legal terms, the anti-legal phenomenon – "dictatorship of proletariat". This placed demand on a special concept of this dictatorship called to prove its fundamental distinction from all other historical forms of dictatorship. The main components of this concept happened to be, firstly, a paradoxical thesis on that this dictatorship is the supreme form of democracy, secondly, the idea of its depersonalized ("class") character, and, thirdly, limitation of its existence by definite historical limits of transition period. Nevertheless, the phantom of Bonapartism, wandering in the heads of witnesses of dispersal of the Constituent Assembly, never left the regime ideologists in peace. Doubts mounted even more upon comparison of the RSFSR 1918 Constitution with its historical analogues – a brief draft organization of 1871 Commune of Paris, which it didn't have time to implement, and the 1793 French Constitution (Convent), which was never put into practice. In all those cases, the constitution either was not operational at all, or its principles were viewed as pure declarations, which could not be implemented under civil war. As a result, according to Stuchka, rather widespread is an opinion that "dictatorship somewhat poorly accords with the words 'written law' ".

This evolution is not due to "degeneration" of a revolutionary elite but is an objective result of renunciation of the principles of civil society and law-based state, which took hold in pre-war Russia to some extent. The renunciation of all known forms of social checks on power takes Russia back to the system of military-service state, where violence was the main method of social administration, and bureaucracy a tool for its implementation.

The model of exporting agrarian revolution (which can be defined as a project of the Communist International (Comintern)) is nothing more than an attempt to compensate the lack of a positive strategy of transformation of agrarian relations with dissemination of their extensive form to other countries. The main strategies of solving agrarian issues through revolution and reform vary. The choice between the two strategies is dependent, however, not only on internal but also on external – geopolitical – factors. In this context, of interest no doubt is an agrarian model, which is associated with the transfer of conflict to the outside world. In world history, the agrarian issue was frequently solved precisely in this way – by moving the excessive agricultural population out by colonizing new territories; by economic emigration of the new poor to colonies (Great Britain); beginning of military expansion especially in the wake of intensive internal social upheavals (e.g. Napoleonic wars). These processes became particularly visible along with the growth of global population and transition from traditional agrarian society to industrial society on global scale in modern and recent times. Though the processes of human migration were known in ancient history too, they came to be especially destructive in recent times (during World Wars). Some researchers justifiably point to agrarian overpopulation, emergence of new poverty and intensification of migratory streams as the basic social causes of destructive movements in the globalization era.

The problem of arable land scarcity with the population growth (the so-called shortage of land or even "land hunger"), which was named as the main cause of agrarian revolution of 1905, could in principle be resolved in two ways. The first one involves transition to a commercial agricultural land use. The advantages of this way (realized in England in the sixteenth century) included concentration of land resources, transition to intensive farming and accumulation of capital in industry. The drawback boiled down to emergence of considerable "excessive" population making up a source for mass protest movements.

The other way suggested a traditional solution of the problem: collectivization of land and a new equalizing redistribution thereof (as part of a "socialization" programme). The advantage of this other way consisted in conservation of temporary social stability in post-revolution period. The obvious flaw comes to an extreme irrationality and inefficiency of this way of farming (continuously reproducing the problem of land shortage on a new level). While giving one-off advantages, this way no doubt led, for the long-term perspective, to stagnation and turned out to be the loser.

A way out of the impasse could be found only in forcible spreading of this solution of the agrarian issue on a global scale. That was precisely the Comintern aim in the post-revolution period. It should be treated as an independent and quite clearly defined way of handling the agrarian issue. Only now does it become possible to reconstruct the key parameters of this project, following the opening of Comintern archives, in particular, those of its analytical centres such as "International Agrarian Institute", "Chinese Commission", etc., which secretly formulated the real strategy of revolution expansion.

This direction of research involves an analysis of agrarian revolution theory as a branch of modern science; review of the key parameters of this theory in a post-revolution period; interpretation of the agrarian issue by Comintern theoreticians; reconstruction of debates on the ways of implementing the agrarian revolution project; identification of the reasons behind the changes in strategy and tactics, as well as the general historical failure of the entire project. The conducted analysis points to existence in Soviet Russia of a coherent plan of handling the agrarian issue through the expansion of revolution. The genuine concept of the world or permanent revolution, advanced by Marx, not only contained any idea of agrarian revolution but was sooner its antithesis. As far as classical Marxism is concerned, solution of the fundamental social conflict of the new time was feasible through victory of proletarian revolutions in the most industrially developed countries. The historical paradox was that the revolutions, staged on behalf of Marxism, were victorious (or gained the greatest momentum) precisely in the most backward countries, having a traditional agrarian society by the beginning of revolutions.

It is Leninism, first formulating the idea of using agrarian revolution for power seizure, which served as a theoretical formula for generalizing this social practice. This theory was the first to generalize the experience of the Russian agrarian revolution of 1905–1907. The theory suggested, in effect, it use the movement of ignorant peasant masses, dissatisfied with their new situation, for overthrowing the existing political system and establishing a one-party dictatorship.

The concept of world revolution, which Comintern assumed as a basis of its activities, has also undergone a drastic transformation. The conflict of two directions (industrial and agrarian trends) was a manifestation of different ideas of progress strategy. The victory of "agrarian" strategy (after the failure of revolution in the West) meant shifting the focus to exploiting the ignorance of the masses in the traditional agrarian society with a view to directing the powerful destructive potential of agrarian revolutions against the leading industrial powers.

The complexity of the situation was due to the failure of solving the agrarian issue in post-revolutionary Russia. The Comintern counted on agrarian revolution precisely at the time of a powerful peasant movement within the country. Hence, a significant importance was attached to debates on the problem. The debates were held at a high professional level with a maximum mobilization of all the then accessible information (primarily coming directly from different countries). Though they were ideologically pointed, but subject to discussion were real problems.

Particular attention was given to the issue of whether the Bolshevik strategy at the time of Russian revolution of 1905–1907 is suitable for analogous coups in other agrarian countries from Mexico to China. The problem setting served as an incentive for the study of social structure of eastern societies, atypical property relations and power in them (Asian mode of production), and the main thing was the search for the mobile social element, which could (given weakness of cities) be used as a tool for power seizure.

The key parameters of the given plan were as follows: preparation of peasant uprisings through a targeted campaign; establishment of peasant unions under control of the party for mobilization purposes; use of lumpen elements in cities. It is the ideas of black redistribution (equalization-distribution model) that served as integrating slogans. This was, in fact, an attempt at exporting the Russian agrarian revolution model (whose real features were not fully understood, hence described in terms of French and other European revolutions).

The failure of this programme in the considered period of time was explained by the inapplicability of the Russian model in eastern countries (underdeveloped communications, weakness of cities, management decentralization, actual absence of uniform public administration and role of the army). No account was taken of the religious and nationalistic concepts of the peasantry. Only a due account of these specifics could produce the expected result (as the subsequent history of the twentieth century demonstrates).

The ruin of this paradigm of the agrarian issue solution in the considered period of time had not only external but also internal implications. The impossibility of imposing the programme of equalizing redistribution of land on other countries resulted, in turn, in its renunciation within this country: a transition to revival of a modified model of a liturgical state in new environments. Realization of this idea in the course of collectivization and accelerated industrialization became possible only given land alienation from producers and creation of a powerful layer of agrarian nomenclature.

Decisive for defining the ways of Soviet constitutional doctrine development was an issue of party/state balance within the system of dictatorship of proletariat. By discarding the theories of national (popular) sovereignty and separation of powers, the Soviet legal doctrine replaced them with the principle of class sovereignty.

Operating from the position of class will, the constitutional development of democratic nations in Western Europe was rejected, and the institute of presidency of the third republic in France or Weimar Germany was perceived as a mere substitute of monarchic power and a premise for fascist regimes of Mussolini, Pilsudski and Kemal, which were the case in point in the 1920s. In this respect, it shared the forecast of several European theoreticians treating parliamentarianism as an obsolescent institute no longer reflecting the real balance of forces in modern society. Quite natural, in this connection, is the interest in management theory, Taylorism and the rationalization concept. The relationship of the rationalization and bureaucratization process, described by Max Weber, is used by Soviet (Petr Stuchka) and later by the Nazi politico-legal theory (Carl Schmitt) as an important argument against parliamentarianism in general. For them "even the modern bourgeois democrats, for example Professor Max Weber, candidly recognize that, of course, a real supremacy in the modern state manifests itself not in parliamentary debates or monarch messages but in real rule".[13] This supremacy is in the hands of a special privileged caste – the officialdom, whose organization is a function of "the scale of modernization of the given state". However, the conclusion of this theory, that "future belongs to bureaucracy", was not at all treated as a warning to the Soviet political system. The comparison of Weber and Lenin's views on bureaucracy and prospects of its development, undertaken in Soviet literature, perfectly exposes the differences between them, sometimes coming to extremes.

The process of party bureaucratization could not help touching upon the Soviets – declarative power bodies, whose constitutionally fixed structure corresponded to that of party organs and intertwined with them. Developed after the October coup, Soviet bureaucracy became a result of a fusion of two trends: bureaucratization from the top (in a descending line), which was a means of spreading power of the new institutions to social structure of the disintegrating traditional society; and bottom-up bureaucratization (in the line of ascent) – manifesting itself in the strife of the new low-level institutions towards consolidation and survival. Modern literature exposed the linkage of Soviet bureaucratization with the agrarian revolution and the policy of war communism. They led to a legal vacuum, uncontrolled redistribution of landed property and, as a consequence, to the restoration of power of traditional institutions of social regulation, i.e. commune and peasants' community. For accomplishing their goals at the stage of war communism, the new institutions (Soviets, committees of the poor and food detachments) were forced to rely on these structures, being connected to them to a considerable extent. This explains the traditionalism of the system of Soviets, its peasant character, tunnel social vision confined by purely distributive and control-repressive functions and, finally, the ease of its manipulation on the part of external, and much better organized force – urban party bureaucracy. The strength of the Bolsheviks compared to other parties (primarily socialist-revolutionary) was their superior organization and ability to create their social basis by making use, to this end, of the traditional, pre-capitalist elements (peasants' community) as well as new ones engendered by capitalist development, namely urban proletariat and raznochinets. These two trends could only briefly fuse in the party nomenclature as a specific organizational layer at the time of civil war. The inevitable conflict of traditional agrarian institutes and the new political and administrative structures made their division unavoidable under modernization, and turned the Soviets into a battlefield of the two opposite trends. The new management layer emerging at the intersection of these two trends has, therefore, integrated several highly heterogeneous social segments. According to Mark Ferro, these were: members of committees and Soviets (primarily urban workers and soldiers); Red Guards (peasants, soldiers and activists of the committees of the poor); civil and military administration of the old regime (civil servants, officers, intelligentsia) siding with the Bolsheviks; and old Bolshevik Guards of professional revolutionaries, as well as bureaucracy of national regions. The development of the system of Soviets resulted in coming to the fore of representatives of lower classes (largely of worker-peasant origin) and actual exclusion of representatives of higher classes, whose lifestyle and education made them socially alien elements.[14] The predominance of the peasant element with their intrinsically peasant psychology and behavioural traditions left an imprint on the new Soviet bureaucracy. It became more conservative, oriented at values such as collectivism, family, power. The new segment of promoted individuals, actively striving towards power, were not satisfied with its slow and gradual acquisition, hence, the deliberate necessity of liquidating the existing ruling group – Leninist revolutionary vanguard. Consolidation of the new Soviet bureaucracy served as a social basis of Stalinism. Bureaucratization of Soviets became a linear trend in the development of the Soviet regime.

Following the disintegration of the Russian empire and growth of nationalism, the key problem turned out to be the constitutional solution of national issue, which was possible on theoretically mutually exclusive principles of federalism and autonomic development. The former (advanced by Lenin) was convenient at the time of power seizure and its retention, for this made it possible to use nationalistic movements for destabilizing the old power and thereafter for consolidation of social basis of the new regime in localities. The latter (advanced by Stalin) was to a greater extent consistent with the Marxist ideological aim towards denationalization and creation of a unitary state some time in the future. Hence, the struggle of the two concepts in Bolshevist leadership was soon of a tactical nature and was overcome at the first signs of strengthening of the dictatorship. The decision was found within the general framework of nominal constitutionalism: while formally consolidating the federal principle (the 1924 Constitution) the party, in reality, was pursuing the course towards a persistent curtailing of the rights of republics and transformation thereof into autonomies. The constitution was drafted in several steps and identified different positions. The adoption of the new constitution, just like of the preceding one, was carried out on party's decision and legitimized by the decision of the First Congress of Soviets, which endorsed policy documents, namely, a "Declaration" and a "Treaty on Formation of the USSR". It is worth noting that these documents were not subject to preliminary legal scrutiny and, which most importantly, were not agreed upon with the republics. This task was assigned to a special CEC commission (which started its activities on 3 February 1923) whose job was to agree the interests of individual republics and the centre. This issue was predetermined, however, by the twelfth party congress (in April 1923), which adopted a relevant resolution, on Stalin's presentation – on creation, within the union CEC, of two chambers, one of which would be elected at the union congress of Soviets, irrespective of nationalities, and the other by the republics but would be approved by the same congress. Note that the very construct of union power organization implied revision of the terms of the "Treaty on Formation of the USSR", for it envisaged a one-chamber structure of the supreme power body – CEC – rather than two-chamber one. It had to be elected at the congress from representatives of union republics in proportion to the population strength in each one of them. The other major body – CEC presidium – had to be made up of representatives from four major republics. Thus the "Treaty" proceeded from the consideration of CEC as the supreme guarantor of rights of nationalities, thereby setting it off against the congress (elected by purely territorial principle) and the government (CPC) referred to as an "executive body of CEC". The Treaty also provided for "suspension" of the central government's decisions by republican CEC and their presidiums, true, "only in exceptional cases". This was, probably, due to the influence of western samples of federal government organization in the form of a special chamber of parliament (primarily of the Weimar Constitution, where the upper chamber was the seat of representatives of individual lands). In any case, this structure emanated from the general desire for the "Declaration" and "Treaty" to persistently realize the principle of a "voluntary unification of equitable peoples", a federative (rather than unitary) state, defending it from the claims of both legislative (congress) and executive (CPC) branches of power. The party congress formula of the two-chamber

CEC, with both chambers enjoying equal rights, came to be an antithesis to this. This formula was deeply thought through: while formally the power structure reflected not only class interests but "purely national demands" too, in reality it hugely minimized their influence on decision-making process (for the final word owed to the congress, which was frequently a decorative entity). Thus, given a formal observation of a federative form of unification, a unitary state model was realized in practice.

In considering the 1924 Constitution from a general historical perspective of nominal constitutionalism, it should be recognized that it played a major role in integrating the disintegrated tsar empire into a new type of unitary state. The ideas of regional separatism and nationalism (born by local party and state elite) were opposed by a concept of strong central power having supranational character. Accordingly, its adoption promoted revival, in a new form, of patriarchal monarchic ideas, objectively leading to consolidation of despotic power. By expressing this trend the constitution failed, however, to complete it. In handling the issues of federative structure of the Union, it (in contrast to the subsequent ones) did not regulate competences of republican and local governments, authorizing supreme bodies of union republics to solve these issues. They were modelled on the centre and represented by a cumbersome structure of congresses – CEC – presidiums. The function of main conductors of central influence in localities was performed precisely by the latter institutions – republican presidiums – the supreme standing power bodies (in-between CEC sessions which, due to their huge membership and transient nature of functioning were unable to effectively oppose central directives). Against this background, rather illustrative is endorsement, after the adoption of the constitution, of several fundamental laws as a follow up. The most important of these were Provisions on CEC USSR and CPC laying down the relationships between them via the new power institution – presidium, whose prerogatives kept on continuously increasing (up to issuing new decrees, amendments to the budget and imposition of new taxes), as well as their relations with the republican power bodies. The constitution, however, testified to the uncompleted process of integration and totalization of control, for the remainder of the issues, linked to organization and authority of central and local republican bodies, were placed under the discretion of republican legislatures. Accordingly, gaining momentum is a process of purposeful limitation of a republics' sovereignty by determining the prerogatives of their supreme power bodies as of subjects of the Union, as well as specification of the nature of their relations with central (All-Union) power bodies.[15] This failure to complete the process of power and control centralization in this country explains both the general direction of constitutional changes towards unification of law and centralization of power and the scale of repressions at later times, resulting in virtual destruction of all previous regional elites opposing the unlimited power of the centre. The role of a formally independent judge in solving these issues is played by Soviet and party authorities. By denouncing, from tactical considerations, the concept of a "uniform and indivisible" Russian empire they, in fact, pursue a course towards its restoration in a new form. For the first time the attention to this was drawn in the Russian émigré literature, which appreciated the process of restoration of the uniform state.

The total integration and absorbing of huge and diverse regions in a uniform state were possible only given a special supercentre possessing monopoly on the interpretation of national interests. These functions could not be performed by public bodies of one republic or a mechanical assembly of their representatives but only by a new supranational and suprastate union possessing a number of political and legal characteristics such as sovereignty, might, infallibility, unity of will. In other words, there was need for a charismatic power embodied in the party and leader.

In studying an authoritarian political regime, it is always very important to identify the relationship between the formal (constitutional) and informal (real) power structures. It is precisely this approach that makes it possible to lay bare the mechanism of power and decision making, on the one hand, and functions of constitutional institutions, on the other. A simple comparison thereof, quite appropriate for clearness, fails to fully explain the phenomenon such as integrity and totality of the whole system. They speak of parallelism of the two systems – nominal and real, of taking the real power out of legal control, or of placing it above constitution. This phenomenon is characteristic, to some or other extent, of all authoritarian regimes of modern and recent times, yet it has different manifestations, which can be exposed given the identification of regime typologies with regard to legitimation formula and the exercise of power in them.[16] Sociological interpretation of this fact, as applied to Soviet dictatorship, is largely dependent upon the general concept of Stalinism. At present, literature deals with three main directions. Firstly, Stalinism is viewed as a classical version of totalitarianism with all the key features inherent in it. As applied to it, the gap between the constitutional forms and real administrative practice is one of the manifestations of formal and real power structures which, however, do not contradict but sooner complement one another for a fuller control of society. This concept has its weakness, namely, it explains this phenomenon only in its final, static form paying no adequate attention to the process of its evolution. Yet, several basic phases are identified relative to Stalinism – its consolidation, revolutionary reforms from the top, and subsequent (post-war) conservative phase. Note that each one experiences the change of ideology and no changes in power regime. The degree of totalization of control over society also undergoes transformation, peaking only upon liquidation of opposition. The other concept explains Stalinism proceeding from the theory of modernization of traditional agrarian society. It treats it as a part of the uniform revolutionary process evolving in Russian society up to the late 1930s. This concept focuses on the system dynamics, Stalinism continuity in relation to a Lenin system. It stresses the conflict between the traditional agrarian society and the industrialization objectives, which is resolved in the form of a specific mobilization political system (whose characteristic components are Soviets and party). The modernization concept tackles the issue of alternative development of the regime, which began to take shape following the rejection of war communism and introduction of the new economic policy, in favour of the objective inevitability of Stalinist revolution from above (collectivization and industrialization manifest in the one-party dictatorship). The third concept, which can be referred to as traditionalistic, proceeds from an assumption that the Soviet regime is a logical extension of the preceding Russian monarchic order, therefore it borrowed many of its essential specifics relative to power organization. One of the distinguishing characteristics is the unlawful nature of social regulation. Many specific features of Soviet authoritarianism are explained in this manner. As for the constitution itself, the system is defined as negation of written law and a turning back to common or conventional law, to a primitive system of "unwritten rules" – behavioural incentives and bans at a subconsciousness level. Accordingly, gaining special significance are informal and frequently irrational methods of functioning orientation in the political system (like the so-called "state machinery law", "telephone law", reading between the lines, etc.). The system not only tolerates these phenomena but legitimizes them by hammering a number of stereotypic attitudes and myths into public consciousness.

On closer examination it turns out, however, that the three reviewed approaches not only contradict but complement one another. They permit the definition of Stalinism as a specific form of totalitarianism evolving and functioning under modernization and resting upon traditional components of Russian monarchic political culture.

Stalinism can be defined as a qualitatively new political system, whose main features are a specific legitimation of regime, a set of national policy goals, mechanisms of power and administration and a style of governance tinted by the dictator's will.[17] In defiance of constitution, the real mechanisms used for exercising power in this political system are rooted not in declarative public authorities but, primarily, in the party machinery. The ruling party organs, established in March 1919, were the five-men strong Political Bureau (Politburo, concerned with main political issues), Organizational Bureau or Orgburo, also five-men strong, engaged in managing party organizations, and a six-men strong Secretariat. The latter institution did not have any definite functions and reported, apparently, to other party organs. By 1944, Stalin added the position of general secretary of the party to Politburo and Orgburo membership. These fatal appointments, made with Lenin and his closest colleagues' consent, were aimed at relieving them from routine organizational work and providing opportunities for concentrating on major political decisions. They resulted from the general underestimation of the bureaucratic factor in modern policy (which was demonstrated above). The unique combination of the three major organizational positions gradually allowed Stalin to exert a decisive influence on the major appointments in the party and state machinery, virtually concentrating the issues of personnel reshuffle into his own hands, influence the advancement of new political initiatives, and act as an umpire in the disputes of political leaders. Within a short period of time, Stalin's secretariat managed to make new appointments of ministers, high military commanders, top party officials and, most importantly, local party figures all over the country. This created a decisive prerequisite for isolating opposition groups in the centre and their political destruction. Supervision of the local party machinery made it possible to exercise a purposeful selection when staffing the top party bodies. The power concentration process resulted in the creation of an informal group or a cabinet of personal assistants of the general secretary, later assigned an official status of "Secretariat of comrade Stalin". The essence of this structure and of its functions was revealed by Boris Bazhanov, Stalin's secretary, who managed to flee.[18]

In social terms, these transformations resulted in the evolvement of a new elite. As some of our special studies into several big reforms of modern and recent times revealed, the adoption of a course toward modernization and its pursuance inevitably imply a split of the elite of any traditional society into three groups: left-, right-wing and moderate (or swamp). The post-revolutionary Lenin elite, whose specifics enhanced this regularity even stronger, was no exception, for it turned out to be (as a result of power seizure in a peasant country) a vanguard deprived of deep social roots. Therefore, the split of the elite has manifested itself in this case in the most pure form, quite explicitly transforming, in institutional terms, into intra-party oppositions (which in different circumstances could serve as a foundation for a variety of modernization strategies and political parties) and tough methods of struggle, which had to result in the liquidation of opponents. The struggle took the form of intra-party purges accompanied by ideological campaigns in mass media. The final phase of this struggle was the annihilation of the entire previous elite and creation of a new one. The political processes in the 1930s (1934, 1937 and 1938) were aimed at depriving these groups of legitimacy within the frameworks of the existing political system and state ideology, hence, enhancing legitimacy of the new rulers.

The significance of the terror within the Stalinism system, which was an important tool of political struggle, gets increasingly clearer against this background. The prominent literature on terror revealed that it is generally an integral feature of totalitarianism, being perhaps a decisive premise for its existence. At the same time, this thesis does not in fact explain the distinguishing nature of Stalin terror which (compared to, say, Hitler's) was directed not only against political opponents but embraced, on an unprecedented wide scale, all strata of society and, in the final count, led to the replacement of the ruling elite. All members of Politburo of revolution time were crushed (except Stalin), 70 per cent of Central Committee members were elected at the "Congress of Victors" in 1934, as well as virtually all the delegates of this congress. Repressions also resulted in annihilation of one half of the army officer corps and virtually all of its high command formed in the course of the civil war.

The new elite differs from the old one by its social origin (mostly from peasantry and lower sections of the population), education (much lower), age (much younger) and social outlook. The main distinction, however, is somewhat different – the new elite was created by the power itself in the literal sense, i.e. thoroughly screened and shaped by the party machinery. It is an extremely homogeneous social layer, detached from society and set off against it, whose status, prestige and well-being are fully controlled by the power. All potential lines of interface with society, save those determined by the system, are blocked. The new elite, in a sense, hangs over society, having exterritorial status (its representatives freely move in geographical terms), exlevel (transference from periphery to the centre and back), exfunctional (they are capable of performing different functions in the party, state, military or police structures) and even timeless character (for the advanced technical facilities and creation of closed information space enable them to manipulate history, modifying it for the sake of the current tasks). The reverse side of this isolation from society is the elite dependence on the power. This control encompasses not only traditional areas of material well-being and career development but also the elite infrastructure: its lines of communication, information system, directions of social mobility and even manner of conduct and lifestyle. In fact, this elite exists as an integral whole only in the continuously dynamic relations with the supreme power, which becomes the supreme arbiter and a symbol of this social structure. It differs from the previous revolutionary vanguard primarily in its personal dependence on the head of this machinery, namely on the party and state leader. The successive modification of legitimizing principles of government, making one recall Polybius' teaching on the circulation of forms of government, becomes the manifestation of the concentration of power. In the classical terms of antique political thought, the democracy which replaced monarchy rapidly gives way to oligarchy of revolutionary leaders (for the Lenin period, the idea of collective leadership was still there); oligarchy, however, is generally replaced, because of its instability, with triumvirate (government of "Lenin's best disciples" at the time of interregnum) and, finally, this last form logically ends up with a tyranny – personal government not connected even with the moral laws, which distinguished monarchy. The circle closes in its original point – personal despotic power. It is legitimized by reorientation of ideology (from the concept of world revolution to the idea of building socialism in one country, and then on to "Soviet patriotism"), legal consolidation of the new system ("most democratic" constitution), and the main thing – cult of leader's personality.

According to contemporary researchers, Stalin's Constitution of 1936 adopted at the height of mass terror and entrenchment of the cult of personality was primarily designed for external use, in particular, for deceiving West European public opinion. None of the West European constitutions offered so many guarantees and rights. As fascism took hold in some European countries, it declared guarantees of all basic democratic rights of the individual; at the time of economic crisis – social security, guaranteed employment, equality of men and women in a social sphere; and given the rising nationalism – rights of the nation and of ethnic minorities. Finally, it is no accident that the adoption of the constitution coincided with the Moscow political processes: that was an attempt to divert the west's attention from the latter, to enlist the support of western democracies under the growing danger of fascism. At the same time, the constitution was designed for internal use too. It proclaimed a new era of revolution development: the end of class struggle in Russia, establishment of representative political institutions and extending political rights and social guarantees to all population (except disfranchised individuals – "enemies of the people"). As a price of these privileges, the constitution demanded from the people ("all Soviet people") total loyalty to the regime and an active struggle with its enemies. The very fact of power's declaration about the establishment of western-type political institutions and proclamation of a sort of "Bill of Rights" created an illusion that the regime evolves towards democratic principles. In the 1930s, it was much more difficult, than in the 1950s and 1970s, to conjecture that this conclusion was contrary to fact. An important characteristic of the 1936 Constitution was also the fact that it half-opened the real power mechanism, reflecting the general trends in its concentration. The constitution marked departure from the principle of class dictatorship towards a wider social base (which was declared to include all "working people", i.e. practically the entire population). In practice, this meant tougher social control on the part of the state, which proclaimed its inseparable unity with society (thereby turning into a total or totalitarian one in the literal sense of the term).

Russian émigré theoreticians accepted the concept of the Thermidor, treating it, however, not as negation of revolution but as its logical completion. For in understanding Stalin's regime, they deemed it reasonable to turn to the traditions of Russian state organization rather than to western dictators. Similarly to the explanation of revolution by analogy with the "Time of Troubles" in the seventeenth century, the establishment of Stalin's regime became a sort of analogy for the restoration of monarchy. Being staunch state supporters, they viewed the process as positive, even treating it as a basis for rapprochement with the Soviet power. They believed that it manifested itself in renunciation of the ideology of world revolution and transition to national development, destruction of Lenin's elite and creation of a new elite, expression of new principles of patriotism. A logical result of this rapprochement or even identification of a Soviet regime with a tsarist one, and of Stalin with Peter the Great (Milyukov's stance during World War II). Thus, the revolutionaries and liberals, while disagreeing in the assessment of social function of Stalinism, unanimously referred to it as Caesarism.

This definition is key to the interpretation of the Soviet Constitution of 1936. In analysing the mechanisms used by this regime for exercising power, Trotsky almost interprets it as totalitarian. He speaks of totalitarian dictatorship as a specific form of authoritarianism, totalitarian party and leader. The distinguishing characteristic of totalitarian dictatorship, compared to other forms of authoritarian dictatorship, comes to a total bureaucratic control of society. Its main consequence is barring any form of opposition. The struggle with oppositions acts as a major phase of consolidation of a dictatorial regime. From this perspective, consideration is given to the struggle with oppositions in the 1920s, which are viewed as phases of bureaucratic power consolidation. The wide-scale purges and political processes become the closing phase of this process. Hence, an explanation of the 1936 Constitution as a means of suppression of the opposition ideology.

Modern science advances different opinions on the nature of Stalin's power: some see it as a consequence of the general process of administration centralization in a totalitarian state, others treat it as a means of artificial maintenance of integrity of a multinational state devoid of organic unity, still others as a consequence of and the main lever for modernizing the country under foreign policy isolation. The concept of totalitarianism and modernization should be recognized as prevailing in modern western writings devoted to Stalinism. All point to the terror machine as the main tool of unification and concentration of power in the party and state. Much less attention is given to the 1936 Constitution as it failed to fix changes in the political system and real power relations. Indirectly, however, it reflected the principal of these, notably, entrenchment of Soviet Caesarism.

In order to understand the main constitutional ideas of the reform era in the 1960s, it is important to identify the main directions of political struggle. The common prerequisite thereof is recognition of inefficiency of the monolithic Stalin system and attempts at its modernization under new circumstances. This implied splitting of the Stalin elite into two groups: conservatives and reformers. In the focus of their political debates lay the attitude to Stalinism as a political system with concentration camps as its manifestation and, at the same time, structural foundation. Both groups were aware of the need for change, differing in the perception of their scale and ways of implementation. The conservatives proceeded from the possibility of gradual transformations initiated from the top, and reformers of fast changes, which ought to cover (though not modify drastically) the entire system. A legitimizing basis of the reform course was provided by the "criticism of the cult of personality" and return to the so-called "Lenin standards", which in this case implied denunciation of the system of mass terror, opening up of camps and some democratization of political life. The main weaknesses of the system were identified in the course of Khrushchev reforms. These were the economic inefficiencies of the centralized planned economy, which were expected to be rectified along the lines of a decentralization programme (alignment of the levels of development of industrial and agricultural sectors, institution of *sovnarkhozes* (regional economic councils) in 1957, stronger personal control of the head of state over local governments through central planning agencies); doing away with social apathy and inertia of society, where violence served as a major institute of social regulation (a programme of ideological destalinization, setting up party control over state security agencies, legal reform of 1958 restoring, in place of collective condemnation by social categories, an element of competitive legal procedure and individual verdict; education reform aimed at liquidation of the legacy of privileged status for entering a higher educational institution, gained through compulsory work); attempts at changing the role of the party in the political system (proclaiming the party in 1961 not only the vanguard but also the party of the whole people, i.e. of peasantry too). Also meriting attention in this connection are the attempts at party reforms, which were planned but not implemented in the Khrushchev era, engendering an especially violent opposition on the part of the party machinery. One of these was a system of regular renewal (rotation) of the party elite (limitation, with reservations though, of tenure on top posts in the Central Committee and Politburo). A much more radical measure came to be the division (in 1962) of the party apparatus into two parallel hierarchies in agriculture and industry. This reform was a consequence (and adjustment) of the preceding one, namely, decentralization of economic management (in *sovnarkhozes*) resulting in consolidation in localities and creation of regional and party lobbies there (forerunners of today's regional elites). The principle of separation of powers, which could not be implemented officially, given the continued political monopoly of the party, turned into purely functional regroupings along horizontal and vertical lines, changing the previous foundation of institutional elites. Finally, especially worth noting, is a populist style of Khrushchev leadership, who appealed to people directly, bypassing the party apparatus (being Gorbachev's predecessor in this respect). The compromise character of Khrushchev's reforms aggravated their inner weakness and led, in the final count, to the loss of wide social foundation by reformers. The objective implication of the reforms turned out to be reinforcement rather than weakening of power of the party apparatus. By abolishing terror as a means of social regulation within the party and its elite, the new leadership failed to create any other (legal) guarantees against power usurpation. Under the circumstances, the ruling layer – "nomenclature" – was the only layer enjoying power and property monopoly. Khrushchev's downfall, in October 1964, was caused by the elite's dissatisfaction with the then current course towards destalinization and debureaucratization of the system. However, prerequisites for the subsequent triumph of bureaucracy had been laid earlier, in part in the course of the reforms *per se*. There is, therefore, an apparent link between the establishment of the Constitutional Commission in 1962 (when Khrushchev was still sitting pretty) and the desire to legally fix the results of destalinization and certain trends in reforming the political system. Also, connected with this is, in the first place, the idea of separation of Soviet and party systems, which would play, at a later phase, a decisive role in demolishing the authoritarian state and its nominal constitutionalism. In the Brezhnev period, the constitution was developed on a new basis. Unlike the preceding Constitution of 1936, primarily oriented at western public opinion (therefore more declarative in terms of rights, and focusing less attention on the party role), this one (as a response to concessions in the Khrushchev era), on the contrary, served to reflect the specific features of "real socialism". Note in this connection a discussion of jurists on which law is more significant – constitutional or public, whose real purpose was to identify theoretically feasible legal guarantees against administrative arbitrariness. These guarantees depended on the will of the ruling layer which, on the one hand, was interested in the stability of their domination and privileges (in relation to other social groups) and, on the other, would like to have some legal guarantees against arbitrariness of tyrannical power in relation to the personality and property of its representatives. In this sense, evolution of nomenclature, as a ruling layer, very much resembles the preceding evolution of nobility, who passed similar phases from service class to a privileged one. The achievement of this status means the transformation of nomenclature into a parasitic layer, opening up a "golden era of bureaucracy". This new social reality pressed for its consolidation in a new Fundamental Law.

The Constitution of 1977, while adhering to the same principles as the preceding one, differed from it in two respects: heavier emphasis was placed on citizens' obligations than on their rights and privileges; and the party role was justified to a greater extent. Only the regulations on the party role turned out to be effective and, in part, the social guarantees of citizens. In the above constitutions, legislation, elections, civil rights are perceived in line with Lenin traditions, i.e. are admissible only given party domination. The specific feature of the constitution development was the lack of alternative options, on the one hand, and the unusually long time taken by the compilation of the final text, on the other. The absence of alternative options (like in the case of the 1936 Constitution) is easily explained by party monopoly, as well as by a consensus on the key issue – on rights and privileges of the ruling circle. Of much higher interest is the time factor reflecting disagreements within the elite and a latent struggle on the issues concerned with guidelines for the political course. Indeed, 15 years elapsed since making a decision on the establishment of a constitutional commission (in 1962) to the nationwide discussion of the constitution (1977). This is in striking conflict with the theory and practice of Soviet nominal constitutionalism proceeding from the fact that the constitution just states the reality – "attained and recorded in writing", hence has a certain pragmatic value and must come into force immediately. Noteworthy is the discrepancy between the time needed for adoption of the new constitution and that for adoption of all preceding constitutions, which (even given the availability of alternative options and debatable opinions) were put into action several months after the establishment of constitutional commission (as the RSFSR Constitution of 1918) or at least the year after the beginning of its activities (the Constitutions of 1924 and 1936). This fact can be explained, in part, by the power struggle playing in this case a significant though far from decisive role. The point is that Brezhnev's regime (1964–1982), which would then be viewed as stagnation, had not acquired its later conservative features straight away, and passed several stages in its development. Being a sort of response to the reforms in the preceding period, this regime, in principle, bent for their conservative revision. It was largely guided by the principles of replacing economic decentralization with rigid planned centralization, administrative regrouping with the principle of "confidence in personnel", regime democratization with reinforcement of its repressive functions.

The Brezhnev Constitution of "developed socialism" in general summed up the most characteristic features of nominal constitutionalism of Soviet society. It retained and reflected a general continuity in relation to the preceding Soviet Constitutions of 1918, 1924 and, in particular, of 1936. The differences from the latter are not fundamental but rather declarative. Constitution verbosity, its legal amorphism and lackadaisical discussion were perfect signs of the start of the stagnation of the regime. Given the erosion of the world communist movement taking shape, the "Fundamental Law" contains an extensive preamble to show the global significance of a Soviet type of state organization, and at the same time link it with patriotic idea. The constitution advances, in principle, the same (as before) legitimizing formula (Article 1) defining the political system as "socialist state of all the people expressing the will and interests of workers, peasants and intelligentsia, working people of all nations and nationalities of this country". Especially demagogical is a formula on that "all the power in the USSR belongs to people" and is realized through "people's deputies" (Article 2). It was stated at the time when "people's deputies" became puppets in the opinion of the thinking segment of society. This constitution was a rather extensive document in relation to rights and obligations. Apart from this, the Fundamental Law was clearly a certain reaction to the preceding reform attempt, and to the latent imminent destabilization of the system. A way out was found in formal consolidation of the leading role of the party.

The formal legal consolidation of this principle in the sixth article of the Constitution of 1977 can also be treated, however, as a result of a certain trade-off. As a matter of fact, definition of a non-legal phenomenon in legal terms always reveals its essence and discloses its place in the political system much better, hence, makes it possible to see contradictions in its development. According to the 1977 Constitution the party (as in the past) is defined in a purely metaphysical form as a "vanguard of the entire people". At the same time, some rational parameters of this phenomenon are provided: the party is "a leading and guiding force of Soviet society, the core of its political system, state and public organizations"; it determines the prospects of social development, directs internal and foreign policy, i.e. endowed with all the attributes of state sovereignty. It is noted at the same time that "all party organizations act within the frameworks of the Constitution of the USSR" (Article 6, Part III).[19] It is significant that the point here is not of the party as a whole (which is above constitution by virtue of ideological function) but only of individual party organizations. Being the developer and guarantor of law, the party, at the same time, had to appeal to law for its own legitimation. This very fact was indicative of a certain (hardly perceptible, though) shift in legitimizing foundations of the regime forced to seek justification in law (let it be purely declarative) and not only in class or "public" will. We have demonstrated above that the social basis of this process of a party's attempts at its own perception in legal terms is, firstly, the desire of the ruling layer to legally consolidate its special status and privileges in society and, secondly, a desire to secure itself against the power. This situation somewhat resembles the one which established itself in pre-revolutionary Russian jurisprudence, which tried to define autocracy in legal terms. The ideology of absolutism, also appealing to "general will", did not rule out, nevertheless, certain legal parameters of expression of sovereign's will. Back then the way out was found in contrasting despotism to monarchy resting on its own fundamental laws. Both in the past and under the new circumstances, this internally contradictory formula could be exposed in a diametrically opposite way – in favour of monarchy or of the party as a bearer of sovereignty and a source of constitutional norms (octroyed constitutionalism), and in favour of these norm as such, which also extended to the power which provided them (contractual principle). This legal construction is a reflection of the compromise character of the entire Brezhnev "collective leadership" striving towards restoration of Stalinism, yet with guarantees from mass repressions. That was precisely the progressive difference between constitutions of 1977 and 1936, containing no legal restrictions of the party power. Inclusion in the new constitution of a party-related article (purely dogmatic, though) made it possible to raise questions, which in the past could not be discussed at all: questions about the relationship of law and party, party and Soviets, and separation of legislative power between them.

Teaching of Soviets has always served as a main means of legitimation of one-party dictatorship as a will on the given type of nominal constitutionalism. This type of public institution has nothing in common with the institutes of parliamentary democracy, but is a body of a quasi-representative nature, in terms of its organization, structure and functions, ideally fit for manipulation from the outside. The Soviets had to create an illusion of the unity of the people and the party, approve its decisions in a constitutional manner and assume responsibility for errors in their implementation. The thesis of the absolute power of the Soviets, as a legitimation basis, has always accompanied the party dictatorship throughout its existence. Although it has undergone some evolution correlating with the official concept of state organization and the party. The official ideologists segregated three phases of this evolution: from Soviets of workers, soldier and peasant deputies (the 1918 Constitution) to Soviets of workers' deputies (the 1936 Constitution) and from these to Soviets of people's deputies (the 1977 Constitution) – "this is how the bodies of people's representation in our country evolved". The final phase of the process was viewed as a full triumph of Soviets as bodies of representative power. The thesis of the state of all the people, which became an acme of Soviet constitutional-legal doctrine, represented a new legitimizing foundation (of people's rather than class sovereignty) and was called to impart some populist features to the patriarchal system of party absolutism. The mobilization function of Soviets also played a significant role. It was realized within the frameworks of a logically meaningless formula of "expansion of Soviet democracy" and "higher role of Soviets" apparently running counter to constitutional proclamation thereof as supreme power bodies. According to official explanations, this meant that the "party leadership is a prerequisite for the regular functioning of Soviets, successful implementation by them of the role of bodies of people's power". Accordingly, a key role was assigned to the party groups in Soviets, whose job was to exert party influence and implement its directives. By the end of the Brezhnev era, the sphere of their strong influence covered over 30 million people, of whom over two million were deputies of different level of Soviets. The main function of the system of Soviets, however, was to divert attention from the authoritarian concept of the leading role of the party.

Approaching the problem of the legitimation formula from the standpoint of the ruling layer, rather than from the official legal ideology, convincingly proves that the evolution of this formula in major Soviet Constitutions clearly fixes the phases of its advent, growth and social degradation. Thus, the 1918 Constitution reflects the fact of its emergence and the desire to establish its domination over society in the form of dictatorship of proletariat, which denies all other social segments the right of participation in politics (through a system of indirect elections and electoral qualification); the Union Constitution of 1924 reflects the fact of the elite regrouping in conditions of tough struggle between the centre and provinces, integration of regional elites into a single all-union one accompanied by the destruction of marginal groups, modification of infrastructure and channels of social mobility. Also, it reflects the growing integration of party and state elites by way of fusion thereof into a uniform system of party nomenclature. The Constitution of 1936 carries the both trends (horizontal and vertical) through to a logical conclusion, and turns into a system of qualitatively new levels, where the party already confronts the entire society as its vanguard, whose place is fixed in a formal, legal way. This monument embodies the very dynamic phase of the development of Soviet elite, when it achieves, for the first time ever, a total control of society, internal unity (thanks to purges) and at the same time has not yet lost its functional purpose – an organizing role in the course of modernization. Later on, upon establishing control of power, it loses this dynamism, increasingly turning into a privileged class. By renouncing all attempts at establishing social or power control of itself (in constitutional ideas in the era of Khrushchev reforms), it achieves its peak form, which simultaneously means the beginning of the end for it as a holistic social phenomenon engendered by the revolution. This closing phase is presented in the 1977 Constitution with its concept of leading and guiding role of the party elite. Being aware of the fragility of its power in conditions of incipient systemic crisis, it looks for ways of holding power under the new circumstances. The period of *perestroika* (restructuring) and the subsequent break-up of the state witnesses the split of the elite itself manifest in the concept of the so-called "social pluralism" and the respective changes in the effective constitution. This process results in the rejection of the old ideology and abrogation of the constitutional principle of the leading role of the party. This process proceeded so painlessly because it did not affect the real power of the elite, which had already found a new way of legitimizing its power. These are the ideas of liberalism and struggle against privileges, so attractive for society. Power converts into ownership (by privatizing state property), politically manifesting itself in the replacement of nominal constitutionalism of a Soviet era with one of the common forms of sham constitutionalism – presidential dictatorship. This system is finally legalized in the Constitution of 1993. That was the way of "professional revolutionary" transformation into modern bourgeois confirming the old truth that there is nothing new under the moon. This path was followed (for shorter periods of time, though) by all the big revolutions of the past, giving philosophers grounds for formulating the principle of "iron rule of oligarchy". Therefore, the Soviet system differs from them not so much in essence as in a much more bloody character, connected with a bigger scale of social crisis devastation in recent times and the specific difficulty of modernizing traditional societies. The real absence of civil society and law-based state in Russia render reforms extremely destructive. Given the lack of middle class, as a social foundation of reforms, we face the phenomenon of a substituted middle class. It is precisely authoritocracy – a specific service layer, being a managerial tool of power in the course of modernization – which acts as this substitute.

The problem of transition from authoritarian to democratic power was always difficult to understand. The main difficulty is determined by a paradoxical status of the authoritarian power itself in a reform environment. Being authoritarian, hence independent of social control, it is theoretically capable of running any transformations at its own discretion. In practice, however, it frequently becomes impotent precisely at the time of reforms running into a powerful opposition on the part of the social structures and institutions which served, in pre-reform times, as its solid foundation. Already Tocqueville had noted this paradox by saying that despotic regimes experience the hardest times when they start reforming themselves. The other difficulty arises from the specific role of law at the time of reforms and revolutions. It is common knowledge that law can perform two main functions – conservation of the existing systems or the changing of them. The ideal situation is where both functions are harmonically combined, forming a continuity of the state legal system. This situation, however, comes to an end at reform times, when the two functions of law come into an insoluble conflict creating a basis for two competing legal frameworks: the old (pre-reform) and the new (emerging in the form of transformations and legitimizing them). Being forced to destroy the old law, the state and the reformatory political elite lose control of it; they have to act in spite of law, in defiance of it, appealing directly to "public opinion". This turns law into a subject of sharp political discussions and ideological debates of conservatives and reformers, when the former blame the new regime for the illegal character, and the latter need to look for arguments in quasi-legal constructions or outside law altogether. The third difficulty arises due to the prevailing authoritarian ideology exerting a reverse hypnotic influence on society and the political elite. It is impossible to carry out reforms in an ideologized (or "totalitarian") state without destroying the very ideology underlying legitimation of power of the ruling regime. Reforms can, therefore, be top-down, rejecting in a stage-wise manner the obsolete ideological frameworks and the administrative political structures behind them. The real history of this process are rooted in the struggle of two groups within the former elite – of ideologists (advocating stability of party religion as a foundation of the regime) and technocrats (stressing scientific and business pragmatism, and finding it possible to sacrifice a number of political postulates for the sake of it). For a long time, this struggle (sometimes hardly visible) does not come to the surface and is not perceived in ideological and political terms. In conditions of the apparent systemic crisis it becomes, however, a detonator of changes, bringing to the forefront the reformatory core of educated bureaucracy (largely economists and managers whose views had formed during the initial attempts at reforms). The process of ousting the party priests from power manifests itself in renouncing ideological dogmatism. There arises a historical chance for ending the deadlock of ideological state through its modernization and Europeanization. The main social conflict on the eve of perestroika can be defined, therefore, as an increasing discrepancy between the system of party ideological domination and the objectives of the nation's modernization. To put it differently, there comes a phase of development (sometimes defined as post-industrial society, which is not quite accurate) when the process of technological change can already proceed without totalitarian ideological mobilization, and the ideology and its bearer – the party – become a barrier on the way to development.

Institution of presidential power in Russia resulted from understanding the impossibility of fast wide-ranging socio-economic reforms on the basis of the old party apparatus (due to its conservatism) or a new "legislative power" of Soviets (due to inefficiency). Firstly (in 1989), this idea was perceived rather critically as there was a fear that the concentration of power would dominate the Soviets and restore the "personality cult". As the crisis mounted, a different strategy of reorganization of the Soviet political system was developed with a view to bringing the role of the party in the state to naught. It suggested a gradual transfer of power from party structures to state ones, which could be implemented only given an independent and formally neutral supreme arbiter. The role of the latter should be played by presidential power, which would become a historic successor of power of the general secretary. The formal termination of relations with the party occurred on 24 August 1991, when Mikhail S. Gorbachev gave up the post of general secretary and membership to the CPSU. On 29 August 1991, Supreme Soviet adopted a historical resolution "On urgent measures for preventing attempts of coup d'etat", which terminated its activities because of participation in the coup d'etat on 18–21 August 1991. This event could not be realized, however, without prior institutional preparation.

The reforms of the political system resulted in transformation of one-party dictatorship into a state permissive of party pluralism. The concept of power inseparability gave way to the principle of separation of powers, the interpretation of these powers and the balance thereof in the political system underwent considerable changes, and a number of top public institutions were introduced, of which the major one is presidential power. The thesis on the vanguard role of the communist party is missing from the new edition of the Fundamental Law, and the wording of its place within the political system (Article 6) was changed so as to rule out power monopoly. The provision on monopoly of socialist ownership was replaced with a thesis on different forms of ownership: state, collective and individual. Most radical changes occurred in the power structure, which was reformed with regard to the principle of separation of powers (which was implemented rather inconsistently, however). The Congress of People's

Deputies becomes the new supreme body of state power to be elected (unlike the Congress of Soviets at the time of first Soviet Constitutions) directly by the population. In turn, it elects a two-chamber Supreme Soviet (headed by presidium) and its chairperson as a "standing legislative and control body of state power" and the Committee of Constitutional Inspection headed by a chairperson, whose main function was to exercise assessment of draft laws from the standpoint of their constitutionality. The institute of presidential power was called to play a major role in the new political system. It would be formed by universal, direct, equal and secret election of head of state – a president, who is given exclusively wide authorities both in legislative and executive areas.[20]

The method of establishment and legitimation of the new presidential power – decision of the Congress of People's Deputies – merits special comment. The very principle of establishment of this power body had no precedent in Soviet history. It sooner resembles archaic assemblies convened in the period of forming monarchical power or during big political crises for a specific purpose of discussion and legitimation of some or other decisions of the monarch.

Under the incipient break-up of the union, there arose an acute problem concerned with the balance of the political system of the heterogeneous institutions such as Congress of People's Deputies (theoretically representing all of the population and "public organizations", i.e. the CPSU), Supreme Soviet (representing the traditional vertical of Soviets as formal bodies of state power) and republics (national representation in the Chamber of Nationalities of the SS) and, finally, the government (council of ministers and the entire central apparatus of public administration). The debates on this problem held during discussions on the Supreme Soviet election procedure identified three main standpoints. The first one was adhered to by separatists (who later quitted the Congress) who set an ultimatum for electing SS by quotas from national republics. The two other positions, however, representing a reaction to the above one, were at variance relative to the interpretation of the balance of Congress and Supreme Soviet prerogatives.

Abolition of party monopoly on power and creation of a new system of central political institutions, having no precise analogues in localities, led to the weakening of central power. It is the conservative opposition to reforms that specifically stressed this point, for it conceived (and, as it turned out, not without reason) administrative decentralization as a threat of state disintegration. Under the circumstances, the functions of a real and formal successor of the party apparatus power had to be performed by a new political structure – the presidential institute. Under political reforms, the latter came to be a key link in the reorganization of public administration, the core of the new vertical hierarchy of executive power. Actually, however, given the post-totalitarian system, the president was called to perform many other functions too, becoming the only guarantor of law and order in this country and who concluded international treaties. This objectively raises the phenomenon of presidential dictatorship resembling its Weimar version. This comparison, quite popular in liberal political science, is rather conventional. Weimar Republic, for all the reservations, was a functioning parliamentary democracy with a system of separation of powers and legal guarantees of political rights. The Soviet-type nominal constitutionalism, on the contrary, ends up by transition as a very specific form of sham constitutionalism, where the scope of presidential power corresponds to that of monarch and even exceeds it. Hence, we notice the similarity of many of the processes of post-Soviet political evolution to those which we mentioned when characterizing Duma monarchy in Russia on the eve of revolution. The main example of these is reinforcement of personal power, when all principal decisions are dependent upon the personal traits of the head of state rather than on the developed laws and procedures. The specific feature of the Soviet, and later post-Soviet, model of presidential power is that, under the emerged complete legal vacuum, it is the only umpire between all political vested interests, itself becoming in turn a subject of conflicting influences.

The introduction of presidential power was accompanied by the creation of two advisory institutions, namely the Council of Federation and Presidential Council. They served to concentrate presidential power in regions and make it more efficient. Presidential Council, however, did not have a definite competence and real power, but had to develop policy alternatives. Hence, its mixed composition included both reform proponents and their conservative critics. An important stage of power concentration came to be the Supreme Soviet decision (as of 24 September 1990) conferring temporary power on Gorbachev (until 31 March 1992) for issuing decrees in the areas of economics, law, security and government appointments. Importantly, he was authorized to introduce direct presidential rule in troubled regions and dissolve (if necessary) the democratically elected governments. That was actually the regime of presidential dictatorship. The further reinforcement of presidential power led to a plan of comprehensive reorganization of the entire state machinery. Its general concept suggested creation of a solid vertical hierarchy of executive power both in localities (by reinforcing republican governments) and in the centre (presidential power). This model – strong centre and strong republics – called to halt the national disintegration of the state and ensured, under power crisis (both that of the party and of Soviets), the creation of a new administrative structure with president as the apex. This is also linked to the reform of major state institutions.

The struggle of political trends has increasingly acquired the form of collision of the union centre and of the Russian core, manifesting itself in the clash between the union and Russian presidents. This power structure was reproduced at the periphery too, leading to the ever-intensive centrifugal trends in the republics. The process of the union state disintegration gained momentum as a result of establishment of presidential power in the republics and of the accompanying institute of a prime minister.

The August 1991 putsch produced a structural and functional crisis of the entire political system; its break-up rapidly extended to horizontal and vertical parameters, paralyzing the very mechanism of power and government. It is worth noting that the crisis was far from unexpected, for it was unfolding precisely along the lines identified in the course of previous attempts at system reform and political discussions that were undertaken throughout the years of perestroika. These were the relations of the union centre and national provinces (thoroughly camouflaged by nominal Soviet constitutionalism but identified in the course of discussion of the draft "Union Treaty") and the inefficiency of executive power (becoming more apparent in the course of all previous attempts at economic reforms and peaking during the political reform launched by Gorbachev). The real significance of the crisis was that it highly accelerated the entire process of the system erosion over time (which itself acts as a major political factor), made the changes revolutionary in character (thereby ruling out reform strategy), deprived the old elite of legitimacy and promoted legitimacy of the new one. The horizontal aspect of the crisis is presented by the changing relations between the centre and the provinces in exercising power. The formula of strong centre and powerless regions (national republics and autonomies) traditional for the Soviet period turned into its antipode. By taking advantage of the sharp weakening of the centre, the national elites, formed under the cover of old ideology, laid their claims on redistribution of power and property. The nationalists' criticism of the union centre was largely targeted at strong state power in general. It would be safe to say that the process resulted in, at this stage, disintegration of the union state and transfer of power from the union centre to republics. A decisive role in the process was played by the position of Russian authorities, which became an assignee of union power. The new political reality was legalized by the Belovezhsky agreements of 1991 – an international legal act registering transformation of former national republics into sovereign states. The agreements pursued two principal goals – on the one hand, they fixed the fait accompli and the established distribution of power and, on the other, legitimized the new Russian state power. The vertical aspect of the crisis consisted of the disintegration of the old structure of legislative and executive power represented by a hierarchy of party institutions and their alter ego – powerless Soviets from top to bottom. This dimension of the crisis is especially important when characterizing the stance of the major power and administrative institutes – the army, security service and bureaucracy – in the course of the coup d'etat, their passivity and temporizing position.

After scrapping the party's monopoly of political power, the consolidation of the new elite in Russia acquired the diarchy character, which had already taken place in history. Two power centres evolve: one around Presidium of Supreme Soviet and the entire vertical hierarchy of Soviet institutions in localities (which become a refuge for old cadres); and another around the president (where proponents of market reforms rallied).

In this case we witness reproduction of the given model in a similar situation of power struggle. For this purpose, a new state-legal structure – "Council of Subjects of the Federation" – was created, made up of representatives of both branches of regional power and, accordingly, symbolizing the uniform support of presidential power. First established as an advisory body under constitutional crisis, this institution then acquired prerogatives of a power body and was legalized (after adoption of the new constitution) as the upper chamber of parliament – Council of Federation. From the very beginning, it opposed the Congress and the Supreme Soviet of the RSFSR. The support of regional elites (where the split was not as pronounced as in the centre or was inexistence at all) is explained by their desire for stability – the unity of administration, economic links and procurement.

The subsequent reform of local government gives rise to ambiguous interpretations. It is interpreted as a liquidation of representative institutions in localities, a simple replacement thereof with heads of administration (who in the past had dual reporting: to the president and the respective council). According to this opinion, the reform did away with Soviets as institutions legally (in some cases actually) independent of the ruling party and executive power, which they became in the wake of the 1990 democratic elections. In other words, the local government reform of 1993 can be viewed, from this perspective, as a counter-reform restoring orders existing before 1991. This thesis, however, does not take into account a number of important aspects, notably, organizational and functional inefficiency of Soviets as local governments, social and genetic proximity of Soviets to the former regime (which explains, in particular, their conservation after the coup in the republics where they performed previous functions), and finally their staff continuity, as well as the remarkable fact that the population simply overlooked their liquidation and did not get out of the customary apathy. Just after the August putsch the Soviets turned into a stiff hierarchical corporation, under absolutely no control of the electorate. There are, therefore, no serious grounds for treating Soviets as civic self-government bodies (like municipalities, zemstvo, city councils, and the like). In any case, weakening of federalism, which had just started to take shape, integration of regions in a uniform system of public administration were a result of an objective process of consolidation of authoritarian presidential power, which there was hardly any serious alternative to in the then real political situation.

The constitution, adopted after the termination of dual power (and liquidation of the system of Soviets in September to October 1993), is of a centralizing nature in terms of the balance of central and local governments. There is no system of social control of power in localities, therefore central institutions of executive power have no analogous structures at lower levels of administration. Lying in the core of the constitution is the principle of separation of powers represented by its three branches. The major power institutes are represented by the RF President, two-chamber Federal Assembly – State Duma and Council of Federation, the Government, the Russian Federation's courts. Formally, the constitution stamps the state structure of presidential republic.[21] On closer examination it turns out, however, that the principle of separation of powers is realized rather inconsistently. The president was given huge powers, again realizing the concept of power domination over social control. Being adopted by referendum, the constitution reflects not so much the democratic alternative to Russia's authoritarian tradition as the closing phase of consolidation of the regime of sham constitutionalism.

5 A contemporary model of Russian constitutionalism in comparative perspective

The Russian Constitution of 1993 has played a critical role in the processes of transition to democracy in Russia and elsewhere. Its adoption has led to the end and definitive renouncement of a grandiose social experiment on building a communist (socialist) society by utilizing physical force. Due to this fact, the current constitution represents a social choice by the Russian society in favour of democracy, liberal values and human rights. On the one hand, this document is a fully-fledged representation of systemic changes seen by the end of the twentieth century worldwide. On the other hand, it is an independent document that to a large extent has determined the course of governmental changes in today's Russia and in other post-Soviet countries. Contemporary discussions of the Russian Constitution, however, put aside the issues of to what extent the constitution has reflected transitional processes around the world; how the process of constitutional modernization has (or has not) fitted into the context of post-Soviet social development in Eastern Europe; how the constitution has impacted on social changes occurring throughout Russia; what areas of social tensions have been revealed during the course of constitutional development; and, finally, given all the above mentioned, what are the prospects for Russia's constitutional system in the future.

The search for answers to these questions is going to determine the content of Chapter 5. Subsequently, the main purpose of this chapter is to analyse the Russian Constitution in a comparative perspective; to identify the commonalities and particularities in Russian constitutional development over the past ten years; and, given this, to determine what is going to be the trend of constitutional development in the future. Speaking about the significance and prospects of the 1993 Constitution, one should look at it from three perspectives: comparative (commonalities and particularities in Russian constitutional development); historical (the past, present and future of the Russian Constitution); and functional (how norms correlate with reality and what mechanisms are used for enhancing social efficiency of the constitution). We believe that an analysis based on these three factors will help answer a widely debated issue of the advisability and prospects of constitutional reform in Russia.[1]

The comparative analysis is conducted, horizontally and vertically, on the basis of methods employed by the contemporary sociology of law that primarily investigates the way legal rules operate in society. This approach seems to be highly relevant to Russia where the constitutional crisis of a transitional period was simultaneously a political crisis affecting economic, social, national, cultural and legal aspects. Therefore, it is necessary to draw a comparison between constitution (in a strictly legal sense of the term) and constitutionalism (a social movement seeking to transform constitutional norms into reality). There emerges a situation resembling the theory of Rudolf Stammler, according to which the formal aspects of law are far more important than the real ones. Law, to some extent, outpaces reality, hence evolving into *a priori* category, a formal logical structure that is independent of society's (social) reality and becomes an accessory. Yet, law by itself can influence society's reality by producing a variety of strategies for regulating and restricting people's reality, which are based on purposeful goal setting. Any changes to society's reality (social relations) should therefore be introduced through rational modification of legal rules. Under this approach, the constitution acts as an independent, indispensable element of institutionalization of new socio-economic relations, which could possibly both accelerate and hamper their development. The constitutional form is still searching for its social content, an idea that has not materialized yet. This approach makes it possible to interpret the very attitude towards the constitution as a motive of social behaviour, and to analyse it pursuant to the theory of rational choice. It also provides an opportunity for reviving the theory of the social contract and for creating a metalaw, i.e. a specific socio-cultural reality enabling one to adapt rational legal rules in the conditions of irrational legal behaviour (or legal nihilism). Finally, this approach permits analysing the process of transition as the dynamics of dissemination of constitutional principles, thereby changing the entire political and legal reality (particularly, by way of the so-called constitutionalization of branch law). Some of the countries apply the notion of "political constitution" that conveys the fundamental commonality of objectives pursued by law and politics in relation to the creation of a new social ethics in a democratic society.

Along these lines, we are going to explore the genesis, relevancy and future prospects of the Russian Constitution. To examine these aspects, we have formulated the following problems: constitution in the context of worldwide transitional processes from authoritarianism to democracy; a constitutional revolution in Russia; the Constitution of the Russian Federation as a turning point in establishing civil society and law-based state in Russia; constitution and federalism; a form of government and a type of political regime in Russia; and potential and strategies for constitutional reform in present-day Russia.

In analysing the cyclical evolution of Russian constitutionalism, we are going to address the following issues: the mechanisms of cycles –

constituent power and constitutional power; decentralization and centralization of political system – the evolving concept of federalism; transition from the separation of powers to their unification – the form of government and the type of political regime in Russia; the conflict of modernization and retraditionalization – strategies for implementing constitutional reforms in today's Russia; and lastly, the third constitutional cycle and possibilities for its adjustment.

The constitution seen in the context of worldwide transitional processes from authoritarianism to democracy

The trend towards enshrining uniform criteria and rules of civil society and law-based state in law has been very strong in the contemporary world, especially in the age of globalization, democratization and dissemination of information via the web. However, the processes of rapid, legal and political modernization in transitional societies often lead to radical transformations in their social structures, political and legal systems. On a global scale, the situation of transition is characterized by the following phenomena: loss of the former regime stability; a search for new ways of consolidation based on new premises; a new political regime coming into play with substantially different characteristics; and lastly, the emergence of specific transitional regimes marked by conflicting traditions of the former and new political authorities. Transitional processes, of course, can go into reverse: instead of shifting from authoritarianism to democracy, they can either transform democracy into authoritarianism or reproduce various modifications of preceding regimes. For example, these processes can modernize sham constitutionalism. In doing so, the constitution acts as a basic tool for ensuring accord or some semblance of accord in a divided society.[2] It can therefore perform completely different social and political functions, ranging from declaring certain ideological goals, fixing the balance of social forces, legitimizing a new political regime to expressing dynamic relationships between a government and society in the course of democratic reforms. The situation of transition manifests itself primarily through a constitutional crisis.

The constitutional crisis, as described in Chapter one, means a situation where either the Basic Law loses its legitimacy (a gap between legitimacy and legality appears); or conflicting social forces fail to agree on certain constitutional norms derived from the existing Basic Law; or the constitution and certain provisions thereof clash with political reality. The constitutional crisis is generally (but not necessarily) linked to the crisis of political regime, which may manifest itself in different ways. During transition from authoritarianism to democracy, the ways of solving constitutional crises are represented by two ideal models for adopting a constitution: the first model is based on contract (consensus model), and the second on disruption of consensus (essentially, an octroyed or delegated constitution).

In literature, the aforesaid dichotomy is usually referred to in written constitutions only. However the logic of legal tradition continuity and rupture also exists, though manifests itself in specific forms, in nations with unwritten constitutions and parliamentary sovereignty (e.g. the UK, New Zealand and partly Israel). While a parliament plays a specific role where it is a constituent and a constitutional power at the same time, according to the principle of unlimited parliamentary sovereignty; the unwritten nature of constitution allows changes or amendments to be easily introduced thereto (this is why unwritten constitutions are often termed flexible). This issue was raised in the classical work of Albert Venn Dicey. Alexis de Tocqueville noted that the British constitution could not be changed because it was not written down, whereas Dicey stressed that the opposite is actually true: the constitution indeed changes constantly, because it was not formally set out in written or statutory form. Since any law may be equally easy or difficult to change in a legal manner, there is no need to write down a constitution. This is possible not only theoretically but also practically, as has been shown by the experience of several dominions that codified conventional norms in their written constitutions in order to secure consensus at the time of constitutional crises (e.g. Australia and Canada). Problems, however, arise nowadays due to the changing form of the British constitution itself. Constitutional changes are carried out along the lines of incorporating the written law, namely European law, into the common law system. The main areas of recent reforms (particularly since 1997) include: the Bill of Rights; proportional representation; the upper chamber reorganization; open government; establishment of quasi-federalism (the devolved administrations in Scotland and Wales); and stronger democratic control over executive authorities. Many people believe that reforms may lead to adoption of a written constitution (there are, at least, three drafts thereof). This logic questions the underlying principles of traditional British constitution. For the adoption of the written constitution (or of the borrowed European Convention on Human Rights) denies the omnipotence of parliament and therefore reduces its role in implementation of future constitutional changes. The point is whether parliament, as sovereign, can limit its own sovereignty, and whether it refers exclusively to the current assembly of parliament or to its future assemblies too. As early as in 1980, a question arose about the possibility of a constitutional revolution – a sharp conflict between the Constitutional Assembly and parliamentary prerogatives (which parliament has to abandon or transfer to somebody else) – which could be provoked by adoption of the written constitution in the UK. It was suggested that parliament introduce constitutional changes and adopt a new oath for the swearing-in of judges, which would ensure continuity during transition to the written constitution. Though constitutional changes in common (case) law countries can be easily implemented (constitutions are usually amended by Acts of Parliament), they implicitly include the mechanisms utilized for consensus building (in the course of parliamentary debates) and their consequences are far more serious compared to the countries with codified laws. This problem can be aggravated by adoption of the written constitution changing the very principles of the common law system. In the UK, the problem of constitutional reforms has been at the heart of many heated debates due to implementation of the programme of constitutional reforms, covering virtually all aspects of British constitutionalism. It is noteworthy that constitutional processes in Russia, Eastern Europe and South Africa have been often referred to as an argument against over-rapid reforms in the UK.

The two models reveal different parameters during transitional periods in countries with codified constitutions. There is contemporary literature written about transitional periods that gives considerable attention to the problem of constitutional changes. The latter is explored using the examples of both stable Western European democracies and unstable modernizing democracies in Asia, Africa and Latin America. Of major significance is the problem of modelling a process of transition to constitutional democracy and the question of the role of a constitution therein. The first, consensus model, might be defined as a deliberate strategy for reaching a consensus among political forces on the fundamental values of civil society and long-term goals of development. The second model, by contrast, can be defined as an insuperable conflict between political forces that leads to a situation where one force establishes dominance over the others and bends them to its will.

The first model, which is quite difficult to implement, is still rarely seen in current governmental affairs around the world today. For example, let us look at the Spanish experience. In Spain, the process of transition from the Franco dictatorial regime to the democratic political system went through several stages. The first stage involved a comprehensive democratization of the authoritarian political system, including the introduction of openness and of liberty to form political parties and various associations; the second stage consisted of the drafting and adopting (through a referendum) of the special law on political reform that laid down (without a formal rupture with the former Franco legislation) a pattern for the future constituent power; and finally, the third stage was determined by an agreement reached between leading political parties within the constituent power *per se*. The entire period of transition resulted in the adoption of the 1978 constitution, which is no doubt legitimate and recognized as one of the best constitutions in Europe today. In comparison with other Southern European countries such as Greece and Portugal, the uniqueness of Spanish transitional process is that the radical reform was carried out in such a way that the real constitutional continuity was preserved in relation to the former dictatorship. The Spanish model of transition to democracy was of great interest to Soviet President Mikhail Gorbachev, who reportedly sought to implement a similar model of consensus-based regime liberalization.

Another example of the consensus model is the South African Constitution. It was drafted and adopted in the conditions of a difficult transition, whereby a racial segregation society was transformed into a modern type civil society. This process also went through the following stages: preliminary consultations and negotiations between the main opposing parties (the governing white minority and the opposition movement led by the African National Congress (ANC) and supported by other parties); formation of the provisional coalition government acting under a special transitional constitution; organization of democratic elections to the Constitutional Assembly whose constitution making was actively supported by all political forces and supervised by the Constitutional Court. The provisional or transitional constitution, though different in contents, coincided with the adoption of the Russian Constitution in 1993. The process of transition ended up with adoption of the South African democratic Constitution in 1996.

The third example of the consensus model is that of several Eastern European countries where new constitutions were adopted following consultations (the so-called "round table discussions") between the communist power and democratic opposition in order to reach a consensus on the basic principles of a future political system and on the legal basis of further democratic reforms. Researchers compare this method of implementing constitutional transformations to a relatively peaceful transfer of power through the "Velvet Revolution" in Czechoslovakia. In several nations, this process passed through an intermediate stage where either an interim constitution ("small constitution" in Poland) was adopted or a political system was transformed, but the old constitution remained intact yet substantially amended (Hungary). Whenever a nation failed to implement the consensus model of transition, it faced a constitutional revolution that frequently led to a forcible coup d'etat (Romania).

The Russian analogue of consensus or contractual model institutions came to be the Democratic Conference and Pre-Parliament it elected, whose activity the October Revolution of 1917 terminated. For a long period of time, it was impossible to undertake any serious study of these institutions due to ideological reasons and to the fact that they had not actually affected the sequence of events during the Russian Revolution. However, this fact does not undermine their significance for typological and comparative studies, being indicative of a certain tradition of such institutions in Russia. All attempts at reaching a consensus failed because of a bitter political struggle and deliberate reluctance by extremist parties to compromise. In particular, Bolsheviks were responsible for this. At the time of World Wars and social revolutions, many extremist political parties categorically denied that parliamentarianism could solve the conflicts. They clung to maximalist demands on solving immediately the conflicts by creating a new type of state, namely, social republic. So, the consensus model could hardly be implemented during the revolution.

Neither was it implemented under the break-up of the Soviet system in the early 1990s. The post-Soviet transitional period could solely rely on the experience of other European nations, which turned away from authoritarianism by utilizing precisely the contractual model, and a new political consciousness of citizens. Several Eastern European countries have chosen exactly this route of transition. However, the consensus model failed once again in Russia. It is generally acknowledged that what lay behind the model's failure was an extreme passiveness of the Russian people manifest in the weakness of many political parties; conservatism of political bureaucracy seeking to retain its leverages over state property seizure; growing nationalism and separatism, which ultimately led to the collapse of the state. All subsequent attempts to reach a consensus between the former political regime and a new system modelled on the Moncloa Pact also came to naught. Thus, the consensus model for adopting a constitution once again gave way to the model of legal continuity rupture. The entire transitional process culminated in the constitutional crisis of 1993, which led to the adoption of a virtually octroyed constitution. The constitution's legitimacy, therefore, became a key problem of subsequent constitutional modernization, resulting in a stiff confrontation between the parliamentary power and presidential power.

The second model (constitutional continuity rupture) is far too often applied compared to the first one. This model is also represented by a number of options. First, a radical social revolution that simultaneously changes property relations, social and political structure, and the whole political and legal system. For example, the constitutions which underwent changes following the French, Russian, Mexican, Chinese and Iranian revolutions. Second, the so-called "constitutional revolution" that transforms the entire political and legal system, rather than radically changing the structure of society in an illegal manner. This is usually exemplified by the US Constitution and constitutional changes occurring at the time of the Glorious Revolution in England. Third, a new constitution imposed on a conquered nation after a military defeat; for instance, the Basic Law promulgated in 1949 for the Federal Republic of Germany (FRG). The contents of the Basic Law were defined, approved and supervised by the allied powers. Although it was originally intended as a provisional constitutional law, this document was eventually adopted as a permanent constitution for Germany. Japan's constitution of 1946 is yet another typical example. This constitution, largely drafted by American lawyers in the occupation authority, profoundly changed legal traditions in Japan. It was adopted under the direct influence of the occupation forces. But it seemed, on the surface, as if some continuity had been preserved. The Japanese Constitution of 1946 was passed as an amendment to the 1889 Meiji Constitution (the Constitution of the Empire of Japan), pursuant to its Article 73. However, this article allowed for different interpretations and had never been applied before because constitutional amendments had either never been introduced or debated. In accordance with the established procedure, the newly drafted constitution was submitted as an amendment to the Diet (Japanese Parliament) on behalf of the emperor. However, the new constitution based on the principle of popular sovereignty was incompatible with the basic principles of the former constitution establishing monarchical sovereignty. Henceforth, no amendments have been made to the current constitution of Japan, although new interpretations have been acquired by some of its articles (primarily, Article 9 due to the so-called "Ashida amendment"). That is the main point differentiating the Japanese Constitution from the German Basic Law, which has undergone numerous modifications. Fourth, a democratic constitution can be adopted in the aftermath of a military revolt. For example, the so-called "Mediterranean constitutionalism", which is illustrated by three Turkish constitutions routinely drafted following their military coups; and especially the Portuguese Constitution adopted by left-wing officers during the Revolution of the Carnations in 1974. Another example of the continuity rupture model is that of Greece where the present democratic constitution, adopted after the fall of the "black colonels" dictatorship, was based on restoration (with active participation by the army) of legal continuity with the constitution preceding the dictatorial regime (this, however, did not avert the breaking of legal tradition). Fifth, the breaking of constitutional and legal tradition is typical of situations where former colonies proclaim new independent nations and enshrine the principle of national sovereignty in their constitutions. For example, despite similar legal prerequisites, British colonies experienced different conditions compared to India where a constitutional transition was implemented through the optimal consensus model; or Pakistan whose constitutional development, due to the constitutional assembly's inability to solve the problem of the Basic Law, has been until recently marked by a series of constitutional upheavals coinciding with military revolts. Finally, legal continuity may be disrupted during the building of a new nation, if a constituent power refuses to comply with international legal norms that actually allowed for its creation. This situation has already happened in the state of Israel and it may take place again during the establishing of an independent Arabian state in Palestine. These different situations could be grouped together under the model of constitutional rupture because they share similar characteristics, namely: an absence of wide citizens' involvement in the search for political and legal compromises; lack of political parties addressing the issues of constitutional reform and restructuring; and lastly, formal rupture of legal continuity between the old constitution and the new one.

The phenomenon of subsequent legitimation is of great importance to the countries where constitutions were adopted in the aftermath of manifest or latent coups d'etat. This legitimation can be carried out in different ways. The most cynical way is justification of a coup d'etat by the constitutional (supreme) court due to the mere fact of the coup success.

In Pakistan, for example, this fact is viewed as a consequence of grassroots support and as a reason for altering the constitution through emergency laws. The phenomenon (of subsequent legitimation) happens today in many nations that have experienced coups d'etat. And it has its own theoretical rationale. Underlying the phenomenon is Kelsen's theory proclaiming that law is always effective law, and any successful coup creating a new effective law cannot be assessed on the basis of the old law. Thus, a successful coup (or "revolution") is regarded as a legal act, while an unsuccessful coup is regarded as an illegal act ("rebellion").

One can point out a number of specific combinations of the consensus model and the rupture model, along with their clearly pronounced options. Interesting combinations are observed in the Latin American countries where constitutional crises coincided with crises occurring in the USSR and Russia. The transitional process from military dictatorships to democratic political systems was primarily based on the Spanish model of contractual transition. This is why many political parties and elite groups were deliberately developing democratic constitutional norms. The constitutional continuity was to some extent disrupted, even then when new constitutions were discussed and adopted through the consensus model (e.g. Brazil and Argentina). Concurrently, the consensus model was not fully implemented because the democratic process was interrupted by the military forces that acted as a unified, corporate, closely knit institution interfering with the process of constitutional development. New circumstances bring reproduction of a situation seen as traditional to Latin America. Military forces act as a guarantor of constitution (either through military intervention or under the constitution), thereby legitimizing their potential participation in the adjustment of constitutional process (e.g. Brazil, Argentina and Chile).

Comparison of democratic transition periods in Brazil and Argentina (which coincided with the transition to democracy in Russia) permits identifying their intermediate type. On the one hand, these countries had not experienced revolutionary upheavals and radical breaking with the former constitutional order; but on the other hand, the process of constitutional revision was non-compliant (e.g. in Brazil) or was inadequately compliant (e.g. in Argentina) with the former constitutional norms. In Brazil, following the relinquishing of power to civil officials by military authorities in 1985, the new government headed by Jose Sarnea promised to launch democratic constitutional reforms. In 1987, the Brazilian Congress proclaimed itself National Constitutional Assembly, which thoroughly discussed and then adopted a constitution of New Republic in 1988. The Brazilian period of transition (1985–1988) was unique because the current constitution was adopted in violation of the revision procedure set forth by Article 48 in the former constitution adopted under the military regime in 1969. Furthermore, this procedure was not adhered to while adopting a constitutional amendment, which stipulated clear-cut procedures for discussing and approving the consensus model. Another deviation from the consensus model of transition is seen in the fact that the army constantly controlled the course of constitutional debates and played a principal role in formulating a number of key constitutional provisions, including rejection of a parliamentarian republic and transition to the presidential one.

Argentina started its democratic transition when the military government lost its legitimacy, because their attempts at democratization and constitutional reforms were thwarted in Malvina. Constitutional changes were introduced pursuant to the Constitution of the Argentine Nation of 1853, which provided for the convocation of a Constitutional Assembly (Article 30). The Constitutional Assembly was convened in 1994. The uniqueness of the Argentine transition process lies in the fact that the Assembly's activities were guided and governed by political parties, which had previously placed certain obligations on the future legislative assembly. The Constitutional Assembly of 1994 was bound by legal restrictions. In other words, its activities were limited by a range of issues that had been stipulated in the previously prepared document, known as "The Core of Fundamental Principles" (1993). However, this document is in turn derived from an earlier agreement by the leaders of two major parties – Raul Alfonsin and Carlos Menem – who made a number of compromises, which were unknown not only to the public but also to their parties (Pacto de Olivios). So, the Argentine transitional process appeared, on the surface, to be similar to the consensus model of transition; but in fact it was rather an agreement between political elites, and even two presidents, on a strategy for democratic transition.

Yet, the least democratic option of transition had occurred in Columbia. The Columbian Constitution, which was in effect until 1991, stipulated such a procedure for amendments that made them exclusively dependent on the will of the Congress (notorious for its clientelist nature of representation). When the Congress rejected a package of constitutional reforms, President Barco used the former constitution for imposing a state of siege. The Congress in particular rejected a constitutional proposal, which enabled citizens to use plebiscite as a way of constitutional reform. The president and his followers organized a public movement (whose nucleus was initially formed of students), which turned into "unofficial plebiscite". The public movement was successful and therefore, the president introduced the stage of siege in order to use emergency laws for holding an official referendum. The referendum approved convocation of the constitutional assembly that led to the adoption of a new constitution. Thus, the entire process of democratic transition was totally unconstitutional, given that under the former constitution only the Congress was empowered to alter the constitution. However, the Supreme Court clearly voiced its opinion for revising the constitution on the grounds that under extreme conditions the president turned to "primary constitutionality" represented by the people's requests for convening a constituent assembly. Other presidents have also resorted to the state of siege and issue of emergency laws for promoting their liberal policies. As for the rest of Latin America, namely Central American and Caribbean countries, they have frequently experienced the situation of constitutional instability, cyclical coups and subsequent legitimation, arising from the problems of post-colonial times.

France is a very good example of the constitution being adopted in a unique way, when Charles De Gaulle headed a real coup d'etat under the systemic crisis of the Fourth Republic. De Gaulle submitted to the French National Assembly a declaration in which he set as a condition for assuming the presidency that the government agreed to constitutional reform. After receiving a vote of confidence from the Assembly, the government presented a draft constitutional law intended to change the very procedure of constitutional revision laid down by Article 90 in the constitution of the Fourth Republic. In fact, the National Assembly introduced changes to the procedure for revising a constitution (the right to initiate this procedure was transferred from the parliament to government) and for making respective decisions (this right was given to the people in the form of referendum). These measures helped break the constitutional deadlock connected with the inability of the regime of parliamentary assembly to implement constitutional reforms aimed at its own self-restriction. The subsequent legislation provided opportunities for the governmental substantial work on drafting a qualitatively new constitution for the Fifth Republic. The constitutional continuity was formally preserved, though many critics denounced this fact. Today, jurists define this unique way of solving problems as a "legal coup". According to the terminology of French authors, the purpose of this "legal coup" (given that it was absolutely impossible to agree with the parliament on the contents of the future constitution) was to adopt the amended article on introduction of changes to the constitution in force (Article 90 of the Constitution of the Fourth Republic). Thus, the procedures for constitutional revision were radically changed, which made it possible to begin drafting the Constitution of the Fifth Republic.

During the past decade, Eastern Europe has seen a variety of almost all main forms of the rupture model, namely: i) revolutions and constitutional revolutions (which in principle might be defined as "velvet revolution"); ii) acute crises triggered by either the collapse of state in a more violent (e.g. former Yugoslavia) or more peaceful form (e.g. the "velvet divorce" in Czechoslovakia); by introduction of constitutions in the aftermath of coups d'etat (e.g. Romania, Albania and all the CIS countries); or by reaction to preceding authoritarian regimes (e.g. a coup d'etat in Poland). A multi-stage adoption of the Polish constitution failed to solve the problem of continuity (as it has been stressed by many critics of the current Polish constitution).

Several types of constitutional transformations can be conditionally identified in Eastern Europe. The fall of a communist regime may, first of all, lead to a situation where the former (nominal) constitution becomes invalid, and the subsequent period (until a new constitution is adopted) is characterized by the application of individual legislative acts of a constitutional nature (e.g. Romania); second, to changes in the effective nominal constitution, which is going to be replaced by a new constitution later on; third, the former constitution could be preserved, yet with substantial amendments giving it a new nature and content (e.g. Hungary); fourth, the option of an interim constitution (e.g. Poland); and lastly, restoration of the former constitution which was valid prior to establishment of a totalitarian regime (e.g. Lithuania).

For a comparative study, it is important to assert that there are two models of transitional processes: one is based on the contract (consensus model) and the other on the disruption of consensus (essentially, the model of delegated constitution). While the former may imply a better expression of the will of the people (via political parties), the latter may boil down to a situation where a victorious side (a party, a state or even a foreign power) imposes its will on the defeated. The consensus model is preferred to the rupture model in terms of stability, legitimacy and continuity of legal development. The rupture model is best suited for introducing the principles of democracy, modernization and constitutionalism into a traditional authoritarian society.

Currently, the political regime of the Russian Federation displays distinct features of transitional regimes. This regime took shape in an underdeveloped civil society whose shaky foundations were destroyed by the subsequent regime at the outset of the twentieth century. Democratic transformations, which had not been properly prepared in advance, led to an acute crisis of legitimacy and split the ruling elite at the end of the twentieth century. The process of legitimation, implemented initially on the basis of former legitimation (nominal Soviet constitutionalism), revealed sharp social conflicts that could be resolved solely through radical (revolutionary) transformation of a legitimate underpinning of the entire political system. Unlike some countries of Southern and Eastern Europe, Russia's transition to democracy was based not on the contractual model, meaning consensus among social movements and political parties, but on the model of legal continuity rupture. Eventually, the Constitution of the Russian Federation was adopted in 1993 not as a result of constitutional reform but as an outcome of constitutional revolution (according to its formal legal assessment) in which course the victorious side imposed its will on the defeated. Therefore, the Russian Constitution is characterized by a number of significant features.

Adoption of the constitution implied a radical discontinuity from the entire previous tradition of nominal Soviet constitutionalism with its class theory of law. A conflict between two fundamentally different types of legitimacy manifested itself in a series of coups d'etat – doing away with the one-party system and the demise of the Soviet Union (1991). The conflict was reproduced on a new level in Russia, and reached its peak when the president dissolved the legislative body in violation of the constitution existing at that time (the RSFSR Constitution of 1978) and irrespective of the Constitutional Court's opinion. The conflict between the new legitimacy and the old legality was resolved in favour of the former. The constitutional revolution found its expression in the new constitution, drafted by the Constitutional Assembly under the president's supervision and submitted by the presidential decree to a nationwide referendum on 12 December 1993.

Constitutional revolution in Russia: contents, stages and specifics

Constitutional modernization is widely known as the process of introducing changes to a constitution which is going to bring its norms into alignment with a new social reality. Society in general can be modernized in a legal or illegal manner. Legal (or constitutional) modernization, in turn, can either maintain or break legal continuity. These two kinds of legal modernization might be defined as a constitutional revolution or coup (they are basically identical, from a legal point of view) and constitutional reform. The latter can be carried out either through constitutional revision by introducing changes and amendments to the constitution or through adoption of a new constitutional legislation aimed at complementing or specifying the Basic Law provisions and their diverse interpretations.

In contemporary science, the two aforesaid models of transformations are defined as constitutional reform and constitutional revolution. Constitutional reform implies such changes to the Basic Law, which are in line with its own provisions and hence foster its legal development in a new socio-political reality. Being a means of constitutional modernization, such reforms may be accomplished through constitutional amendments or judicial interpretation of constitutional norms. Besides, they can be sometimes rather radical. Constitutional modernization is feasible, providing that the procedures for constitutional reforms are set down in the constitution itself and simultaneously there is a broad social consensus in relation to their application. It clears the way for controllable constitutional changes implemented through the contractual model of transition from authoritarianism to democracy. Constitutional revolution (or constitutional coup) means that there will be radical changes to the Basic Law that are not based on its own provisions and therefore create an entirely new constitution. These changes can be implemented in a formal way (in the form of the newly adopted constitution) or carried out along with the old constitution being preserved (whereby the phenomenon of the so-called "parallel constitution" appears).

The Russian process of transition clearly exhibits some specific features typical of Eastern European countries. First, constitutional transformations lagged behind (were tardy). Second, they coincided with radical social, economic and political transformations, whose analogues were hardly seen in other countries. Third, these transformations turned out to be closely connected with the problem of national identity (in this respect, they posed questions which other nations had already solved in the previous century). Fourth, it was a crisis of the entire political and legal system, which produced a vacuum of power (since the party and the state were integrated under the system of nominal constitutionalism). Fifth, modernization generated specific disproportions between the logic of social reforms (movement towards democracy and parliamentarianism) and the logic of constitutional reforms (movement towards a law-based state). All of these specific features taken together made the constitutional process convulsive.[3]

The period of transition consists of movement from the system of nominal constitutionalism to a real one with an explicit tendency towards sham constitutionalism. Nominal constitutionalism can be defined as the system where the constitutional norm is not effective at all. The classical principles of liberal constitutionalism which are governing human rights and power relations (the separation of powers) are not entrenched in the political system. The constitution legalizes an unlimited power, a dictatorship, which is *per se* unconstitutional. Therefore, this system is constitutional in name alone. And it does not have constitutional norms for power restriction in reality. Theoretically, the constitution is the embodiment of new legitimacy principles (sovereignty of the people, the nation or the class) and authoritarian administration institutions (the authoritarian one-party dictatorship). In principle, this type of constitutionalism corresponded to the totalitarian model of state and was clearly embodied therein. Its real, rather than declared, goal is to strengthen one-party dictatorship. All Soviet Constitutions (starting with the RSFSR Constitution of 1918) should be recognized as a historical expression of this kind of constitutionalism. Nominal constitutionalism had its own rigid logic, which one cannot overlook, particularly in comparative studies. The main distinctive feature of nominal constitutionalism is the supremacy of ideology over law, and of party over state (the resolutions of highest party authorities have never referred to the constitution authority). In this sense, the constitution itself forms part of this ideology and thus, can change accordingly. All constitutional rights and liberties, which are fixed by such constitutions (regarded as "the most democratic" by their advocates), therefore turn out to be fictitious even from a formal legal perspective, since they are entrenched as a conditional rather than absolute value regulated by the purpose of building a socialist and communist society (which, being a utopian ideal, defies any rational scientific interpretation and thus cannot be put into legal terms). Similar reservations were inherent in all the

Soviet-type constitutions, starting with the Stalin constitution of 1936 (Article 152), including the Brezhnev constitution of 1977 (Article 50) and even its modified Gorbachev version of 1991 (Articles 50–51). The entire logic of evolving nominal constitutionalism is also determined by the supremacy of ideology over constitutional law. Researchers assert that as the revolutionary legitimacy of Eastern European communist regimes was losing its strength, their constitutions began developing "towards reality". The trend manifested itself in a series of constitutional amendments made in the 1970s to introduce provisions on the leading role of the party (which was a real nucleus of power and government, but had never been previously mentioned in constitutions). A turning point came to be the inclusion in the 1977 constitution of a provision on the party's leadership (Article 6), which was abrogated only in the course of perestroika in 1990. This evolution, to some extent, prepared the processes of democratization and enabled certain nations to carry out negotiations ("round table discussions") between the party and the opposition. Yet, on the whole, it could not lead to an organic and evolutional transformation of a one-party dictatorship. Until the last minute of its existence, the system of nominal constitutionalism was characterized by a total differentiation between what was written in the constitution and the reality of everyday life.

Under the circumstances, it was impossible to make an overnight transition from nominal to real constitutionalism. A specific transitional process was needed to gradually do away with the dualism of nominal and real law (which was the focal point of perestroika); replace ideological monopoly with ideological pluralism (of course, within the framework of "socialistic pluralism" at the first stage); the doctrines of class-differentiated approach with the principles of civil society (acceptance of universal social values); one-party dictatorship with a permissible variety of forms of political expression (at first, restricting them to "informal public associations"); and lastly, annihilation of rigid ideological censorship ("glasnost" (openness)). These measures are to be followed by political actions to secure a consensus among political forces and to liberalize the political and legal system. All this terminology is part and parcel of any transitional period (it is especially close to Spanish tradition), and its narrowness is due to reformers' reluctance to call a spade a spade, primarily for the sake of consensus in a divided society.

The situation of transition is therefore objectively related to the emergence of a specific phase of nominal constitutionalism. On the one hand, the phenomenon of transition from nominal to real constitutionalism is observed. On the other hand, political decision making (due to objective conditions of constitutional crisis and forced "hypocrisy" of power) turns out to be deliberately withdrawn from the sphere of constitutional control. This goal can be accomplished through conferring vast legal powers on the head of state; maintaining flaws or lacunas in the constitution; and consequently, through establishing procedures for discrepancy adjustment and constitution interpretation, giving priority to the head of state. In such a way a specific political legal regime of sham constitutionalism emerges, which is capable of affecting the transition situation by leading it either to a real constitution or reproduction of authoritarianism in one of its myriad historical modifications. The choice largely depends on national historical traditions and transitional process particularities.

The act of adopting the constitution for the Russian Federation in 1993 had completed three long periods of Russian constitutional development. These include, first of all, the period of transition from absolutism to monarchical constitutionalism, represented by a shift from the first constitutional drafts to the fundamental state laws of 23 April 1906, and on to the declaration of the Republic in 1917. Second, the period of nominal constitutionalism that came about via the constitutional coup, forcible dissolution of the Constituent Assembly in 1918, to embrace the Soviet-era basic nominal constitutions (the RSFSR Constitution of 1918, the USSR Constitution of 1924 and RSFSR Constitution of 1925; the USSR Constitution of 1936 and RSFSR Constitution of 1937; the USSR Constitution of 1977 and RSFSR Constitution of 1978). Finally, the transitional (post-Soviet) period (1989–1993) embraced the adoption of the amendments that were introduced to the USSR and the RSFSR constitutions remaining in effect at the time, and included in the 1992 constitution edition (modified and amended).[4] Thus, the transitional period has absolutely clear-cut constitutional and institutional contours: it runs from 1989 (when the Congress of People's Deputies began its work and Mikhail S. Gorbachev launched constitutional reforms) to 1993 (adoption of the Constitution of the Russian Federation on 12 December 1993).[5]

Russia's transitional process can be divided into three main phases. The first phase (1989–1991) consists of attempts at partial reforms of the constitutional and political system (as related to the vision of possible reforms of nominal constitutionalism). Although the formal legality of these reforms is questioned by their opponents, they no doubt developed along the line of the old legitimacy. It is proven by the fact that the new legislation appealed to the old ideological attributes and some of them were borrowed from the 1920s rhetoric, which was used prior to the establishment of Stalin's regime. Transformations were aimed at strengthening "socialist democracy", rather than constitutional democracy. Gorbachev introduced a number of constitutional changes. The major changes were carefully implemented to permit the alternative forms of ownership, greater number of social initiatives, promotion of glasnost, federalism and separation of powers, as well as to abolish the party monopoly on power.

Decisions to reform the constitution were made by the party authorities in 1988. The main institution of constituent power – the Congress of People's Deputies that approved constitutional amendments – was not even mentioned in the 1977 constitution. Introduction of the office of the president became the chief result produced by the reforms. It was needed to strip the party structures of their power, de-ideologize society and make staff selection. The USSR Law on "Establishment of the Office of the USSR President and Introduction of Modifications and Amendments to the Constitution (Fundamental Law) of the USSR" was adopted after many heated debates at the Congress of People's Deputies on 14 March 1990. The first president was elected at that congress. But future presidents would be selected through direct national elections. The president was invested with extraordinary wide powers, including control over the cabinet of ministers. These changes were fixed in the Law "On Modifications and Amendments to the Constitution (Fundamental Law) of the USSR in view of Improvement of the Public Administration System", approved by the Congress on 26 December 1990. Gorbachev liberalized the legal system in order to legitimate the new institution of presidency, restructure ministries and Soviets, and to prevent a further fragmentation of the party and state. The new (substantially modified) edition of the 1991 constitution obliged the party, voluntary associations and other organizations to observe the constitution and other laws (Article 4). At the same time, running counter traditions, the improved party platform of 1990 said that the communist party and all organizations thereof were operating under the constitution and Soviet laws. However, Gorbachev's power, unlike that of Yeltsin, never relied on direct popular elections. The presidential form of government power was also accepted by republics, which provoked destabilization and separatism. The office of the president was established by a majority of votes in the RSFSR referendum on 17 March 1991. Thus, the power of the Russian president, unlike that of the Union president, gained a wider popular legitimation.

Therefore, a question related to the legality and legitimacy of the first phase was raised and debated from the outset of the transitional process. Although Gorbachev's reforms appeared real, actually they were not. Radical changes boiled down to revision of the constitutional system that was out of step with the content of the former fundamental law and procedures for introducing changes stipulated thereby. However, it is noteworthy that these changes were sanctioned by the highest party authorities playing (as was demonstrated) a decisive role in interpretation of the constitution (pursuant to Article 6), under nominal constitutionalism. A question arises as to how legal were the self-restrictions actually imposed by the communist party – the dilemma encountered by all authoritarian regimes at the stage of radical modernization. This question could be answered solely through a new interpretation of popular sovereignty where it performs its power directly via the system of new democratic institutions, rather than being delegated by the leading and guiding force.

The first phase can be compared to attempts at implementing similar reforms by Caetano's regime in Portugal and Suares' government in Spain at the initial stage of their transitional processes. In both countries, prominent governmental figures of the former regime tried to carry out a top-down liberalization, whereby they wanted to maintain continuity with the former regime. To this end, the reformatory elite was consolidated to oppose its conservative part, which in Spanish lexicon is defined as a "bunker". Yet, the phenomenon of one-party dictatorship was not so widespread in Southern Europe as it was in the Soviet Russia. Hence, this parallel can be drawn only with necessary adjustments.

The second phase, which essentially consists of constitutional revolution, covers the period from the August Coup of 1991 to the Coup of 1993. It was in-between these two coups d'etat that the future of Russia's constitutional system was determined. At the core of the second phase lies a conflict between the old legality and the new legitimacy.

The second phase started with a liberal coup attempt by the State Emergency Committee 18–19 August 1991, which became known as the "August putsch". Nevertheless, those advocating the Soviet legitimacy still do not accept this event being treated as a coup. They justified themselves by their desire to protect the former Soviet Constitution (which was revised and actually became ineffective), to prevent the union from breaking apart (as a result of introduction of the confederative system) and to restore the party monopoly on power. A state of emergency was imposed under the respective legislation. This action cannot be defined as a "coup" or "conspiracy" because it was intended not to change but, on the contrary, to preserve the existing system and was headed by the state leaders. Therefore, the leaders contrasted a false coup (seen through their eyes as the August putsch) against a real coup (staged by democrats). However, the arguments do not take account of the fact that most coups, not to mention putsches (in their specific German form), were staged by the elite leaders and sometimes by the head of state (this point differentiates coups from the revolution in a sociological context). In the Russian context, it was an attempt to restore the former Soviet system by doing away with constitutional innovations instituted at the first phase of democratic transition. That is how exactly the State Committee's actions were interpreted in the subsequent presidential decrees that stopped the party's functioning, announced dissolution of its executive structures and seizure of its property.[6] The very occurrence of the coup attempt and the crushing thereof, in any case, demonstrated that the contractual model of transition had failed and could not be implemented in the USSR (in contrast to Spain, whose example Russia followed at the initial phase of constitutional reforms).

The second phase of transitional process clearly manifests itself in a conflict between constituent power and constitutional power. Constituent power is defined as a power which creates basic norms. In other words, it means the power to write and adopt the wording of a fundamental law. Classic examples of constituent power are democratic institutions whose mission is to express the principle of popular sovereignty through adoption of fundamental constitutional principles. These institutions can have different formation procedures and enjoy wide powers, more or less. They can also be driven by different power ambitions. The most famous institutions are as follows: the Long Parliament in England, the Philadelphia Convent in the USA, the Convent in France, and the Constituent Assembly or parliament performing constituent functions in Russia. In some instances, the constituent assemblies, which were formed to draft a constitution, either did not fulfil their function (e.g. Israel) or failed to reach a consensus (e.g. Pakistan). The constituent power incapable of creating a constitution is indicative of political polarization and the failure of a democratic transitional period. The second (constitutional power) is defined as political institutions whose powers and procedure rules are set down in a fundamental law. The conflict between the constituent power and constitutional power manifested itself during the Congress of the People's Deputies, which brought about many changes aimed at the political structure democratization and liberalization. However, this conflict is reproduced at a new level after the August coup and the demise of the Soviet Union. In Russia, the transitional process is characterized by one distinctive feature (the phenomenon which is rarely seen, but not unique to Russia) – the emergence of two competing centres of constituent power, namely the Supreme Council Committee and the President.

The constitutional crisis, which arose in the post-Soviet Russia, showed that the parliament and president had divergent views on the constitution. Members of the parliament were elected under the old Soviet Constitution of 1978. Hence they could easily alter the constitution to their own advantage (for all Soviet-type nominal constitutions could be amended relatively easily) and use its wording against the objectively increasing (as a result the putsch's failure) power of the president. As for the president, he became the first head of state elected by a nationwide vote. Therefore, his liberal reforms were widely supported by the population. Finally, after the coup attempt, he was temporarily given emergency powers (which, however, he tried to retain later on). Russia's transitional situation almost corresponds to the concept of constitutional deadlock that, as some authors believe, leads to adoption of the presidential form of government during a period of transition (as illustrated by constitutional crises in Latin America). In fact, this way of crisis resolution creates a dualistic legitimacy. Put more precisely, two competing legitimacies – parliamentary and presidential – come into play. Both institutions of power are constitutional and formed on the basis of democratic elections. But they have radically divergent views on ways of resolving acute socio-economic and political crises. The conflict of the parliament and president covered a whole host of problems related to Russia's transitional process, including economic reforms, privatization of state owned property, foreign policy, military and administrative reforms. While the Supreme Council pinned its hopes on the former Soviet legitimacy and constitution, the president built his legitimacy upon the fact of being nationally elected and defeating the instigators of the conservative coup. As the conflict escalated, the two sides persisted in their efforts to revise the constitution. The Supreme Council strived to establish a parliamentary republic and turn the president into a ceremonial figure. The president, in turn, did not want to cede his power to the anti-liberal parliamentary majority. But at the same time he could not resolve the conflict in a constitutional manner by dissolving the Supreme Council and adopting a new constitution. In the conditions of "constitutional deadlock", another coup attempt was a real solution to the problem.

The coup was aimed at abolishing the dual power (or "dual anarchy"). Its main stages of development are well known. First, as early as March 1993, a decree was adopted to introduce a special form of government until the power crisis was resolved. This rendered any decisions void, which were made by government agencies to revoke presidential decrees. Then, on 21 September 1993, the president issued Decree No 1400 "On Gradual Constitutional Reform in the Russian Federation". The decree implied dismissal of the Supreme Council and Congress of People's Deputies, suspension of the constitution and of the Constitutional Court sittings, as well as holding a referendum on a new draft constitution and elections to a new parliament. Thereafter, the president adjourned the court sessions until the new constitution was adopted. In response to his actions, the Constitutional Court Chairman on behalf of the Court stated that "the president has staged a coup", made an attempt to "usurp power" and establish "tyranny". During the coup, the Supreme Council was forcibly dismissed and the Soviet system was annihilated. Following the coup, the new constitution conferring large powers on the president, was approved by the majority of votes in the referendum on 12 December 1993. The president's opponents clearly demonstrated that the new regime was illegal as it came to power by violating the previous constitution. They specifically stressed that the special Constitutional Assembly formed under the presidential decree was unlawful. They also noted that the constitution was drafted and discussed in a non-democratic way, and the president had no legal right to submit the constitution's wording for a nationwide discussion by his decree of 15 October 1993 (which contravened the existing law on referendum as of 16 October 1990). Thus, it was concluded that the current constitution lacked legitimacy and needed to be revised. The implementation of a radical constitutional reform and the introduction of many amendments to the constitution was also suggested. Until recently, the amendments have been primarily aimed at changing the form of government and the system of separation of powers in the current constitution, switching from the parliamentary republic to the mixed one, and introducing the system of checks and balances in relation to the presidential power. However, it would be naive to interpret Russia's constitutional crisis only as a collision between the parliament and president. For the Supreme Council can be called "parliament", with considerable reservations only (because the concepts of Soviet democracy and parliamentary democracy are absolutely incompatible). Equally, the institution of presidential power, which has inherited many functions from general secretaries, is far from being the equivalent of similar western forms. Russia was faced with the dilemma of whether to opt for formal democratic norms and passively observe the restoration of conservative forces, or for real political measures capable of moving these forces away from power.

The general dynamics shows substantial similarities between constitutional crises occurring in Russia at the beginning and at the end of the twentieth century. Therefore, it is enough to analyse only the unfolding of the 1993 constitutional crisis. An immediate result of abolishing the one-party system and proclaiming the constitutional principles of democracy, human rights and separation of powers came to be the emergence of dual power and of two opposite centres of power, namely the Supreme Council and President. The members of parliament (Supreme Council deputies), which were selected in the course of comparatively democratic elections in 1990, proceeded from the legitimacy of the old RSFSR Constitution of 1978 formally investing the parliament (Supreme Council) with full powers. The Supreme Council, of course, cannot be treated as a parliament in the true sense of the word; and the formal declarations of its powers had nothing to do with the reality of every day life. Nevertheless, those opposing a strong presidential power used the constitutional legitimacy as a sound argument and reason for its restriction. A conflict between the two kinds of legitimacy – parliamentary and presidential – broke out under the circumstances. Typologically, the conflict bears a close resemblance to the conflict between the Duma and monarch of the early twentieth century.

In this perspective, the so-called Stolypin coup d'etat is of interest. In characterizing the dismissal of the Duma as a "coup d'etat", contemporary historiography accepts the scenario suggested by the opponents of autocracy, namely liberal constitutionalists. Such a version is undoubtedly acceptable. Furthermore, from today's views on the separation of powers and parliamentarianism, it appears to be quite convincing. Liberals (at the time of the Vyborg Appeal) assumed that the very fact of the Duma being dissolved in the conditions of acute political conflict should be treated as a coup. Yet, the dissolution of the Duma did not contravene the legislation which operated at that time. In accordance with the "Establishment of the State Duma" (Article 3), "under a decree of the imperial majesty, the State Duma may be dissolved prior to the expiration of a five-year term". The complexity of a dilemma facing the liberal opposition is shown by the fact that even Constitutional Democrats dissented in their views on the issue. It was Fedor F. Kokoshkin who played a decisive role in labelling the dissolution of the Duma (and revision of the electoral law) as a coup. He justified his evaluation based upon the fact that the tsar manifesto on dissolution was missing a date for the new elections for the Duma. In doing so, Kokoshkin referred to the second part of Article 3: "By the same decree the new elections for the Duma shall be scheduled". The monarchy also had certain legal arguments for justifying its standpoint. Their reasoning was based on the octroyed nature of Russian Fundamental Laws: as the laws are granted by the monarch, they theoretically can be revoked or, at least, revised. It is clear that in the context of constitutional discussions of the early the twentieth century, this situation could be handled differently, even in relation to some formal legal arguments of law discipline of those times and to the interpretation of the whole system of monarchical constitutionalism therein. The real practice of monarchical constitutionalism was yet more distanced from the system of separation of powers envisaged by the constitution. The main reason for this fact was an increasingly broad application of emergency decrees (pursuant to Article 87 of the Code of Fundamental State Laws as amended on 23 April 1906).

In both cases (at the beginning and at the end of the twentieth century) the opposition relied on constitutional provisions, and the head of state could only counterbalance them with his greater legitimacy. In the case of autocracy, this legitimacy emanated from the tradition of monarchical statehood in Russia. In the case of the president, it stemmed from the president's personal democratic legitimacy. In both cases, the unfolding confrontation was not only and not so much a conflict between the two branches of power – legislative (parliament) and executive (head of state) – as a reflection of radically divergent views on Russia's future political structure. The two conflicts were resolved in a similar way, too. Their solution was found in dissolution of the parliament by the head of state. At the beginning of the twentieth century, Petr A. Stolypin dissolved the State Duma. Liberals evaluated his action as a coup d'etat, although it was actually based on the monarch's legitimate prerogatives. At the end of the twentieth century, the denouement of the conflict became even more dramatic because there were practically no legal arguments for its dissolution.

During the post-Soviet constitutional crisis, theoretically it was possible to choose between different strategies of presidential actions. After crushing the putsch of 1991, the President could hold new elections for the old Supreme Council, thereby securing a majority of votes for further peaceful implementation of his constitutional reforms. Yet, the President had another option which was to reach a consensus with the effective majority of the Supreme Council. Note the consensus seemed to be more attractive as it allowed him to avoid the rupture of legal continuity and ensure a greater legitimacy of new democratic institutions. So, the President preferred the second option which he later recognized as a mistake. The branches of power once again failed to reach a consensus in the post-Soviet Russia, just as they had not achieved it earlier in the pre-Soviet Russia (where the two strategies had been tested for the first time on relations between the parliament and monarch). However, the two sides have traded places during the constitutional crisis of recent times. In the pre-Soviet Russia, there was a conflict between the Duma and the Tsar. The former was a bearer of the ideas of western democracy and parliamentarianism. The latter was a bearer of the patriarchal values of Russian statehood. Let us compare this with the conflict between the Supreme Council and Russian President. The former was a protector of obsolete Soviet legitimacy. The latter was a supporter of western type democracy and constitutional principles of separation of powers. Nevertheless, in both cases, the conflict resolution raised grounds for accusations of unconstitutionality (on the part of the Vyborg Appeal in the first case, and on the part of the Constitutional Court in the second). The constitutional crisis of 1993, as you know, was solved through the use of physical force: the coup d'etat crushed the opposition parliament and concurrently permitted adopting the new democratic Constitution. However, the coup did not eliminate the objective reasons for confrontation which were reproduced in new forms thereafter (up to 1999, all the subsequent State Duma elections were won by the opposition). Therefore, the actions taken by the head of state during the coup were illegal, but legitimate. Accordingly, the conflict of legitimacy and legality acts as a dominant factor in the course of Russian constitutional crises.

The very method of constitutional crises resolution objectively leads to a growing authoritarianism and a strengthening autocratic regime. Hence the mechanisms for exercising the power inherent in Russian statehood is maintained and continuously reproduced under the new circumstances. Such conflicts are primarily triggered not by political parties or voluntary associations representing the wider strata of society, but by the institutions of power such as elites, bureaucracy and army. In recent times, this leads to some sort of plebiscite regime recognizing its continuity in relation to monarchical and dictatorial traditions. The trend manifests itself in a curious combination of ideological symbols taken from two different political traditions: democratic and patriarchal-monarchical.

The second phase can be compared to the constitutional coups staged in the Mediterranean countries, like Portugal, Greece, Turkey; and, in some way, to the camouflaged coup by Charles de Gaulle in France (where the legal tradition was continued only because they had changed the very procedure for revising the constitution of the Fourth republic).

The third phase could be defined as a subsequent legitimation of the new political regime and of the constitution created therein. The phenomenon of subsequent legitimation is well known from the literature on constitutional coups. Such legitimation is realized by the victorious side through referendums, plebiscites or constitutional court decisions. The legitimacy of the constitution can be backed up by the fact that a legal system in the true sense of the word had been unthinkable before the constitution was adopted. It was a Soviet system of nominal constitutionalism, and any attempts to reform the system at the final stage of its establishment can be hardly seen as legitimate. To put it bluntly, the newly adopted constitution replaced one illegitimate regime with another. In other words, the next coup occurred within the law. It would explain why a certain way was chosen for drafting and adopting the new constitution. The presidential draft of the Constitution was drawn up by the Constitutional Assembly, which was set up and fully controlled by the President. As for adoption of the constitution, the logic of conflict with the Supreme Council played a crucial role here. The concept of Constituent Assembly and the idea of giving constituent power to the Congress of People's Deputies (as was proposed by the Supreme Council) were rejected. The search for a consensus (contractual model) between the two competing centres of constitution making – the President and Supreme Council – yielded no results (and political parties were as usual not involved in the process). While the Supreme Council advanced the strategy for adopting the draft constitution at the Congress of People's Deputies (scheduled to open on 17 November 1993), the President forestalled them by staging the coup and then adopting a strategy for approving the draft constitution in a referendum. The referendum of 25 April 1993 enabled the President to adopt his draft and ensure its legitimacy. As the President relied on regional support in the conflict with the Supreme Council, it had some bearing upon the constitutional regulation of federalism and the upper chamber status. The Constitution was adopted by the referendum on 12 December 1993, which actually meant the subsequent legitimation of the constitutional coup results. The line of subsequent legitimation continued and was consolidated by the next parliamentary and presidential elections.

A political document, which was formally released to the international audience, can be viewed as an official version of events during the coup d'etat, therefore a reason for imposing a state of emergency.[7]

The basic arguments underpinning the subsequent legitimation can be divided into legal arguments (appeal to national and international norms); those related to the forced usage of means (a sort of principle of forced self-defence); and teleological arguments represented by statements (made before and after a coup) on the aims of actions undertaken.

The state of emergency, which was introduced in Moscow in October 1993, became a forced measure under the political crisis provoked by the resistance of the Congress of People Deputies to the attempts of the executive power at establishing a law-based state and implementing liberal economic reforms. According to the official version of the coup d'etat, the president's actions were contrary to Article 121–126 of the RSFSR Constitution of 1978 stipulating that the presidential powers shall not be used for suspending any legally elected bodies of state power. However, the document questioned the legitimacy of the article itself, which was introduced into the Constitution during the unfolding crisis of power. It was done to counterbalance a debated issue about the presidential right to announce early parliamentary elections in Russia. Under the circumstances, the president resorted to "forced emergency measures to dissolve the Supreme Council and the Congress so that to break the legal deadlock and allow Russians to have a say at elections" at a time when "all political measures for resolving the crisis were exhausted".

Despite appearing to be quite complex, the problem of legitimacy of the state of emergency was solved in a paradoxical way with reference to Article 56 of the 1993 Constitution that was adopted after and, obviously, as a result of the imposed state of emergency. The constitution did not work during the political crisis in Russia, as the crisis itself became constitutional in nature (counterparts failed to agree on the contents of a future Fundamental Law). Therefore, the situation was regulated by the Law "On the State of Emergency" of 17 May 1991 that specified terms, grounds and procedures for imposing a state of emergency, the forms of public administration and measures to be taken under the state of emergency, as well as respective guarantees of rights and responsibilities of citizens and officials. The contrast between legitimacy and legality becomes pronounced. The anti-constitutional actions of the president serve as a safeguard of the "fundamental principles of constitutionalism", namely the "principle of rule by the people and that of separation of powers", unity and integrity of the state and national security. The presidential actions appear to be aimed at protecting the democratic system from the conspirators who had "mutinied" against legal authorities and unleashed "bloodshed, street riots and raids" in the capital (3 October 1993). To safeguard the security of the nation and its citizens, the president imposed a state of emergency and undertook measures to secure his regime on the evening of 3 October 1993. In doing so, he acted in accordance with the Law "On the State of Emergency" and the International Pact on Civilian and Political rights:

> As the opposition refused to give up the struggle and the militants continued their actions threatening the life and health of the population, the president had to crush the mutiny.

Finally, the subsequent legitimation involved a retrospective reference to the aims of presidential actions in order to prove his democratic intentions. The key argument lies here in the fact that the Decree on Gradual Constitutional Reform in the Russian Federation as of 21 September 1993 specified the date for the Duma elections, guaranteed their freedom, and provided for the full scope of human rights and fundamental freedoms including the right to participation in national administration and liberty to form associations and conduct political activities. In addition, there were other grounds, notably the political statements of the president and government expressing their desire to solve the crisis peacefully, according to the "universally recognized rules of political struggle with the opposition".

The international legal legitimacy of the coup was determined (in the absence of stronger reasons) by such a strange argument as that of the president having observed "the principle of proportionality enshrined in the International Pact on Civilian and Political Rights". In view of this principle it boiled down to minimization of "human losses" and giving mutineers a chance to "freely leave the parliament building".

A comparative analysis of the Russian model of transitional period allows one to reveal its specifics and particularities. This model is determined by the rupture of legal continuity while overcoming the deadlock of Soviet nominal constitutionalism. The deadlock could not be broken through preserving legal continuity. For the nominal character of the previous legal system practically ruled out any rational application of Soviet constitutional norms. In Russia and over post-Soviet countries, the transition to democracy was conductive to radical changes in property relations, national relations and structures of power. Thus, debates on the constitution were, at the same time, the means of choosing a social development strategy. Unlike many other constitutional crises, the Russian crisis embraced cultural, institutional and economic factors along with legal and technical ones. The constitutional problem historically evolved by manifesting itself repeatedly in the fact that legal modernization outpaced the reform of social structures. Hence, the polysemy of the term "constitution" in the Russian political context: fundamental law, supreme attribute, frameworks of civilized forms of struggle and strategic lines of future political system. These general factors seriously impeded (if permitted at all) the implementation of the contractual model of transition to democracy. Was this feasible in Russia?

Theoretically, such reform was feasible (as shown by political events of some of the Eastern European countries) only given a preliminary preparation of public opinion. Hence, the ruling elite had to be consolidated at a new level around the strategic goals of constitutional reform. At the present time, some researchers note the signs of such consolidation within the Chinese communist elite (particularly, under the influence of Russian experience) that has decided to conduct an interesting social experiment. They are gradually developing a social consensus and constitutional changes not so much along the line of amendments to the constitution as along the line of semantic changes to key ideological terms fixed therein. We do not know how successful the Chinese experiment will be. However, it evidently relies on the specifics of nominal constitutionalism whose advantage lies in the fact that ideology and law are intertwined. Therefore, legal norms could be treated in different ways (some may be contradictory) due to their ideological interpretation and explanation (Politburo performs the function of Constitutional Court). Another example is the evolution of the Iranian post-revolutionary constitution whose operation can be also radically changed according to the interpretation of Islamic principles. In Russia, however, the systemic crisis of one-party dictatorship ruled out the possibility of such an internal or organic transformation of nominal constitutional norms. Eventually, the model of legal continuity rupture prevailed and opened the way for a constitutional revolution.

Russia's constitutional crisis chiefly consisted of conflicts between legitimacy and legality, constituent power and constitutional power, the federation and the subjects of the federation and between the constitutional branches of power. On the whole, it was a long series of coups d'etats where each coup was legalized (in contravention of constitutional procedures, almost every time). Until recently, the supporters of Soviet legitimacy (of a one-party system) in Russia employed as an argument the fact that the radical political changes of the last decade of the twentieth century had always led to the rupture of legal continuity. They even speak about a "three link coup d'etat" (the anti-party coup in August 1991, the anti-union coup in December 1991 and the anti-Soviet coup in 1993) (well, they would say that: a coup may consist of three links . . .). Nevertheless, the thesis can be accepted from Kelsen's normativist standpoint treating law solely as an effective law. In this case, the history of Russian coups should be traced from toppling the monarchy and overthrowing the Provisional Government to dismissing forcibly the democratically elected Constituent Assembly and adopting the first Soviet Constitution (which was a purely nominal act, just like all the subsequent Soviet Constitutions). Thus, the Soviet period could be defined (in legal terms) as a permanent coup d'etat. This formula of French publicists of the Fifth Republic is more suitable for the twentieth century Russia, whose first and final stages were marked by constitutional revolutions and ruptures within the law. The problems of Russian transitional period were very well understood among the Latin American countries where coups had played an essential role in the adoption of liberal constitutions. Two revolutions (of 1917 and of 1993) can be noted in the history of Russian constitutionalism, if it is compared to Mexico. However, the uniqueness of Russian constitutionalism is manifested in the impact of social forces, which every time determine the entire process beyond legality. The same phenomenon can be easily tracked in the constitutional reforms implemented over the last decade by Brazil, Peru, Argentina and Mexico.

It is worth noting that in the struggle with "communists", "democrats" have used the classical tactics of coup d'etats of the twentieth-century far more effectively compared to the former. Curzio Malaparte, a political observer, noted that a key element of these tactics was subsequent legal legitimation of the actual power seizure. In opposition to Kelsen who believed that only a successful coup d'etat could be treated as legitimate (since it independently positions itself within the frameworks of positive constitutional law), contemporary researchers (and political practitioners) have reached the contrary conclusion: a coup cannot be successful without its legal (simultaneous and subsequent) legitimation and in this sense legitimation is already implicitly present during the coup as a key criterion of its success. Russian communists were well aware of this fact. Therefore, they have been staging coups and simultaneously legitimizing them since 1917. Virtually all of the considerable constitutional changes in the republican Russia resulted from the coups d'etat. Yet, some coup attempts were made to impede these changes (a sort of constitutional "counter-coup"). So, the palace (inner-party) coup, which overthrew Khrushchev in 1964, was secretly prepared over a long period of time and appeared on the surface as an ordinary conspiracy to seize power. However, this coup also meant embarking on a new political course, which manifested itself in the rejection of the material prepared by Khrushchev's constitutional commission. The next Constitution of 1977 was adopted in a new epoch and it was based on different ideas.

The history of post-Soviet constitutional reforms can be defined, to paraphrase the well-known term, as a "permanent constitutional revolution" going through all the main stages: from comprehension of legitimacy crisis and attempts to solve it through partial reforms to crisis resolution in the form of a new constitution with its subsequent legitimation. At all of these stages, society was a mere background against which political groups were struggling with each other. Dual power ruled out any possibility of the contractual model implementation, which could hamper reforms and transform them into a latent form under the circumstances existing in Russia. Parties (even if compared to the humble representation of opposition public opinion in the course of round table discussions in Eastern Europe) were not in the least represented in Russian constitutional process. Decisions were made not so much under established procedures by the commissions independent of executive power as by the very small groups supporting political leaders. The openness of constitutional debates was also criticized. Finally, the political expediency of adopted rules was preferred to their scientific examination. Suffice to mention here the questions that most frequently arose in the process of constitution making and provoked a wide-ranging discussion in society during democratic transition, but had never been a subject of open constitutional debates in Russia. These include: procedures for adopting a new constitution; application of constitutional principles and norms borrowed from other countries; continuity of the new constitution in relation to the previous constitutional legal development in Russia; holding a referendum for discussing and often deciding on the form of government (primarily, the issue of the monarchy's future addressed by Southern Europe); the concept of separation of powers and prerogatives of the head of state; the type of federalism and the problem of the upper chamber structure; the role of religion and church in public life, especially in the light of educational problems (which were extremely relevant to the Catholic Southern European countries and to some countries of Eastern Europe), restitution of property (which was significant for a number of Eastern European countries); and lastly, problems with the trial of leaders of the former dictatorial regime and their accomplices (which were particularly urgent for Latin America, Southern Europe and for a number of Eastern European countries). Unlike the Eastern European countries where constitutional changes were implemented through "velvet revolution" smoothly evolving into "velvet counter-revolution", the Russian conflict was traditionally resolved by Blut and Eisen.

The constitution was adopted in the heat of political confrontation. It embodied both the merits and demerits of the continuity rupture model. In particular, the merits of the constitution are its liberal stance on human rights, commitment to the market economy and pro-western orientation. However, Russia, as Bruce Ackerman put it, didn't missed its "constitutional moment" (the culmination of national and social upsurge calling for adoption of a constitution corresponding to the true aspirations of society and to the level of national development). The Russian Constitution resulting from the rupture of legal continuity, a genuine constitutional revolution, in this sense did not mean implementation of the contractual model of transition from authoritarianism to democracy but implied the delegated method of transition (virtually it was octroyed from above by the victorious side). The conflict between the new legitimacy and the old legality was resolved in favour of the former. Hence, there emerged a legitimacy deficit and the necessity of long subsequent legitimation for the constitution. The main contradiction of this transitional process – adoption of the democratic constitution by non-democratic means – is not unique to Russia in recent times. Nevertheless, Russia's transitional process has most clearly revealed the fundamental inconsistency of modernization – between goals (declaration of a law-based state) and means (strengthening of authoritarianism in the form of a plebiscite democracy).

The constitution as a phase in establishing civil society and law-based state

Analysing the Russian Constitution of 1993 in the context of modernization processes enables one to identify its historical significance and peculiarity. The analysis also reveals inconsistencies in the Russian Constitution as related to its contents, purposes and adoption procedure. The constitutional revolution resulting from accelerated modernization produced, as was demonstrated, an important result – the democratic constitution was introduced by authoritarian means. The way in which the new constitution was adopted (via the constitutional coup and subsequent legitimation) could not but affect its contents. Hence, there is an evident discrepancy between the declaration of rights and a more authoritarian model of power (which makes the first part of the constitution less feasible). This situation upholds national historical traditions. In Russia, since the times of Peter the Great, the state power has often acted as a tool of modernization supporting it even more vigorously than society itself. It is precisely the state that implemented key reforms aimed at Russia's modernization and Europeanization in the pre-revolutionary period. In doing so, it relied on western legal norms which were later entrenched in the practice of traditional society. And the new Russian Constitution was essentially adopted in such a way. The "advantage of backwardness" rested upon the fact that under a constitutional revolution (when the state power was not practically bound by old legal norms), it was possible to adopt any western models and treat them flexibly enough to adjust to the national context.

This fact should be taken into consideration when addressing the problem of norms borrowed from foreign constitutions during the adoption of the 1993 Constitution. Since information on the constitution drafting is restricted, we still do not know much about the motive and nature of major borrowings in the Russian Constitution. This problem was mainly highlighted by the foreign experts who were in one way or another involved in debates on the Russian Constitution (e.g. Michel Lesage, Stephen Holmes). A study into the western constitutions in Eastern Europe could be useful only when the opinions of comparativists were taken into account as to what degree one or another institution corresponds with the aims and specifics of living law and with the conditions required for its proper operation. In Russia, constitutional drafters initially concentrated their attention on the US experience (like in some other countries of Eastern Europe). The parliamentary constitutional commission was interested not only in the US Constitution but also in the constitutions of several states. In the conditions of struggle for power between the Supreme Court and President, there arises, as was demonstrated, the conflict between two concepts of constitution and state structure, hence two alternative directions for possible borrowings: the draft constitution prepared by parliamentary commission gravitated to a semi-presidential system, whereas the presidential side pressed for a presidential system. The first draft was based on the Weimar Republic Constitution of 1918 and to a larger extent on the Soviet Constitutions (especially on the RSFSR Constitution of 1978), providing for an ostensibly strong parliament along with a real one-party dictatorship. By contrast, the second (presidential) draft included several provisions of US constitutionalism. Among them observers noted the following: the president's exclusive right to control of executive authorities; the president's right of vetoing any act passed by the parliament, which is subject to approval by a two-thirds majority; the right to be elected for a six-year term on the basis of a nationwide vote, in tandem with a prime minister who automatically becomes the speaker of the upper chamber. The influence of the US model peaked at the beginning of 1993 when Russian experts met with US specialists (and the latter criticized the Russian draft of constitution). By the end of the year, as the constitutional crisis was coming to a head, the Constitutional Assembly formed by the President for bringing two drafts together found out that many elements of the US Constitution were unsuitable for Russian conditions. Thus, by the time the final constitutional draft was prepared, initial euphoria over the US Constitution was replaced by modest interest in continental European models, historically less influential but more adaptable. Under the circumstances, Russian specialists began looking at the constitutions of France, Germany, Belgium, Spain and Italy. According to Robert Sharlet:

> The 1993 Constitution of the Russian Federation could be seen as a constitutional equivalent of the European watermelon made up of components produced in several countries advantage of backwardness.[8]

What prompted the Constitutional Assembly to change its priorities so radically at the critical moment of constitutional crisis, which seems even stranger given that the US Constitution is considered a model of the presidential system implementation? Robert Sharlet singles out several features of the US constitutional model that make it impractical for the former Soviet bloc countries to implement it. These features include: state minimalism falling beyond the perception of the state as a prerequisite for economic development in a transitional period; the absence (due to the concise nature of the US Constitution) of provisions regulating the process of public administration (hence, it is unclear how governmental agencies can put the constitution into practice); while the American Bill of Rights is focused on negative rights, positive rights enjoy popularity in the post-Soviet states. And finally, the fact that operation of the US Constitution can be solely ensured by a special judiciary: constitutional interpretation falls within the jurisdiction of the Supreme Court and subordinate federal courts, each of them treating the constitution as a legal and regulatory document. Thus, the model in question can be hardly realized in the countries that do not have the tradition of independent judiciary entitled to judicial control.

We believe, however, that the US model was rejected for political rather than purely juridical reasons. Some of these reasons can be compared to those underlying the rejection of the US model in France (though such ideas were frequently advanced during the period of the Fifth Republic). The main reason is that if one tries to integrate the over-rigid model of separation of powers inherent in the US Constitution into a different social context, it will inevitably entail the risk of recurrent constitutional crises in relations between a parliament and president (which is mitigated in the USA by the independent judiciary and the stable two-party system). In most of the countries that have borrowed this model, it works inadequately, and what is more, often becomes a major factor contributing to dysfunction and causing coups d'etat. Therefore, some countries try to modify the system either through a less rigid separation of powers (reception of the French variant in one form or the other) or by concentrating them (as was done by Latin American countries). Under the Russian constitutional crisis, this argument, intentionally or unintentionally, was to play a decisive role (although we do not have any documentary proof of discussions being held on this issue).

Therefore, a way out was found in the combination of constitutional borrowings implying reception of the constitutional norms constitutional drafters deemed as most relevant to the Russian situation. The Constitution of the Russian Federation contains in its sections the principles which are borrowed from the constitutions of different countries. The interpretation of human rights came under the influence of international and European charters on human rights, and constitutions of the fourth generation; the formation of an asymmetric federalism model was affected by the constitutions of Spain, Belgium and possibly by that of India, in part. The traditional influence of German constitutionalism was reflected in the general interpretation of federalism, the upper-chamber concept and the Constitutional Court structure. German constitutionalism also impacted on parliamentary elections, providing for a mixed (proportional and majority) voting system and a five per cent barrier for parties to get into the Duma. The system of separation of power, particularly presidential power, was affected by the US and French Constitutions. However, in the Russian Constitution the system of balances was eliminated, which is represented by the Congress' exclusive right for legislative activity in the USA and by the principle of cohabitation in France. The US Constitution had a major influence on the procedure of president dismissal and the mechanism of constitutional amendments. The French influence (a dichotomy between organic and ordinary laws) manifests itself in the difference between constitutional federal laws and ordinary federal laws, which is envisaged by the Constitution of the Russian Federation. Furthermore, the western (French) law indirectly contributed to restoration of the provision on citizen's constitutional right of trial by jury, which was introduced by the judicial reform in the nineteenth century and left its mark on the liberal concept of the judicial reform carried out these days.[9]

The drafting of the Russian Constitution is therefore characterized by a pluralism of borrowing sources, which is in principle (though to various degrees) typical of all the constitutions of catch-up democratization. So, the Spanish Constitution was mainly affected by German and Italian models, the Greek Constitution by German, French and Italian models, the current Polish constitution by German and French models, etc. In general, the most common constitutional norms, such as those fixed in international acts on human rights, become practically universal. And it is often difficult to say which country they originate from. Thus, the very fact that the Russian Constitution includes borrowed principles follows the common practice of constitution making. However, the final outcome has no doubt proven not only its viability but also its effectiveness during acute constitutional crises over the past decade.

The 1993 Constitution is an undeniable achievement compared to the previous phase of nominal constitutionalism. Russia is defined as a "democratic federative law-based state with the republican form of government" (Article 1, part 1), as well as a social (Article 7) and secular (Article 14) state whose bearer of sovereignty and the only source of power "is its multinational people advantage" (Article 3). The rights and liberties of man, whose interpretation was profoundly influenced by international and European charters on human rights, are declared to be the "supreme value" and protection thereof – a "duty of the state" (Article 2). The important component parts of the legal system are a consolidation of alienable natural rights (Article 17, part 2), ideological plurality (Article 13, part 1), the freedom of public associations' activities (Article 30, part 1), prohibited censorship and the freedom of the mass media (Article 29, part 5), with the guaranteed freedom of literary and scientific creativity (Article 44, part 1), prohibition on the propaganda inciting "social, racial, national or religious hatred" and superiority (Article 29, part 2). For the first time in Russian history, the principle of separation of powers was clearly articulated (Article 10). The right of legislative initiative was given to the supreme executive, legislative and judicial power (Article 104, part 1). The Russian Constitution (unlike the preceding Soviet Constitutions) has created a professional parliament: the deputies to the State Duma shall work on a permanent professional basis and may not be employed in the civil service (Article 97, part 3). Judges shall be independent and shall obey only the Constitution and the federal law (Article 120, part 1). An important practical and concurrently symbolic step came to be adoption of the principles of presumption of innocence, adversarial court proceedings and trial by jury (Article 49, part 1 and Article 123, part 4). In other words, the basic ideas of the pre-revolutionary judicial laws of 1864 have been revived. These ideas had a strong impact on the liberal concept of judicial reforms in Russia. Thus, the constitutional coup resulted in adoption of the Fundamental Law which had initially a limited scope of democratic legitimacy but created prerequisites for a civil society and law-based state.

Conflict dynamics is of essential importance for human rights. The rights and liberties of man and citizen may be restricted by the federal law only to the extent required for the protection of the fundamentals of the constitution system, morality, health, rights and lawful interests of other persons, for ensuring the defence of the country and the security of the state (Article 55, part 3). Hence, of fundamental significance is the interpretation of such notions as "defence" and "security". For an overbroad interpretation thereof may lead to heavy restrictions on rights and liberties.

The 1993 Constitution of the Russian Federation and the political system it created opened the way for democratic development of legislative and executive powers (the mixed majority-proportional system), and for adoption of the principle of separation of powers and functioning of a multi-party system (as was demonstrated by all subsequent Duma elections which were dominated by the left-wing opposition until recently, namely prior to the 1999 parliamentary elections). Since 1993, Russia's political regime has been displaying characteristics that are typical of many contemporary presidential systems in general. These characteristics include: firstly, dual legitimacy which leads to a continuous struggle between the two branches of power and blocks economic reforms (under transition to market economy); secondly, the frequent replacement of governments which is done by the president not for objective reasons but tactical considerations of political struggle; and lastly, a continuous confrontation in relations between the parliament (dominated by the opposition) and the president (many attempts at constitution revision, demands on impeachment, usage of any mistakes committed by the administration in order to increase a personal political potential). Furthermore, unstable presidential systems are usually characterized by autocratic regimes, impulsive leadership and paternalistic relations between officials within the state machinery. However, the main and decided advantages, which have legitimized a strong presidential regime in the eyes of the population, are curbing centrifugal tendencies and ensuring the continuity of power, and political stability during the transitional period. Russia's current constitution is a reflection of social compromise in the divided society that has resulted from post-Soviet stiff confrontation between democracy and authoritarianism.

The historical role and, in a way, teleology of the Russian Constitution should be recognized as its distinguishing feature. The constitution was drafted and delegated under the stiff confrontation of the old regime forces with the nascent new regime. No matter what specific goals and objectives the coup instigators pursued, their historical legitimacy involved democracy and struggle against totalitarianism. The constitution's authoritarian nature and way of adoption were referred to as forced measures against the conservative supporters of the old regime restoration (known as neo-Stalinists).

At the same time, it was repeatedly stressed that the political regime established by the 1993 Constitution owed its creation to the old Russian monarchical tradition, in many respects. In Russia, the imperial system used to position itself as a guarantor of order and stability both within the country and beyond. It was predicted that other options would be disorder, anarchy and chaos. Finally, this system and especially statehood has always been an instrument of modernization and society's Europeanization. The imperial model could take on various forms (for example, forcible modernization in the form of a "regular state" implemented by

Peter the Great or liberal reforms carried out by Alexander the Second in the 1860s), but a reformatory impulse did not always come from the top. The same thing has happened nowadays. Besides, these trends have gained considerable momentum over recent years.

The legitimation of constitution underwent profound changes: initially it was based on the ideas of democracy, anti-totalitarianism, federalism and revolutionary liberalism, then those ideas gave way to the ideas of revival of national grandeur, state unity, patriotism and strong power. Although the notion of "imperial consciousness" had been earlier criticized for denouncing the Soviet system, later it increasingly acquired positive connotations leading to the restoration of the Soviet imperial symbols (the flag, the emblem and the hymn). In this context, the legitimating premises of a constitutional system are no longer dominated by motives related to the post-Soviet mentality crisis. Rather, they are filled with the elements of historical consciousness including the imperial epoch archetypes. The legitimizing formula of the current regime increasingly resembles that of the old imperial regime (including symbols, rhetoric and the paternalist image of governmental actions). It is noteworthy that the constitution does not quite rule out (permits) this kind of interpretation as well.

Contradictory views on the constitution and its historical significance are typical of both contemporary literature and society at large. Some authors state that the constitution is liberal in nature and forms a solid basis for the new Russia. The others assert that the Russian Constitution is "nominal rather than real" and treat it as a document of a transitional period "because of the debatable legitimacy of its promulgation and the president's unrestricted right to issue decrees".[10] While some of them consider the principles of human rights, federalism, separation of powers and the multi-party system declared in the constitution to be a real thing and a safeguard of democracy; the others doubt that the declared principles are a fait accompli and a guarantee against the restoration of authoritarianism. The majority of researchers claim the constitution is to some extent inconsistent and stress its conformity with the objectives of Russian authoritarian modernization.

By summing up these historical observations, we can say that the 1993 Constitution, to a certain extent, not only disrupts the historical continuity but also restores it by bringing back the situation that emerged in the wake of the first Russian revolution and was characterized by alternative directions of constitutional development. The 1993 Constitution completes the Russian constitutional cycle which got underway in 1905. Having passed through the 100-year cycle of revolutionary upheavals, Russian society has essentially returned to its original form with a different social content, of course.

The 1993 Constitution became a turning point in the movement towards civil society and law-based state, which marked the beginning of the transition from nominal constitutionalism to a real one. A comparative study into the adoption of the constitution, specifics of its contents and subsequent developments allows us to make a number of general observations.

When examined in comparative perspective, the Russian model of constitutional transformations exhibits both the general features, which are typical of all countries under transition from authoritarianism to democracy, and Russia's specific features, which originate from its historical traditions and transitional period peculiarities. Constitutional transformations in Russia, as described, have certain analogues in various regions of the world. The processes of transition to democracy everywhere manifest themselves in the phenomenon of constitutional modernization. Being an objective result of a rapid transition from the authoritarian model to the democratic one, the constitutional crisis primarily shows itself in a conflict between legitimacy and legality, that is between the new system of democratic values and the old, usually, repressive system of political legal institutions and norms. Given a widening deficit of legitimacy of the existing legal system, the idea of a new constitution catches on among the people and comes to the forefront of the campaign for society renewal led by political forces. Finally, the constitutional crisis is settled either through the contractual model of adopting a new democratic constitution (implemented through the consensus reached by political forces, which society was gradually preparing for) or through the model of legal continuity rupture. It is precisely the second model that was implemented in Russia, thereby determining the entire logic of subsequent constitutional process.

As the constitutional crisis grew worse, Russia could not solve it with the contractual model (through a radical constitutional reform) and had no choice but to disrupt the legal continuity by a constitutional revolution. Why did Russia, unlike many other countries, opt once again for the second variant instead of the first one? The question is still at the heart of all debates on the constitution, its legitimacy and development prospects. When answering this question, one should point out a number of common cultural characteristics: specific historically evolving relations between the state and society in Russia; absence of the infrastructure of civil society with its key components such as private property, individual rights, autonomous judiciary; and lastly, the historical tradition of top-down modernization – radical changes in public relations introduced by bureaucracy with a view to fostering catch-up development. These characteristic features of Russian historical process did not only remain unchanged after the revolutions of the early twentieth century, but, conversely, they assumed a special grotesque expression in the totalitarian state. It was exactly these features that the constitutional revolution of 1989–1993 so clearly manifested. The crisis of one-party dictatorship led (for the second time during one century) to collapse of the state, modified property relations and a new system of political and administrative institutions.

This meant that society had firmly rejected the whole system of nominal constitutionalism. Interestingly enough, the constitutional revolution in the post-Soviet Russia (intentionally or unintentionally) used the terminology of the preceding revolutions: Russian, French and American. The transitional period could be defined as a constitutional crisis manifesting itself in the conflicts of a nominal constitution and a real one, legitimacy and legality, constituent power and constitutional power, federation and subjects thereof, parliament and president. A solution to the crisis is found in the permanent constitutional revolution persistently destroying the most important underpinnings of the old regime. The revolution inevitably entails a whole series of legal coups accompanied by subsequent legitimation of their results. It was rather easy to use the mechanisms of subsequent legitimation for new legal norms, since the masses of people (in contrast to democratic transitional periods in other countries) were callously indifferent to the constitution.

Constitutional modernization, Europeanization and catch-up development, which found their expression in the revolutionary logic of creating a new law, have led to the adoption of the 1993 Constitution that outpaced its time in terms of several vital parameters.

Mechanisms of cycles: constituent power and constitutional power

In literature, it has been described how the different models for adopting constitutions in the period of transition (via contract or continuity rupture) determine the contents and operation of constitutions in society. However, a transitional situation differs from stable periods by the fact that it speeds up changes and necessitates the analysis of constitution in terms of its dynamics as well as statics. To understand the mechanisms of cyclicity and the overcoming thereof, one should look at the correlation between constituent power and constitutional power. The first (constituent) power is defined as a power which creates norms. In other words, it means the power to draft and adopt a fundamental law. The second (constitutional) power fixes political institutions, their powers and procedure rules in the fundamental law. The crisis of the transitional period manifesting itself in a serious gap between constituent power and constitutional power, lays the foundations for subsequent phases of constitutional cycles. Since such a gap emerged at the initial stages of all Russian constitutional cycles, it might open up in the future too. Therefore, it is advisable to examine the provisions of a constitutional revision, which are laid down by the current constitution, to see how they could be practically applied under the transition from authoritarianism to democracy (taking account of not only legal, but also political arguments affecting the constitutional revision).

There is a traditional concept dividing constitutions into flexible, rigid and mixed. It is easy to change flexible constitutions because it can be done by parliament acts. However, the consequences of changes are quite serious and virtually irrevocable. Rigid constitutions, by contrast, are difficult to alter; but, if necessary, it can be done through introducing other changes. There can be also a rigid constitution adjusted by judicial interpretation (the USA). Mixed constitutions include various combinations of flexible and rigid ones.

In recent times, rigid constitutions are mostly seen in societies under transition from authoritarianism to democracy. It is linked with the aspiration to consolidate radical changes in society, on the one hand, and to ensure no return to authoritarianism, on the other. That is the essence of all the South European constitutions which set forth very complex procedures for their alteration (e.g. Greece, Portugal, Italy). A similar approach is characteristic of other post-communist constitutions of Eastern Europe. Russia's Constitution is no exception and is defined as rigid. It is worth mentioning that the future of the constitutions of transitional periods is not only and so much determined by provisions on their alteration as by the nature of their adoption and political conditions. So, the contract constitutes an invisible pillar of the entire "constitutional building" in the countries where transition was carried out via the contractual model. Therefore, the fixed procedures of constitutional amendments are designed for maintaining the established balance of political parties; and the procedure of constitutional revision turns to be the second consultation on the issue of contract preservation. Under the circumstances, any constitutional changes require the involvement of all major political parties. Constitution is not only a legal act but also a political contract. Such a situation unfolded in the FRG and Spain; and is now partly seen, perhaps, in Hungary (where the ruling party coalition even halted adoption of a new constitution in order to hold onto power). It is also due to the fact that the political elite (for example, in Spain) is reluctant to apply the procedure of constitutional revision without valid reasons. The reverse effect of this situation is that opponents accuse the constitution of becoming sacred and solid.

Another option is seen when a rigid constitution adopted in the course of constitutional revolution and legal continuity rupture, embodies the dominance of one force or power over the others. In that case, the rigidity of constitutional revision procedure fixes coup results and becomes directly proportional to the force of opposition. The Russian variant of rigid constitution is an example of this trend. A question arises: is it possible to revise the Russian Constitution of 1993, what are revision mechanisms, and what kind of political reality stands behind the possible constitutional changes? Contemporary literature on legal issues provides many ways of constitutional revision (some of them are unlawful, of course) that can be arranged in decreasing order of their sweeping nature, as shown below.

First: through a constitutional revolution or a coup (when a constitution randomly changes without resorting to revision procedures enshrined therein; for example, the adoption of the RF Constitution in 1993). In the course of its development, society repeatedly encounters a situation where the dynamic political force (a parliament, a president or a monarch) striving for supremacy and domination, yet constrained by old constitutional norms, has to change those norms in an illegal manner (e.g. Napoleon III whom the French Constitution did not allow to run for another term). This course of events is undesirable for society, since it leads to constitutional coups and to the crisis of legitimacy. In such conditions, over-rigidity becomes a drawback of the constitution. Along these lines one can interpret proposals to change the duration of presidential mandate, to probe into public opinion and to prepare the latter for introduction of imperial presidency.

Second: through the revision of the entire RF Constitution when chapters 1, 2 and 9 are modified by the Constitutional Assembly (it practically means a radical constitutional reform). It is recognized that the distinguishing features of the Russian Constitution include the separation of constituent and constitutional powers and application of various procedures for modifying different constitutional provisions. The constituent power (Constitutional Assembly) is responsible for constitutional revision (making changes to chapters 1, 2 and 9), whereas the constitutional power is responsible for introduction of amendments. The Constitutional Assembly was sometimes treated as Russia's contemporary analogue of the Constituent Assembly. This statement is, however, premature because the principles of assembly formation are vague. We know what has happened to the constitutional consultative bodies and many other similar institutions formed in different countries in modern and recent times. Although these institutions essentially represented the constituent power, they were actually formed and fully controlled by the executive power.

Debates on the principles of Constituent Assembly formation (and alternative strategies related thereto) illuminated the following issues: formation principles, terms of power, procedure rules and the assembly's prerogatives in constitution making. The institution of Constitutional Assembly envisaged by the RF Constitution of 1993 was, most likely, borrowed from the US Constitution (where this institution is referred to as Convent, and regulation of its functioning is also uncertain). Therefore, it is no surprise that the issues linked to the Russian Constitutional Assembly are similar to those arising in the USA in relation to the procedures of convocation and functioning of the Federal Convent. The Federal Convent (pursuant to Article V of the US Constitution) shall be convened by the Congress at the request of states' legislatures. This institution can be potentially set up at any time, though it has never been convened to discuss constitutional amendments. No one knows how they managed to form such a convent as this. In fact, the 1787 Philadelphia Convent was convened in conditions which could not make it a model for future convents called by the legislatures of states with a view to discussing amendments. This situation raised three sets of questions: how such a Convent can be summoned; if it is possible to limit the range of issues for discussion; how the Convent should be organized and conducted; and what measures can be undertaken by the Congress and states in response to the Convent's actions? Since these questions are not regulated by the legislation, they would cause much concern under constitutional crisis.

Conversely, countries of Southern Europe (e.g. Greece, Spain and Portugal) and most of the East European countries used to assign constituent functions to the parliament (except the Bulgarian Constitution). However, in the wake of decadence of the Weimar Republic and modern German doctrine, when investing their parliaments with constituent powers (given the required qualified majority and conformity with the established procedure for consideration of draft laws on amendments), those countries usually specifically stipulated that the constitution might be changed only through a special law on its alteration or by introducing substantive limitations on its revision, in some instances. For example, they could list the constitutional provisions that could not be changed under any circumstances. The revision procedure is, sometimes, completed by a referendum whose results determine a final decision on the future of constitutional reform.

The formation procedure for the Russian Constitutional Assembly is still unclear, thus the latter's political orientation remains in question (recent drafts on the Constitutional Assembly confirm the doubts). The problem of constituent power has always been linked to the issue of legitimacy of the Russian Constitution. Opponents view the constitution as illegitimate, while supporters speak of its historical and popular legitimacy as opposed to the legal one. The opposition criticized the way in which the constitution was adopted, referring to falsification of the vote (referendum) results. They proposed to adopt a new constitution based on consensus among various political forces within the framework of a more representative and legitimate body – Constitutional Assembly or other constituent authority (Zemstvo Council, Constituent Assembly, Congress of People's Deputies). The problem, however, consisted not in what form of constituent power to choose and what historical name this institution would be given to, but in the latter's capacity to build a consensus on the constitution in society. Such consensus or realization of the contractual model is feasible, only providing that political parties are in agreement. Otherwise, all the efforts of constituent power would be frustrated by discord and division in society. This can be exemplified by Democratic Conference, Pre-Parliament and Constituent Assembly during the revolution of the beginning of the twentieth century, and the failure of analogous institutions during the constitutional revolution at the end of the twentieth century (to this we should add the institutions of consensus search such as the Congress of People's Deputies, abortive attempts to set up a common constitutional committee during the conflict of parliament and president, unproductive agreements on consensus between social and political forces, the recent failure to convene a new Democratic Assembly and Civil Forum). Furthermore, these examples show that the institutionalization of consensus in a divided society usually does not eliminate contradictions. Therefore, the examples of successfully doing away with authoritarianism in a contractual manner (the Spanish model) are very seldom found. Given the immaturity of political parties and the absence of a culture of compromise, the idea of a new constituanta appears to be feeble in the present-day Russia. The lack of strong parties and public associations may also result from the new Federal Law on Political Parties. Therefore, the initiative of convening a Constitutional Assembly and adopting a new constitution can bring benefits solely to the forces which are sure that the expected results will be achieved. That means that constituent power can be externally controlled. Given the existing balance of forces, it is fairly easy to undertake such an action and find a good reason for it (for example, the necessity of altering the constitution due to creation of a new union state). However, this action can undermine the regime's constitutional legitimacy in the long run.

Third: by altering the Russian Constitution by introducing amendments (under the procedure prescribed by the constitution, decisions of the RF Constitutional Court and the Federal Law of 4 March 1998, "On the Procedure of Adoption and Enactment of Amendments to the Constitution of the Russian Federation").[11] The Russian mechanism for making amendments, borrowed from the US Constitution, appears to be extremely rigid. As a matter of fact, this mechanism was devised in the USA so as to prevent federalists from altering the constitution and was intended to safeguard the rights of the states from any attempts at establishing an overcentralized model of federalism (in the USA, it was precisely federalists that promoted these ideas; they supported the unified federative state and struggled with its opponents – confederates). This motivation was, of course, present during the adoption of the Russian Constitution (it is suffice to mention conflict norms in the Constitution and the Federative Treaty of 1992). At the same time, Russia obviously had another strong motivation (typical of all post-communist countries). It aimed to avert restoration of the one-party (communist) system by making the amendment procedure as cumbersome as possible. That is why the mechanism for introducing amendments was not only adopted but the Constitutional Court also explained how it should be properly applied, thereby preventing the prevailing Duma opposition from changing the constitution.

It would be wrong to say that the Russian Constitution is fully protected from radical changes implemented via amendments. For it provides neither for broad substantive restrictions, as the Portuguese constitution does, nor for limitations under emergency situations, as the Spanish Constitution does, nor for provisions prohibiting the revision of certain norms under whatever circumstances, as does the Basic Law of the FRG does.

There is not such a binding element as a strong and independent system of conventional norms whose observation is ensured by historical tradition and independent judiciary (for example, the UK whose unwritten constitution can be easily changed by the Parliament's decision). Theoretically, much depends on what forces initiate amendments, and how the latter are approved, passed and adopted as legally substantial modifications. It is clear that the usage of different methods of constitutional revision already represents a certain political choice based on objectives pursued by the ruling elite or counter-elite. Given this interpretation, the question should be put another way: who can actually introduce amendments to the constitution, how and under what circumstances?

Fourth: by revising the Russian Constitution through its interpretation by the RF Constitutional Court (particularly, while considering lacunas, omissions and discrepancies in the constitution, solving conflicts between the constitution and federal constitutional laws). Interpretation can take on various forms, including interpretation of norms of the constitution on its proper revision, as was demonstrated by the Constitutional Court's interpretation of Article 136.[12] Some authors have advanced the idea of granting the RF Constitutional Court the right to initiate constitutional amendments (by submitting proposal on amendments). This idea is questionable because it not only contrasts with the global experience but also denies the role of the court as a negative legislator, turns it into a potential rival of the legislature and eventually does not rule out the possibility of its politicization (which, as is well known, occurred in the past).

Fifth: through revision of the RF Constitution by adopting new constitutional or federal laws that, as is well known, can transform the scope of basic constitutional definitions and the hierarchy of their values. Besides, it can be done not necessarily by an individual law but by their totality. These changes, implemented without a formal revision of the constitution, have already resulted in a virtually parallel constitution. Russia's current constitution has undergone substantial modification in all of its most important sections (by federal constitutional laws). These changes are made along the following lines: vertical separation of powers (transition from contractual federalism to a centralized one, creation of a new administrative and territorial system, changing the status of subjects of the Russian Federation and their role in the interpretation of federalism in general); horizontal separation of powers (changing of the functioning of the upper chamber through a radical revision of its formation procedure, institution of the State Council which is not envisaged by the constitution, reform of the judiciary and procuracy, giving more powers to the president for re-enforcing the vertical hierarchy of power, etc.); relationships between the state and society (revision of the status of social organizations and political parties, an incipient restructuring of the electoral system, etc.). It is asserted that the real prerogatives of the presidential powers are to be drastically increased (the model of imperial presidency).

Sixth: by implementing the presidential "decree" law and modifying the legislation through the revision of law application (completely changing the political regime, for example, by delegating powers to courts and to the administration or imposing a state of emergency, etc.). By the way, it is precisely the simple laws that had changed the Weimar Constitution. Therefore, the Russian Constitution is in principle not protected from again facing a situation where radical constitutional changes could be introduced by the decisions of parliament or RF president.

Seventh: by changing the actual conditions of life without revision of law (it is possible, in particular, to provoke such actual conditions). These changes in their totality (for example, new public ethics and ideology, regime of administrative structures, media and business) transform the whole spectrum of constitutional norms, including those enshrined in the sections on fundamental rights, federalism, system of state power and form of government. To some extent, these changes reflect a tendency towards reconstitutionalization, implying a return to the discussions held on the eve of adoption of the RF Constitution in 1993.

If the parliament is dominated by one party in power and the state power as such is actually removed from legal control (as happened in a number of countries during reconstitutionalization), it probably means the end of a regular constitutional cycle – one of those which repeatedly emerged, climaxed with stagnation and was followed by a new constitutional revolution. It is easy to turn the parallel constitution (given the existing balance of forces) into an effective one. Theoretically, this process can lead to a lifelong presidency (for example, as was demonstrated in several CIS states). The effectiveness of such a system depends on who is the bearer of supreme power. However, it does not contain any internal checks and balances; therefore difficulties may arise during succession to power (plots, confronting clans, etc. replace the selection of elites during democratic parliamentarian elections).

Let's turn to a classic example: the Weimar Republic was destroyed by a gradual revision of the constitutional regime, with the formal constitutional frameworks remaining intact. Such changes were feasible because the prevailing positivist legal doctrine was treating leniently the very fact of revision of the Weimar Constitution. In the process, a decisive role was played by the following factors: the parliament was keeping aloof from political affairs; the competences of legislative power were delegated to executive ones ("decree" law); and emergency laws were introduced.

As a rule, constitutional rigidity is always counterbalanced by the possibility of an extra-legal, non-legal or quasi-legal procedure of revision. Despite the popular opinions, the constitution (as shown by the comparative analysis) does not in the least bit hamper its revision and therefore permits constitutional cyclicity. Furthermore, in the absence of other restraining mechanisms an over-rigid constitution provokes constitutional changes along the main directions in extra-constitutional space. From this perspective, the trends in constitutional development, seen over the past decade, give extremely useful information on the following parameters: decentralization and centralization of the political system – the evolving concept of federalism; transition from separation of powers to their unification – the form of government and type of political regime; conflict of modernization and retraditionalization – the strategy of constitutional reform in today's Russia.

Decentralization and centralization of a political system: the evolving concept of federalism

Alteration of centralization and decentralization periods is a constant in Russian political (constitutional) history. The whole social system became unstable due to the amorphousness and vulnerability of society including its upper layers; weakness of the middle class and absence of the western traditions of struggle for freedom, intelligentsia maximalism; and, above all, the external, imposed nature of state origin under implementation of social transformations. In principle, the social system was characterized by two opposite conditions: mechanical stability evolving into apathy (under the reinforcement of state origin); and the reverse condition – destabilization turning into an anarchical protest against the government (because of the latter's impotence). In the absence of former stability, there emerges a trend towards the "sovereignty parade", i.e. decentralization leading to a collapse (for example, during the Times of Troubles, the civil war of the early twentieth century and the breakdown of the Soviet system in the late twentieth century). As soon as the system recovers, there emerges a trend towards "collecting lands" which leads to centralization and even to absolutism. The post-Soviet period also displays the alternation of decentralization and centralization phases described by academicians and historians (e.g. Sergey M. Soloviev, Vasily O. Klyuchevskiy and Pavel N. Milyukov).

Development of post-Soviet federalism permits identifying the following key phases: i) the beginning of the transition from Soviet nominal federalism (virtual unitary system) to a real one – this phase got underway by the end of the 1980s and ended with the collapse of the USSR and declaration of state sovereignty in Russia in 1991; ii) the incipient destabilization of the Russian Federation and achievement of shaky consensus – adoption of the 1992 Federative Treaty and the 1993 Constitution; iii) the conflict development of federalism throughout 1993–2000; and iv) the recent phase of evolving federalism since 2000 up to the present day.

From a long historical perspective of relations between the centre and regions, the evolution of federalism could be described as the alternation of several models of state structure. The "strong centre – weak regions" model prevailed during the Soviet period. In the post-Soviet period, the two first phases had the reverse logic: the "weak centre – strong regions" model predominated. Finally, the last two stages – adoption of the 1993

Constitution and launch of reforms in 2000 – are characterized by intensification of international processes and gradual restoration of the "strong centre – weak regions" model. Thus, we can assert that the post-Soviet federalism has been evolving through certain cycles embracing three main phases: the virtually unitary Soviet model; collapse of this model; and consolidation of federalism on a new base, along with the increasing powers of the federal centre.

The constitution has reflected a transitional phase in the development of Russian federalism. Crisis of the one-party system resulted in the power crisis and political vacuum. Consequently, the centrifugal force quickly gained momentum and induced the breakdown of the Soviet Union, which was followed by the incipient destabilization of the Russian Federation as such (regional conflicts sometimes involved the usage of troops and arms by confronting sides). Decentralization also had an objective economic rationale (regional elites were controlling the allocation of resources under privatization). Finally, at that time the growing nationalism as a social phenomenon which was restrained by the communist system for a long period of time peaked, manifesting itself in political demands for national sovereignty (contrary to the effective legislation but following the tradition of the old Soviet legitimacy with its views on the right of all nations for self-determination). Reaction to the spontaneous process of decentralization was society's automatic and, in a way, systemic (in terms of the self-preservation of state integrity) appellation to the strong presidential power. The adoption of the constitution in 1993 is a crucial phase in the evolution of Russian federalism. Of fundamental importance are Articles 4 and 5 included in chapter 1 "The Fundamentals of the Constitutional System". Article 4 consolidates the sovereignty of the Russian Federation, supremacy of the constitution and federal laws throughout the entire territory of the Russian Federation and guarantees its integrity and inviolability. Article 5 sets down the common principles of Russian federalism. It entrenches the equality of all subjects of the Russian Federation: republics, territories, regions, federal cities, an autonomous region and autonomous areas. Russia is defined as a federal state based on the delimitation of scopes of authority and powers between the national, regional and local levels (Article 1 and Article 5, part 3). The significance of federalism-related problems is confirmed by the fact that chapter 3 "The Structure of the Russian Federation" carefully regulates the status of the federation and subjects thereof. Beyond the jurisdiction of the Russian Federation and the powers of the Russian Federation on issues within the joint jurisdiction of the Russian Federation and the subjects of the Russian Federation, the subjects of the Russian Federation shall exercise the entire spectrum of state power (Article 73). The regions were given a number of exclusive prerogatives. The republics defined their status within the frameworks of their constitutions; and territories, regions and federal cities within the frameworks of their statutes. The republics have the right to institute (in addition to the national Russian language) their own state languages (Article 68, part 2). Pursuant to chapter 8 "Local Self-Government", the bodies of local self-government enjoy financial powers, approve the local budget, establish local taxes and levies (Article 132, part 1). At the same time, the major legislative acts – Declaration of the State Sovereignty of the RSFSR as of 12 June 1990 and the Federative Treaty as of 31 March 1992 – were not declared void with the adoption of the RF Constitution.

The correlation between the Federated Treaty and the RF Constitution merits special comment. Under the incipient collapse of the state, republics signed the Federated Treaty on 31 March 1992, and on 10 April 1992 it was incorporated into the RSFSR Constitution of 1978 which operated at that time. The Treaty had legally fixed the sovereignty of republics inside the Russian Federation and assigned the status of subjects of the Russian Federation to territories, regions and federal cities. It is acknowledged that the key result of the Treaty is delimitation of scopes of authority between the federal bodies of state power and the bodies of state power of republics, territories, regions, federal cities, autonomous regions and autonomous areas inside the Federation. However, the Treaty defined republics as "sovereign states" and not merely "subjects of the federation", directly referred in its preamble to the "declarations on the state sovereignty of republics inside the Russian Federation" and guaranteed "republican citizenship" and not only citizenship of the Russian Federation.

The Federative Treaty could be evaluated as a forced compromise in the conditions of constitutional crisis. Despite prevailing superficial opinions, one should not build on the assumption that federalism, as a universal phenomenon of these days, is good or bad as such. Federalism is a recognition of the existing political reality that can evolve either into confederalism or a unitary state in the long run. Accordingly, the Treaty (and the principles set forth therein) may be good or bad depending on what is considered to be a long-term goal. Obviously, from the very beginning the parties to the Treaty – the federal centre and regions – had different views on the use of this document. The federal centre treated it rather as a forced concession prompted by the conditions of the current stage of power consolidation. The regions (primarily, national republics) regarded the Treaty as consolidation of their rights acquired in the post-Soviet period and of their new status (sovereign republics). We have witnessed how the collapse of the USSR resulted in the decentralization of the RSFSR, when all of its autonomous republics and regions declared themselves to be a sovereign state inside Russia. The most fanatical supporters of secession (Chechnya and Tatarstan) strived for the status of independent states. Given the vacuum of power, several regions (Tatarstan, Yakutia and Bashkorstan) adopted the constitutions establishing their status as independent states and international law subjects.

The Federative Treaty of 1992 is an essential component of the Russian statehood built up under the crisis of central power; and, in this sense, there was no alternative to it at that time. Conclusion of the Treaty, like the preceding historical documents that appeared after the fall of the Russian Empire in 1917, became feasible (and reasonable) under disintegration of the unitary state maintained exclusively by one force – the communist party, which in such capacity succeeded to autocracy. The essential features of political reality came to be the vacuum of power in the centre and its consolidation in the regions, which had actually (if not legally) turned into sovereign states. The entire logic of the 1993 constitutional crisis and subsequent political stabilization are mostly determined by this structure of relations between the centre and subjects of the Russian Federation. This fact becomes evident from the review of materials of the Constitutional Assembly and the whole scope of activities relating to the drafting of the new constitution. That also explains the system of separation of powers fixed in the constitution, specifically the framework of the upper chamber (Council of Federation), its structure, procedure of formation and exclusive power prerogatives.

The RF Constitution of 1993 established the priority of constitutional provisions over the Federative Treaty, which was cautiously removed from the constitution. It was removed from the final constitutional draft that was adopted by the Constitutional Assembly just prior to holding a referendum on the wording of the constitution on 12 December 1993. Provisions of the Treaty underwent serious modifications (the final constitutional draft deleted the word "sovereignty" in the respective article of the draft at the very last phase of discussion). After adoption of the constitution in 1993, the concept of contractual federalism strongly influenced both theory and practice: the Russian Federation and several republics signed treaties on delimitation of the scope of authority and reciprocal delegation of powers; incidentally, the meaning of these norms was also assessed ambiguously. Sometimes they were interpreted by republics as modification of the constitutional status of the Federation and its subjects. Besides, the Constitutional Court of the Russian Federation has always stressed that such interpretation of the treaties is unlawful because the Russian Constitution has priority over all the legal acts including treaties on delimitation of the scope of authority.[13]

Recent reforms question (if not formally, then actually) the system of separation of powers that took shape during the transitional period, implying a shift from the contractual model of federalism to the constitutional one (yet more centralized). The shift is seen as an objective trend within the process of reconstitutionalization, which is indicative of reinforcement of the federal centre at the expense of subjects of the Federation. However, it is important to take account of three factors: first, reform of the historically developed system of compromises between the centre and regions (enshrined in treaties between them) should not be exclusively formal and imposed in nature (it, as already shown by history, turns the problem inward without resolving it); second, federalism (and the system of separation of power built upon it) is a vital prerequisite for a pluralistic democracy and a means of preventing power usurpation; and lastly, the federal intervention or direct presidential government (as demonstrated by worldwide experience) should be regarded as an emergency measure rather than a system of permanent control over the regions.[14]

Dissenting views on Russian federalism are reflected by three stances: acceptance of the existing model; denial of this model; possibilities for its improvement through partial modifications. These stances correspond, to a certain extent, to the proposed concepts of the model of bicameralism that can be strong (when two chambers are essentially on equal footing in legislative process, but the upper chamber can block the lower chamber's decisions, like the US Senate does) or weak (when this symmetry and congruence between two chambers is non-existent, like in the UK, France and Spain) or can represent some sort of intermediate option (for example, the FRG that formally has the weak model of bicameralism, but the Bundesrat can block the part of legislative acts related to federalism).

In Russia, there are different views on the formation procedure of the Council of Federation (that has changed three times over the past decade), on the chamber's role in settlement of constitutional and political conflicts (when broad constitutional powers of the upper chamber, stipulated by Article 102 of the Constitution, were not used) and on its functioning in the capacity of political institution. There are five models, at least: corporativist model, model of regional representation, model of legislative filter, model of impartial arbiter, and that of buffer in relation to regions. However, to make this complete, it is important to mention such an extreme stance as the abolition of the upper chamber or its replacement by the State Council, whose prospects and procedure rules have not yet been defined.[15]

The key criterion for identifying true federalism and distinguishing it from the false one is that subjects of the Federation must have the right to control constitutional changes. As long as the regions enjoy this right only nominally and in the form stipulated by the Federal Law "On the Procedures of Adoption and Enactment of Amendments to the Constitution of the Russian Federation", they can hardly exercise this control in practice. It has been shown by the recent adoption of fundamental legislative acts (Land Code of the Russian Federation, Federal Law "On Political Parties" and Federal Constitutional Law "On the State of Emergency") that the opposition formed by regions and many members of the upper chamber by no means creates an insurmountable obstacle.[16] This fact manifested itself most explicitly in the adoption of the Russian Land Code.[17]

Thus, the contractual model of transition to federalism turned out to be unpopular in post-Soviet Russia. Neither was it in demand in relation to adoption of constitutional principles in general. Russia's incipient transition from nominal federalism to a real one soon became subject to adjustment towards centralization whose scope and strength are seen more clearly today.

From separation of powers to their unification: form of government and type of political regime in Russia

The processes of political system decentralization and centralization manifest themselves in relation to both the very principle of separation of powers and its implementation. In Russia, actualization of the concept of separation of powers (both horizontally and vertically) used to coincide with the periods of liberal reforms and Europeanization, and the tendency towards power concentration with periods of conservative counter-reforms, search for "original" principles and renunciation of Europeanization. The principle of separation of powers and its interpretation quite explicitly reflect the cyclical nature of constitutionalism. The first phase of the cycle (criticism of the current system) generally has as its target the imperfection of the existing mechanism (striving towards separation of powers); the second builds its renovated construction in a positive constitutional law; and the third one works for agreeing this rational construction (frequently estranged from reality) with political and legal reality (the principle of separation of powers is either fully discarded or treated in a different way: separation of branches or functions of one power). Thus, different interpretations of separation of powers determined the boundaries of constitutional cycles throughout the French constitutional history. It is debates on parliamentary, presidential and mixed forms of government that best determine this logic in the course of constitutional cycles in different countries.

The international discussion as to which form of government and type of regime best suited the policy of democratic consolidation of society remained quite current throughout the post-Soviet transitional period in Russia.

Discussions on the contractual model for the transitional period rendered a conclusion that a parliamentary (or mixed) form of government is more preferential than a presidential one. With this in mind (proceeding from the aforementioned comparative analysis of transitional models in Southern Europe and South America), turning to East Europe and specifically to Russia prompted a researchers' conclusion on inadequacy of the Russian presidential constitution.

Critics of the Russian Constitution did not, however, offer any real alternative in the exceptional situation of transition from nominal constitutionalism to a real one. The point is that in this type of transitional society (missing not only a legal system but also the entire infrastructure of democracy: federalism, public organizations, parties, vested interests) the problem turns sooner to self-identification and articulation of various interests than to the choice between weak and strong models of presidency. While in Latin American countries the democratic transition was exercised under army supervision, it is precisely presidential power that acted as the driving force of transition in Russia.

In today's Russia, like in many transitional societies, it is very difficult to distinguish between the form of government and political regime. Nevertheless, for the sake of clarity it should first be reasonable to review the very constitutional norms stamping a specific form of government (their foreign sources and discussions on their constitutional contents), then to clarify the nature of their functioning concentrating on what is generally referred to as regime and, finally, to address the problem of their balance and synthesis taking us, as a result, to the uniform problem of political and legal regime.

The key and probably most debatable specifics of the 1993 RF Constitution is the model of separation of powers prescribed in it. In Western Europe, there is a variety of modifications of parliamentary or mixed regimes. Heated debates on the form of government, characteristic of transitional periods in countries of Southern Europe, didn't go beyond the formal frameworks of presidential-parliamentary form of government, even at times of maximum reinforcement of executive power (in Greece under Konstantinos Karamanlis, in Portugal during the dictatorship of Revolutionary Council). Thereafter, the situation tilted even more towards parliamentarianism, through constitutional amendments.

In the post-communist countries of Central and Eastern Europe, the problem of restriction of power of head of state was the focus of round table discussions, and unambiguously solved in favour of parliamentary (Hungary) or mixed parliamentary-presidential form (Poland, Romania). In the states with formerly monarchical regimes (e.g. Albania, Hungary, Romania, Yugoslavia) the issue of monarchy restoration, though there is a certain number of its proponents (Bulgaria, Albania), did not have a strong impact on the choice of the form of government during the transitional post-Soviet period. Parliamentary republic was established in the bulk of the countries in the region (Albania, Hungary, Slovakia, Czech Republic, Estonia), and in the form closest to the German model of rationalized parliamentarianism (a president is elected by parliament). Also represented is a mixed republican regime in a variety of forms of parliament-president relationships. While some fraction of such regimes is closer to parliamentary-presidential form, as the decisive role in pursuing political course is played by prime minister (Bulgaria, Slovenia), then the other gravitates towards presidential-parliamentary type as the president has a decisive influence on the government course (e.g. Lithuania, Poland, Romania). For all the conventionality of this typology, it illustrates the scale of choice of government forms in countries of Southern and Eastern Europe in transitional periods.[18] Even in Turkey, with its traditions of sultanism and army's meddling with politics, the political system evolution essentially involved movement from parliamentary republic to a parliamentary-presidential one. The current non-liberal constitution of Turkey, adopted after the military coup in 1982, did not create presidential political regime but instituted a specific semi-parliamentary system where president, elected by parliament from professional politicians, acts as a "power broker in a political game". The dominant system for the majority of democratic states in Asia and Africa, after they gained independence, turned out to be either the Westminster (parliamentary) system or one of the numerous modifications of the French (Gaullist) model of separation of powers.

Best-known systems with a strong presidential power are the ones in the USA, and the mixed forms thereof such as the Weimar Republic and the Fifth Republic in France (at the time of Gaullism) in the twentieth century. In the former case, the choice was determined by the impact of the concept of an English monarchical system, and in the second and third cases by the desire to adjust the so-called "party regime" leading to instability of parliamentary majority and instability of governments. Given the current constitutional crisis in Italy, suggestions on reception of Weimar and Gaullist models were also motivated by the absolute power of parties and instability of coalition governments.

In Russia, there have been no such reasons. The Russian Constitution, largely based on American and French models (and its drafts were also influenced by the constitution of Weimar Germany), established the regime of a strong presidential power. While being distinct from the known forms of parliamentary and mixed republics, Russia's constitution also fixed radical distinctions of the Russian political regime from the classical presidential form (such as that in the USA, other presidential systems, and even dictatorships in Latin American countries disguised as presidency), for there is no extremely rigid model of separation of powers.

Contemporary scholars argue about the form of government existing in Russia. According to one opinion, Russia is a mixed republic whose nature is referred to as semi-presidential, semi-parliamentary and even "non-preparliamentary" (this is rather a journalistic term expressing the struggle towards an extended parliamentarianism). The most immediate analogue of this system could be seen in the Fifth Republic in France. It was termed a mixed form of government, though the very formula is quite ambivalent as it covers political regimes featuring different trends (from the trends close to parliamentary to those close to "republican monarchy").

It is only right, therefore, that the proponents of this point of view (the mixed form of government in Russia) are looking for analogues to Russia's regime not so much in contemporary states as in historical forms of the regime, comparing it with dualistic constitutional monarchies. According to this opinion, Russia's form of government "retains the majority of components of dualistic regime where public authority is dominated by president". It should be noted, however, that legal literature of the past did not agree on whether dualistic monarchy is an independent and stable form of government (as Paul Laband and George Jellinek assumed, for example) or is just an interim and unstable transitional step towards a parliamentary republic (as Ademar Esmein believed). Also, as is seen from past history, dualistic monarchies (being unstable combinations of the opposite types of legitimacy: popular and divine) gravitate towards one of the pure forms – parliamentary monarchy (British or Belgian types) or to monarchical constitutionalism regime in German, Dual and Russian Monarchies, where it had all the attributes of sham constitutionalism. This discussion is applicable to any modern mixed regime, including the Russian one, if it is interpreted in terms of a mixed or dualistic form of government. A distinguishing characteristic of the Russian "edition" of this system is a real supremacy of the head of state who, while not being the head of an executive branch of power in constitutional terms (unlike the US president), performs this function in reality, keeping up the traditions of monarchical and Soviet periods. In this case, it would probably be more appropriate to speak of a mixed form not as a real but as a potential one. Note, however, that treating the Russian regime as a mixed form of government has prompted a host of amendments to the RF Constitution, boosting the regime evolution towards strengthening parliamentarianism and accountable government (the logic and terminology of these amendments correspond to those of Russian liberals during the first constitutional cycle).

The other point of view treats the Russian form of government as a presidential republic. The nearest analogue is the US presidential model (though sometimes the concept of "presidential republic" is interpreted in broader terms and includes also the French model, which may function as a presidential republic). The main arguments of this standpoint stress the legal and actual precedence of presidential power in Russia. It is precisely where the proponents of the mixed form of government in Russia see the proofs of its presence (as components of constitutional accountability of government), its opponents find confirmation of their case (in the form of weakness of these components).

And, finally, the third opinion defines the Russian model as a super-presidential republic. It is specific in that, given some (sooner formal) attributes of a presidential system, it lacks a real separation of powers for the president is vested with huge executive and legislative powers. The concept of a super-presidential system was developed as applied to regimes in Latin America. The numerous dictatorship regimes (Argentina, Brazil, Venezuela, Uruguay, Chile) have elevated this power to an absolute level. Some of its essential components were retained, however, upon transition to democracy. The main characteristic feature thereof is the president's prerogative to issue emergency decrees (the so-called "decretos de necesidad y urgencia") with which the president can exercise radical legislative reforms and current administration over the head of parliament. In Latin America, only presidents of Argentina, Brazil and Columbia may issue statutory decrees in any policy area. These decrees turn into law, however, only upon their subsequent endorsement by Congress. Otherwise the president risks impotency. Thus an attempt at liberal economic reforms through such decrees, undertaken by President Color in Brazil, failed and forced him to resign. In some cases (Peru, 1993) the "executive decree" law is confined by fiscal issues. The concept of a super-presidential republic or "hyper-presidency" implies (in Argentina) an actual (but not constitutional) orientation of the whole system of separation of powers to the president. The super-presidential regime in Chile, in the wake of adoption of the authoritarian constitution in 1980 and of constitutional reforms in 1989–1991, vested the president with the right to dissolve the chamber of deputies, impose veto, issue decrees and emergency executive powers.[19]

It is important to note, in comparative perspective, that the real presidential powers are far from always arising directly from constitutional provisions. In reviewing the Mexican Constitution of 1917, the term "meta-constitutional power of president" is used. Mexican scholars generally use the term "presidencialismo" so as to concurrently define the presidential system of government and stress the exceptional concentration of powers (constitutional and all others) in the hands of the Mexican President.[20]

According to the RF Constitution of 1993, the prerogatives of Russia's president exceed those of his Latin American counterparts. Left-wing authors criticized the "decree" law of Russia's president in relation to the so-called "anti-communist decrees". But it has much longer traditions and is rooted in the history of the specific type of constitutional monarchies in Eastern Europe which, at the final phase of their existence, were governed with emergency decrees. The problem of the "decree" law and the so-called emergency-decree legislation has always been important for monarchical states, especially in Germany and Russia. According to the 1906 Fundamental Law of the Russian Empire (Article 87) the emperor enjoyed an important prerogative to issue such decrees, valid as provisional law, in-between State Duma sessions (intermission, which he could initiate himself). These decrees were, however, to be subsequently approved by the State Duma upon resumption of its activities and, given no approval, the validity thereof terminated.

Pursuant to Article 88 of the RF Constitution of 1993, Russia's president shall, under the circumstances and procedures envisaged by the Federal Constitutional Law, impose a state of emergency on the territory of the Russian Federation or in areas thereof, and in the event of aggression against the Russian Federation or an immediate threat thereof shall introduce martial law on the territory of the Russian Federation or in individual areas thereof (Article 87). In both cases the president has to immediately notify the Council of Federation and State Duma of this. Only in these two cases the presidential decrees must be approved by the Council of Federation (items 'b' and 'c', Part 1, Article 102 of the RF Constitution). It does not follow from the constitution, however, that the Council of Federation's refusal to approve the presidential decree on the introduction of martial law automatically implies the repeal of martial law. The latter is introduced by the president, who is the supreme commander-in-chief of the armed forces (Part 1, Article 87), and only he may abrogate it. Yet, the refusal of the Council of Federation to approve the respective presidential decree renders it to be in conflict with the RF Constitution, hence, the president is obliged to repeal the decree.

Handling the problem of state of emergency is very important for unstable democracies. The issues related to its imposition and restriction of rights and liberties in the country are regulated in Article 56 of the RF Constitution of 1993 in line with Article 4 of the International Pact on Civil and Political rights. The RF president, however, has an opportunity to govern by decrees both under the state of emergency and without imposition thereof. While in the former case the decrees must be approved by the upper chamber, then in the latter they need not be. The paradox is that when the president imposes the state of emergency in the country as a whole or in individual areas thereof (Article 88 of the RF Constitution) then the respective federal constitutional law "may institute individual restrictions of rights and liberties with identification of the extent and term of their duration" (Part 1, Article 56). But when no state of emergency is imposed, the rights and liberties may be restricted by federal law indefinitely, if the authorities believe that "this is required for the protection of the fundamentals of the constitutional system, morality, health, rights and legitimate interests of other persons, for ensuring the defense of the country and the security of the state" (Part 3, Article 55). This implies a practical possibility, under crisis, for realizing virtually all the measures of the state of emergency given no formal imposition thereof (which was the case in the course of the Chechen War). The power of the president, who "is guarantor of the constitution" (Part 2, Article 80), increases even more given a broad interpretation of his powers associated with the protection of constitution and sovereignty of the state, mechanisms of institution of the state of emergency and martial law. The point is of the so-called latent or "dormant" powers, which are not directly inscribed in the constitution, but can be inferred through its interpretation.[21]

Of principal significance in this context is the issue of administrative prerogatives, law enforcement and opportunities for restricting administrative arbitrariness. The specifics of the Russian political system, compared to other super-presidential systems, are also quite apparent. In the countries where the components of mixed forms are represented more clearly, parliament has a real possibility of influencing the political course of the president. But the main distinction is that in Latin American constitutions the "decree law" is significantly limited compared to that in Russia, and the possibility for its application is linked to the imposition of state of emergency (from where the expression "emergency decrees" descend). According to Russia's constitution, the "decree" law is virtually unlimited, thereby extending monarchical tradition.

We reviewed the arguments of the proponents of three basic views of the Russian form of government. The analysis reveals that all of them have legitimate grounds for existence. As a matter of fact, many provisions of the Constitution of the Russian Federation are formulated ambiguously, are misleading, deliberately vague, and can be interpreted in different ways. Even more so as the form of government is a sort of ideal based on classical constitutions, however from a legal standpoint, none of the considered models adequately reflects Russian specifics.

The political regime model laid down in the RF Constitution has its distinguishing characteristics. It differs not only from parliamentary and mixed regimes but also from the classical model of presidential republic in the USA. As was mentioned above, both the American and French influences are quite apparent in the presidential power regulation. The main distinction from the mixed form (as it is represented in the Weimar Republic, Fifth Republic and also in other numerous modifications thereof) is the lack of parliamentary control over the government and the possibility of its dismissal by censure. In France, this system was perfected during "cohabitation" resulting in the evolution of French system towards bigger parliamentarianism. The Russian presidential system differs from the one existing in the USA and is characterized by a rigid separation of powers in the lack of checks and primarily an exceptional prerogative of the lower chamber with respect to law making, and vesting the president with the functions of head of executive branch of power. Finally, the Russian model differs from Latin American versions of super-presidential regimes in the lack of rigid constitutional separation of powers (which Latin American constitutions borrowed from the USA), on the one hand, and much broader interpretation of the "decree" law, which is far from confined by emergency situations, on the other. As a matter of fact, Russia's president combines the status of constitutional monarch, president in presidential republic and prime minister in parliamentary republic.

Russia's president is above the system of separation of powers, performing the functions of guarantor of the constitution and umpire (in the broadest sense of the Gaullist term "arbitration"). Quite applicable to the Russian system, therefore, are the notions expressing different ways of power concentration in democratic states, which in different times were suggested for defining the head of state: Weimar Republic – "ersatzkaiser" (Hugo Preis), Gaullist France – "republican monarch" (Michel Debre), the UK – "elected dictator" (Lord Hailsham). All of these are combined in a highly ready-witted notion of "President of All Russia" designating a synthesis of democratic and monarchical powers. The RF president power makes one recall the constitutions of East European monarchical states at the turn of the nineteenth to twentieth centuries with their sham constitutionalism. Yet, in relation to the acts of Russia's president (who is formally head of state but not of executive power) no institute of countersign is envisaged, which distinguishes him from constitutional monarch and sooner brings him closer to "republican monarch". As a matter of fact, the institute of countersign is present in US-type presidential republics where, given a rigid separation of powers, the president is head of executive power, but is missing from French-type mixed republics, where the president is head of state. Hence, the following conclusion is valid: the power of Russia's president (apart from the virtually unfeasible impeachment procedure) is really limited (and in this it differs from a monarchical one) only by the term of office and non-hereditary nature of power devolution.

What is more, normative definitions fail to explain the specifics of the regime, which are associated with extra-constitutional and extra-legal clouts and have always been strong. It is impossible to understand the nature of the Russian presidential regime of a post-Soviet type if no account is taken of the meta-constitutional power of president including a set of symbolic and real powers not directly fixed in the constitution. In describing political and legal regime in Russia it would, therefore, be reasonable to use political science rather than formal legal terms. Therefore, scientific literature makes mention of a "hybrid" form of government, "latent monarchy", a dualistic form of government (these notions have also been borrowed from the history of European constitutionalism of a monarchical period), and some authors give up the task of typology, defining the Russian model as an "atypical" form of government.

How to explain Russian specifics? We believe, it can be explained by the historical tradition of monarchical statehood (as was the case in the Weimar Republic and in France). This system also resembled, by a number of parameters, the Russian constitutional law of the monarchical period, and in this sense restored historical continuity of state legal tradition. Instead of Congress and Supreme Soviet (embodying the principles of Soviet legitimacy) a two-chamber parliament was set up, whose lower chamber was given its former historical name – State Duma, and the upper one somewhat resembled the Council of State (which has increased even more now). Finally, the power of the president is largely similar to that of the monarch as was laid down in the preceding Russian law both by virtue of its practically absolute character and the scope of authority, which the new president was vested with. In this connection, as was mentioned above, the so-called "decree" right of the president is considered (Article 90 of the RF Constitution). These powers immeasurably increase in cases of imposition of martial law or state of emergency.

Indeed, the Russian political system is designed so that the RF president is above the system of separation of powers, acts as an umpire between branches of power and as a guarantor of constitution. This construction bears a strong resemblance to the system of constitutional monarchy pursuant to the Fundamental Law of the Russian empire of 1906; the empire was subject to controversy whether the system was really a restriction of a monarchical power. In due course, we mean to interpret the system as "sham constitutionalism" meaning a specific etymological sense of this concept in the course of transition from absolutism to law-based state in the form of constitutional monarchy. This is, no doubt, a transitional model capable of evolving in different directions and expressing an unstable balance between democracy and authoritarianism. Some authors refer to it as a "hybrid form of government", "dualistic regime", "proto-democracy", "post-totalitarian democracy", "delegated democracy", "presidential democracy", "controlled democracy", etc. This regime can be defined as "authoritarian democracy" were this notion not a sort of *contradicio in adjecto*. All the definitions express an opinion made up of a unique combination of democracy and authoritarianism, whose contradictory relations are each time dialectically reproduced at a new convolution creating a similar synthesis. On this basis, there can emerge and exist various forms of restricted democracy and authoritarianism.

Conflict of modernization and retraditionalization: constitutional reform strategies in modern Russia

An important characteristic feature of constitution adoption at the time of constitutional revolutions is as a rule an advanced character of constitutional provisions in relation to reality. Different research projects defined this process as constitutional modernization and constitutional "catch-up" development. It is common knowledge that the incorporation of democratic principles of civil society and law-based state, federalism, separation of powers and human rights in constitution in societies under modernization does not yet lead to their implementation and, moreover, runs into serious problems, of which the key one is the ineffectiveness of many of the new provisions. This concerns primarily the principles of federalism, the system of checks and balances, and the multi-party system. The adoption of these principles can give rise to tension between constitutional provisions and political structures, which in theory is resolved in two ways: adaptation of the provisions to reality or reality to the provisions. This interaction generally results in a new synthesis, in the emergence of hybrid forms reflecting the contradictory nature of constitutional modernization. These changes give rise to the well-known process of reconstitutionalization, i.e. a new interpretation of constitution or a mere revision thereof (actual or formally legal) in line with the current conditions and interests. This process evolves under the slogans of strengthening constitutional principles, restoration of their relationships with the broken historical tradition, improving their effectiveness, as well as restoration of manageability and vertical power hierarchy.

A paradox under the circumstances is that a gradual renunciation of liberal principles may be (and indeed turns out to be in the short-term) more rational than continuing to be literally guided by them, for it is more consistent with the political reality, historical traditions and public perception stereotypes under the abatement of public expectations. This logic of political process evolution manifests itself in cyclical models of constitutionalism in many countries under modernization, alternating coups d'etat of different political orientation.

Two approaches were clearly discernible during the past decade in Russia. One of these presses for social transformation on the basis of constitution, while the other seeks to revise it as it is inconsistent with legal awareness of the people or the rational principle of administration. These disputes are related with the problem of constitution effectiveness. An analysis of the advanced ideas concerned with constitution revision (as the majority of them did not gain a status of amendment proposals) allows one to state that these ideas are largely concerned with the revision of the issue of separation of powers.

One line of the conflict involving the desire to resolve it with amendments is linked, from the very beginning, to problems of federalism. These are: uncertainties of joint jurisdiction of the federation and its subjects (Article 71–73 of the RF Constitution) wherein the former is capable of taking up all of the prerogatives of the latter; difficulty for the subjects to challenge the constitutionality of laws emanating from executive or legislative authorities; lack of budget federalism, freedom of defining and securing their interests (Article 75), establishment of and maintaining their own administrative and representative institutions (Parts 1 and 2, Article 77), handling the issues of appointments to executive posts with no need for approval from the president (Article 78). These issues are linked with discussions on bicameralism and changes in the status of the upper chamber. According to some experts, the constitution should definitely deprive the president of the specific prerogatives realized in relation to subjects of the federation. Accordingly, the proponents of centralization pressed for a radical revision of the constitutional principles of federalism (up to an outright renunciation thereof), of the status of subjects of the federation (towards a bigger constitutional accountability thereof) and handling the problem of the upper chamber, which should stop being a lobbyist of regional elites (up to its disbandment and transition to a one-chamber parliament).

The other line of conflict is a reflection of the relationships between parliament, government and president. We saw that different interpretations of the existing form of government and political regime tendencies are behind the amendment contents. They are similar to the ones advanced by different political forces, say in France, with respect to the 1958 Constitution. Communists pushed for a parliamentary system and cancellation of strong presidency, Gaullists for maintaining the mixed system with a strong presidential power and, finally, liberals for the reception of the US presidential system. In Russia, these approaches, voiced in the course of draft constitution discussions at the time of the conflict, are still intact. The thesis of the parliamentary system in Russia and cancellation (or restriction) of presidency allowed the communists (making up the opposition majority in State Duma) to look forward to the restoration of the Soviet system. The concept of existence of an analogue of the mixed system (parliamentary-presidential or "non-preparliamentary") in Russia made it possible to raise the question of constitutional accountability of government, accountable ministry or at least "partially accountable" ministry (as was the case in some liberal amendments). Finally, individual academics and practitioners did not hide their preference for the US system seeing in it an optimal solution for Russia's problems. The interpretations of this system stressed the features resembling the Russian one and shading the fundamental distinctions.

The third line of conflict concerned amendments relative to judicial authority, the office of public prosecutor and municipal administration. These also included amendments on revising interpretations of constitutional accountability of subjects of the federation and the possibility of appealing against their actions in court, on the prerogatives of the chambers of parliament with respect to appointment to and dismissal from office of judges and procurators, on the assessment of constitutionality of presidential decrees. The point was, on the whole, of a package of problems related to judicial reform and the problem of independence of judges. For maintaining and strengthening the separation of powers in Russia, the amendment authors believe, there is need for a clear division of prerogatives of the three branches of power.

The analysis of the trends in Russian constitutionalism development along the three lines show their interrelationships (variations along the three lines correspond to the cyclical model). The general manifestation of the trend becomes a search for the model of power enabling combination of democratic legitimacy and a sufficiently authoritarian control allowing the inevitable (but unpopular) reforms. This model is present to an extent in the plebiscite democracy. In countries with the mixed form of government (Weimar Germany and Gaullist France) the plebiscite democracy regime allowed combination of the democratic legitimacy system and existence of a strong national leader – the president, capable of expressing popular will over the head of parliament and political parties. It was precisely this advantage that was attributed to it by liberal thinkers such as Max Weber and Michel Debre. They did not rule out (and probably foresaw) a situation where a strong presidential power would be forced, and find itself in a position, to limit the liberal institution potential for exercising unpopular but necessary reforms. The key way of securing such a charismatic status of president were plebiscites or the equivalent thereof in the form of referendums (the theory of head of state legitimation was developed by French scholars such as Carre de Malberg or Rene Capitan).

The regime of plebiscite democracy, whose historical prototype is generally considered to be Bonapartism, was interpreted in more or less liberal terms in different countries (from authoritarian regimes in Southern Europe to Gaullism and Peronism). Everywhere, however, this regime performed similar historical functions permitting democratic legitimation of authoritarian modernization.

In Russia, the prerequisites for the regime of a plebiscite democracy emerged only in the post-Soviet period. An important role, in the course of a tough confrontation of the union and Russian centres of power, was played by the occurrence of the first direct election of Russia's president. Thereafter, under the constitutional crisis, referendums promoted consolidation and legitimation of presidential power. They led to the development of a populist regime. This regime resorted to plebiscites for confirming its power, shunning the support of political parties, independent mass media and other public organizations inherent in civil society. The referendum mechanism was built into the RF Constitution of 1993, and the then RF president was vested with a prerogative of announcing a referendum (item "c", Article 84). The presidential prerogatives on announcing a referendum, however, were later regulated (and drastically limited) by Federal Constitutional Law as of 10 October 1995. Its adoption by the then oppositional State Duma for precisely restricting the head of state in the use of referendum, for formal and financial reasons, reflects understanding of the mechanisms of a plebiscite regime and possibilities of its utilization for the revision of constitution. Issues restricting fundamental rights and guarantees of their implementation could not be put to referendum, neither could changes in the schedule dates of parliamentary and presidential elections, earlier termination or extension of the term of office of the president and both chambers of parliament.[22] This is, no doubt, one of the reasons as to why no referendums were held after the adoption of the 1993 Constitution.

Naturally, the Russian model of plebiscite democracy differs from the French one: in the latter case, the president may announce a referendum only as agreed with the prime minister accountable to parliament, in the former this is not the case; in the Gaullism period, the constitutional custom according to which president's defeat at the referendum led to his resignation was operational, but not in Russia. Under the current circumstances, the laws on referendums can easily be revised. Finally, the Russian president may pursue his policy without a referendum. Elections, determining the political course of the nation, can be viewed as an analogue of referendums in the plebiscite regime.

The Russian political regime at the transitional period was defined as plebiscite democracy. The latter is a historically evolved concept of democracy as an immediate involvement of the people in public administration through universal and direct parliamentary elections. Underlying the definition is the similarity of this type of election with a plebiscite on the major political and constitutional issues. Transition from the qualification parliamentary democracy to a plebiscite one implies a sharp increase in populism and the role of political parties called to express sentiments of political masses in parliament. This process, realized in European nations by the beginning of the twentieth century, led to the destabilization of parliamentarianism as such and the established forms of law-based state for it provided the masses of people, short of political culture, with real opportunities for involvement in political decision making. This explains the criticism of plebiscite democracy, the search for adjustments, for example, in the form of the concept of rationalized parliamentarianism and strong presidential power. The plebiscite democracy rapidly transforms into democratic Caesarism, which corresponds to the model of authoritarian modernization and controlled democracy.

In comparative perspective, modern Russian political regime has acquired a number of key attributes of democratic Caesarism. If the plebiscite democracy regime is characterized by legitimation through plebiscites (referendums), then democratic Caesarism no longer needs it. It manoeuvres between the forces of a previous system, craving for revenge, and the forces pushing for modernization. Its characteristic manifestations come to be a dual legitimacy (democratic and authoritarian-paternalistic), limited parliamentarianism, distrust of political parties, centralism, super-party technical government, bureaucratization of state machinery and the concept of strong presidential power. Being an objective consequence of complex processes in a transitional period, any centrist political regime can rely on different social forces, hence, has a choice of political trajectory. Democratic Caesarism is a qualitatively new phase in regime consolidation, which is being built in the conditions of a limited and controlled democracy. In Russia, this situation emerged in the wake of elimination of dualism of parliament and president, creation of a new party in power, neutralization of public organizations and regional opposition and the beginning of agrarian reform. At present, these tendencies are rationalized, institutionalized and, so to speak, symbolically manifest themselves in the concept of imperial presidency. If there is a need for a uniform formula, illustrating the evolution of Russian constitutionalism over the past ten years, then it is as follows: from plebiscite democracy to democratic Caesarism.

Until recently, the question "Should the constitution be changed?" has been deemed to be crucial in Russian society. To resolve the question of whether or not it is worth replacing the constitution at the given instant in time, it is necessary to consider not only and not so much the legal aspects of the problem, as the political and psychological ones. In present-day Russia, there are no political forces capable of confronting the incipient executive power expansion. All alternative centres of influence, which were feeble in the past too, have once and for all lost any capacity to oppose the authorities: regional elites found themselves "moved away" from power (as a result of establishment of federal areas); the parliament represented by two chambers, acting until recently as a confrontation centre, is completely controlled by the executive power using the presidential majority (and the new procedure of forming the upper chamber); political parties lost their role and became systemic and controlled (the new law on political parties: some of its provisions seemed to be borrowed from the analogous law of Turkey or states of controlled democracy in Latin America); and mass media have been directly or indirectly deprived of independence. Judicial system also fits into the uniform vertical power hierarchy (some observers ascertain the actual restriction of judge independence). The Constitutional Court of the Russian Federation demonstrates loyalty to all actions of the authorities, refusing to oppose the presidential decrees on transformation of federalism. Different groups within the state machinery form a hierarchy of proximity to the power centre. External control is, naturally, there but it can be alleviated by way of media control and a series of aural agreements with leaders of the western nations based on their desire to promote stability and the alliance for fighting the external enemy. This revision of constitutional provisions significantly alters the functioning of the RF Constitution rendering it more authoritarian. There arises an issue of its estimation in the long-term.

There is every ground to believe that the evolving centrist system of controlled democracy expresses some objective trends in the development of Russian society and is consistent with the current situation and historical tradition. As follows from history, it can give a certain boost to stabilization and promotion of social reforms. The negative implications of the system are also apparent: the growing inertial stability, separation of power from society and, in the final count, the possibility of arresting the course of reforms. Like any system of unstable constitutionalism, the centrist system is a transitional period phenomenon, which can have different modifications and legal interpretations in the future. Hence, the solution to these problems: i) de facto constitution revision has to be taken as an objective fact (fait accompli); ii) de jure constitution revision under the current circumstances is highly undesirable for the nation also risks losing the democratic gains fixed in it; iii) it seems reasonable to maintain the 1993 Constitution, if possible, even being aware of the fact that it is progressively less consistent with reality. The constitution must be viewed as a certain declaration, which can be fleshed at with new democratic contents and remain legitimate in the future. Some may argue that it is a wasted attempt at retaining the form without real contents. If this be the case, it is better than legally registering changes in its contents.

At present, nobody needs constitutional reform: it is no longer needed by the opposition (which is unable to influence the situation); it is not yet needed by the authorities (for it will shatter the subsequent fragile legitimacy, and produce nothing in exchange for the sense of real power);

it is senseless for subjects of the federation and the federal centre (as relations between them are regulated within the frameworks of the new extra-constitutional vertical power hierarchy).

This is not to infer that the constitutional reform is not possible in the future. Should evolutionary changes reach a new qualitative phase, the reform will not be long in coming. And this will occur when the recent constitutional cycle completes its full turn.

Third constitutional cycle and possibilities for its adjustment

Since the constitutional revolution of 1993, Russia has passed through the constitutional cycle, which is nearing its completion. The cycle comprises three phases: a resolute renunciation of nominal Soviet constitutionalism (the first phase); transition to the real one associated with revolutionary adoption of the 1993 Constitution (the second phase); and the subsequent set-in of an unstable balance of law and reality along with an ever-stronger gravitation of the entire system towards authoritarianism (the third phase).

The mechanism of the given cycle development was fully consistent, just like in the course of the preceding Russian cycles, with the logic of constitutional modernization: the constitutional revolution of 1993 constitutes a radical breakup with the past, renunciation of its norms and values, contrasting it with the principles of liberal constitutionalism. At the same time, the declaration of these principles in no way implied their implementation, taking into account the strong resistance to them. Following the failure of several attempts at restoring the previous system, the struggle of the old and new laws focused on the problem of procedures and their effective implementation.[23]

It is precisely at this phase that a disguised (latent) constitutional retraditionalization becomes possible under the slogans of bringing legal provisions into correspondence with the "demands of life". Given the rising apathy of broad masses of the population (inevitable in the wake of considerable social upheavals), active resistance to reforms, and the necessity of their defence, there arises an objective possibility for reconstitutionalization, i.e. transition to sham constitutionalism.

The major parameters of reconstitutionalization, identified in the comparative perspective of constitutional cycles in different countries, are represented in present-day Russia. They comprise: a general contraction of political space; transition from decentralization to centralization and from one model of federalism (contractual federation) to another (centralized federation), as well as from separation of powers to integration implying an actual restriction of separation of powers framework (by creating a powerful governmental group in the lower chamber of parliament, revising the procedure of forming the upper chamber of parliament and establishment of a new institute, namely, the Council of State). The most significant component turned out to be the enlargement of presidential power. This construction can be completed with a broad interpretation of the powers of the head of state as guarantor of the constitution, especially under conflict and emergency circumstances; the respective transformation of the court and procurator's office and also of the concept of administration delegated authority. On the whole, there are signs of transition from plebiscite democracy to democratic Caesarism.

An analysis showed that all of these modifications are of an evolutionary nature but lead to real changes in the constitution. Consideration has been given to ways of constitution revision without alteration of its wording permitting implementation of a definite political strategy; also exposed were the major parameters of changes, made after the constitution adoption, which may lead to its formal and actual transformation along the mentioned line in the future (this was shown when reviewing the balance of the constituent and constitutional powers). All of the above illustrates that the latest, third big cycle of Russian constitutionalism is nearing completion.

The key question is as follows: is constitutional cyclicality adjustment feasible? Cyclicality law, as applied to societies under modernization, has an objective nature, and in this sense cannot be controlled. The less these societies are prepared for the institution of democratic constitutions, the more rigidly the spontaneous phase transition manifests itself during the next cycle. This does not imply, however, that the force of constitutional cyclicality law is in no way amenable to adjustment. On the contrary, it is precisely the knowledge of this law that permits outlining the methods of adjustment with regard to the experience gained in other countries. Note that when some politicians appeal to the necessity of "improving the efficiency of constitutional provisions", with a view to destabilizing the constitution, they also intuitively use the force of this law, but to an opposite end.

There are three ways of adjusting constitutional cyclicality law with a view to alleviating its destructive implications.

The first one involves the possibility of influencing this system from the outside by identifying the ever-growing asymmetry of constitutional provisions (and their prototypes in European law) and the practice of their national implementation. This approach could not be fully applied in the course of the preceding constitutional cycles, but is quite feasible at the current phase.

The second method involves the possibility of retaining a strong independent judicial control over constitutionality. This control makes it possible, on the one hand, to exercise changes in the constitution by way of its judicial interpretation (for bringing closer its provisions and the reality) and, on the other, to identify constitutional deviations capable of resulting in the negative transformation of constitutionalism. In case of control failure, its functions pass directly over to the independent institutions of civil society and to public opinion.[24]

The third method suggests application of educational technologies for securing social consensus in relation to constitution as a separate value. The point is to create a sort of metalaw – a social consensus in relation to constitution value irrespective of the current ideas of administration rationality. A part of these efforts involves behavioural education of the very political elite in observing constitutionality, for it needs be aware of the inefficiency of an actual return to the one-party system.

These technologies of constitutional cyclicality alleviation serve to adapt the necessary social transformations to the existing laws, and changes in the latter to conserving the general legality and legal continuity of social development. Hence, the task came down to preventing the force of cyclicality law, which would lead to a disruption of legal development (which has already occurred in the Russian constitutional history of the recent time on three occasions). The proponents of legal voluntarism, dreaming of the fastest completion of the third constitutional cycle possible, can, according to this theory, be opposed by the following argument: completion of any constitutional cycle implies nothing else but the beginning of the next one. Depending on how and with what the third big cycle of Russian constitutionalism completes, it would be possible to forecast the contents and goals of the fourth cycle.

Conclusion

Constitutional reforms in a traditional social environment are feasible only given the relevant institutions and channels of communication. The attainment of this goal is impossible through a one-off action, for there is need for a stable support of social initiatives. Hence, reformers should focus not so much on managerial issues or even purely administrative transformations as on problems of social psychology in society, its ability to accept some or other innovations and adapt them to a certain level of consciousness, perception and lifestyle. As a result, this kind of reform may not be non-recurring and straight-line in character.

In Russia, the constitutional movement of modern times is a strongly pronounced, consistent and deep phenomenon. One of the forms of its manifestation were the systematically developed projects of legal limitation of absolutist power. First Russian constitutionalists – bigwigs and authors of gentry projects (1730) – mimicked their proposals on oligarchic orders in Sweden and Poland rather than the English unwritten constitution. Borrowing of European Enlightenment ideology did not go beyond perception of the enlightened absolutism model with its concept of "legal monarchy" as the mouthpiece of the common good of subjects. Dealing with the constitutional issue in the wake of French revolution helped identify a whole range of western samples used by Russian constitutionalists and reflecting different orientations of their projects. These were primarily, apart from the constitution of the United States which was a common basis of the constitutional process, constitutions of the French revolution – a model of the 1791 Constitution, a model of the 1793 Constitution, and a number of Bonapartist constitutional acts and, finally, the monarchical Constitution of the 1814 Restoration. The first one is behind the projects of successive constitutional monarchy, the second underlies Jacobinic-centralizing dictatorship evolving into Bonapartism, the third one serves as the basis for the octroyed (or governmental) constitutionalism. In Russian history, all three models are represented in constitutional projects quite explicitly. The first one underlies a moderate liberal constitutional tradition originating in Muraviov's constitution and closing with the Constitutional Democrat programme (and the projects of the

Liberation movement, related to it); the second one – radical revolutionary tradition from Pestel to Bolsheviks; and the third one – top-down political reforms carried out by the governments from Speransky to Stolypin (projects of Loris-Melikov, Valuev, Witte).

Most significant for the liberal constitutionalism of the second half of the nineteenth century to the early twentieth century, however, was the German model of constitutional monarchy with a strongly pronounced monarchical principle. This model was a substantial modification of the respective principles of French constitutionalism, a new synthesis thereof allowing the combination of the principles of law-based state and a strong monarchical power. Both in Germany and Russia, its rationality was due to the historically established pattern of society/state relations, the latter's role in the modernization process. The German model remained significant for Russian constitutionalists in subsequent periods of time also. In spite of the close attention to the French models at the time of preparation of the Constituent Assembly (explained by the borrowing of the very idea from French constitutional tradition), the concept of presidential republic bears a strong resemblance to its Weimar option.

The use of western models is characteristic of modern Russian constitutionalism also. The focus of attention, no doubt, is the US Constitution, which is the yardstick for all projects. Also influential are the doctrines of social liberalism and neo-conservatism, manifest in the constitutional practice of other nations. Turning to Russian constitutional tradition (e.g. Zemstvo constitutionalism at the turn of the century) is also valuable from this perspective, for it can be interpreted as a certain consequence of neo-conservative orientation. Constitutional projects initiated by public authorities (represented by its major political institutions such as Supreme Soviet and President) evidenced continuity of the essential features of the preceding octroyed constitutionalism.

A special problem, when studying the political philosophy of liberalism and constitutionalism, is analysis of the so-called Soviet constitutionalism, which is, on the one hand, a historical continuity of the sham monarchical constitutionalism of previous time and, on the other, is a radically different, qualitatively new political phenomenon. Characteristic of it is a new way of power legitimation (presenting it as a direct expression of the people's will) and, at the same time, severe toughening (compared to the preceding monarchical phase) of authoritarian forms of government (in the form of dictatorship of proletariat, of the party and leader). In not one of the preceding forms of imaginary constitutionalism did the contradiction between liberal norms and absolutist reality achieve such huge dimensions: in the former, the point was sooner of a certain precedence of monarchical institutions over representative ones, but not of negation of the latter. Under communist dictatorship, we are witnessing a unique combination of constitutional rights declaration and an outright denial of any constitutional guarantees, negation of law in general and constitution, in particular, as a way of regulation of relations between the state and society. Under these circumstances, law is deprived of its independent value, becoming a form of ideological education and coercion. The main distinguishing characteristic of this type of constitutionalism and organization of government is the gap between the reality of communist dictatorship and the written constitution, carried to its extreme, which can be overcome exclusively with coercion. We believe that nominal constitutionalism is the most appropriate definition of this type of constitutionalism. The latter should, therefore, be recognized as the eventual form of sham constitutionalism, whose true purpose is disguising party dictatorship.

Reconstruction of the key phases of nominal constitutionalism evolution, in contrast to real mechanism of power (which is thoroughly concealed), is not too difficult for the researcher. It is precisely by virtue of its affectation, declarative nature and even forced imposition from above, that the Soviet nominal constitutionalism is represented by the strongly pronounced stages, whose boundaries are marked by five constitutions – of 1918, 1924, 1936, 1977 and (as the beginning of a new phase) of 1993.

The main contradiction of Soviet constitutionalism, manifesting itself back in the first 1918 constitution, is the desire to justify, in legal terms, the anti-legal phenomenon such as dictatorship of the proletariat. In this connection, a need arose to develop a special concept of this dictatorship called to prove its radical distinction from all other historical forms of dictatorship. The main components of this concept were, firstly, a paradoxical thesis illustrating that this dictatorship is the superior form of democracy, secondly, an idea of its depersonalized (class) character and, thirdly, limitation of its existence by definite historical bounds of a transitional period. Nevertheless, the phantom of Bonapartism, wandering in the heads of eyewitnesses of dispersal of the Constituent Assembly, never left the regime ideologists in peace. Doubts arose even more upon comparison of the RSFSR 1918 Constitution with its historical analogues – a brief draft organization of the 1871 Commune of Paris, which it didn't have time to implement, and the 1793 French Constitution (Convent), which was never put into practice. In all those cases, the constitution either was not operational at all, or its principles were viewed as pure declarations, which could not be implemented during civil war.

Throughout the development of nominal constitutionalism there have been signs of ideology precedence over law, which was manifest in the key ideological dogmas written in constitution. From this perspective, it would be appropriate to speak of the general continuity of the legitimizing formula, which largely served for justification of ideologically determined state construction and the party's right to power. Nevertheless, the legitimizing formula has been evolving along with concurrent changes in social contents of power. If the legitimizing formula problem is approached from a sociological analysis rather than an official legal ideology standpoint, then it would be possible to see that the evolution of this formula in the main Soviet Constitutions clearly reflects the stages of evolvement of the new ruling layer, its growth and social degradation. Thus, the 1918 Constitution reflects its inception in the form of authoritocracy – a specific layer exercising government functions. Within the frameworks of dictatorship of proletariat formula all other social strata are removed from politics (with a system of non-direct and qualification elections); the 1924 Union Constitution reflects the elite regrouping under a sharp struggle between the centre and provinces, integration of regional elites in a single all-union one accompanied by elimination of marginal groups, modification of infrastructure and channels of social mobility. The renunciation of dictatorship of proletariat formula can first be discerned in the 1936 Constitution, which declared "power of working people" but still carried a mention of dictatorship. This monument embodies the most dynamic phase of Soviet elite evolution when it first secured a total control of society, internal unity (thanks to purges) and at the same time has not yet lost is functional purpose – its organizing role in the course of modernization. At a later date, upon gaining power, it would lose this dynamism, increasingly turning into a privileged class. By repulsing all attempts at establishing social or public control over itself (in constitutional ideas of the Khrushchev reforms era) it reaches its peak, which simultaneously means the beginning of its end as a holistic social phenomenon engendered by revolution. This closing phase is presented in the 1977 Constitution with its concept of the leading and guiding role of party elite. Being aware of the fragility of its power in conditions of incipient systemic crisis, it looks for ways of holding power under the new circumstances. The period of perestroika and the subsequent break-up of the state witnesses the split of the elite itself, manifest in the concept of the so-called "socialist pluralism" and the respective changes in the effective constitution. This process ends with the rejection of the old ideology and abrogation of the constitutional principle of the leading role of the party. This process proceeded so painlessly because it did not affect the real power of the elite, which had already found a new way of legitimizing its power. This system was finally legalized in the Constitution of 1993.

The basic trend in the current phase of political development of Russia is exposed in the comparative-historical perspective. It must be defined as an objective transition from nominal constitutionalism to a sham one, which theoretically opens up opportunities for political system movement towards genuine constitutionalism in the future. We showed earlier that the sham constitutionalism phenomenon contains certain contradictions, and simultaneously opens up alternative opportunities for the development of political process. The structure of the 1993 Constitution, primarily the inscribed pattern of separation of powers, the balance between legislative and executive branches of government and, most importantly, presidential prerogatives within the frameworks of central government institutions, makes it possible to interpret it within the framework of this tradition.

Thus, the political theory of Russian constitutionalism is a paradigm interpreting relations between the state and society in a modernization period. The Russian constitutionalism theory is an independent component of the political culture of society, justification of its legal evolution, hence, a stabilizing factor. A theoretical analysis of the problem is especially important along the following lines: justification of the possibility for a way out of the fundamental social conflict not through revolution leading, in the final count, to reproduction of authoritarianism in new forms, but through radical socio-economic and political reforms purposefully undertaken by the state; development of a model of transition from an authoritarian government to a modern pluralistic democracy given continuity of power and government legitimacy; identification of specific features of theoretical underpinnings, constitutionalism strategy and tactics at the time of accelerated political modernization.

In defining liberalism as a political movement aimed at safeguarding human rights, some or other version of liberalism must be treated in terms of the mechanism of goal accomplishment in specific conditions. Russian liberalism defines the direction of its evolution via the concept of constitutionalism. In reviewing the efforts of Russian liberals in the late nineteenth to early twentieth centuries, we see that constitutionalism acts as their political philosophy. Given this approach, it becomes possible to interpret the political programme and political activities which, while varying in the course of changes in the political situation, still remain intact relative to basic values of liberalism and constitutionalism. Accordingly, we receive a certain cognitive model, which can be used for interpretation of political regimes and political conflicts in a wide comparative perspective.

How do you avoid revolution and at the same time swing society from an authoritarian system to a legal one? For the modern world, this is the key problem, an issue of survival. Constitutionalism is a concept generalizing theory, experience and technology of response to this challenge. It first emerges as a hope, a movement of the most far-sighted segment of society, and then gradually takes the form of institutions and political systems. Isn't it strange that we know so little of this social phenomenon? This book is a first attempt at presenting a holistic case of Russian constitutionalism in an historical perspective. The author focuses attention on the specific model of constitutional technologies in transition-type societies assuming that the Russian experience can serve as a basis for development of a uniform theory of constitutionalism in transitional societies.

The state seems to be playing a special role in planning both social and legal transformations. It is the state machinery rather than civil society that is a key tool here. Cutting through the reviewed period, therefore, are society/state relations, given the priority and relatively limited opportunities for administrative reforms. Characteristic of reforms in Russia and East European countries are drastic changes in relations between society and state, in property relations, legal systems, constitutional structure and political institutions. The development of market economy, political democracy and human rights require reforms in the administration framework, civil service, court and procurator office. The administrative reform problem lies precisely at the intersection of the major directions of current policy. Administrative reforms are generally defined as a modification of public administration systems in terms of three major parameters: first, the restructuring of the system of political institutes and public institutions; second, the reorganization of civil service, makeup of management machinery or bureaucracy; and third, alteration of the nature of an administrative system attitude to society in general and to its various social groups, in particular. It follows from this interpretation that the scope of the very notion of administrative reforms can vary markedly depending on the nature of society/state relations, the role of the latter in regulating social processes. Then this scope must, apparently, be adjusted depending on the historical phase of society evolution. Finally, an essential prerequisite for limiting this scope is the place of administrative power itself within the political system (it is apparently different in traditional monarchy, a one-party dictatorship system or in a system claiming implementation of separation of powers principle). This complicates a direct adaptation of historical reform experience, yet permits its utilization at a technological level.

The idea of any administrative reform leads to improving administration efficiency. Democratic and anti-democratic regimes, federative and unitary states, stable civil societies and those in transition and modernization would accomplish this goal in different ways, however. The history of autocratic Russia offers three models of reform (and ideological justification thereof) pursuing modernization of social relations. The first one involves an accelerated "catch-up" development implemented exclusively by way of administrative regulation aimed at a rapid accomplishment of strategic goals. As social consciousness generally rated the place of the power in the political system depending on its military potential, this modernization alternative frequently aims at achieving the respective results precisely in this area. This is best illustrated by Peter's reforms, who rapidly created industry, fiscal system, education system, the army and the navy.

The other modernization model is represented by reforms in the 1860s, which enjoyed the support of much wider social segments recognizing the need for transformations (so-called "educated classes"). The main distinguishing characteristic of this reform model was that it proclaimed drastic social restructuring and put it into law straight away, which promoted the involvement of all strata of society in the reform. The latter opened opportunities for society's involvement in the transformations aimed at creating civil society and a law-based state.

The third model is linked with building a sufficiently wide social movement capable of initiating (via new parliamentary institutions) reforms towards civil society and a law-based state. An analysis of Russian liberalism and constitutionalism of the late nineteenth to early twentieth centuries from this perspective shows that they have been developing within the frameworks of a certain wider social system, being at the same time an important independent part and a stabilizing factor.

The failure of liberal reforms in the course of the twentieth-century revolutions can be explained by both society's unpreparedness for reforms and the conservatism of public administration itself. Inherent in this type of system, sooner characterized by mechanistic than organic unity, are only two mutually exclusive states – stability turning into stagnation, or destabilization connected with a vacuum of power. The changeover of these phases is subject to the well-known cyclicity, manifesting itself in Russian history in a successive alternation of periods of more stringent and weaker public control of society, reforms and counter-reforms. The only possibility of overcoming this cyclicity suggests transition from the mechanical type of social organization (where individuals are incorporated in the state-built class-administrative institutions) to an organic one, i.e. civil society (where individuals enjoy the whole range of individual rights and equal protection of the law). This concept, developed for explaining the liberalism strategy in the early twentieth century, is as significant to this day.

The Soviet-type systems are inefficient because they are missing the internal flexible tools of self-regulation and self-tuning, given the expansion and complication of administrative tasks. As for government organization, Soviet-type nominal constitutions were characterized by negation of the separation of powers principle. It was contrasted with the principle of unity of power always representing one ruling class (under "developed socialism") – all working people. This power is formally exercised directly by the working people or via a framework of representative bodies – Soviets, exercising control of all public bodies.

The Soviets combine legislative and executive powers (and judicial power too, as the procurator's office and courts were accountable to the respective level of Soviet). Soviet deputies exercise their mandate on a part-time basis and are accountable to the electorate who have the right to recall them. Hence, they are not professional members of parliament, their functions are limited. National-level Soviets (supreme Soviets or councils of state) used to be convened several times a year for short sessions, and the rest of the time it is the presidiums, formally elected by them, which were running on a full-time basis and nominally performing the functions of the head of state (a kind of collective head of state, rather rare in world practice, where it is generally personified). The government was formally appointed by supreme Soviets and was accountable to them.

With the passage of time, coalescence of legislative and executive branches of government turned to be increasingly evident: the deputy corps included party, administrative and business managers and, which is most illustrative, heads of courts and procurator's offices. A mandate in a respective level of Soviet came to be a supplement to the managerial position. Membership of several Soviets was also possible. Soviets were short of time and professionalism for making decisions (which were exercised by presidiums, executive committees in cooperation with administrative institutions). The term "Soviet power" was void of real meaning.

The trend in the integration of party and state machineries was at its peak by the end of existence of the communist system: it manifested itself in that the party leader also became the head of state. In heading the two offices – party and state – he acted mostly via the former. Constitution, laws and elections played a "decorative role". Elections to state and party bodies, appointments to state posts were predetermined by the party oligarchy and the first secretary from the list of nomenclature of the respective level, endorsed by the respective party committee. These lists of different levels of nomenclature were a sort of reserve, from which the personnel for managerial positions in all branches of government were drawn. Despite the doctrinal and constitutional negation of the principle of separation of powers, this system (especially with time) allowed some of its external resemblance, at least in the form of separation of functions of different structures. Nevertheless, a real combination of all these functions did occur at personnel level, exercised precisely because of the centralized political control of the personnel and reallocation thereof.

In historical retrospective, Soviet nomenclature can be interpreted as a sort of historical analogy of service gentry, as it passed, over a shorter period of time, similar phases of evolution – from a really functioning tool of management and war to a privileged layer largely concerned with egoistic motives of preserving its status, prestige and well-being. This comparison allowed us to speak earlier of potential identification of a specific layer – authoritocracy, whose specific characteristics and phases of evolution make it possible to distinguish it from other historically privileged layers – ruling classes and castes, economic classes, in the Marxist sense of the term, and bureaucracy. Thirdly, it would be wrong to agree with the thesis on the identical social nature of phenomena such as nomenclature and bureaucracy. We saw that the former should sooner be compared with other ruling classes or ruling elite; the latter is represented in this system only by its upper echelons.

The main contradiction of Russian political and legal development in the past decade, which is inherent in all regimes undertaking a radical modernization, lies between the goals (creation of civil society and law-based state modelled on democratic countries) and tools, which inevitably acquire authoritarian character (due to the necessity of neutralizing the destructive public movements and suppression of irreconcilable opposition). This contradiction manifested itself in the developed and adopted Russian constitutional model: between a wide interpretation of human rights, federalism perceived in quite a western way, and a rather authoritarian interpretation of separation of powers, turning presidential power into an independent political infrastructure having no direct constitutional analogues in the present-day world.

Constitutional modernization, Europeanization and the "catch-up" development, expressed in revolutionary logic of new law creation, led to the adoption of the 1993 Constitution, which was ahead of its time by a number of parameters. Therefore, the major problem of the subsequent constitutional reforms was the need for doing away with the increasing discrepancy between the law and reality, for adequate methods of linking the declared rules and reality. Both, in the past and nowadays it was and is necessary to press for practical implementation of constitutional rules rather than bringing the constitution down to the level of backward social reality. It was clear that, given legal nihilism as well as a serious opposition, the constitutional rules can be made effective only from the top. This required a powerful, autonomous and independent guarantor of constitution – presidential power. In Russia, it is precisely presidential power that was a demiurge of constitution, the only force capable of upholding its provisions in the course of subsequent crises and, finally, a supreme umpire in disputes between branches of government. Russia's constitution is, in the first place, a "presidential constitution" (in a specifically Russian perception of the term "presidency"). The late twentieth century witnessed an emergence of a sort of "second edition" of the dual system of government, which took off in Russia back in the course of the first constitutional experiment in the early twentieth century.

In due course, we suggested interpreting this system as sham constitutionalism meaning a specific etymological sense of this notion in the course of transition from absolutism to law-based state. Russian presidency is, no doubt, a transitional model, capable of evolving in different directions, reflecting an unstable balance between democracy and authoritarianism. Hence, its definitions in political science literature such as a "hybrid form of government", "dualistic regime", "post-totalitarian democracy", "protodemocracy", "delegation democracy", "guided democracy" and the like. It would be safe to refer to it as "authoritarian democracy" were it not a contradictory definition. All of these definitions, in effect, try to express a subtle essence constituting a unique combination of democracy and authoritarianism, whose conflicting relationships are each time reproduced in Russia at a new cycle of historical spiral, producing a similar synthesis.

Ascertaining the transitional period in this country's development already introduces certain frameworks for a solution to the problem. The point is the historically unique case of transition from a centrally planned economy to a market one, on the one hand, and from the authoritarian one-party regime to a political system based on democratic principles.

Here, an instable system is defined as a system lacking fully-fledged legal recognition and regulation of basic values of market economy: private property, fiscal system, budget federalism, independent and equitable jurisdiction, as well as transparent (in legal terms) decision-making procedures. Hence, the main contradiction of an instable legal systems is that no key rules of the game are established, and they are developed following the passage of the respective laws or, at best, concurrently with them (most frequently, however, contrary to them).

Under the circumstances, the administrative reform requires the solution to the following strategic problems: unity of the state and identification of trends in Russian federalism; separation of ownership and power; creation of rational bureaucracy – an effective civil service; institution of public (parliamentary) and judicial control of bureaucracy; creation of an ethical climate in society making corruption morally unacceptable.

According to a number of analysts, the mechanism of modern reform and the tactics of its implementation largely relate to Soviet bureaucratic tradition: constitutional institutions do undergo transformation but the meaning thereof is radically changed at the personnel level. The process of power concentration has entered its ultimate stage. It manifests itself in building a uniform and rather autonomous (from society) vertical hierarchy of government. Given this interpretation, power development strategy suggests that policy should be formulated by a narrow layer of top bureaucracy (presidential administration, officials in the reformed Council of Federation and plenipotentiaries in federal areas) rather than any collective government body. In part, this is Duma (where there is a guaranteed majority) but not parties, elected heads of regions and the government headed by prime minister. Of course, this implies, on the whole, reinforcement of bureaucratic hierarchy and expansion (both formal and actual) of administrative power prerogatives.

The classical Weber concept of bureaucracy treats it as a historical product and, simultaneously, a driving force of rationalization of the political system of modern times. Historically, this process starts in the period of formation of European absolutist states and peaks in parliamentary regimes, where the entire vertical hierarchy of executive power, headed by the cabinet, comes to be under the control of legislative power. Apparently the Soviet public administration system, having nothing in common with separation of powers, was sooner a negation of rational bureaucracy. Soviet bureaucracy was a real consequence of the application of utopian social theory in a backward agrarian society, hence the result of not only modernization but also of retraditionalization of this society. It is in general very hard to distinguish between the ruling layer of bureaucracy and the upper strata of bureaucracy. If bureaucracy was indeed available under the Soviet regime then it was sooner of a traditional nature, being an antithesis of rationalism: an oral instruction instead of law; combination of functions instead of their separation; instead of professional ethics its negation. The main specific feature of the ruling layer of the Soviet regime (including higher segments of bureaucracy), however, is a real opportunity for disposing of property.

These specifics of the given ruling layer predetermined its role under the crisis of Soviet regime. The relevant literature advanced a concept of "nomenclature revolution". The gist of this revolution boils down, apparently, to transforming the administrative control of public property, on the part of the ruling layer on the whole, into a formal legalization of its ownership by individual owners. In comparison with other biggest revolutions of the past (primarily English and French), however, this process should sooner be defined as restoration. When the opposition blamed the regime in Thermidorian degeneration it, no doubt, was erroneous (as restoration of private property did not take place). An analysis of socio-political processes in the post-Soviet regime, however, discerns in it some trends towards Bonapartism – a centrist political regime seeking a wide social support in the disunited society and striving to promote development of a proprietary class.

Clearly, given globalization, modernization and ever-faster political development, the classical forms of political regimes and ruling elites cannot fully correspond to their ideal types formulated on the basis of historical materials. Then come trends towards synthesis, combined development and emergence of hybrid forms. Indeed, the modern Russian ruling circles constitute manifestation of these trends, combining feudal-communist components of old nomenclature and bourgeois-bureaucratic and technocratic components of transitional societies. This helps explain the conflict between business and power. First, this reveals the inefficiency of the Russian state in comparative perspective; second, the relationship of state machinery inefficiency and high level of corruption; and third, the nation trails in terms of executive power modernization.

The main problem is a significant lagging behind in modernizing the executive power system compared to the pace and qualitative changes in all other areas of social and economic development in Russia throughout the reform period. The negative phenomena also include: state machinery not amenable to social control; fusion of government and business leading to their criminalization; evolvement of a specific bureaucratic bourgeois; and power seizure by business.

Business representatives speak of a new troubling phenomenon – business "seizure" by bureaucrats, seeing in it, however, a "by-product of, on the whole, positive process of public structure consolidation". This form of administrative power use by top officials includes concurrent holding of administrative offices and doing business; transition from high administrative offices to executive positions in big corporations and vice versa; attempts at exercising indirect control of business through public bodies in the form of quasi-legal examination of conflicts; and traditional procedures legalized in the notions of "guardianship" and "supervision" of business structures.

This results in a "system of administrative capitalism" which, on authors' estimates, is "no less ruinous for economic and social future of Russia than oligarchic capitalism in the 1990s".

State machinery, as a tool for exercising power in society, should not be a hindrance to economic development, a source of administrative barriers for businesses and citizens, a closed system interested in self-reproduction, using power prerogatives for corporate interests. Such a system is self-sufficient, stagnant and vigorously resists modernization attempts.

The philosophy of the current administrative reform is a liberal concept of state non-interference in economy (in effect – the theory of a state "night guard"), minimum of state, which should not direct business but rather provide favourable social and legal environments for its performance. Authors speak of the necessity of renunciation of the "excessive state" and transition to an "effective state". This is achievable through specification of functions and application by public administration of the new information technologies widely used in business.

The idea of separation of powers and ownership, control and management implies creation of a rational civil service. As public bodies should not manage projects but rather regulate processes, a radical idea is advanced suggesting renunciation of sectoral principle of public administration structure (inherited from the Soviet power) and transition to functional principle (as more acceptable in market economy). This takes the form of a suggestion to scrap all sectoral ministries and hand their functions over to executive bodies of a different level (functional ministries, services, agencies, inspections) and to self-regulating organizations.

A desire to prevent performance of conflicting functions by one and the same agency (legal regulation, supervision, provision of public services, management of public property) is realized in the proposed new system of federal bodies. The major criterion of its structure is separation of agencies performing political and regulating functions (federal ministries) on the one hand, and agencies directly managing public property, on the other. Also instituted is an intermediate category of agencies, which have to combine conflicting functions for accomplishing the goals set to them. The key requirement to the latter is, therefore, the maximum publicity and collective nature of their activities. Accordingly, a system of federal executive bodies is built including federal ministries, federal services, state inspections, federal commissions, all-Russia agencies. It is precisely the latter institution which is, while not performing regulating and supervisory functions, the key federal executive body in charge of managing public property (including intellectual property and allied rights, budget funds and government debt), as well as performing individual business functions on behalf of the state.

The administrative reform, perceived in this way, involves optimization of state functions and executive power structure; improvement of legal and economic mechanisms of handling government tasks, creation of an effective civil service with the built-in anti-corruption mechanisms. Referred to as excessive were functions and competences legally assigned to public authorities, which are not, however, performed in practice; which cannot be realized due to their vague and declarative character; due to the inadequate level of administration to which they were assigned; by virtue of mutual contradiction thereof within the frameworks of one agency (conflicting functions); not supported with adequate resources (financial and informational); duplicating functions and, finally, those violating the current laws.

An important component of administrative reform implementation becomes the transparency of the administrative system and decision-making procedures. In modern times, the administrative justice institute is concerned, in the first place, with the legal defence of individual rights from their infringement by the state. The formation of administrative justice reflected recognition of the objectively existing contradictions between the state and individual, between public and private laws. Principles of constitutionalism can, therefore, be effectively realized only given legal guarantees of administration lawfulness and control of public administration and bureaucracy. And the guarantee of rights provides citizens with an opportunity for challenging unlawful actions of public authorities in court: this places demand on a special network of administrative justice bodies or, given its absence (e.g. in the present-day Russia), an opportunity for citizens to go to civil courts of higher jurisdiction.

A distinguishing characteristic of all Soviet-type administrative and legal systems, extending the imperial tradition in this respect, was that the administrative management was fully controlled by political power (the party and government), treated exclusively as a tool for achieving its ends. The administrative system of the state was closed for the external world, based on self-control and managed through the executive power dictate. The huge powers of public prosecutors relative to control of administration, including in effect the right of handling legality issues, in no way rendered this system more democratic, for the procurator's office itself was a part of the repressive state machinery. The external control on the part of society or independent court was non-existent, the principle of court retrial was either not realized or extremely limited, and the procedures of challenging administrative decisions were established to the benefit of administration itself. One of the major goals of administrative system reform in the post-communist period was, therefore, setting up of external institutions with respect to the executive branch of government and at the same time authorized to exercise supervision and control of administration. That is how there emerged the well-known institute of ombudsman – commissioner on human rights, parliamentary commissions and voluntary inspections expressing the need for independent control of the authority activities.

The need for an independent system of administrative justice in Russia is still a task to be solved. In the background of recent attempts at judicial reforms in Russia, the "quasi-judicial" (British) type of administrative justice, exercised under supervision of courts of general jurisdiction, looks quite attractive but hardly feasible; the "managerial" (French) type is viewed as inefficient, slow and too bureaucratic; and preference is given to the third – "court" (or German) – type of administrative justice featuring all of the advantages of an effective judicial examination.

The current system of dispute resolution in the area of public and municipal administration (in the course of civil trial in common law courts) is recognized as ineffective and biased. Doubted was the very possibility of ensuring an objective consideration of a dispute, one of the parties to which was a public body vested with power. Also argued was the fairness of court decisions relative to regional authorities, for the latter provide a considerable financial support to courts of general jurisdiction because of their underfunding. It is generally believed that the problem can be solved by establishing a network of federal administrative courts, not linked to the current administrative and territorial division, and an institute of special ombudsman for defending human rights from the government meddling with business.

The conducted analysis renders a conclusion that administrative reform in Russia does not at all come down exclusively to restructuring administrative institutions and civil service. It is precisely because society and state in Russia (in contrast to western countries) constituted an integral system in modern and recent times, separation thereof turns into a major prerequisite for administrative reforms. In national history, large-scale administrative reforms coincided with those of property relations and political system. Hence, the administrative reform in Russia is a reform of the state.

A review of the current law governing administrative reforms points to the existence of two key strategies in modern Russia – liberal and conservative-bureaucratic. They vary drastically in perception of the reform, its scope, goals and even implementation technologies.

The first strategy operates around the liberal concept of civil society precedence in relation to state, treats administration as a purely auxiliary tool of society, perceives the major purpose of reform as that of turning the executive department into a transparent and efficient institution. The technology of reform implementation involves, therefore, institutes of social control and the necessity of a wide public discussion.

The other strategy gives a clear priority to the state, seeing in it the only uniting force at the time of radical social transformations. The purpose of reform is seen as optimization of administrative control of society, building a solid vertical hierarchy top-down. This model of guided democracy proceeded from an idea that society is unable to articulate its own interests, to set priorities and be guided by them, hence the need for administration's assistance. Accordingly, the reform technology revives the old absolutist and Soviet tradition of closed discussion of reform.

Both the strategies use the notion of control, yet interpret it quite differently: one presses for the necessity of social control over bureaucracy, the other of bureaucracy over society. Naturally, the interpretations of the very process of administration and its efficiency come to be diametrically opposite: for some people, effective administration primarily involves the development of legal frameworks for social initiatives; for others, expansion of delegated powers of different levels of administration for implementing the decisions made by the supreme authority. The second strategy is, apparently, prevailing over the first one now, which implies reproduction of the Russian historical tradition of reform and counter-reform alternation at a new stage.

Therefore, all attempts to reduce the administrative reform to partial (important as they may be) issues of revision of the network of institutions, structure and functions of civil service, service ethics and, the more so, issues of lobbyism, fighting corruption and (most recently) raising officials' pay are just a palliative diverting from a meaningful analysis. What is seen as a conflict of administrative institutions or efficiency of bureaucratic machinery is just a manifestation of structural conflict of transitional society.

It should be recognized that the resolution of this conflict in an administrative domain requires an explicit legal regulation of administrative institutions (restriction of supervisory functions compared to administration functions); greater transparency of state machinery activities (primarily the accessibility of the required information); securing social control of officialdom performance (in the first place, an opportunity for the citizen to sue the official, and the guarantee of an objective consideration of the case in court).

The author deems it possible to interpret the phenomenon of Russian constitutionalism along the lines of constitutional cycles theory – periodically alternating phases of tougher and weaker constitutional regulation of society. This allows him to concentrate on the aspects of reforms, which had been absolutely ignored by researchers. He finds it possible to speak of the strategy and tactics of such reforms, forecasting not only a successful phase thereof, but also the inevitable rollbacks manifesting themselves in the processes of reconstitutionalization, constitutional retraditionalization, which may come to a direct retreat to pre-constitutional order.

Thus, the author managed to formulate the traditional dilemma of democracy and authoritarianism with new concepts pointing to the specific independent role of constitutional rules, institutions and elite groups acting as a key element in the choice of the respective strategy in traditional-type societies. Finally, this approach makes it possible to proceed from the predominantly meaningful frameworks of constitutionalism to modelling different situations and scientific development of social technologies of constitutional reform implementation in societies not prepared for this historically.

All of the above renders a conclusion that the Russian historical case of constitutionalism should be treated as a core research phenomenon in a global perspective when answering the question whether the classical model of western democracy and constitutionalism can be effectively adapted to other regions of the world. Or the latter will deform the classical model *per se* in a long historical perspective.

In contrast to traditional literature on constitutionalism, perceiving it as a stable social phenomenon, an important research task is, therefore, classification of the variety, from sociological standpoint, of its forms – real, nominal and sham. The author shows that the true choice of modern society is already exercised not along the line of the dilemma – constitutionalism and its negation – but along the line of a choice between real and nominal constitutionalism with a big variety of intermediate options of these two ideals. It is precisely this area, that the author defines as a transitional type of constitutionalism, that is the field of collision of different stakeholders. This is an area of unstable equilibrium where the purposeful reinforcement and utilization of the respective technologies may produce a decisive effect.

In exploring Russian constitutionalism in a long historical perspective and in comparison with the general process of modernization in modern and recent times, the author presented a typological model of a specific type of constitutionalism in transitional societies, identifying characteristic features of the given constitutionalism. This cognitive model can be used for interpretation of other political processes and identification of vectors thereof in the contemporary world.

Notes

1 Constitutionalism as a theoretical issue in transnational societies

1 Alexis de Tocqueville, *L'Ancien régime et la Revolution*, Paris: Gallimard, 1967.
2 A. N. Medushevsky, *Sravnitel'noe konstitutsionnoe pravo i politicheskie instituty*, Moscow: Gosudarstvennyi Universitet – Vysshaya Shkola Economiki (The State University – Higher School of Economics), 2002.
3 Y. Guchet, *Histoire Constitutionnelle de la France*, Paris, 1993.
4 Conde E. Alvarez, *Curso de derecho constitucional*, 2nd edn, Madrid: Tecnos, 1996, vol. 1, pp. 74–75.
5 E. Rabasa, *La constitucion y la dictadura: Estudio sobre la organizacion politica de Mexico*, 3rd edn, Mexico City, 1956, pp. 244–245.
6 A. Cabanis and M. L. Martin, *Les Constitutions d'Afrique francophone: Evolutions récentes*, Paris, 1999, p. 15.
7 J. de Maistre, *Considerations sur la France: Essai sur le principe generateur de constitutions politiques*, Paris, 1907.
8 H. Kelsen, *Reine Rechtslehre, Einleitung in die Rechtswissenschaftliche Problematik*, Leipzig und Wien, 1934.
9 C. Schmitt, *Verfassungslehre*, Berlin, 1970.
10 J. Linz and A. Stepan, *Problems of Democratic Transition and Consolidation: Southern Europe, South America and Post-Communist Europe*, Baltimore: The Johns Hopkins University Press, 1996.
11 A. N. Medushevsky, *Istoriya russkoi sotsiologii*, Moscow: Vysshaya Shkola, 1993.
12 A. N. Medushevsky, *Demokratiya i avtoritarism: rossiiskii konstitutsionalism v sravnitel'noi perspektive*, Moscow: ROSSPEN, 1998; A. N. Medushevsky, 'Democracy and Tyranny in Modern and Recent Times', *Russian Studies in Philosophy (Liberalism in Russian Political Philosophy)*, vol. 33, No. 3, winter 1994–1995.
13 M. Weber, *Zur Russischen Revolution von 1905: Schriften und Reden 1905–1912*, Tübingen: Mohr (Paul Siebeck), 1989.
14 M. Ya. Ostrogorsky, *Demokratiya i politicheskie partii*, Moscow: ROSSPEN, 1997.
15 *Rossiiskie liberaly*, Moscow: ROSSPEN, 2001.

2 Proto-constitutionalism in Russia's traditional society

1 A. N. Medushevsky, *Utverzhdenie absolutisma v Rossii: Sravnitel'noe istoricheskoe issledovanie*, Moscow: Tekst, 1994.
2 RGADA, F. 1255 (Palata ob Ulozhenii 1700 g.), D. 1, Part 1–3.
3 Ukaz Petra I o poryadke nasledovaniya dvizhimykh i nedvizhimikh imushchestv ot 23 marta 1714 g., *Rossiyskoe zakonodatel'stvo* X–XX vekov, Moscow, 1986, vol. 4, pp. 295–300.

4 I. T. Pososhkov, *'Kniga o skudosti i bogatstve' and other essays*, Moscow, 1951.
5 D. A. Korsakov, *Votsarenie imperatritsy Anny Ioannovny*, Supplements, Kazan, 1980.
6 Ekaterina II, *Nakaz Komissii o sochinenii novogo Ulozheniya*, St Petersburg, 1907.
7 A. Ya. Polenov, 'Ob unichtozhenii krepostnogo sostoyaniya krest'yan v Rossii', *Russkiy arkhiv, Istoriko-literaturny sbornik*, God tretii, 1869, pp. 510–541.
8 E. S. Shumigorsky, 'Rassuzhdenie o nepremennykh gosudarstvennykh zakonakh grafa N. I. Panin', *Imperator Pavel I: Zhizn' i tsarstvovanie*, St Peterburg, 1907, Supplement 1, pp. 4–13.
9 A. Haxthausen, *Studien über die inner Zustande, das Volksleben und insbesondere die ländlichen Einrichtungen Russlands*, Hannover: Von A. Freiherrn von Haxthausen, 1847.
10 *Manifesty i ukazy E. I. Pugacheva*, Moscow: Nauka, 1975.
11 'Doklad grafa Panina, predstavlenny Ekaterine II vmeste s proektom teksta manifesta', *Sbornik Imperatorskogo Russkogo istoricheskogo obshchestva*, St Petersburg, 1871, vol. VII, pp. 202–209.
12 E. S. Shumigorsky, 'Proekt N. I. i P. I. Paninykh "O fundamental'nykh pravakh, ne primenyaemykh na vse vremena nikakou vlast'u"', *Imperator Pavel I: Zhizn' i tsarstvovanie*, St Petersburg, 1907, Supplement 1, pp. 13–20.
13 Zapiska A. A. Bezborodko, *Sbornik Imperatorskogo Russkogo Istoricheskogo Obshchestva*, St Petersburg, 1881, vol. 29, pp. 643–646.
14 V. P. Semennikov, 'Proekt Vsemilostiveishei gramoty, Rossiyskomu narodu zhaluemoi', *A. N. Radishev: Ocherki i issledovaniya*, Moscow: Progress, 1923, pp. 180–194.
15 M. M. Speransky, 'Plan gosudarstvennogo preobrazovaniya grafa Speranskogo', *Vvedenie k Ulozheniu gosudarstvennykh zakonov*, St Petersburg, 1905; M. M. Speransky, *Proekty i zapiski*, Moscow-Leningrad, 1961.
16 N. K. Shilder, 'Gosudarstvennaya ustavnaya gramota Rossiiskoii imperii 1820', *Imperator Aleksandr I*, St Petersburg, 1898, vol. 4, supplements.
17 'Russkaya pravda P. I. Pestelya i sochineniya, ei predshestvuushchie', *Vosstanie dekabristov: Dokumenty*, Moscow, 1958, vol. VII.
18 N. M. Druzhinin, 'Tekst Konstitutsii N. M. Muravieva', *Izbrannye trudy: Revolutsionnoe dvizhenie v Rossii v XIX veke*, Moscow, 1987.
19 K. D. Kavelin, 'Zapiska ob osvobozhdenii krest'yan v Rossii', *Sobranie sochineniy K. D. Kavelina*, St Petersburg, 1898, vol. 2.
20 A. N. Medushevsky, 'Tekhnologiya demokraticheskikh reform v obshchestvakh perekhodnogo tipa: K pereosmysleniu velikikh reform v Rossii', *Vestnik Evropy*, 2003, vol. 9, pp. 186–203.
21 RGALI. F. 436. Op. 1. D.; OR RGB. F. 548.
22 'Vsepoddanneishaya zapiska stats-sekretarya P. A. Valueva', *Vestnik prava*, 1905, book 9 (November), pp. 226–233.
23 'Proekt novogo uchrezhdeniya Gosudarstvennogo soveta', *Vestnik prava*, 1905, book 9 (November), pp. 234–270.
24 Turgenev Foundation, Paris. BN. Slave. F. 7.
25 *Konstitutsiya grafa M. T. Loris-Melikova: Materialy dlya eie istorii*, London, Free Russian Press Foundation, 2nd edn, Berlin, 1904, *Byloe*, 1918, No. 4–5 (32–33), pp. 134–164.
26 *Grazhdanskoe Ulozhenie*. Kniga Pervaya. Polozhenie obshchie. Proekt Vysochaishie utverzhdennoi Redaktsionnoi komissii po sostavleniu Grazhdanskogo ulozheniya s ob'yasneniyami, St Petersburg: Gosudarstvennaya tipografiya, 1903–1905.
27 V. V. Leontovich, *Istoriya liberalisma v Rossii: 1752–1914*, Paris, 1980.
28 A. N. Medushevsky, 'Costituzioni e riforme amministrative in Russia e in

Europa occidentale nel secolo XIX', *Annali. Instituto Universitario Orientale*, Napoli, 1994; 'Administrative Reforms in the Russian Empire: Western Models and Russian Implementation', *Peter the Great and the West: New Perspectives*, L. Hughes (ed.), London: Palgrave, 2001.

3 Constitutional platform of Russian liberalism and its implementation under the transition from a monarchy to a republic

1 For more information on the political philosophy of Russian constitutionalism see also: A. N. Medushevsky, *Demokratiya i avtoritarizm: rossiiskii konstitutsionalizm v sravnitel'noy perspective*, Moscow: ROSSPEN, 1998.

2 *Juristen. Ein biographisches Lexicon. Von der Antike bis zum 20. Jahrhundert. Hrsg. von M. Stolleis*, München: Beck, 1995; A. N. Medushevsky, *Die Französische Revolution und die Naturrechtstheorie in Russland, Echo und Wirkungen der Französischen Revolution bei den slawischen Völkern und ihren Nachbarn*, Wien, Peter Lang, 1996.

3 A. N. Medushevsky, 'Vom Untertan zum Staatsbürger: Das russische Modell', *Staatsbürgerschaft in Europa. Historische Erfahrungen und aktuelle Debatten*, Hrsg. von Ch. Conrad und J. Kocka, Hamburg, 2001.

4 RGASPI. F. 279 (Fund of P. B. Struve and 'Osvobozhdeniye' magazine). Op. 2. D. 220.

5 RGASPI. F. 279. Op. 2. D. 220., Pisma v redaktsiu s izlozheniem programmy Soyuza Osvobozhdeniya i istorii prinyatiya 'Deklaratsii' (Letters to the editor containing the platform of the Union of Liberation and the history of adoption of the 'Declaration').

6 RGASPI. F. 279. Op. 3. D. 224. L. 109–112 (Proekty Konstitutsii Souza Osvobozhdeniya) (Constitutional drafts of the Union of Liberation).

7 Manuscript 'Osnovnye Polozheniya' (Main Thesis), ibid. L. 78–107.

8 Correspondence between B. Kistyakovsky and P. Struve, ibid. F. 279. Op. 1. D. 80. L. 87–91.

9 *Draft of the Fundamental Law of the Russian Empire*, developed by the Committee of the Bureau of All-Zemstvo congresses, Paris: Societe Nouvelle de Librairie et edition, 1905.

10 'Izbiratel'ny Zakon', *Konstitutsionnoe Gosudarstvo*, St Petersburg, 1905, pp. 550–551.

11 GARF. F. 575 (Muromtsev). The archives of Kokoshkin do not contain materials on his work on the draft (GARF. F. 1190).

12 F. F. Kokoshkin, S. A. Muromtsev i zemskie s'ezdy, *Sergei Andreevich Muromtsev*, Moscow, 1911, pp. 205–250.

13 Full transcriptions of the most prominent western constitutions are dated by 1905: V. M. Gessen and B. E. Nolde, *Sovremennye konstitutsii*, St Petersburg, 1905; Texts of the main Basic Laws of foreign states translated by F. F. Kokoshkin, Moscow, 1905.

14 G. Jellinek, *Allgemeine Staatslehre*, 3-e Auflage, Berlin, 1921.

15 'Papiers de Paul Boyer', Bibliothèque Nationale Francaise. Manuscrits. N. A. F. 18861. F. 104–105 (Pis'mo S. A. Muromtseva ot 13/26 iyulya 1902).

16 'Vysochaishy manifest ot 17 oktyabrya 1905 goda', PSZ, 3rd collection, vol. XXV, section I, No. 26803.

17 P. B. Struve, 'Revolutsiya, Rossiiskiie liberaly: kadety i oktyabristy', *Documents, memoirs, articles*, Moscow: ROSSPEN, 1996, p. 403.

18 V. A. Maklakov, *Vlast' i obschestvennost' na zakate staroi Rossii*, vol. 3, p. 403.

19 A. Tyrkova-Williams, *Na putyakh k svobode*, 2nd edn, London: Overseas Publication Interchange, 1990, pp. 96, 206, 246–247.

20 D. N. Shipov, *Vospominaniya i dumy o perezhitom*, Moscow, 1918, pp. 446–460.

21 P. N. Milyukov, *Istoriya vtoroi russkoi revolutsii*, 1st edn, Kiev, 1919, vol. 1, pp. 5–12.
22 Texts of the drafts published in the book *Konstitutsionnoe Gosudarstvo*, St Petersburg, 1905.
23 See also A. N. Medushevsky, 'Konstitutionelle Projecte in Russland am Anfang des 20. Jahrhunderts und ihre deutschen Prototypen', *Reformen im Russland des 19. und 20. Jahrhunderts. Westliche Modelle und russische Erfahrungen*, Frankfurt am Main, V. Klostermann, 1996.
24 *Polozhenie o vyborakh v Uchreditel'noe sobranie narodnykh predstaviteley, Proekt podkomissii byuro*, Moscow: Tipografia O. L. Somovoy, 1905 (Regulations for Elections to the Constituent Assembly of the Popular Representatives. Draft of the Subcommission of the Bureau).
25 *Polozhenie ob Uchreditel'nom sobranii.*
26 'Postanovlenie Vremennogo pravitel'stva ob obrazovanii Osobogo soveshchania dlya podgotovki Proekta Polozheniya o vyborakh v Uchreditel'noe sobranie', *Uchreditel'noe sobranie Rossii 1918*, Moscow, 1991, p. 10 (Resolution of the Provisional Government on formation of the Special Counsel for Preparation of the Draft Regulations for Elections to the Constituent Assembly).
27 'Zaklyuchenie Yuridicheskogo soveshchaniya o poryadke otkrytiya Uchreditel'nogo sobraniya i yuridicheskom polozhenii posle ego otkrytiya Vremennogo pravitel'stva', *Uchreditel'noe sobranie Rossii*, 1918, pp. 23–27 (Conclusions of the Legal Conference on the Procedure of the Opening of the Constituent Assembly and the Legal Status of the Provisional Government after the Opening, Constituent Assembly of Russia).
28 'Draft law on establishment of the Provisional executive power', ibid, pp. 30–31.
29 P. A. Sorokin, *Dal'nyaya doroga*, Autobiography, Moscow: Terra, 1992, p. 137.
30 *Zaklyuchenie Yuridicheskogo soveshchaniya o poryadke otkrytiya Uchreditel'nogo sobraniya i yuridicheskom polozhenii posle ego otkrytiya Vremennogo pravitel'stva*, Uchreditel'noe sobranie Rossii, 1918, p. 23 (Conclusions of the Legal Conference on the Procedure of the Opening of the Constituent Assembly and the Legal Status of the Provisional Government after the Opening).
31 On Formation of the Special Assembly, ibid, pp. 10–11.
32 'Regulations for the Elections to the Constituent Assembly'. Resolution of the Provisional Government of 25 March 1917, ibid. pp. 10–11.
33 'Decree of the All-Russian Central Executive Committee on dissolution of the Constituent Assembly dated 6 January 1918 (19 January)'. Telegrams of the western observers are dated respectively by 20 January (7 January old style).
34 GARF. F. 1792. (Yuridicheskoe Soveshchanie Legal Conference). Op. 1. D. 4. L. 186–194.
35 GARF. F. 1792. Op. 1. D. 4. L. 196–199.
36 Materials of the debates: GARF. F. 1792. Op. 1. D. 4. L. 201–215.

4 Nominal constitutionalism under Soviet dictatorship

1 H. Kelsen, *Reine Rechtslehre, Einleitung in die Rechtswissenschaftliche Problematik*, Leipzig und Wien: Franz Deuticke, 1934.
2 B. Mirkine-Guetzevitch, *Les Constitutions Européennes*, Paris: PUF, 1951, vol. 1, p. 85.
3 L. Kolakowski, *Die Hauptsträmungen des Marxismus. Entstechung. Entwicklung. Zerfall*, München-Zurich, R. Piper und Co. Verlag, 1981, Bd. 2. S. 63.
4 A. Borcke, *Die Ursprung des Bolshevismus. Die Jakobinische Tradition in Russland und die Theorie der revolutionären Diktatur*, München: Johannes Berchmans Verlag, 1977, S. 484–485.

5 E. Karr, *Bol'shevistskaya revolyutsiya 1917–1923*, Moscow: Progress, 1990, vol. 1–2.
6 P. N. Milyukov, *Istoriya vtoroi russkoi revolyutsii*, Moscow: ROSSPEN, 2001.
7 A. G. Goykhbarg, *Osnovy chastnogo imushchestvennogo prava*, Moscow, 1924, pp. 7–8.
8 U. B. Pashukanis, *Obshchaya teoriya prava i marksizm: Opyt kritiki osnovnykh yuridicheskikh ponyatiy*, Moscow: Izdatel'stvo Sektsii prava i gosudarstva sotsialisticheskoy Academii, 1924, p. 16.
9 M. Reisner, *Pravo. Nashe pravo. Chuzhoe pravo. Obshchee pravo*, Moscow-Leningrad: Gosizdat, 1925.
10 P. I. Stuchka, *Izbrannye proizvedeniya po marksistsko-leninskoi teorii prava*, Riga: Latviyskoe gosudarstvennoe izdatel'stvo, 1964.
11 N. N. Sukhanov, *Zapiski o revolyutsii*, Moscow: Politizdat, 1991, vol. 1, pp. 129–130.
12 Constitution (the Fundamental Law of the Russian Socialist Federated Soviet Republic. Adopted by the Fifth All-Russian Congress of Soviets on 10 July 1918), SU RSFSR, 1918, No. 51, Article 582.
13 C. Schmitt, *Die geistesgeschichtliche Lage des heutigen Parlamentarismus*, München und Leipzig, 1923; M. Weber, *Gesammelte politische Schriften*, Tübingen, 1968; P. I. Stuchka, op. cit., pp. 167, 171, 200.
14 E. X. Karr, *Russkaya revolyutsiya ot Lenina do Stalina*, Moscow: Inter-Verso, 1990; M. Ferro, *Des Sovietes au communisme bureaucratique: Les mécanismes d'une subversion*, Paris, 1980.
15 On the drafts of the first Soviet Constitutions see G. S. Gurvich, *Istoriya sovetskoi konstitutsii*, Moscow, 1923; N. I. Chelyapov, *Gosudarstvennaya sistema (konstitutsiya proletarskoi diktatury i burzhuaznaya demokratiya)*, Moscow: Vlast' Sovetov, 1928; V. I. Ignatiev, *Sovetskii stroy*, Moscow-Leningrad: Gosizdat, 1928.
16 Berg van den G. P., 'Elements of Continuity in Soviet Constitutional Law', *Russian Law: Historical and Political Perspectives*, Leyden: Sijthof, 1977, p. 227.
17 D. R. Little, *Governing the Soviet Union*, London: Longman, 1989, p. 65.
18 B. Bazhanov, *Vospominaniya*, Moscow, 1990.
19 *Constitution (Fundamental Law) of the Union of Soviet Socialist Republics*, Moscow: Pravda, 1977. Konstitutsiya (Osnovnoy zakon) Soyuza Sovetskikh Sotsialisticheskikh Respublik.
20 *Konstitutsiya (Osnovnoi zakon) SSSR. S izmeneniyami i dopolneniyami, vnecennymi zakonami SSSR ot 1 dekabrya 1988 g.; 20 dekabrya, 23 dekabrya1989 g., 14 marta i 26 dekabrya 1990 g.*, Moscow: Izvestiya Sovetov narodnykh deputatov SSSR, 1991.
21 *Konstitutsiya Rossiyskoi Federatsii. Prinyata vsenarodnym golosovaniem 12 dekabrya 1993*, Moscow: Yuridicheskaya literatura, 1993.

5 A contemporary model of Russian constitutionalism in comparative perspective

1 A. N. Medushevsky, *Sravnitel'noe konstitutsionnoe pravo i politicheskie instituty*, Moscow: Gosudarstvenny Universitet – Vysshaya Shkola Economiki (The State University – Higher School of Economics), 2002.
2 Literature on transitional processes in the world: *Constitution Makers on Constitution Making. The Experience of Eight Nations*, R. A. Goldwin and A. Kaufman (eds), Washington, 1988; *Constitutionalism and Democracy. Transitions in the Contemporary World* (D. Greenberg, S. N. Katz, M. B. Oliviero and S. C. Wheatley (eds)), 1993; *Constitutional Policy and Change in Europe*, J. J. Hesse and N. Johnson (eds), Oxford: University Press, 1995; *The Revolutions*

of 1989, V. Tismaneanu (ed.), London and New York: Routledge, 1999; *Democracy and Political Change in the Third World*, J. Haynes (ed.), London: Routledge, 2001.
3 These problems are highlighted in the following works: *Konstitutsiya kak factor sotsial'nykh izmenenii*, Moscow: CKI MONF, 1999; *Konstitutsiya Rossiyskoi Federatsii s kommentariyami Konstitutsionnogo Suda RF*, 2nd edn, Moscow: INFRA-M, 2000; *Konstitutsionnye prava v Rossii: dela i resheniya*, Moscow: Tsentral'ny Evropeyskii Universitet, 2002. *Ispolnenie reshenii konstitutsionnykh sudov*, Moscow: Institut Prava i Publichnoi Politiki, 2003.
4 *Konstitutsiya (Osnovnoi zakon) SSSR. S izmeneniyami i dopolneniyami, vnecennymi zakonami SSSR ot 1 dekabrya 1988 g.; 20 dekabrya, 23 dekabrya1989 g., 14 marta i 26 dekabrya 1990 g.*, Moscow: Izvestiya Sovetov narodnykh deputatov SSSR, 1991.
5 Konstitutsiya Rossiyskoy Federatsii, Moscow: Yuridicheskaya literatura, 1993.
6 Ukaz Presidenta RSFSR 'O gosudarstvennom perevorote', *Vedomosti S'ezda narodnykh deputatov i Verkhovnogo Soveta RSFSR*, 1991, No. 34.
7 'Periodicheskii doklad Rossiyskoi Federatsii, predostavlyaemy komitetu OON po pravam cheloveka v sootvetstvii so stat'ei 40 Mezhdunarodnogo pakta o grazhdanskikh i politicheskikh pravakh', *Prava cheloveka v Rossii: Mezhdunarodnoe izmerenie*, Moscow, Prava cheloveka, 1995, pp. 29–31 (Razdel 'Chrezvychainor polozhenie').
8 R. Sharlet, 'Pravovye transplantatsii i politicheskie mutatsii: retseptsiya konstitutsionnogo prava v novykh nezavisimykh gosudarstvakh', *Konstitutsionnoe pravo: vostochnoevropeyskoe obozrenie*, 1999, No. 2 (27), p. 18.
9 For more information on the debates see *Konstitutsionnoe soveshchanie. Stenogrammy. Materialy. Dokumenty*, Moscow, 1995, vol. 1–14; *Konstitutsionnoe soveshchanie: Informatsionny byulleten*, 1993, No. 1–3 (avgust–dekabr).
10 E. P. Hoffmann, 'Can Viable Constitutionalism Take Root in Post-Soviet Russia?', in A. I. Baaklini and H. Desfosses (eds), *Designs for Democratic Stability. Studies in Viable Constitutionalism*, New York: Sharpe, 1997, p. 246.
11 *Sobranie zakonodatel'stva Rossiiskoi Federatsii*, 1998, No. 10, Article 1146.
12 Postanovlenie Konstitutsionnogo Suda RF ot 31 oktyabrya 1995 goda No 12-P po delu o tolkovanii stat'i 136 Konstitutsii Rossiiskoi Federatsii, *Sobranie zakonodatel'stva Rossiyskoi Federatsii*, 1995, No. 45, Article 4408.
13 *Konstitutsiya Rossiiskoi Federatsii s kommentariyami Konstitutsionnogo Suda RF*, 2nd edn, Moscow: INFRA-M, 2001.
14 *Administrativno-territorial'noe ustroistvo Rossii: Istoriya i sovremennost*, Moscow: Olma-Press, 2003.
15 *Sovet Federatsii. Evolutsiya statusa i funktsii*, Moscow: Institut Prava i Publichnoi Politiki, 2003.
16 For the review of the adopted legislative acts see: *Sovet Federatsii i konstitutsionnye protsessy v sovremennoi Rossii*, 2002, No. 1.
17 A. N. Medushevsky, 'Power and Property in Russia: The Adoption of the Land Code', *East European Constitutional Review*, 2002, vol. II, No. 3 (summer).
18 *Konstitutsii gosudarstv Tsentral'noi i Vostochnoi Evropy*, Moscow, 1997; *Konstitutsionnoe pravosudie v postkommunisticheskikh stranakh*, Moscow, 1999.
19 S. Morgenstern and B. Nacif (eds), *Legislative Politics in Latin America*, Cambridge: University Press, 2002.
20 Maria del Refugio Gonzalez and Sergio Lopez Ayllon (eds), *Transiciones y Diseños Institucionales*, Mexico: Universidad Nacional Autonoma de Mexico, 2000.
21 A. N. Medushevsky, 'Agrarian Reform: Difficulties in Implementing Land Legislation at the Current Stage', *The Transformation and Consolidation of Market Legislation in the Context of Constitutional and Judicial Reform in Russia*, Ana-

lytical Report 2003, A. N. Medushevsky and L. Skyner (eds), Moscow: Institut Prava i Publichnoi Politiki (Institute of Law and Public Policy), 2004, pp. 6–11.

22 *Konstitutsiya Rossiyskoi Federatsii: Problemny Kommentarii*, Moscow: Tsentr konstitutsionnikh issledovanii, 1997.

23 A. N. Medushevsky, 'Konstitutsiya Rossiyskoi Federatsii 1993 goda i bol'shie tsikly rossiiskogo konstitutsionalisma', *Konstitutsionnoe pravo: vostochno-evropeiskoe obozrenie*, 2003, No. 4 (45), pp. 37–58.

24 *Konstitutsionnyi Sud kak garant razdeleniya vlastei*, Moscow: Institut Prava i Publichnoi Politiki (Institute of Law and Public Policy), 2004.

Index